revise

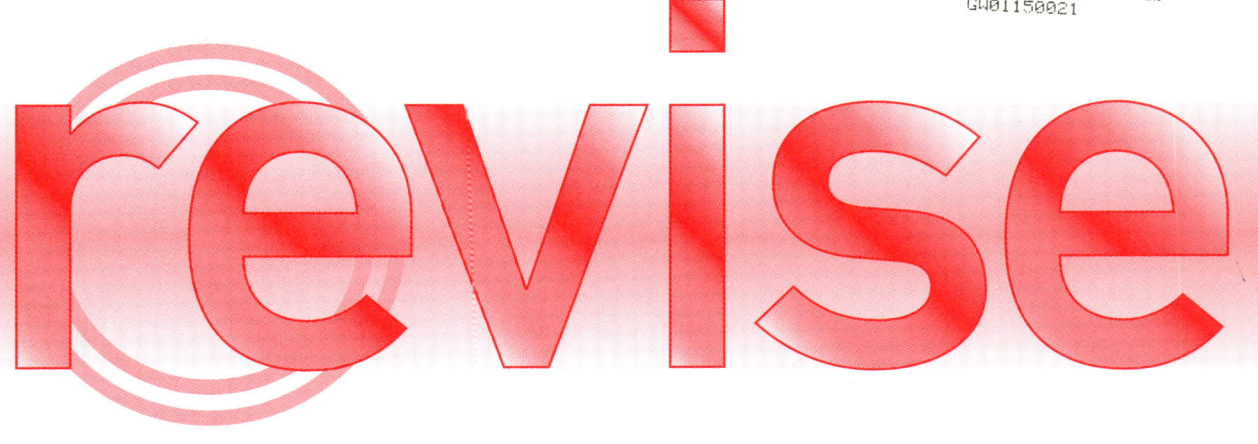

GCSE
Science: Single Award

Eileen Ramsden, David Applin and Jim Breithaupt

with Tony Buzan

Hodder & Stoughton

A MEMBER OF THE HODDER HEADLINE GROUP

Key to symbols

As you read through this book you will notice the following symbols. They will help you find your way around the book more quickly.

shows a handy hint to help you remember something

shows a short list of key facts

means remember!!!

says Did you know this? – interesting points to note

gives worked examples to help you with calculations and equations

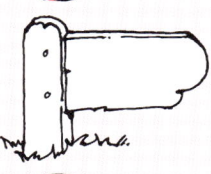

points you to other parts of the book where related topics are explained

shows a sequence of linked processes

refers you from a diagram to a checklist of related points

Acknowledgements

Copyright photographs have been used, with permission, from the following sources: Planet Earth Pictures (p.19); Science Photo Library (pp. 28, 72)

ISBN 0 340 66387 1

First published 1997
Impression number   10 9 8 7 6 5 4 3 2 1
Year   2001 2000 1999 1998 1997

The 'Teach Yourself' name and logo are registered trade marks of Hodder & Stoughton Ltd.

Copyright © Eileen Ramsden, Jim Breithaupt, David Applin 1997
Introduction copyright © 1997 Tony Buzan

All rights reserved. No part of this publication may be reproduced or transmitted in any form or by any means, electronic or mechanical, including photocopy, recording, or any information storage and retrieval system, without permission in writing from the publisher or under licence from the Copyright Licensing Agency Limited. Further details of such licences (for reprographic reproduction) may be obtained from the Copyright Licensing Agency Limited, of 90 Tottenham Court Road, London W1P 9HE.

Designed and produced by Gecko Ltd, Bicester, Oxon
Printed in Great Britain for Hodder & Stoughton Educational, a division of Hodder Headline Plc, 338 Euston Road, London NW1 3BH by Scotprint Ltd, Musselburgh, Scotland.

Mind Maps: Patrick Mayfield
Illustrations: Peter Bull, Simon Cooke, Chris Etheridge, Ian Law, Joe Little, Andrea Norton, Mike Parsons, John Plumb, Dave Poole, Chris Rothero, Anthony Warne
Cover design: Amanda Hawkes
Cover illustration: Paul Bateman

Contents

Revision made easy	4

Life processes and living things — 9
1	Introducing biology	10
2	Organisms in the environment	16
3	Cell activity	24
4	Humans as organisms	38
5	Inheritance and evolution	65
Answers		81

Materials and their properties — 87
1	Matter and the kinetic theory	88
2	Elements, compounds and equations	91
3	Separating substances	95
4	The structure of the atom	98
5	The chemical bond	102
6	The periodic table	106
7	Acids, bases and salts	110
8	Air	115
9	Water	121
10	Rocks	123
11	Metals and alloys	126
12	Reaction speeds	131
13	Fuels	134
14	Alkenes and plastics	138
Answers		140
Periodic table		148
Mind Maps		149

Physical processes — 157
Mind Maps		157
1	Beyond the Earth	164
2	Energy resources and energy transfer	172
3	Radioactivity	179
4	Waves	186
5	The electromagnetic spectrum	192
6	Force	197
7	Electricity and magnetism	204
Equations you should know		212
Answers		213

Index	220

Revision made easy

The four pages that follow contain a gold mine of information on how you can achieve success both at school and in your exams. Read them and apply the information, and you will be able to spend less, but more efficient, time studying, with better results. If you already have another *Hodder & Stoughton Revision Guide*, skim-read these pages to remind yourself about the exciting new techniques the books use, then move ahead to page 8.

This section gives you vital information on how to remember more *while* you are learning and how to remember more *after* you have finished studying. It explains

- how to use special techniques to improve your memory
- how to use a revolutionary note-taking technique called Mind Maps that will double your memory and help you to write essays and answer exam questions
- how to read everything faster while at the same time improving your comprehension and concentration

All this information is packed into the next four pages, so make sure you read them!

Your *amazing* memory

There are five important things you must know about your brain and memory to revolutionise your school life.

1. how your memory ('recall') works *while* you are learning
2. how your memory works *after* you have finished learning
3. how to use Mind Maps – a special technique for helping you with all aspects of your studies
4. how to increase your reading speed
5. how to zap your revision

1 Recall *during* learning – the need for breaks

When you are studying, your memory can concentrate, understand and remember well for between 20 and 45 minutes at a time. Then it *needs* a break. If you carry on for longer than this without one, your memory starts to break down! If you study for hours non-stop, you will remember only a fraction of what you have been trying to learn, and you will have wasted valuable revision time.

So, ideally, *study for less than an hour*, then take a five- to ten-minute break. During the break listen to music, go for a walk, do some exercise, or just daydream. (Daydreaming is a necessary brain-power booster – geniuses do it regularly.) During the break your brain will be sorting out what it has been learning, and you will go back to your books with the new information safely stored and organised in your memory banks. We recommend breaks at regular intervals as you work through the *Revision Guides*. Make sure you take them!

2 Recall *after* learning – the waves of your memory

What do you think begins to happen to your memory straight *after* you have finished learning something? Does it immediately start forgetting? No! Your brain actually *increases* its power and carries on remembering. For a short time after your study session, your brain integrates the information, making a more complete picture of everything it has just learnt. Only then does the rapid decline in memory begin, and as much as 80 per cent of what you have learnt can be forgotten in a day.

However, if you catch the top of the wave of your memory, and briefly review (look back over) what you have been revising at the correct time, the memory is stamped in far more strongly, and stays at the crest of the wave for a much longer time. To maximise your brain's power to remember, take a few minutes and use a Mind Map to review what you have learnt at the end of a day. Then review it at the end of a week, again at the end of a month, and finally a week before the exams. That way you'll ride your memory wave all the way to your exam – and beyond!

Revision made easy

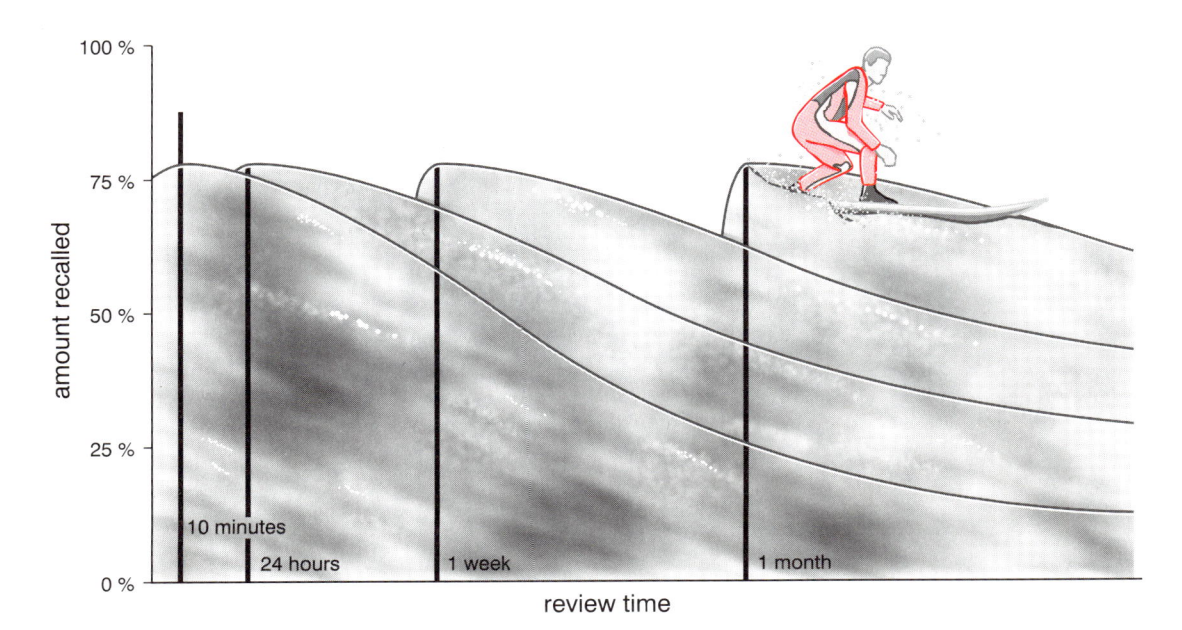

[Graph: amount recalled (y-axis, 0% to 100%) vs review time (x-axis) with markers at 10 minutes, 24 hours, 1 week, and 1 month, showing memory recall curves resembling ski slopes]

Amazing as your memory is (think of everything you actually do have stored in your brain at this moment) the principles on which it operates are very simple: your brain will remember if it (a) has an image (a picture or a symbol); (b) has that image fixed and (c) can link that image to something else.

3 The Mind Map® – a picture of the way you think

Do you *like* taking notes? More importantly, do you like having to go back over and learn them before exams? Most students I know certainly do not! And how do you take your notes? Most people take notes on lined paper, using blue or black ink. The result, visually, is *boring*! And what does your brain do when it is bored? It turns off, tunes out, and goes to sleep! Add a dash of colour, rhythm, imagination, and the whole note-taking process becomes much more fun, uses more of your brain's abilities, *and* improves your recall and understanding.

A Mind Map mirrors the way your brain works. It can be used for note-taking from books or in class, for reviewing what you have just studied, for revising, and for essay planning for coursework and in exams. It uses all your memory's natural techniques to build up your rapidly growing 'memory muscle'.

You will find Mind Maps throughout this book. Study them, add some colour, personalise them, and then have a go at drawing your own – you'll remember them far better! Put them on your walls and in your files for a quick-and-easy review of the topic.

How to draw a Mind Map

1. Start in the middle of the page with the page turned sideways. This gives your brain the maximum room for its thoughts.
2. Always start by drawing a small picture or symbol. Why? Because a picture is worth a thousand words to your brain. And try to use at least three colours, as colour helps your memory even more.
3. Let your thoughts flow, and write or draw your ideas on coloured branching lines connected to your central image. These key symbols and words are the headings for your topic. The Mind Map at the top of the next page shows you how to start.
4. Then add facts and ideas by drawing more, smaller, branches on to the appropriate main branches, just like a tree.
5. Always print your word clearly on its line. Use only one word per line. The Mind Map at the foot of the next page shows you how to do this.
6. To link ideas and thoughts on different branches, use arrows, colours, underlining, and boxes.

How to read a Mind Map

1. Begin in the centre, the focus of your topic.
2. The words/images attached to the centre are like chapter headings, read them next.
3. Always read out from the centre, in every direction (even on the left-hand side, where you will have to read from right to left, instead of the usual left to right).

Using Mind Maps

Mind Maps are a versatile tool – use them for taking notes in class or from books, for solving problems, for brainstorming with friends, and for reviewing and revising for exams – their uses are endless! You will find them invaluable for planning essays for coursework and exams. Number your main branches in the order in which you want to use them and off you go – the main headings for your essay are done and all your ideas are logically organised!

POLYALKENES

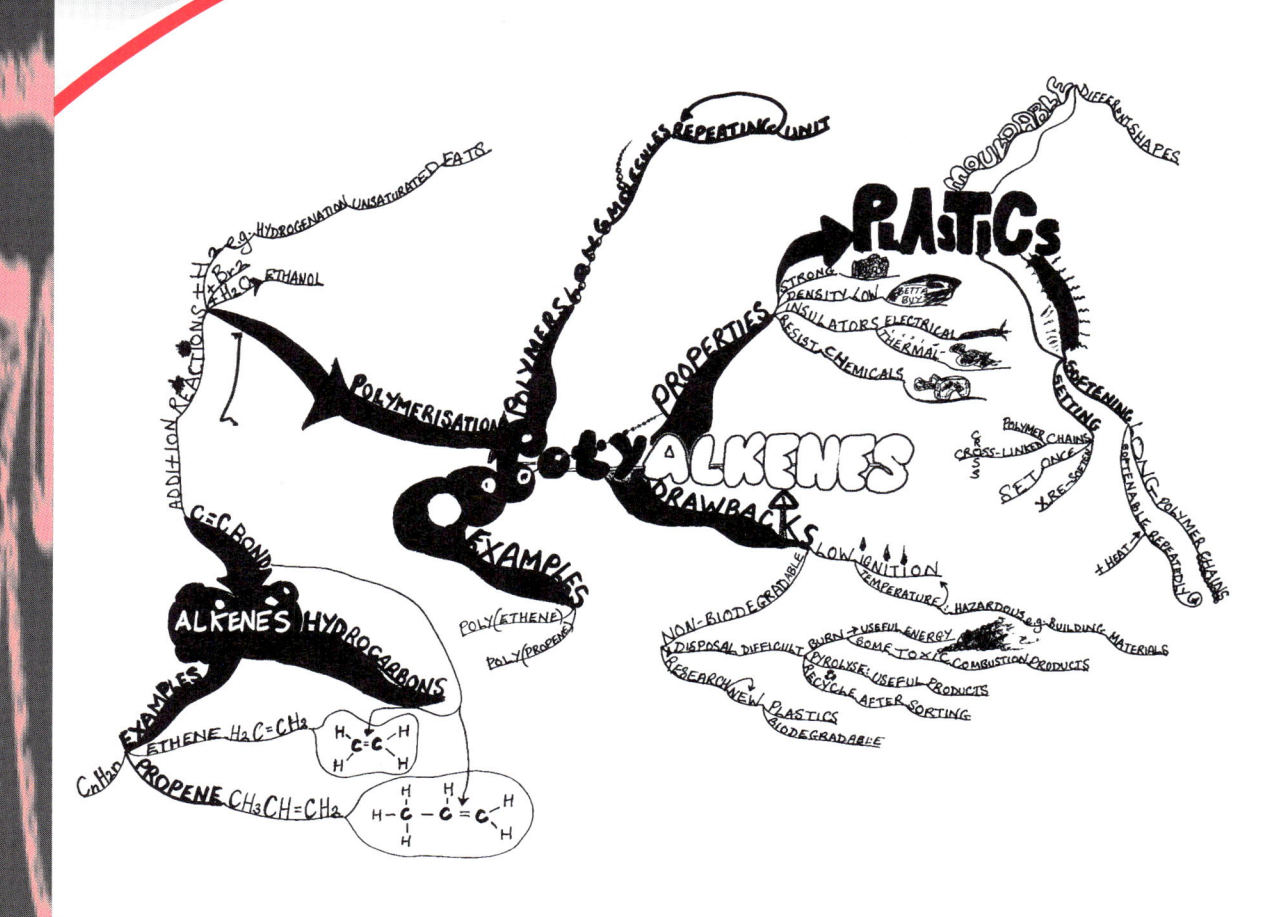

Mind map (initial)

- POLYMERISATION
- POLYMERS
- PROPERTIES
- DRAWBACKS
- EXAMPLES

Mind map (expanded)

POLYALKENES

- **POLYMERISATION** — POLYMERS (6 + 6 + 6 + 6 + 6 molecules) → REPEATING UNIT
- **ADDITION REACTIONS** + H₂ e.g. HYDROGENATION UNSATURATED FATS
  - + Br₂
  - + H₂O → ETHANOL
- **ALKENES** — HYDROCARBONS — C=C BOND
  - EXAMPLES:
    - ETHENE H₂C=CH₂ (H₂C=CH₂ structural)
    - PROPENE CH₃CH=CH₂ (H–CH₂–C=CH₂ structural)
    - C$_n$H$_{2n}$
- **EXAMPLES**
  - POLY(ETHENE)
  - POLY(PROPENE)
- **PROPERTIES** → PLASTICS
  - STRONG
  - DENSITY LOW
  - INSULATORS — ELECTRICAL, THERMAL
  - RESIST CHEMICALS
  - MOULDABLE — DIFFERENT SHAPES
  - SETTING:
    - CROSS-LINKED POLYMER CHAINS — SET ONCE — X RE-SOFTEN
    - LONG POLYMER CHAINS — SOFTENABLE + HEAT REPEATEDLY ☺
  - e.g. BUILDING MATERIALS
- **DRAWBACKS**
  - LOW IGNITION TEMPERATURE → HAZARDOUS
  - BURN → USEFUL ENERGY, SOME TOXIC COMBUSTION PRODUCTS
  - NON-BIODEGRADABLE — DISPOSAL DIFFICULT
  - PYROLYSE — USEFUL PRODUCTS
  - RECYCLE AFTER SORTING
  - RESEARCH NEW PLASTICS — BIODEGRADABLE

Revision made easy

4 Super speed reading

It seems incredible, but it's been proved – the faster you read, the more you understand and remember! So here are some tips to help you to practise reading faster – you'll cover the ground more quickly, remember more, *and* have more time for revision!

★ First read the whole text (whether it's a lengthy book or an exam paper) very quickly, to give your brain an overall idea of what's ahead and get it working. (It's like sending out a scout to look at the territory you have to cover – it's much easier when you know what to expect!) Then read the text again for more detailed information.

★ Have the text a reasonable distance away from your eyes. In this way your eye/brain system will be able to see more at a glance, and will naturally begin to read faster.

★ Take in groups of words at a time. Rather than reading 'slowly and carefully' read faster, more enthusiastically. Your comprehension will rocket!

★ Take in phrases rather than single words while you read.

★ Use a guide. Your eyes are designed to follow movement, so a thin pencil underneath the lines you are reading, moved smoothly along, will 'pull' your eyes to faster speeds.

5 Helpful hints for exam revision

Hints & Tips

Start to revise at the beginning of the course. Cram at the start, not the end and avoid 'exam panic'!

Hints & Tips

Use Mind Maps throughout your course, and build a Master Mind Map for each subject – a giant Mind Map that summarises everything you know about the subject.

Hints & Tips

Use memory techniques such as mnemonics (verses or systems for remembering things like dates and events, or lists).

Hints & Tips

Get together with one or two friends to revise, compare Mind Maps, and discuss topics.

And finally...

⭐ *Have fun while you learn* – studies show that those people who enjoy what they are doing understand and remember it more, and generally do it better.

⭐ *Use your teachers* as resource centres. Ask them for help with specific topics and with more general advice on how you can improve your all-round performance.

⭐ *Personalise your* **Revision Guide** by underlining and highlighting, by adding notes and pictures. Allow your brain to have a conversation with it!

Your brain is an amazing piece of equipment – learn to use it, and you, like thousands of students before you will be able to master 'B's and 'A's with ease. The more you understand and use your brain, the more it will repay you!

GCSE Science: Single Award and this Revision Guide

Tailor-made for *Science: Single Award*

This Revision Guide is not intended to replace your textbooks. As tests and examinations approach, however, many students feel the need to revise from something a good deal shorter than their usual textbook. This Revision Guide is intended to fill that need. It covers all the syllabuses for *Science: Single Award* for the different Examining Groups, and nothing more. If you want to read more for interest, then you can refer to a more extensive text.

Getting the most out of the Guide

We have tried to depart from the textbook style by presenting material in the form of lists, charts, tables, concept maps and Mind Maps. When using the book, it is a good idea to study one of the topics and then close the book and try to draw the scheme of reactions or relationships you have been studying. In this way you will know whether you have been really concentrating or just sitting with the book open in front of you.

Each revision topic begins with a set of Test Yourself questions to give an idea of how well you have already grasped that topic. You could work through the questions again after you have revised the topic. The improvement should be encouraging! There is a set of Round-up questions at the end of each topic. Work out your Improvement Index from your score on the Round-up questions compared with your first score on the Test Yourself questions.

Organising your time

Make a timetable for homework and revision, and keep to it. You have a lot of subjects to cope with. Leave space in your timetable for your leisure activities. Planned use of time and concentrated study will give you time for your other activities and interests as well as work.

When the exam arrives

The night before the exam make sure that you have everything you will need: your pen and spare cartridge, pencils, rubber, calculator, etc. Decide what you are going to wear and get everything ready. You want to avoid any last minute dithering.

Be optimistic. You have done your revision and can have confidence that it will stand you in good stead. Do not sit up late at night trying to cram. A last-minute glance through the Mind Maps you have made yourself is as much as your brain can take in at the last minute.

In the examination room, read the instructions on the front of the paper before you set pen to paper. Do not spend more time than you should on any one question. If you can't answer a question, move on to the next question and return to the unanswered question later. Attempt all the questions you are supposed to answer. Make sure you turn over every page! Many marks have been lost in exams as a result of turning over two pages at once. If you suffer a panic attack, breathe deeply and slowly to get lots of oxygen into your system and clear your thoughts. Above all, keep your examination in perspective; it is important but not a matter of life or death!

We wish you success.

Eileen Ramsden, Jim Breithaupt, David Applin

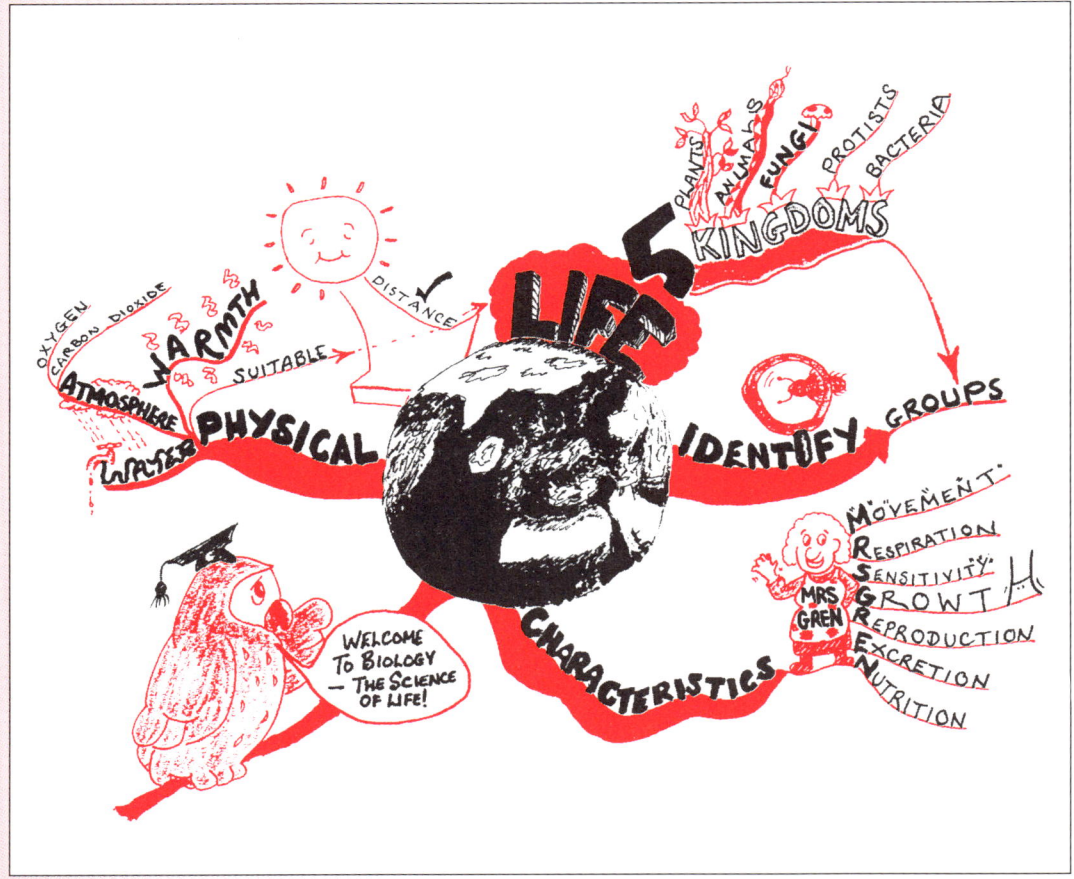

Life processes and living things

1	**Introducing biology**	**10**	**5**	**Inheritance and evolution**	**65**
1.1	Living on Earth	10	5.1	Reproduction	65
1.2	Characteristics of life	11	5.2	Asexual reproduction in plants	68
1.3	Grouping living things	11	5.3	Monohybrid inheritance	70
1.4	Identifying living things	14	5.4	Biotechnology	73
			5.5	Variation	75
2	**Organisms in the environment**	**16**	5.6	Evolution	76
2.1	Introducing ecology	16			
2.2	Distribution of organisms	18		**Answers**	**81**
2.3	Population size	19		**Index**	**220**

3	**Cell activity**	**24**
3.1	Cells at work	24
3.2	Cell division	25
3.3	Cells, tissues and organs	30
3.4	Chemicals in living things	33
4	**Humans as organisms**	**38**
4.1	Food and diet	38
4.2	The digestive system	42
4.3	Blood	46
4.4	Senses and the nervous system	48
4.5	Sense organs	49
4.6	Hormones	54
4.7	Maintaining the internal environment	55
4.8	Health and disease	58

Introducing biology

How much do you already know? Work out your score on page 81.

Test yourself

1 What would happen to the ground temperature if Earth were a) nearer to the Sun b) further from the Sun? [2]

2 a) List the processes which tell you that something is living. [7 × ½]
  b) Put a tick (✓) next to the processes which you think apply to animals. [7 × ½]
  c) Put a cross (✗) next to the processes which you think apply to plants. [6 × ½]
  d) Do plants and animals have the same characteristics? If not, how are they different? [1]

3 Using the forget-me-not and oak tree as examples, explain the meaning of the words 'annual' and 'perennial'. [3]

4 a) What is a biological key used for? [1]
  b) Why are features like exact colour, size and mass not suitable for including in a biological key? [3]

5 List the physical features of soil which make it a suitable place for earthworms to live. [4]

1.1 Living on Earth

preview

At the end of this section you will:
- understand why Earth is a suitable place for living things (organisms)
- know that soil, air and water are the physical environments in which organisms live.

Why the Earth can support life

Earth is a planet in orbit round a star we call the Sun. It is the only planet we know of that supports life.

★ Earth is close enough to the Sun for its surface temperature to be in the range in which life can exist. The temperature at the Earth's surface varies between −70 and 55 °C.

★ Earth is massive enough to have sufficient gravity to hold down an atmosphere of different gases essential for living organisms.

★ The layer of ozone which surrounds Earth reduces the amount of ultraviolet light from the Sun reaching the planet's surface. Too much ultraviolet light destroys living things.

Limits on life

- 9000 m limit for springtails (tiny insects) which feed on pollen and seeds blown up by the wind
- 6000 m limit for flowering plants
- 4500 m limit for farming
- 100 m deep limit for plant-like phytoplankton

Mount Everest – highest mountain
permanent snow
tree line
sea level
light – photosynthesis possible
Mariana Trench – deepest part of the ocean

soil forms a thin layer covering most of the Earth's land surface

air forms an atmosphere of gases around the Earth

biosphere – the places on Earth where there is life

water (fresh and salt) covers 75% of the Earth's surface

Ocean depths – no light. Life here depends on falling dead organisms, and thermal and chemical energy from deep sea vents.

Earth's physical environment

The diagram on the opposite page shows that soil, air and water form Earth's environment:

★ **Soil** is formed when the weather, the roots of plants and the different activities of animals break down rocks into small particles.

★ **Air** consists of: 78% nitrogen; 21% oxygen; 0.03% carbon dioxide; and less than 1% water vapour, argon, xenon and other gases.

★ **Water** fills the seas, oceans, rivers and lakes. About 2% of the Earth's water is locked up as ice, in the soil, in the bodies of living things or is vapour in the atmosphere.

1.2 Characteristics of life

At the end of this section you will know the characteristics of life:
- Movement
- Respiration
- Sensitivity
- Growth
- Reproduction
- Excretion
- Nutrition.

Handy hint
The mnemonic **Mrs Gren** will help you remember the characteristics of living things.

More about MRS GREN

The characteristics of life are the features that are common to all living things:

★ **Movement**: animals are able to move from place to place because of the action of **muscles** which pull on the **skeleton**. Plants do not usually move from place to place; they move mainly by **growing**.

★ **Respiration** occurs in cells, and releases energy from food for life's activities. **Aerobic** respiration uses oxygen to release energy from food. **Anaerobic** respiration releases energy from food without using oxygen.

★ **Sensitivity** allows living things to detect changes in their surroundings and respond to them.

★ **Growth** leads to an increase in size. **Development** occurs as young change and become adult in appearance.

★ **Reproduction** produces new individuals.

★ **Excretion** removes the waste substances produced by the chemical reactions (called **metabolism**) taking place in cells.

★ **Nutrition** makes food (by the process of **photosynthesis**) or takes in food for use in the body.

Remember
- **Respiration** releases energy from food.
- **Gaseous exchange** takes in oxygen for respiration and removes carbon dioxide produced by respiration.
- **Excretion** removes wastes produced by metabolism.
- **Defecation** (or egestion) removes the undigested remains of food.

1.3 Grouping living things

At the end of this section you will:
- understand that groups of living things are named according to Linnaeus' system of classification
- know the major groups of plants and animals
- understand binomial names.

Classification

Living things which have features in common are grouped together. Organising living things into groups is called **classification**. Some characteristics are unique to the group; other characteristics are shared with other groups. Groups therefore combine to form larger groups. The largest group of all is the **kingdom**. Each:

- kingdom contains a number of **phyla**
- phyl**um** (singular) contains a number of **classes**
- class contains a number of **orders**
- order contains a number of **families**
- family contains a number of **genera**
- gen**us** (singular) contains one or more **species**.

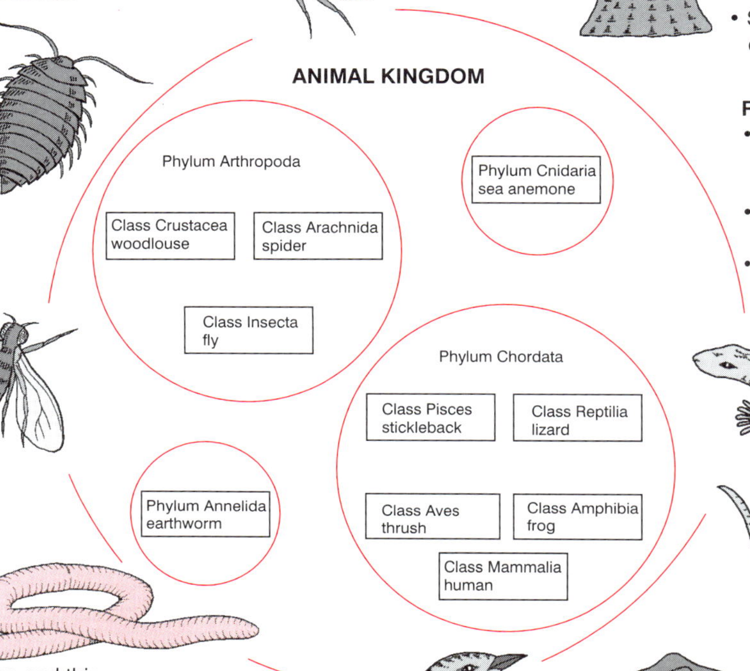

Life processes and living things

Arachnids
- The body is made up of two parts.
- There are 8 legs.
- Scorpions, mites and harvestmen are close relatives of spiders.

Cnidarians
- The body has no front or re[ar]. Its parts are arranged even[ly] in the round.
- Tentacles surround an opening which is both mouth and anus.
- Stinging cells are used to capture prey.

Crustacea
- The body is made up of two parts.
- There are 14 legs.
- Woodlice are the only crustacea that live on land.
- Crabs, lobsters and prawns are close relatives of woodlice.

Reptiles
- Skin is dry and covered w[ith] scales that restrict water [loss] from the body.
- Lay eggs, each protecte[d] by a hard shell.
- As a result, water is not necessary for breeding.

Insects
- The body is made up of three parts: head, thorax and abdomen.
- There are six legs.
- There are usually two pairs of wings, but flies have one pair.

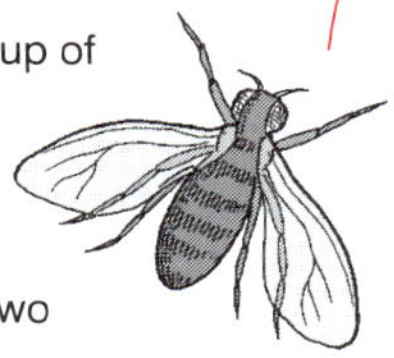

ANIMAL KINGDOM

Phylum Arthropoda
- Class Crustacea — woodlouse
- Class Arachnida — spider
- Class Insecta — fly

Phylum Cnidaria — sea anemone

Phylum Annelida — earthworm

Phylum Chordata
- Class Pisces — stickleback
- Class Reptilia — lizard
- Class Aves — thrush
- Class Amphibia — frog
- Class Mammalia — human

Worms
- The body is long and thin.
- The body is made up of many segments.

Fish
- The body is covered with scales.
- Fins control the position of the body in water.
- Gills are surfaces for gaseous exchange.

Birds
- The body is covered with feathers which:
  - make flying possible
  - keep in heat
  - keep out water.
- The beak is specialised (adapted) differently in different species to deal with different foods.
- Birds lay eggs, protected by a hard shell.

Amphibians
- Live on land but breed in water.
- Young are swimming tadpoles.
- Development of young into adult is called a metamorphosis.
- Soft skin loses water easily in dry a[ir].

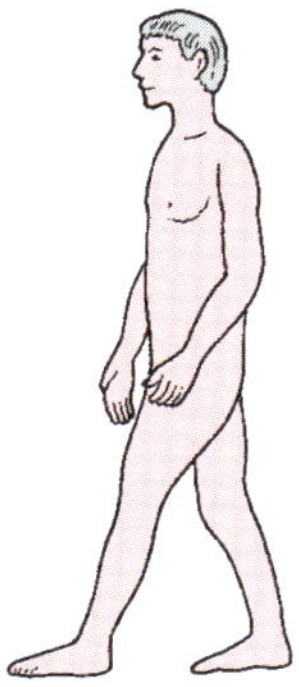

Mammals
- Hair helps conserve body heat.
- Young feed on milk produced by the female's breasts (mammary glands).
- Have a small tail bone called the coccyx.

Groups within groups – the major groups of the Animal kingdom and the Plant kingdom, with an example of each. Each major group of plants is called a Division rather than a Phylum.

Introducing biology

Mosses
- Mosses quickly lose water in dry air. As a result, mosses live in damp places.
- Roots are absent.
- As a result, water is soaked up by capillary movement over the leaves.
- Stalks grow from moss plants, each carrying a spore capsule filled with spores.
- Each spore is able to develop into a new plant.

REPRODUCE BY MEANS OF SPORES

PLANT KINGDOM

Division (= Phylum) Mosses

Division (= Phylum) Ferns

Division (= Phylum) Seed plants
- Class conifers
- Class flowering plants

Ferns
- A waxy layer waterproofs the plant's surfaces, reducing water loss in a dry atmosphere.
- Roots draw water from the soil.
- Spore capsules containing spores grow in patches on the undersides of leaves.
- Each spore is able to grow into a new fern plant.

REPRODUCE BY MEANS OF SEEDS

Forget-me-not: annual – flowers and produces seed in one growing season. The plant then dies.

Oak tree: perennial – produces seeds year after year. The plant survives for many years.

Conifers
- Seeds are contained in cones.
- Covered with leaves all year round ('evergreens').
- Roots draw water from the soil.
- Waxy layer waterproofs plant surfaces.

Flowering plants
- Seeds are contained in fruits.
- Leaves of trees/shrubs fall once a year ('deciduous').
- Roots draw water from the soil.
- Waxy layer waterproofs plant surfaces.

Life processes and living things

The genus and the species identify the individual living thing, rather like your first name and surname identify you. For example, humans belong to the genus *Homo* and have the species name *sapiens*; barn owls are called *Tyto alba*.

Since the name of each living thing is in two parts, the method of naming is called the **binomial system**. Notice that the genus name begins with a capital letter, the species name begins with a small letter, and the whole name is printed in italics.

The Swedish naturalist Carolus Linnaeus (the Latin version of his name) published *Systema Naturae* in 1735. The book established the system of naming organisms that we use today.

The five kingdoms

There are five kingdoms. Living things in each kingdom obtain food in different ways. Their structure and body chemistry are different. Each kingdom, therefore, represents a way of life which all its members share. Pages 12–13 show the major groups in the Animal kingdom and Plant kingdom. The other kingdoms are:

Kingdom Fungi – organisms made up of cells that form thread-like structures called **hyphae**.

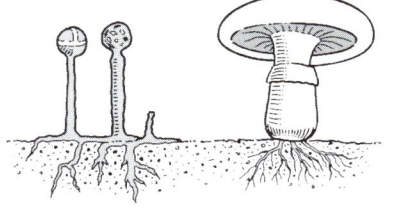

Kingdom Protista – single-celled organisms.

Kingdom Bacteria – single-celled organisms. The cell body is simple in structure compared with the cell body of protists.

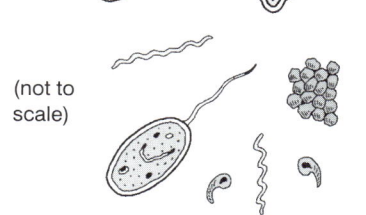

(not to scale)

1.4 Identifying living things

preview

At the end of this section you will:
- know that a key is a set of clues that help identify a particular organism or group of organisms
- understand how to use a dichotomous key
- know that a dichotomous key can be written in different ways.

What is a key?

A **key** is a means of identifying an unfamiliar organism from a selection of specimens. A key consists of a set of descriptions. Each description is a clue that helps in the identification. A set of clues makes the key.

The easiest type of key to use is called a **dichotomous** key. 'Dichotomous' means branching into two. Each time the key branches, you have to choose between alternative statements. The alternative statements may be presented diagrammatically as a chart, or written in pairs or **couplets**. For example, a key to amphibians would begin:

		yes	no
1	The animal has a tail.	**newts**	go to **2**
2	The animal has no tail.	**frogs and toads**	go to **3**

and so on ...

By comparing the pairs of statements with the organisms, you will eventually find one that fits. This identifies the organism. A key is therefore the route to a name. Different keys are used to name different living things.

When making a key, it is important to choose features that are characteristic of the type of organism rather than of the individual itself. For example, shape or proportions and patterns of colour are fairly constant in a type of organism and are therefore useful clues in a key. Size and shades of colour vary from individual to individual and are of limited use.

Introducing biology

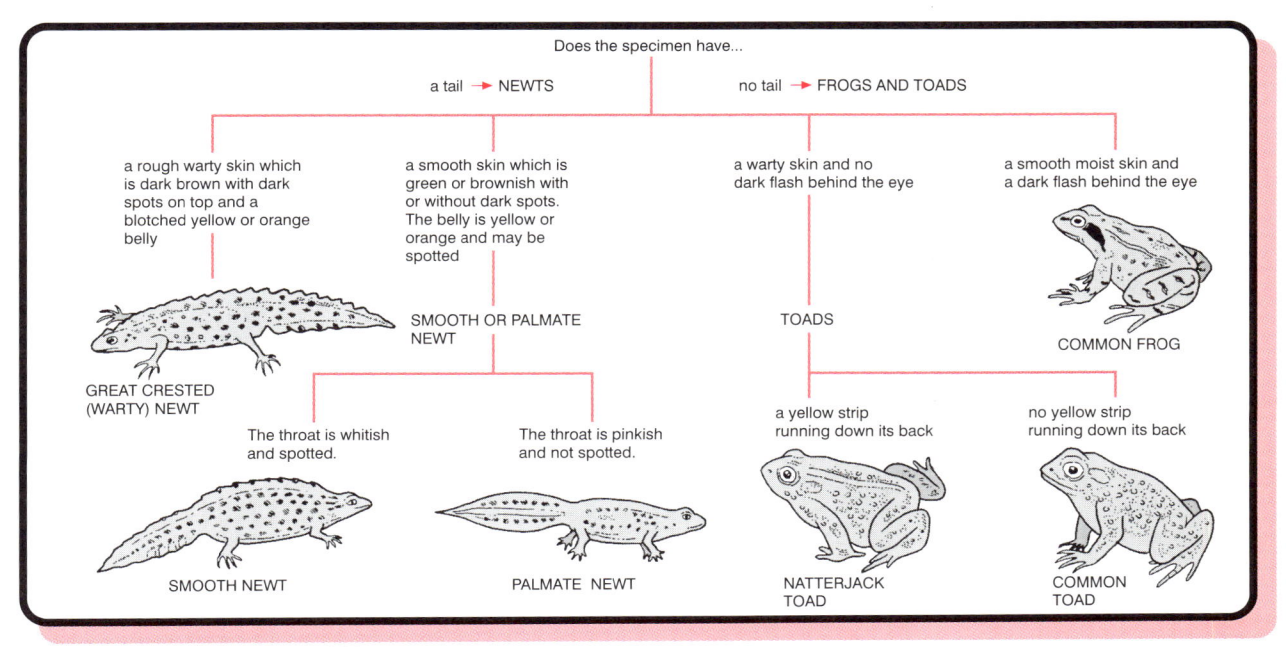

Different ways of writing a key to amphibians

round-up

How much have you improved?
Work out your improvement index on page 81.

1 What would happen to Earth's water if Earth were
   a) nearer to **b)** further from the Sun? [2]

2 a) Which gas is used during aerobic respiration to release energy from food? [1]
   b) Which gas is produced during aerobic respiration? [1]

3 a) Distinguish between respiration and gaseous exchange. [3]
   b) Distinguish between excretion and defecation. [2]

4 In the 1890s, when people saw cars for the first time, many thought that the cars were alive. Imagine that you are a reporter writing a short article for the local newspaper reassuring the populace that although cars seem to move under their own steam, they are not alive. [8]

5 Match each characteristic of life in column **A** with its description in column **B**.

A characteristics	B descriptions
movement	making or obtaining food
respiration	responding to stimuli
sensitivity	removing waste substances produced by cells
growth	producing new individuals
reproduction	releasing energy from food
excretion	changing position
nutrition	increasing in size

[7]

6 Different types of animal are listed in column **A**. Match each type with the correct description in column **B**.

A animals	B descriptions
insect	no legs
worm	eight legs
spider	two legs
bird	six legs

[4]

7 Briefly describe how a biological key is used. [4]

8 Briefly explain how the binomial system of biological names works. [4]

9 A key can be written in couplets. What are 'couplets'? [1]

15

Organisms in the environment

2

How much do you already know? Work out your score on page 81.

Test yourself

1. Match each term in column **A** with the correct description in column **B**.

A terms	B descriptions
biosphere	the place where a group of organisms lives
community	all the ecosystems of the world
habitat	a group of individuals of the same species
population	all the organisms that live in a particular ecosystem

   [4]

2. What is competition? [2]

3. Give reasons for the rapid increase in the human population. [4]

4. Weigh up the benefits in food production of intensive farming against the costs to the environment. [5]

2.1 Introducing ecology

preview

At the end of this section you will understand that:

- an ecosystem is a self-contained part of the biosphere, such as a pond or an oak wood
- the community consists of the organisms that live in a particular ecosystem
- the habitat is the place where a group of organisms live
- a niche is the role each species has in its habitat
- a population is a group of organisms of the same species living in a particular place at the same time.

Some ecological terms

Ecology involves studying the relationships between organisms and between organisms and the environment.

The diagram on page 10 shows how all the places on Earth where there is life form the **biosphere**. Each organism is suited (**adapted**) to the place where it lives. This place consists of

- an **environment** of air, soil or water
- a living **community** of plants, animals, fungi and microorganisms.

Environment and community together form an **ecosystem,** which is a more or less self-contained part of the biosphere. 'Self-contained' means that each ecosystem has its own characteristic organisms not usually found in other ecosystems. These organisms are the living (**biotic**) community of the ecosystem. The physical environment is the non-living (**abiotic**) part, consisting of air, soil or water. The diagram opposite shows the different components of an oak wood ecosystem.

The flow chart below shows the hierarchy of ecological terms.

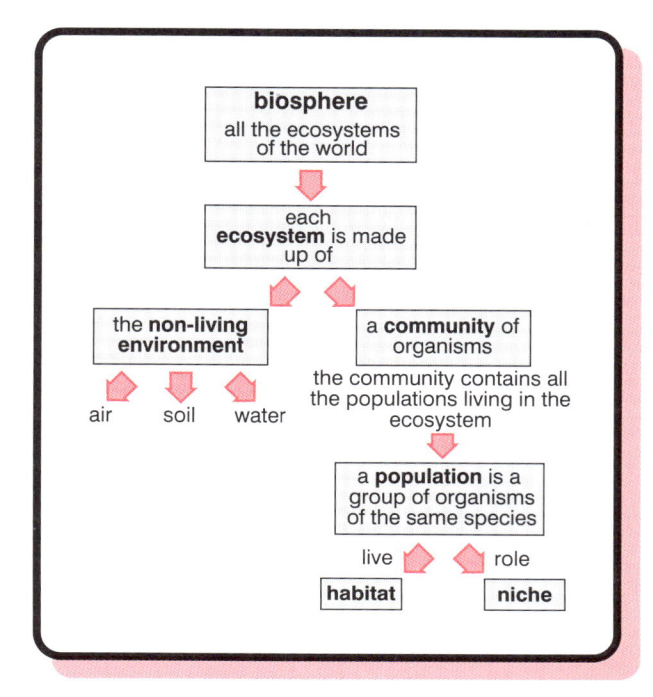

```
                    biosphere
             all the ecosystems
                of the world
                      ↓
                   each
              ecosystem is made
                   up of
                  ↙      ↘
        the non-living    a community of
        environment         organisms
         ↙  ↓  ↘         the community contains all
       air soil water    the populations living in the
                              ecosystem
                                 ↓
                          a population is a
                          group of organisms
                          of the same species
                          ↙            ↘
                        live           role
                      habitat         niche
```

COMMUNITY

key
1. oak tree
2. hazel
3. holly
4. bluebell
5. wood anemone
6. primrose
7. moss on tree trunk
8. pigeons, rooks living in canopy
9. bluetits, woodpeckers living further down tree
10. great tits, warblers living in shrubs
11. wrens, blackbirds living on ground
12. toadstools on rotting log
13. woodlice in detritus
14. earthworm pulling leaf into burrow
✓ falling leaves

Organisms in the environment

PHYSICAL ENVIRONMENT
There may be up to 90% less light inside the wood than outside when the canopy is fully developed.

* canopy fully developed
** leaf fall

light outside wood
light passing through canopy

month: J F M A M J J A S O N D

THE ECOSYSTEM

HABITATS
- canopy layer
- shrub layer
- field layer
- ground layer
- detritus layer

EXAMPLE HABITAT
decomposers (which break down dead organic matter) at work on dead wood

decomposed dead material

FUNGI Page 14.

NICHE: Fungal hyphae decompose dead wood, releasing minerals into the environment.

- wall of hypha
- wood
- digested wood
- food absorbed into hypha
- enzymes secreted
- cytoplasm
- digested wood
- tip of hypha
- enzymes

Fungi and bacteria feed on the dead wood causing decomposition.

Woodlice and other wood-eating animals break up the tree into pieces called **frass**, increasing the surface area exposed to attack by fungi and bacteria.

Earthworms pull dead leaves into their burrows for food.

Nitrates and phosphates are absorbed in solution by the roots.

Decomposition releases gases and minerals into the soil.

nutrients essential for the growth of plants

The components of an oak wood ecosystem

Life processes and living things

2.2 Distribution of organisms

preview

At the end of this section you will:
- understand the effect of environmental factors on the distribution of plants
- know that competition affects the distribution of organisms
- understand that different adaptations enable plants and animals to survive.

Competition between organisms

The distribution of organisms (where living things are found in the environment) is affected by different factors.

★ Physical factors include
  - the amount of light
  - the abundance of water.

★ Biological factors include
  - **intraspecific competition** – competition between individuals of the same species
  - **interspecific competition** – competition between individuals of different species
  - **interactions** between predators and prey
  - **adaptations** of organisms for survival in different environments.

Fact file

★ **Competition:** in nature organisms that are rivals for something that is in limited supply are competitors. The 'something' is a resource like water, light, space, food or mates.

★ **Adaptation:** organisms are adapted (suited) for the environment in which they live and for their role (niche – see pages 16–17) in that environment.

Different factors affect the distribution of organisms. Some examples follow.

Example 1: intraspecific competition for light

In a wood, the branches of full-grown trees spread in all directions. They touch the branches of neighbouring trees, forming a continuous layer. This is the **canopy** which shades out plants beneath. When a tree is blown over, light floods through the gap in the canopy, stimulating vigorous plant growth on the woodland floor. This sunlit clearing becomes an arena for intense competition between tree seedlings sprouting from thousands of seeds, and then forming saplings (young trees). Many competitors start out but there is limited space for spreading branches, which also overshadow slower-growing rivals. Many young trees perish along the way. Only the one that grows the fastest will fill the gap in the canopy, finally cutting off the sunlight that signalled the start of the race many years previously.

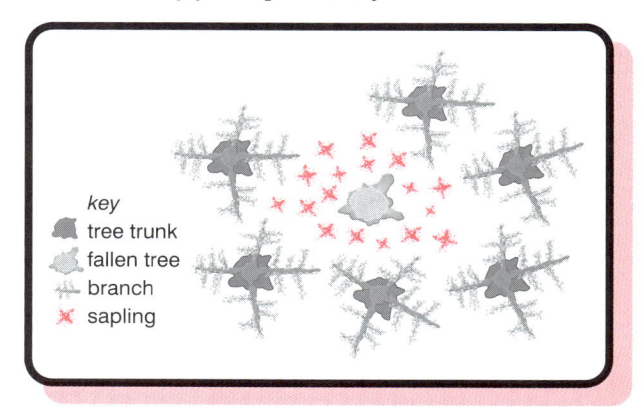

key
- tree trunk
- fallen tree
- branch
- sapling

Which sapling will survive to fill the gap? The length of the branches determines the distance between neighbouring trees, producing a continuous canopy and a regular pattern of tree trunks. The sunlit clearing caused by the fallen tree breaks the pattern and provides opportunities for new plant growth and competition between saplings to complete the canopy once more.

Example 2: intraspecific competition for water

The cacti in the photograph opposite are widely spaced apart, and they look as if they have been planted out in a regular arrangement. The pattern appears because although many tiny cactus seedlings sprout in a particular area, there is only enough water for some of them to grow into mature plants. Growing cacti are the competitors and water is the resource in short supply.

Organisms in the environment

Example 3: interspecific competition

Competition between different species is usually greatest among individuals that occupy the same trophic level. This competition for the same resource often leads to one species replacing another (called **competitive exclusion**). For example, when two species of clover (both producers) were grown separately, they grew well. However, when grown together one species eventually replaced the other. The reason was that the successful species grew slightly taller than its competitor and overshadowed it.

Example 4: predator and prey

Predators are adapted to catch prey, and prey are adapted to escape predators. The table summarises their different strategies.

predator	prey
eats a variety of prey species, reducing the risk of starvation should one prey species decline in numbers	large groups (e.g. herds of antelope, shoals of fish) distract predators from concentrating on a particular individual
catches young, old and sick prey	stings and bitter taste deter predators
catches large prey which provides more food per kill	warning coloration tells predators to avoid particular prey
moves to areas where prey is plentiful	camouflage conceals prey
	shock tactics startle predators
	prey tries to run/swim/fly faster than pursuing predator

Strategies for predator success and prey survival

Cacti in the Arizona Desert, south-western United States, where rainfall is erratic and infrequent

2.3 Population size

preview

At the end of this section you will:
- **know how populations increase in size**
- **understand that the impact of human activity on the environment is related to population size**
- **be able to identify specific effects of human activity on the environment.**

The size of a population

★ A **population** is a group of individuals of the same species living in a particular place at the same time.

★ **Births** and **immigration** increase the size of a population.

★ **Deaths** and **emigration** decrease the size of a population.

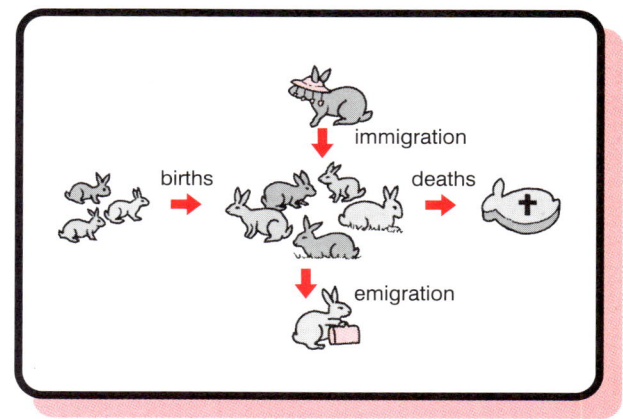

Factors affecting the size of a population

Population growth

The graph overleaf shows that populations grow in a particular way. **Limiting factors** stop populations from growing indefinitely. They include:

shortages of
- food
- water
- oxygen
- light
- shelter

build-up of
- poisonous wastes
- predators
- disease
- social factors.

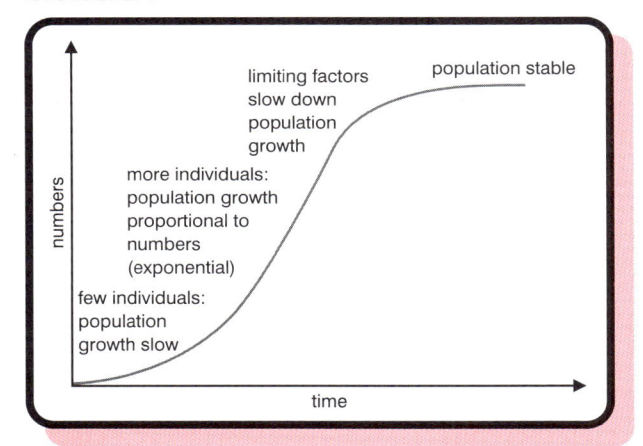

Life processes and living things

Population growth curve

Notice that

- fluctuations in predator numbers are *less* than fluctuations in prey numbers
- fluctuations in predator numbers *lag* behind fluctuations in prey numbers.

Why is this? There are fewer predators than prey, and predators tend to reproduce more slowly than prey.

Predator and prey populations

Predation affects the numbers of the prey population. The number of prey affects the predator population: if prey is scarce, then some of the predators will starve. The graphs below show the relationships between the numbers of predators and prey.

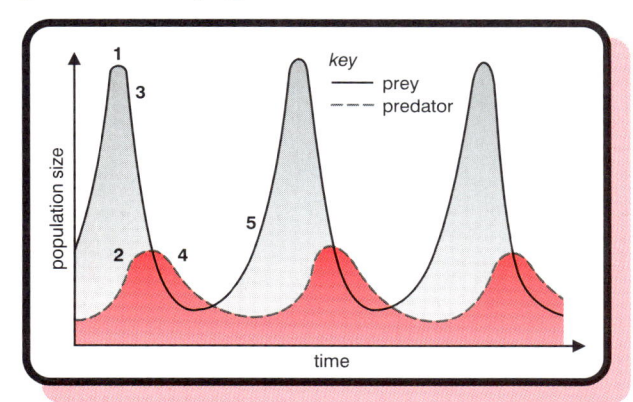

The human population

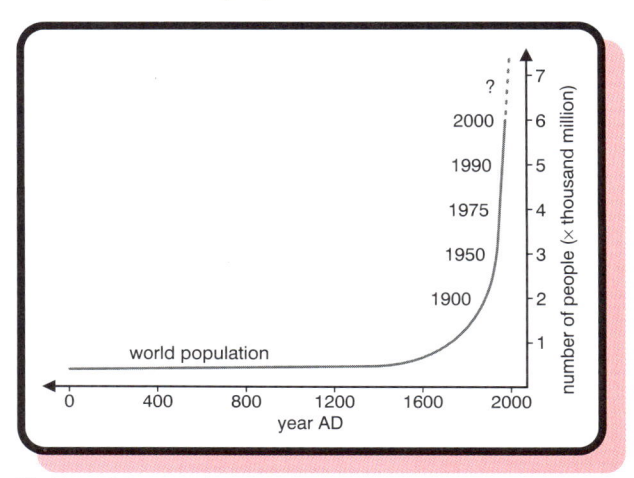

World population growth over the past 2000 years showing predicted future increase based on present trends

This graph shows that the human population has grown dramatically since the beginning of the nineteenth century. Although the populations of Europe, North America and Japan (developed countries) are levelling off, the populations of Latin America, Asia and Africa (developing countries) are still growing rapidly as a result of

- improvements in food production
- more drugs for the treatment of disease
- improved medical care
- improved public health.

Predator–prey relationships

1. Prey breed and increase in numbers if conditions are favourable (e.g. food is abundant).
2. Predators breed and increase in numbers in response to the abundance of prey.
3. Predation pressure increases and the number of prey declines.
4. Predator numbers decline in response to the shortage of food.
5. Predation pressure decreases and so prey numbers increase … and so on.

The rate of population growth is affected by the number of young people in the population, particularly women of child-bearing age. The table on the next page summarises the problem.

A large proportion of the world's population is young so the problems listed in the table are global. The problems are particularly acute in developing countries.

Organisms in the environment

problem	result
present birth rate high	adding to the rate of population increase
future birth rate high	as children in the population 'bulge' grow older and have their own children, adding further to the rate of population increase
social services inadequate	large numbers of children put strain on the educational system, medical services and housing

Problems of a young population

In Britain (and other developed countries) the problems are more to do with a population that has an increasing proportion of old people. The diseases of old age (cancer, arthritis, dementia) take up an increasing proportion of the resources available for medical care.

Human impact on the environment

1.5 million years ago: early humans probably moved from place to place in search of food. They hunted animals and gathered plants. Their impact on the environment was no more than that of other medium-sized animals.

10 000 years ago: about 12 million people lived in the world. In the Middle East they harvested wild wheat and other grains. When the grain was ripe, a family could probably gather over a year's supply in just a few weeks. People had little impact on the environment beyond their village.

2000 years ago: people had started to farm. Skills in crafts and tool-making developed. Villages became larger and some grew into towns. People had a much greater impact on the environment – farming the land, using raw materials.

Today: about 6 billion (thousand million) people live in the world. In developed countries, food is produced by relatively few people. Industry and technology use raw materials, often obtained from developing countries where environments may be stripped of resources. Pages 22–3 show the impact of human activities on today's environment.

round-up

How much have you improved? Work out your improvement index on page 82.

1. Look at pages 16–17. List the different components of an ecosystem. [6]

2. Explain the differences between
   a) intraspecific competition and interspecific competition
   b) adaptation and survival
   c) camouflage and warning coloration. [6]

3. The graph shows long-term changes in the numbers of snowshoe hare and its predator the Canadian lynx.

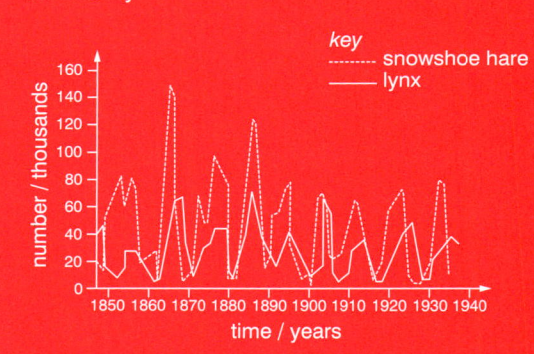

   key
   ---------- snowshoe hare
   ———— lynx

   a) Why do the highs and lows in the numbers of lynx lag behind the highs and lows in the numbers of snowshoe hare? [3]
   b) Although the numbers of snowshoe hare and lynx fluctuated between 1850 and 1940, what do you think is the *overall* trend in the population growth of each species between these years? [1]
   c) In 1890, if disease had virtually wiped out the lynx population, what do you think would have happened to the numbers of snowshoe hare? [1]
   d) If the lynx population had recovered from the effects of disease by 1910, what then do you think would have happened to the numbers of snowshoe hare? [2]
   e) If the lynx population had never recovered from the effects of disease, what then do you think would have happened to the numbers of snowshoe hare? Briefly explain your answer. [2]

Well done if you've improved. Don't worry if you haven't. Take a break and try again.

Life processes and living things

HUMAN IMPACT ON THE ENVIRONMENT

RESOURCES

Resources are the raw materials needed to satisfy human demands for food, homes, hospitals, schools and manufactured goods.

- **Renewable resources** are replaced as fast as plants and animals can reproduce and grow. If a resource is over-used it will decline. Damage to the environment also limits the production of renewable resources.

CASE STUDY: Fishing in the North Sea

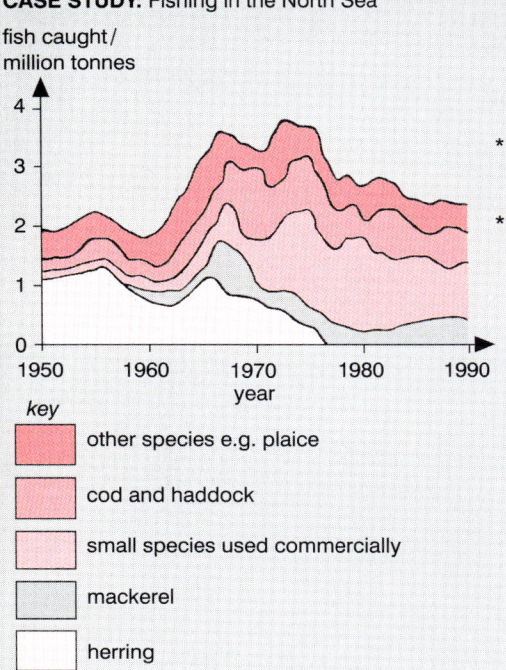

fish caught / million tonnes

[Graph showing fish catches from 1950 to 1990, ranging 0–4 million tonnes]

key:
- other species e.g. plaice
- cod and haddock
- small species used commercially
- mackerel
- herring

Catches of fish are reduced because of:
* **overfishing:** increased efficiency of fishing methods catches more fish than are replaced by reproduction
* **pollution:**
  - nutrients (e.g. nitrogen and phosphorus) from sewage works and surplus artificial fertilisers enter rivers which discharge into the North Sea
  - pesticides used to protect crops enter rivers which discharge into the North Sea
  - metals (e.g. mercury, cadmium, copper) from different industrial processes

---

- **Non-renewable resources** cannot be replaced when used up. For example, there are only limited amounts of fossil fuels (coal, oil, natural gas) and metals.

CASE STUDY: World reserves of metals
The table shows estimated world reserves of some metals vital for the manufacture of goods and technological development. Work out how long reserves of each metal will last at present rates of use.

iron ore	annual use	1.6 billion tonnes
	reserves	216.4 billion tonnes
copper	annual use	10 million tonnes
	reserves	570 million tonnes
tin	annual use	226 thousand tonnes
	reserves	4.2 million tonnes

Answers (to the nearest whole number)
Iron ore: 135 years
Copper: 57 years
Tin: 19 years

How human activities exploit resources and land and produce pollution

Organisms in the environment

Land use destroys habitats, driving thousands of species of plants and animals to the verge of extinction. The pressures are
- economic development
- growing human populations
- the increasing need for food to feed people.

} increase the use of land

CASE STUDY 1: Land use in the United Kingdom
Out of 24 million hectares of land in the UK:
- 19 million hectares are used for agriculture
- 1.7 million hectares are used for housing.

Quarrying (gravel, limestone, sand and sandstone) for building materials and the disposal of household waste account for some of the rest.

CASE STUDY 2: Exploiting tropical rainforest
Rainforests girdle the equator covering 14.5 million km² of land. The vegetation recycles carbon dioxide and oxygen through photosynthesis.

Moisture absorbed by the forest evaporates back into the atmosphere, to fall as rain thousands of miles away. Rainforest is being cleared at a rate of 100 000 km² each year for:

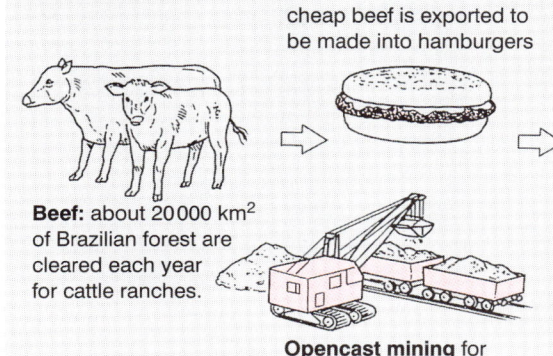

cheap beef is exported to be made into hamburgers

Beef: about 20 000 km² of Brazilian forest are cleared each year for cattle ranches.

Opencast mining for metals causes much damage to rainforest.

After clearing, nutrients disappear and soil is soon exhausted. Semi-desert develops: the ranchers move on to clear a new area.

Logging: only 4% of trees are felled for timber, but another 40% are damaged or destroyed in the process.

POLLUTION

Pollution is the result of industry making goods that maintain our standard of living.
- **Air** is polluted by gases, dust and smoke from vehicles and industry.
- **Water** is polluted by wastes from factories and runoff of agrochemicals.
- **Land** is polluted by agrochemicals and the dumping of rubbish and waste.

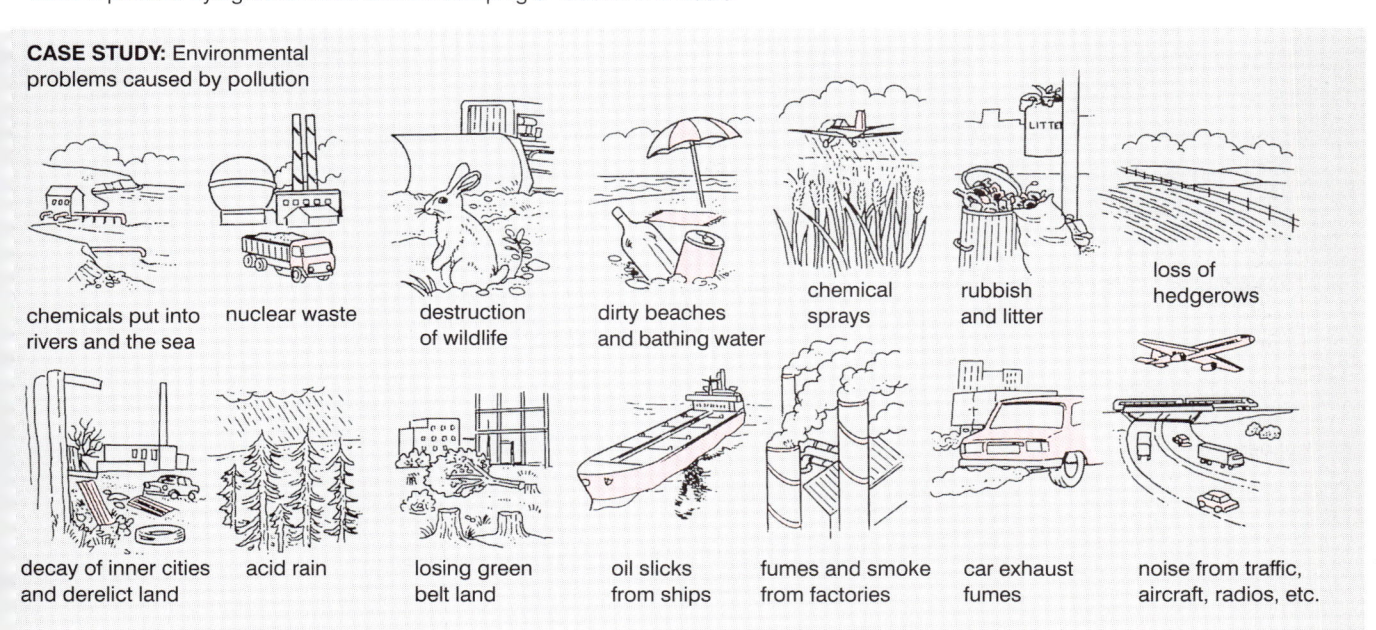

CASE STUDY: Environmental problems caused by pollution

- chemicals put into rivers and the sea
- nuclear waste
- destruction of wildlife
- dirty beaches and bathing water
- chemical sprays
- rubbish and litter
- loss of hedgerows
- decay of inner cities and derelict land
- acid rain
- losing green belt land
- oil slicks from ships
- fumes and smoke from factories
- car exhaust fumes
- noise from traffic, aircraft, radios, etc.

23

Cell activity

How much do you already know? Work out your score on page 82.

Test yourself

1. Match each of the structures in column **A** with its function in column **B**.

A structures	B functions
mitochondrion	partially permeable to substances in solution
cell membrane	where energy is released from the oxidation of glucose
chloroplast	fully permeable to substances in solution
cell wall	contains the chromosomes
nucleus	where light energy is captured

   [5]

2. What is a clone? [1]

3. What is formed by the replication of DNA? [2]

4. a) Why do the cells of a tissue undergo mitosis?
   b) In mitosis, what is the relationship between the number and type of chromosomes in the parent cell and in the daughter cells? [5]

5. Briefly explain the meaning of 'haploid' and 'diploid'. [4]

6. Complete the following paragraph using the words below. Each word may be used once, more than once or not at all.

   types   organism   tissues   organs   cells   an organ

   Living things are made of _____ . Groups of similar _____ with similar functions form _____ that can work together as _____ . A group of _____ working together form _____ system. [6]

7. Cellulose and chitin are important building materials in living things. Give an example of the use of each. [2]

8. Briefly explain the difference between saturated and unsaturated fats. [2]

9. What is a nucleotide? [4]

3.1 Cells at work

preview

At the end of this section you will know that:
- all living things are made of cells
- plant cells and animal cells have structures in common but are also different from one another
- mitochondria and chloroplasts are structures in cells which convert energy from one form to another
- different types of cells are each specialised to perform a particular biological task.

Cell functions

The structures that make up a cell are organised in a way that depends on the **functions** of the cell (the way it works).

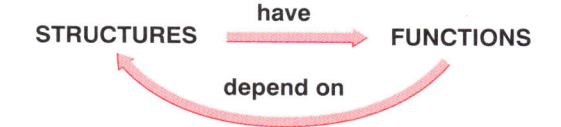

STRUCTURES ⇄ FUNCTIONS
(have / depend on)

Fact file

★ Most cells are too small to be seen with the naked eye.

★ The light microscope helps us see the structure of cells.

★ The transmission electron microscope reveals cell structures too small to be seen under the light microscope. It enables us to see the fine structure of cells in great detail.

★ The human body is constructed from more than 200 different types of cell.

How cells work

The diagram on pages 26–7 is the concept map for **cells at work**. The numbers on the diagram refer to the checklist of points.

3.2 Cell division

preview

At the end of this section you will:
- know that new cells (daughter cells) are formed when old cells (parent cells) divide into two
- understand that the cytoplasm and nucleus divide during cell division
- know that a cell may divide in two ways: mitosis and meiosis.

How cells divide

On pages 28–9 is the concept map for **cell division**. Study it carefully.

Remember
★ The **cells of the body** divide by **mitosis**.

★ The **cells of the sex organs** that give rise to the sex cells (**gametes**) divide by **meiosis**. Sex cells are produced in the sex organs:
- the testes of the male and the ovaries of the female in mammals
- the anthers (male) and the carpels (female) in flowering plants.

SEXUAL REPRODUCTION Pages 65–7.

Mitosis and meiosis

The nucleus contains **chromosomes**, each consisting of **deoxyribonucleic acid** (**DNA**) wound round a core of protein. In cell division, the chromosomes are passed from the **parent** cell to the new **daughter** cells. 'Daughter' does not mean that the cells are female. It means that they are the new cells formed as a result of cell division.

CHROMOSOMES AND DNA Pages 35–7.

Mitosis produces daughter cells with the same number of chromosomes as the parent cell. The daughter cells are described as **diploid** (or **2n**).

Meiosis produces daughter cells with only half the number of chromosomes in the parent cell. The daughter cells are described as **haploid** (or **n**).

The importance of mitosis

The daughter cells each receive an identical full (diploid) set of chromosomes from the parent cell.

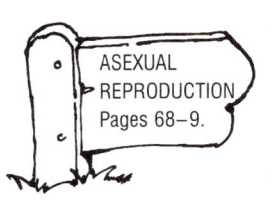

ASEXUAL REPRODUCTION Pages 68–9.

As a result, the parent cell and its daughter cells are genetically identical. They form a **clone**.

As a result, mitosis is the way in which living things

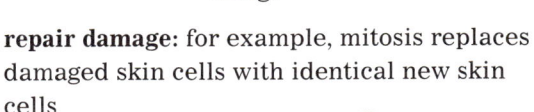

- **repair damage:** for example, mitosis replaces damaged skin cells with identical new skin cells
- **grow:** for example, the root of a plant grows because root tip cells divide by mitosis to form new root tissue

DEVELOPMENT Page 65.

- **reproduce asexually:** for example, parts of stems can sprout roots and grow into new plants. The new individuals are genetically identical to the parents and are therefore clones.

The importance of meiosis

The daughter cells each receive a half (haploid) set of chromosomes from the parent cell.

As a result, during fertilisation (when sperm and egg join together), the chromosomes from each cell combine.

As a result, the fertilised egg (**zygote**) is diploid but inherits a new combination of genes contributed (50:50) from the parents.

VARIATION Pages 75–6.

As a result, the new individual inherits characteristics from both parents, not just from one parent as in asexual reproduction.

Life processes and living things

Checklist for cells at work

1 ★ During photosynthesis, oxygen is released into the environment.

   ★ During aerobic respiration, oxygen is used to release energy from food.

   As a result, photosynthesis and aerobic respiration are stages in a cycle, the by-products of one forming the starting point of the other.

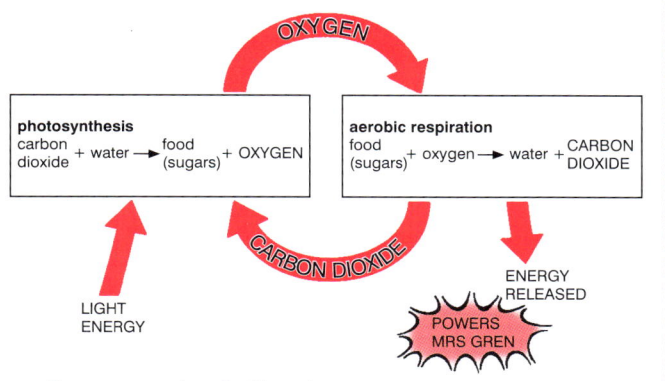

photosynthesis
carbon dioxide + water → food (sugars) + OXYGEN

aerobic respiration
food (sugars) + oxygen → water + CARBON DIOXIDE

LIGHT ENERGY

ENERGY RELEASED
POWERS MRS GREN

The oxygen–carbon dioxide cycle

2 ★ There are different types of cell for different functions.

   ★ Each type of cell is suited (**adapted**) for its function in the animal body or plant body.

   ★ A sheet of cells which covers a body surface is called an **epithelium**.

   ★ Red blood cells do not have nuclei.

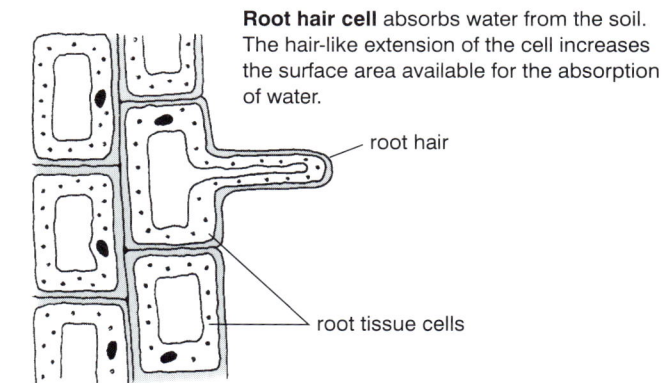

Root hair cell absorbs water from the soil. The hair-like extension of the cell increases the surface area available for the absorption of water.

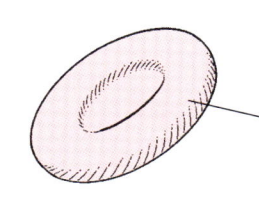

— root hair
— root tissue cells

Red blood cells transport oxygen around the body. They contain haemoglobin which combines with oxygen.

flattened disc shape increases surface area for the absorption of oxygen

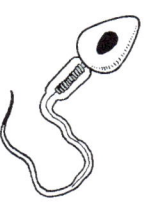

VARIETY OF CELLS

sperm – the male sex cell which swims to the egg

tail-like flagellum lashes from side to side

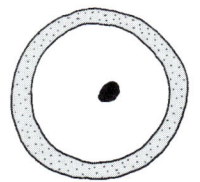

ovum (egg) – the female sex cell which is fertilised when a sperm fuses with it

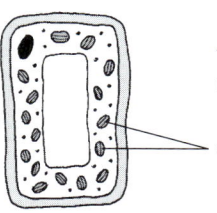

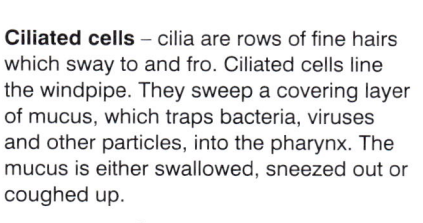

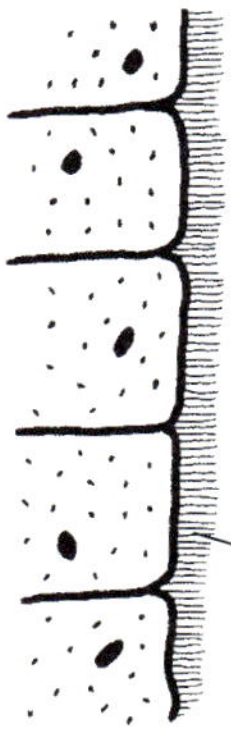

Ciliated cells – cilia are rows of fine hairs which sway to and fro. Ciliated cells line the windpipe. They sweep a covering layer of mucus, which traps bacteria, viruses and other particles, into the pharynx. The mucus is either swallowed, sneezed out or coughed up.

— cilia

The **leaf palisade cell** contains numerous chloroplasts.

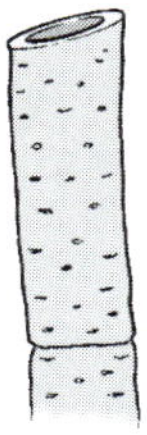

— chloroplasts

Xylem cells form tubes in the stem, roots and leaves, transporting water to all parts of the plant.

Cells at work

Cell activity

SUNLIGHT ENERGY

captured by chlorophyll

chloroplast

PHOTOSYNTHESIS

PLANT CELLS TRANSFORM ENERGY

CONVERTED TO CHEMICAL ENERGY

$6CO_2 + 6H_2O \rightarrow C_6H_{12}O_6 + 6O_2$
carbon dioxide, water, sugar (glucose), oxygen

CELL STRUCTURE

mitochondria where energy is released from the oxidation of glucose

nucleus contains the chromosomes which carry genes

chloroplasts contain chlorophyll which captures light energy

cell wall made of cellulose, fully permeable to substances in solution

vacuole contains cell sap – a solution of sugar and salts

cytoplasm is jelly-like material which fills the cell, giving it shape

ANIMAL CELL

PLANT CELL

cell membrane is partially permeable to substances in solution

STRUCTURES FOUND IN ANIMAL *AND* PLANT CELLS

STRUCTURES FOUND *ONLY* IN PLANT CELLS

SUGAR

CHECK LIST 1

ANIMAL AND PLANT CELLS TRANSFORM ENERGY

OXYGEN

mitochondrion

oxidation of sugar (glucose)

MRS GREN Page 11.

AEROBIC RESPIRATION

MOVEMENT
RESPIRATION
SENSITIVITY   POWERS

GROWTH
REPRODUCTION
EXCRETION
NUTRITION

ENERGY

CHEMICAL ENERGY RELEASED

$C_6H_{12}O_6 + 6O_2 \rightarrow 6CO_2 + 6H_2O$
sugar (glucose), oxygen, carbon dioxide, water

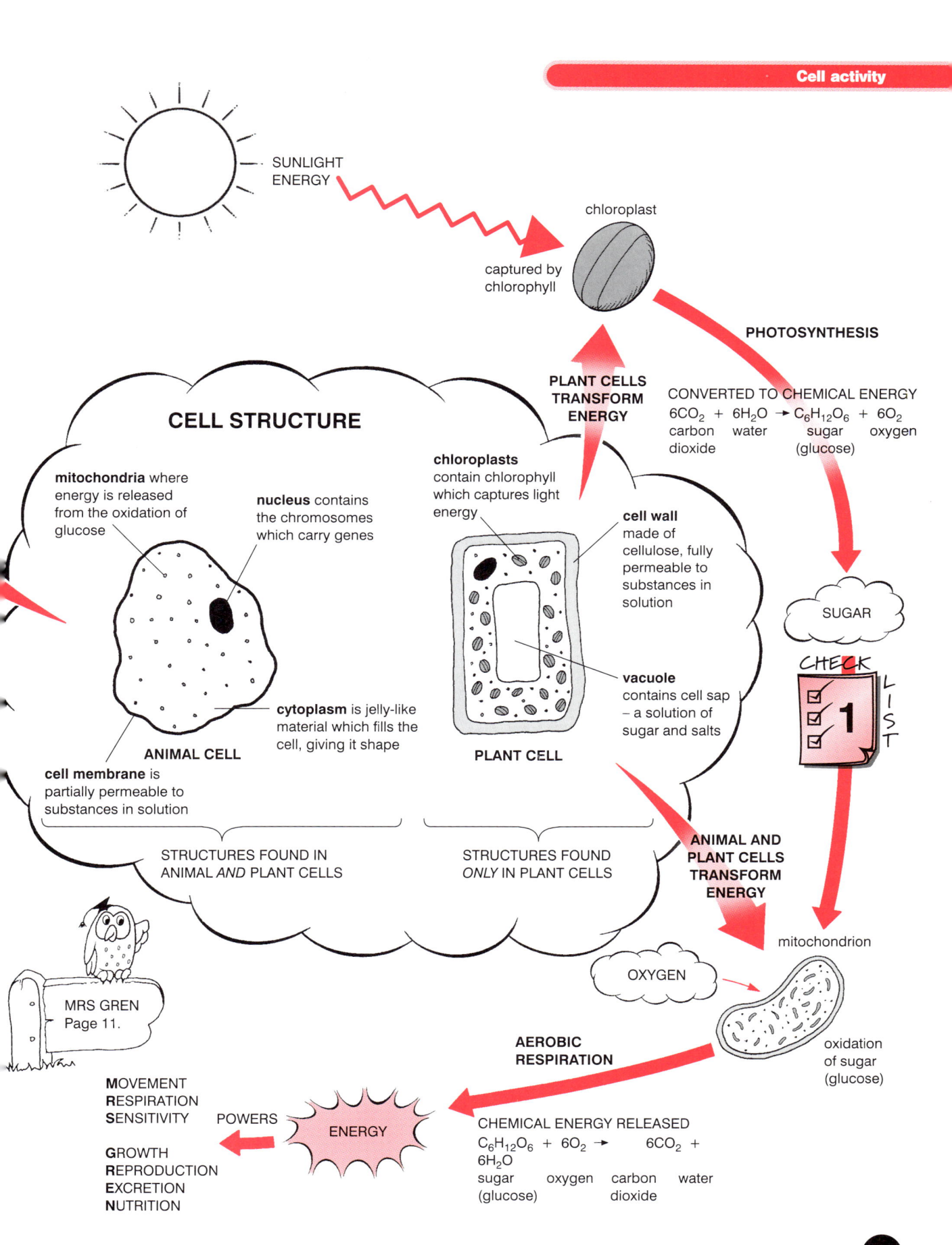

27

Life processes and living things

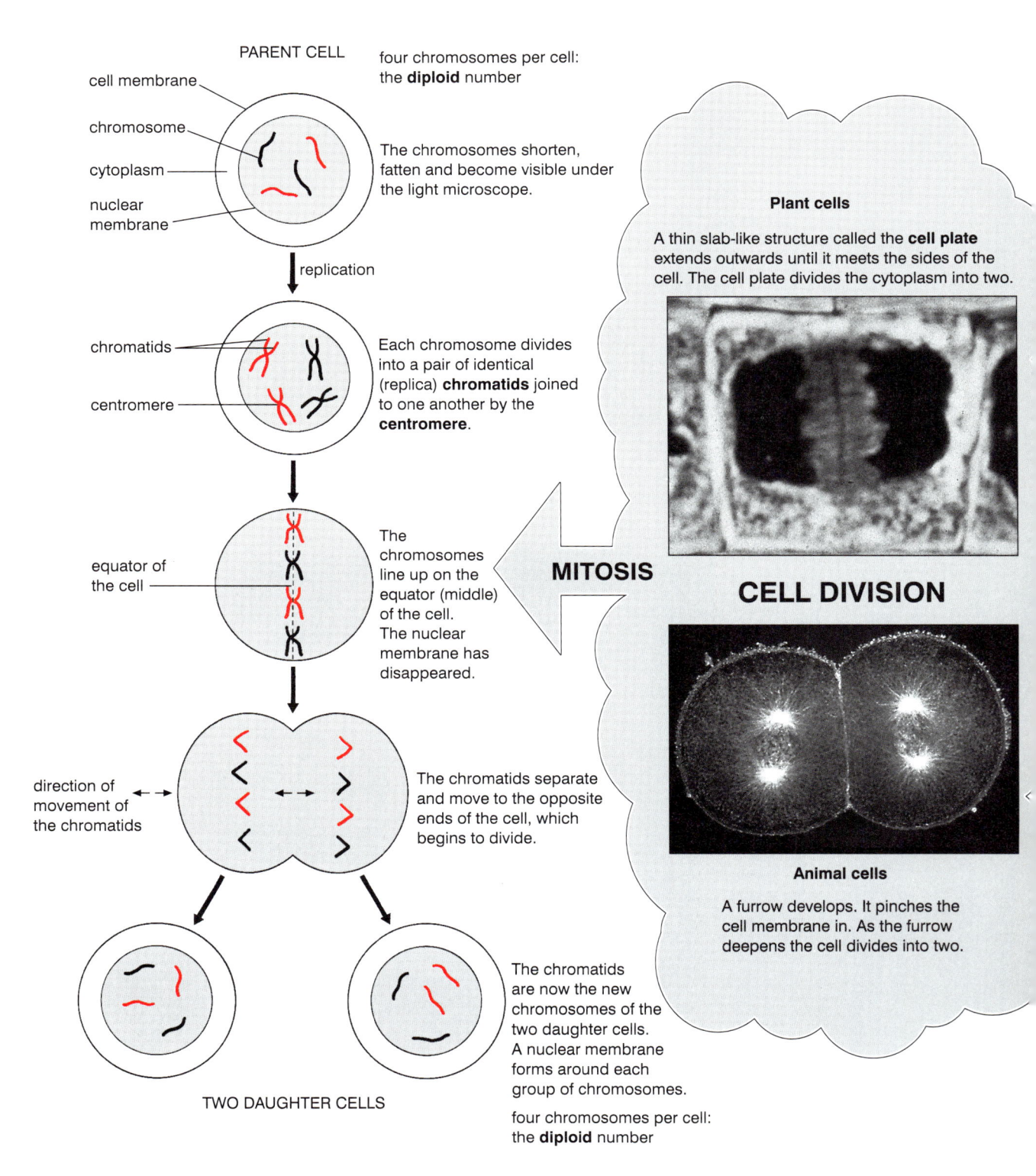

CELL DIVISION

MITOSIS

PARENT CELL — four chromosomes per cell: the **diploid** number

- cell membrane
- chromosome
- cytoplasm
- nuclear membrane

The chromosomes shorten, fatten and become visible under the light microscope.

↓ replication

- chromatids
- centromere

Each chromosome divides into a pair of identical (replica) **chromatids** joined to one another by the **centromere**.

- equator of the cell

The chromosomes line up on the equator (middle) of the cell. The nuclear membrane has disappeared.

- direction of movement of the chromatids

The chromatids separate and move to the opposite ends of the cell, which begins to divide.

TWO DAUGHTER CELLS

The chromatids are now the new chromosomes of the two daughter cells. A nuclear membrane forms around each group of chromosomes.

four chromosomes per cell: the **diploid** number

Plant cells

A thin slab-like structure called the **cell plate** extends outwards until it meets the sides of the cell. The cell plate divides the cytoplasm into two.

Animal cells

A furrow develops. It pinches the cell membrane in. As the furrow deepens the cell divides into two.

Cell division

Cell activity

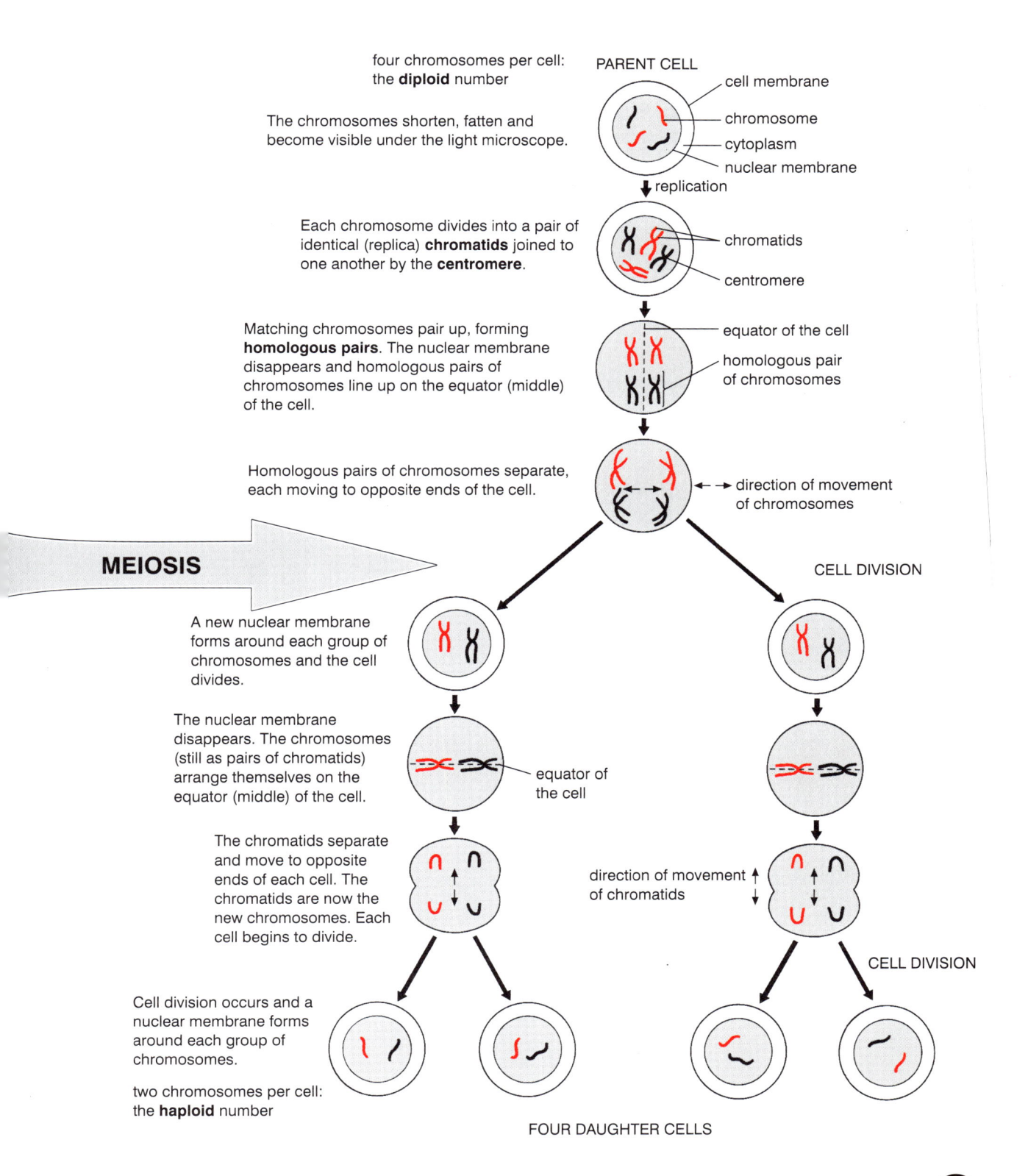

PARENT CELL

four chromosomes per cell: the **diploid** number
- cell membrane
- chromosome
- cytoplasm
- nuclear membrane

The chromosomes shorten, fatten and become visible under the light microscope.

↓ replication

Each chromosome divides into a pair of identical (replica) **chromatids** joined to one another by the **centromere**.
- chromatids
- centromere

Matching chromosomes pair up, forming **homologous pairs**. The nuclear membrane disappears and homologous pairs of chromosomes line up on the equator (middle) of the cell.
- equator of the cell
- homologous pair of chromosomes

Homologous pairs of chromosomes separate, each moving to opposite ends of the cell.
- direction of movement of chromosomes

MEIOSIS

CELL DIVISION

A new nuclear membrane forms around each group of chromosomes and the cell divides.

The nuclear membrane disappears. The chromosomes (still as pairs of chromatids) arrange themselves on the equator (middle) of the cell.
- equator of the cell

The chromatids separate and move to opposite ends of each cell. The chromatids are now the new chromosomes. Each cell begins to divide.
- direction of movement of chromatids

CELL DIVISION

Cell division occurs and a nuclear membrane forms around each group of chromosomes.

two chromosomes per cell: the **haploid** number

FOUR DAUGHTER CELLS

Life processes and living things

3.3 Cells, tissues and organs

preview

At the end of this section you will:
- understand that cells are organised into tissues, tissues into organs, and organs into organ systems
- know about the importance of the surface area to volume ratio for living processes
- understand that organ systems are specialised for exchanging materials.

Building an organ system

Here is the concept map which revises **cells**, **tissues** and **organs**.

Plants and animals are **multicellular**: they are made of many types of cells. Each type of cell is specialised to perform a particular biological task.

★ A group of similar cells makes a **tissue**.

VARIETY OF CELLS Page 26.

★ Different tissues together make up an **organ**.

★ Different organs combine to make an **organ system**.

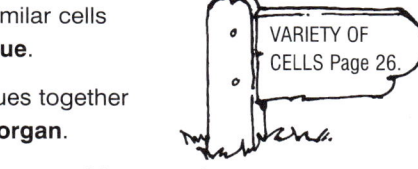

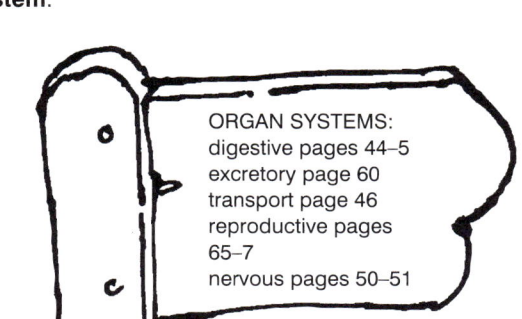

ORGAN SYSTEMS:
digestive pages 44–5
excretory page 60
transport page 46
reproductive pages 65–7
nervous pages 50–51

The heart and blood vessels transport blood to all parts of the body.

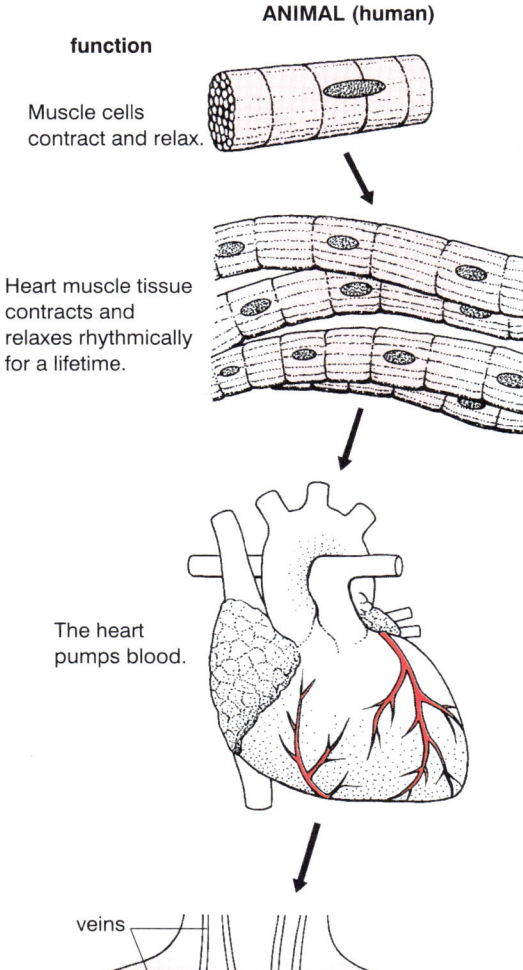

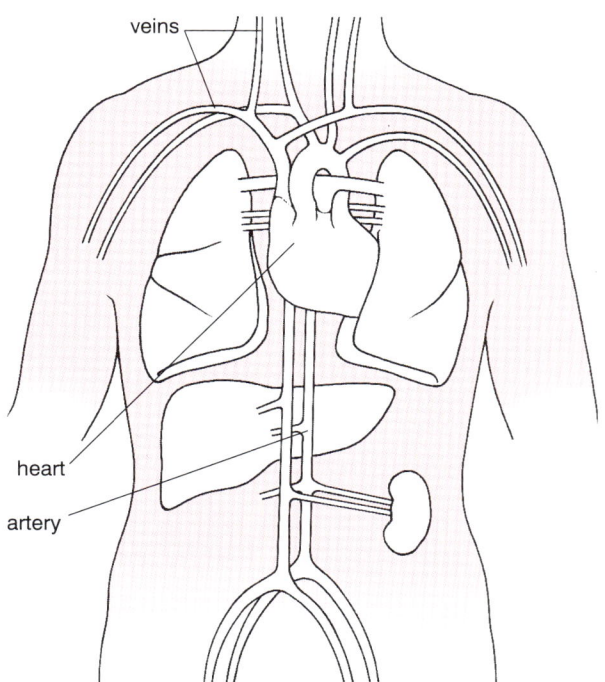

ANIMAL (human)

function

Muscle cells contract and relax.

Heart muscle tissue contracts and relaxes rhythmically for a lifetime.

The heart pumps blood.

veins

heart

artery

Cells to organ systems

30

Cell activity

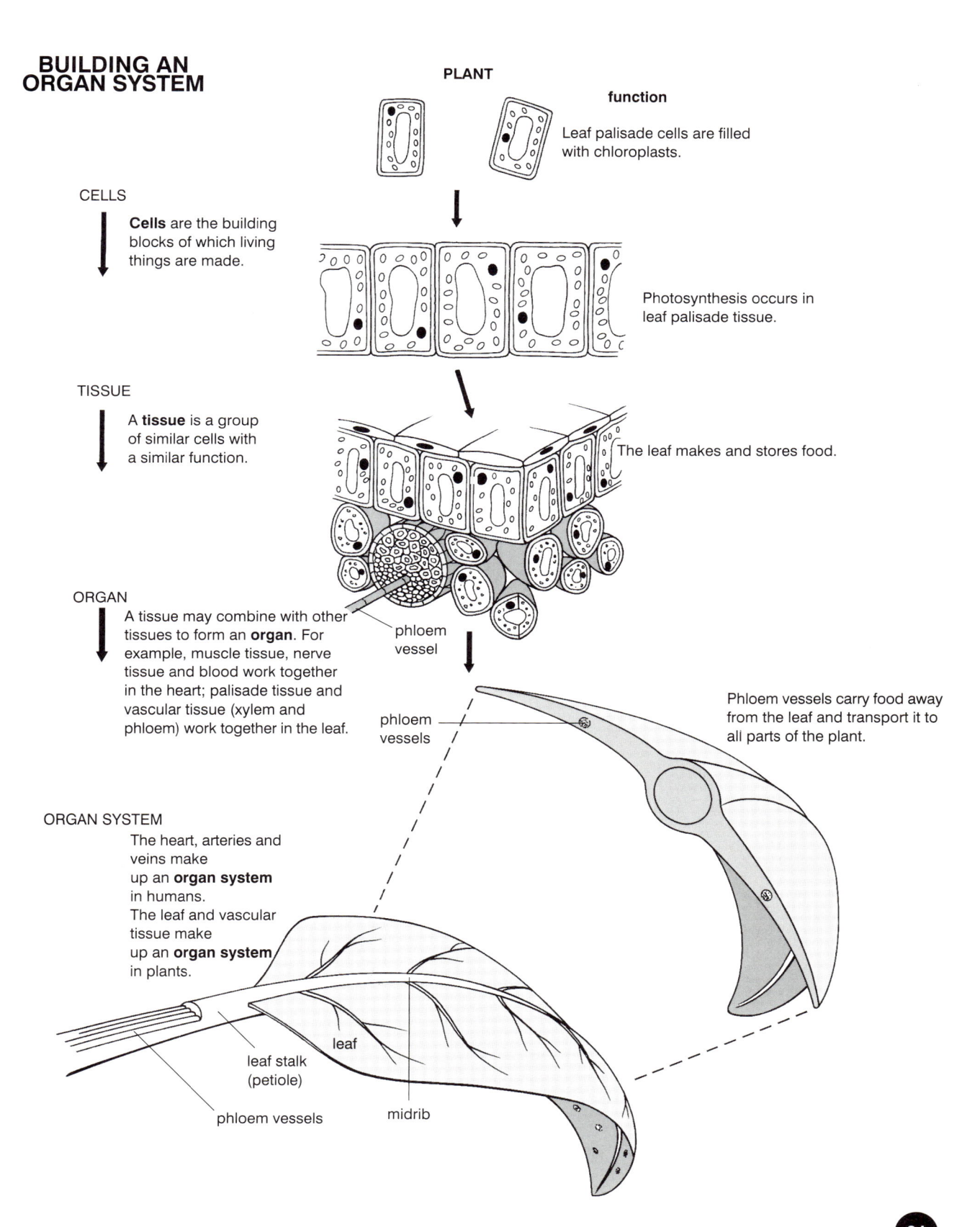

BUILDING AN ORGAN SYSTEM

PLANT

function

Leaf palisade cells are filled with chloroplasts.

CELLS
↓
Cells are the building blocks of which living things are made.

Photosynthesis occurs in leaf palisade tissue.

TISSUE
↓
A **tissue** is a group of similar cells with a similar function.

The leaf makes and stores food.

ORGAN
↓
A tissue may combine with other tissues to form an **organ**. For example, muscle tissue, nerve tissue and blood work together in the heart; palisade tissue and vascular tissue (xylem and phloem) work together in the leaf.

phloem vessel

Phloem vessels carry food away from the leaf and transport it to all parts of the plant.

phloem vessels

ORGAN SYSTEM

The heart, arteries and veins make up an **organ system** in humans. The leaf and vascular tissue make up an **organ system** in plants.

leaf stalk (petiole)

phloem vessels

leaf

midrib

31

3 Life processes and living things

Surface area to volume ratio

All cells (tissues, organs, organisms) exchange gases, food and other materials with their environment. The exchanges occur mostly by diffusion across surfaces. Look at the calculations for surface area (SA), volume (V) and surface area to volume ratio (SA/V) here.

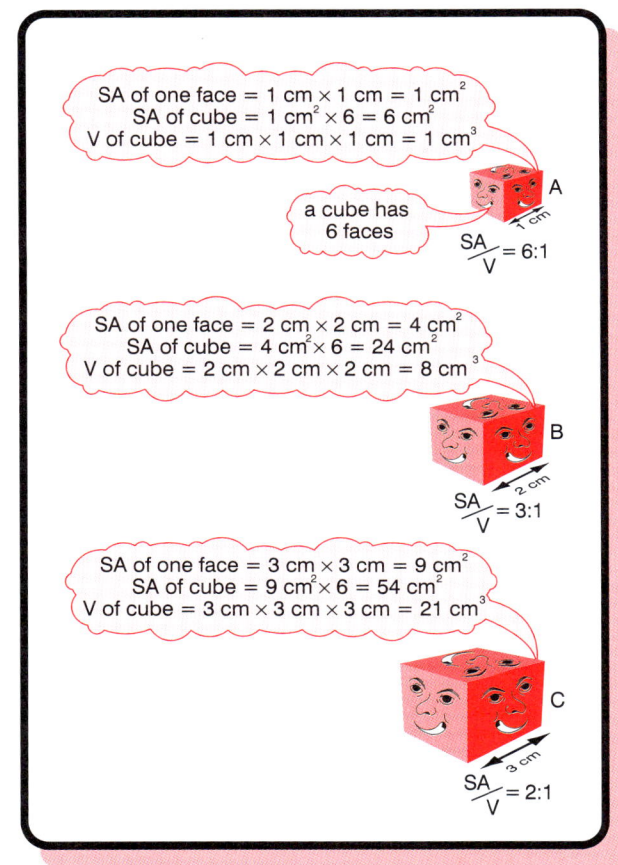

Cube A (1 cm):
SA of one face = 1 cm × 1 cm = 1 cm^2
SA of cube = 1 cm^2 × 6 = 6 cm^2
V of cube = 1 cm × 1 cm × 1 cm = 1 cm^3
a cube has 6 faces
SA/V = 6:1

Cube B (2 cm):
SA of one face = 2 cm × 2 cm = 4 cm^2
SA of cube = 4 cm^2 × 6 = 24 cm^2
V of cube = 2 cm × 2 cm × 2 cm = 8 cm^3
SA/V = 3:1

Cube C (3 cm):
SA of one face = 3 cm × 3 cm = 9 cm^2
SA of cube = 9 cm^2 × 6 = 54 cm^2
V of cube = 3 cm × 3 cm × 3 cm = 21 cm^3
SA/V = 2:1

Cubic arithmetic

- The SA/V of cube B is half that of cube A.
- The SA/V of cube C is two-thirds that of cube B and one-third that of cube A.

Remember
The LARGER the cube becomes, the SMALLER its SA/V.

★ Surface area increases with the **square** (power^2) of the side.

★ Volume increases with the **cube** (power^3) of the side.

Cells (tissues, organs, organisms) are not cube shaped, but the calculations apply to any shape. For example, as a cell grows it

- takes in more food and gases
- produces more waste substances.

After the cell reaches a certain size, its surface area becomes too small to meet the needs of the larger volume of living matter inside.

At this point, the cell divides into two smaller daughter cells. This restores the ratio of surface area to volume because the surface area to volume ratio of a daughter cell is greater than that of the parent cell.

As a result, sufficient food and gases can pass across the cell surface into the cell.

As a result, wastes can pass across the cell surface out of the cell.

Organ systems specialised for exchanging materials

We all exchange gases, food and other materials between our body and the environment. The exchange happens slowly by diffusion across body surfaces. Different organs and organ systems are specialised to increase the available surface area for the exchange of materials with their surroundings. They make the SA/V as large as possible.

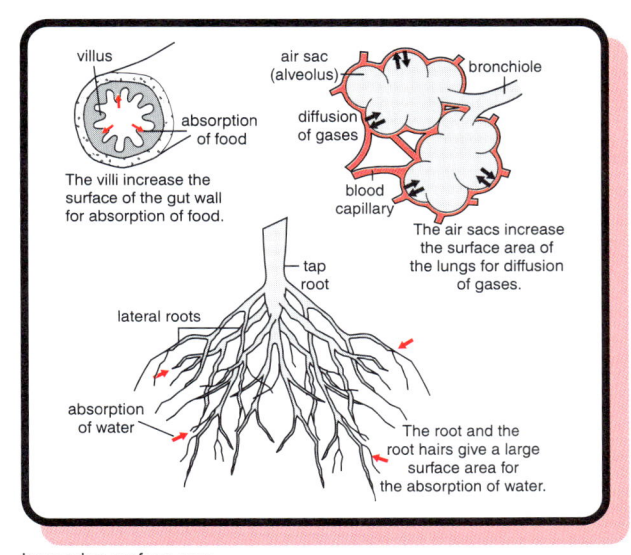

The villi increase the surface of the gut wall for absorption of food.

The air sacs increase the surface area of the lungs for diffusion of gases.

The root and the root hairs give a large surface area for the absorption of water.

Increasing surface area

3.4 Chemicals in living things

preview

At the end of this section you will:
- understand that living things are made from the same elements as other types of matter
- know that carbohydrates, lipids, proteins and nucleic acids are important chemicals in living things
- understand that atoms of carbon are able to combine to form long chains.

Elements for life

All matter is made of chemical elements. Of these elements, six make up more than 95% by mass of living matter. They are:

- carbon (C)
- hydrogen (H)
- nitrogen (N)
- oxygen (O)
- phosphorus (P)
- sulphur (S).

Hints & Tips: The symbols of the elements arranged in order of abundance in living matter make the mnemonic **CHNOPS**.

Compounds for life

Important compounds in living things are

- **carbohydrates**: a major source of energy and structural materials
- **lipids**: stores of energy
- **proteins**: for building bodies
- **nucleic acids**: carry a code which tells cells how to make proteins.

Fact file

Carbon is the most common element in the substances that make up living things. Carbon atoms can combine to form long chains. Many of the carbon compounds in living things have large molecules (**macromolecules**) formed by small molecules combining.

Carbohydrates

Carbohydrates are compounds containing the elements carbon, hydrogen and oxygen. There are three categories:

Monosaccharides are simple sugars. Sweet-tasting **fructose** and **glucose** are examples. Both have the formula $C_6H_{12}O_6$. The six carbon atoms form a ring. Sugars (especially glucose) are an important source of energy in all living things.

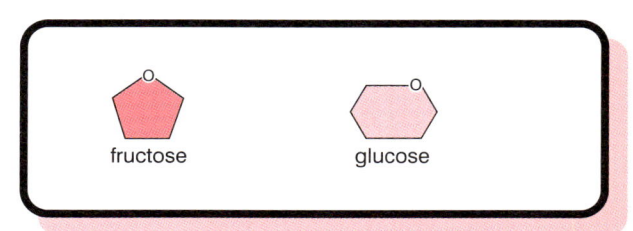

The formula of fructose and glucose in shorthand form

Disaccharides are more complex sugars. They are formed when two monosaccharides combine. For example, two molecules of glucose combine to form one molecule of **maltose**:

2 glucose → maltose + water
$2C_6H_{12}O_6 \rightarrow C_{12}H_{22}O_{11}(aq) + H_2O$

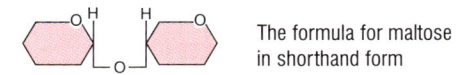

The formula for maltose in shorthand form

A molecule of fructose and a molecule of glucose combine to form one molecule of **sucrose**:

glucose + fructose → sucrose + water

Polysaccharides are carbohydrates whose molecules contain hundreds of sugar rings. For example, **starch**, **cellulose** and **glycogen** are polysaccharides. Their molecules consist of long chains of glucose rings.

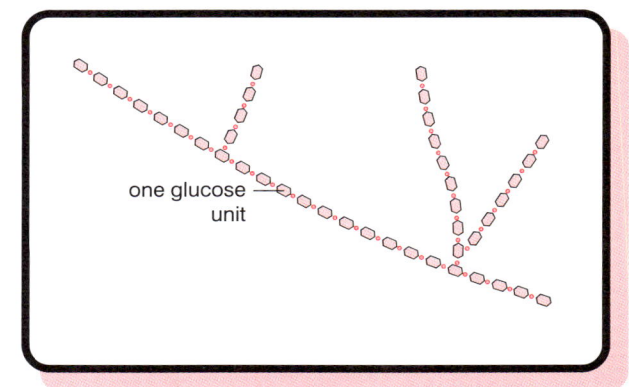

Part of a starch molecule

Life processes and living things

Polysaccharides differ in the length and structure of their chains. They are important storage and structural materials in living things.

★ **Starch** is a food substance stored in plants. Their cells convert the starch into glucose, which is oxidised (respired) to release energy.

★ **Glycogen** is a food substance stored in animals. Liver cells convert glycogen into glucose, which is oxidised (respired) to release energy.

★ **Cellulose** is an important component of the cell walls of plants.

★ **Chitin** is an important component of the exoskeleton of insects.

Lipids

Lipids are compounds containing the elements carbon, hydrogen and oxygen. There are two types of lipids: **fats**, which are solid at room temperature; and **oils**, which are liquid at room temperature.

Fats and oils are compounds formed between two constituents: **fatty acids** and **glycerol**. A molecule of glycerol can combine with three fatty acid molecules to form a **triglyceride** molecule and three molecules of water. Fats and oils are mixtures of triglycerides.

glycerol + fatty acid ⟶ triglyceride + water

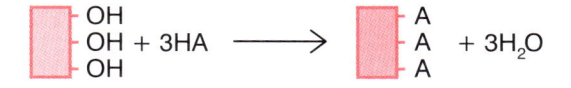

$$\begin{matrix} \text{OH} \\ \text{OH} \\ \text{OH} \end{matrix} + 3\text{HA} \longrightarrow \begin{matrix} \text{A} \\ \text{A} \\ \text{A} \end{matrix} + 3H_2O$$

Making a triglyceride

Saturated and unsaturated fats and oils

Fatty acids (and therefore the fats and oils of which they are a part) may be

- **saturated** – the carbon atoms are joined by single bonds, *or*
- **unsaturated** – the carbon atoms have double bonds between them (see page 138). If there is one double bond in the molecule, the compound is **monounsaturated**. If there is more than one double bond in the molecule, the compound is **polyunsaturated**.

Fats and oils are important as

- components of cell membranes
- sources of energy
- sources of the fat-soluble vitamins A, D and E
- insulation which helps keep the body warm
- protection for delicate organs.

Proteins

Proteins are compounds containing the elements carbon, hydrogen, oxygen, nitrogen and sometimes sulphur.

Amino acids are the building blocks which combine to make proteins. Two or more amino acids can combine to form a **peptide**, which can combine with more amino acids to form a **protein**.

Fact file

★ **Peptides** have molecules with up to 15 amino acids.

★ **Polypeptides** have molecules with 15–100 amino acids.

★ **Proteins** have still larger molecules.

There are 20 different amino acids that combine to form proteins. The protein made depends on the type and number of amino acids joining together.

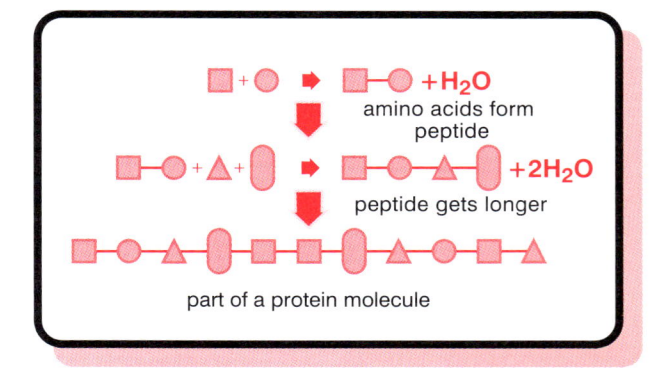

How amino acids combine to form peptides and proteins. Each shape represents a particular type of amino acid.

Cell activity

Proteins are important because

- they are the materials from which new tissues are made during growth and repair
- **enzymes** are proteins which control the rates of chemical reactions in cells
- **hormones** are proteins which control the activities of organisms.

HORMONES Pages 56–7.

Enzymes in action

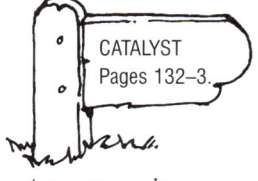

Enzymes are made by living cells. They are **catalysts** which control the speeds of chemical reactions in cells. There are thousands of different enzymes in a cell. Enzymes also speed up the digestion of food in the gut.

CATALYST Pages 132–3.

Enzymes are

- **specific** in their action – each enzyme catalyses a certain chemical reaction or type of chemical reaction
- sensitive to changes in **pH**
- sensitive to changes in **temperature**.

The substance that the enzyme helps to react is called the **substrate**. The substances formed in the reaction are called **products**.

The features of enzymes are shown below.

Nucleic acids

There are two important nucleic acids – **deoxyribonucleic acid (DNA)** and **ribonucleic acid (RNA)**.

★ DNA makes up the chromosomes in the nucleus of the cell. The **genes** that carry information from parents to offspring are lengths of DNA. They carry the **genetic code** which tells cells how to assemble amino acids in the correct order to make proteins.

★ RNA occurs in the nucleus and cytoplasm of the cell. It transfers the information in the genes to the places in the cell where proteins are made.

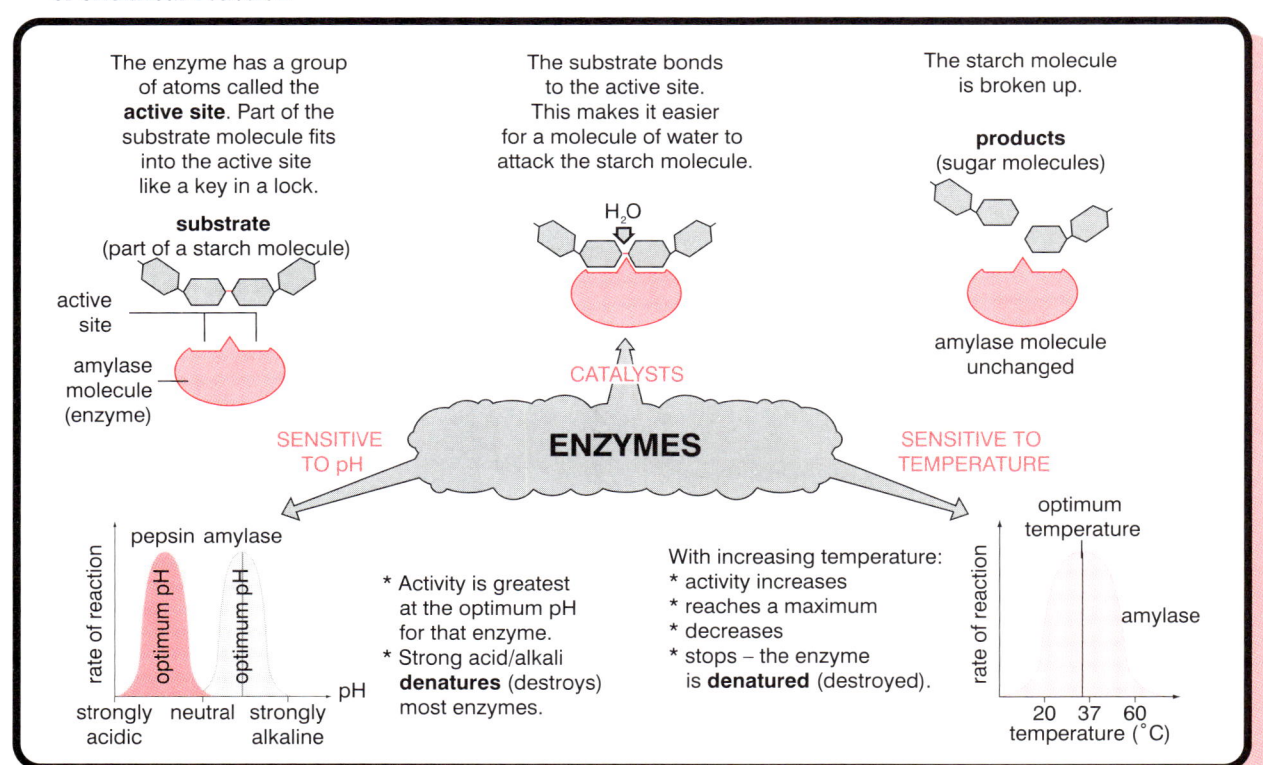

The enzyme has a group of atoms called the **active site**. Part of the substrate molecule fits into the active site like a key in a lock.

substrate (part of a starch molecule)

active site

amylase molecule (enzyme)

The substrate bonds to the active site. This makes it easier for a molecule of water to attack the starch molecule.

H_2O

The starch molecule is broken up.

products (sugar molecules)

amylase molecule unchanged

CATALYSTS

ENZYMES

SENSITIVE TO pH

pepsin amylase

rate of reaction

optimum pH

pH

strongly acidic | neutral | strongly alkaline

* Activity is greatest at the optimum pH for that enzyme.
* Strong acid/alkali **denatures** (destroys) most enzymes.

With increasing temperature:
* activity increases
* reaches a maximum
* decreases
* stops – the enzyme is **denatured** (destroyed).

SENSITIVE TO TEMPERATURE

rate of reaction

optimum temperature

amylase

20 37 60
temperature (°C)

Enzymes in action

Life processes and living things

The structure of DNA

DNA and RNA are large complex molecules made from lots of smaller molecules called **nucleotides**.

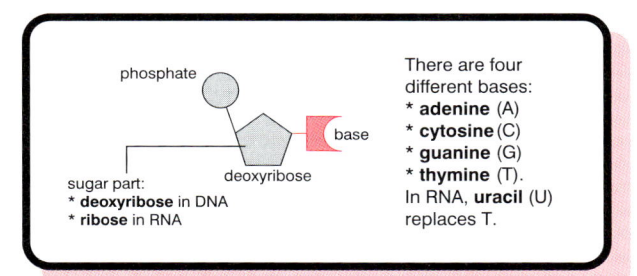

There are four different bases:
* **adenine** (A)
* **cytosine** (C)
* **guanine** (G)
* **thymine** (T).
In RNA, **uracil** (U) replaces T.

sugar part:
* **deoxyribose** in DNA
* **ribose** in RNA

A nucleotide molecule

★ Many nucleotides join together, sugar to phosphate, to form a long strand.

★ Two of these strands link together by **base pairing** to form a molecule of DNA.

★ The double strand twists into a spiral called a **double helix** – two intertwined spiral strands.

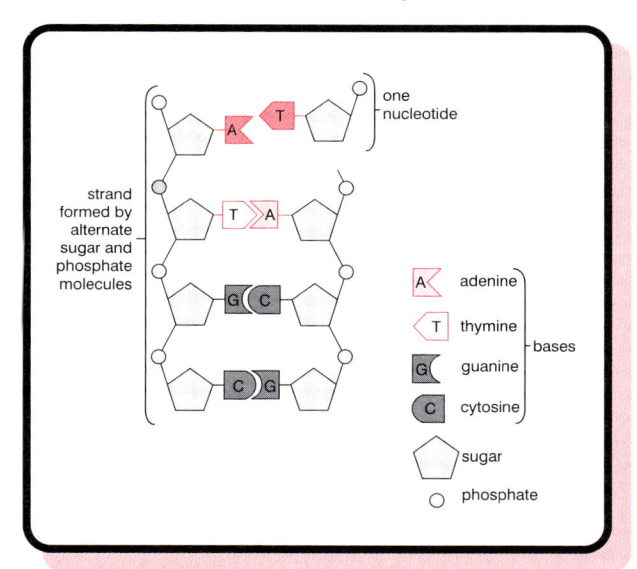

Part of a molecule of DNA

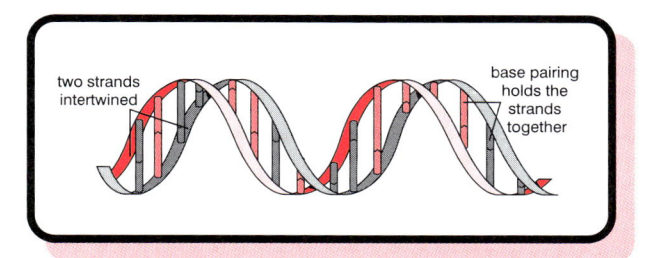

The double helix: two spiral strands connected by their bases

★ A **chromosome** consists of folded strands of DNA coiled round a protein core. The DNA part of the structure controls the inheritance of characteristics.

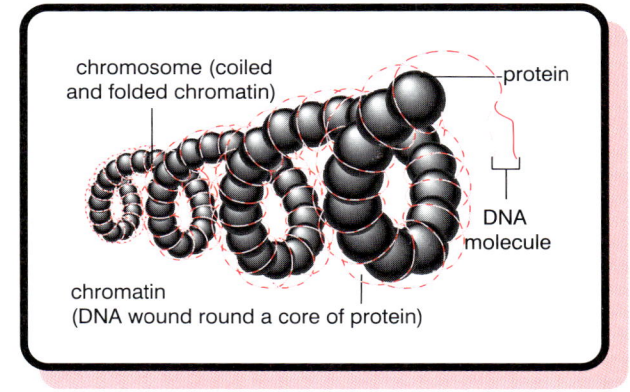

The structure of a chromosome

DNA replication

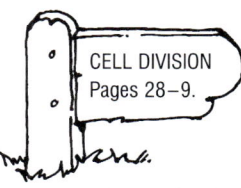

In cell division, the chromosomes **replicate** – they form an identical copy of themselves. This means the DNA molecule must make a copy of itself. The diagram below shows how this happens.

CELL DIVISION
Pages 28–9.

Now you can see why the daughter cells formed by mitosis are genetically identical to each other and to their parent cell. The two new molecules of DNA are each a replica of the original because of the base pairing. A always pairs with T, and G always pairs with C. All the cells in the body that die are replaced by mitosis, so they stay the same.

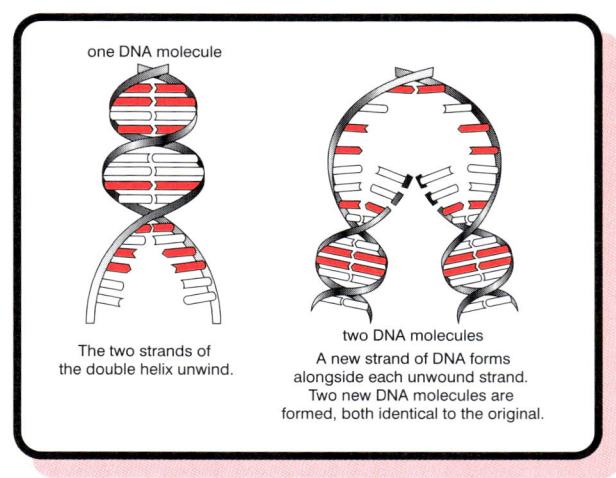

one DNA molecule

The two strands of the double helix unwind.

two DNA molecules
A new strand of DNA forms alongside each unwound strand. Two new DNA molecules are formed, both identical to the original.

DNA replication

Mutation

Hundreds of thousands of nucleotides a second can be adding to the replicating DNA. Occasionally the wrong base adds by mistake. Then the new DNA formed is slightly different from the original. The change is called a **mutation**.

The genetic code

★ A **codon** is the length of a DNA molecule that codes for one amino acid. It is three nucleotides long.

★ A **gene** is the length of a DNA molecule that codes for one complete protein.

★ So a gene is a long line of codons in a particular order.

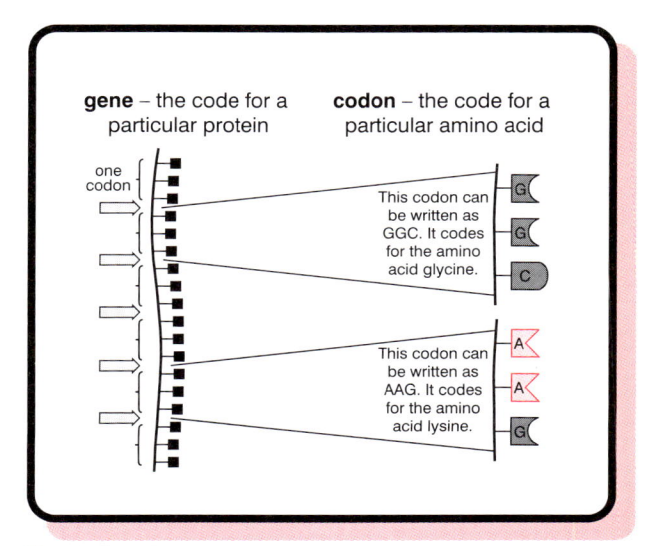

The genetic code

round-up

How much have you improved?
Work out your improvement index on page 82.

1 Complete the following paragraph using the words below. Each word may be used once, more than once or not at all.

chloroplasts   nucleus   membrane   cilia   vacuole mitochondria   cytoplasm   flagellum   cellulose

A cell is surrounded by a _____ which forms its surface. Inside is the jelly-like _____ in which are different structures. For example, the _____ contains the chromosomes and _____ are the structures where energy is released from the oxidation of glucose. Only plant cells have a cell wall, and _____ which trap light energy. The wall of plant cells is made of _____. Inside plant cells there is a large space called the _____ which is filled with cell sap. [7]

2 Which of the structures listed below are found in
 a) animal cells and plant cells **b)** plant cells only?

nucleus   cell membrane   cell wall   large vacuole mitochondria   chloroplasts   cytoplasm [7]

3 Why is mitosis important for maintaining the health of the tissues of the body? [1]

4 Compare and contrast the processes of mitosis and meiosis by listing the similarities and the differences in different columns. [8]

5 Below is a series of words that describe the organisation of living matter. Arrange the words in the correct sequence, beginning with the simplest level of organisation and ending with the most complex.

organs   cells   organisms   organ systems tissues [5]

6 Match each substance in column **A** with its function in column **B**.

A substances	B functions
fat	carries the genetic code
cellulose	insulates the body
DNA	a component of the plant cell wall
polypeptide	a food substance stored in the liver
glycogen	enzymes are made of this substance
protein	made of about 40 amino acids

[6]

7 a) The following is a sequence of bases for a length of DNA. How many codons are there in the sequence, assuming the first codon begins at the left-hand side and there is no overlap?

T T A G G A C T G A T C

b) If each codon codes for one amino acid, how many amino acids are coded for in this length of DNA? [2]

Humans as organisms

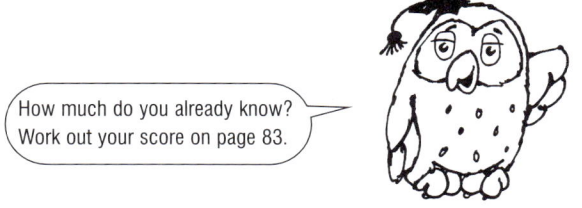

How much do you already know? Work out your score on page 83.

Test yourself

1 The nutrients in food are listed below. Use these nutrients to answer the following questions.

   carbohydrates   fats   proteins   vitamins   minerals

   a) Which nutrients give food its energy content? [3]
   b) Which nutrient is a source of energy, but is most important in the body for growth and repair? [1]
   c) Which nutrient releases the most energy per gram? [1]
   d) Which nutrients are needed only in small amounts, but play an important role in the control of metabolism? [2]

2 Match each term in column **A** with its correct description in column **B**.

A terms	B descriptions
ingestion	the removal of undigested food through the anus
digestion	digested food passes into the body
absorption	food is taken into the mouth
egestion	food is broken down

   [4]

3 The different components of blood are listed in column **A**. Match each component with its correct description in column **B**.

A components	B descriptions
plasma	contain haemoglobin
red blood cells	promote the formation of blood clots
white blood cells	contains dissolved food substances
platelets	produce antibodies

   [4]

4 The components of the reflex arc are listed as follows: sensory neurone, effector, relay neurone, receptor, motor neurone. Write the components in their correct order. [4]

5 What is the function of each of these parts of the ear?
   a) the eardrum   b) the bones of the middle ear
   c) the pinna   d) the hair cells [8]

6 What are hormones and how are they transported around the body? [2]

7 Distinguish between the roles of the hormones insulin and glucagon in keeping the blood glucose level steady. [2]

8 The structures of the kidney tubule and its blood supply are listed below. Rewrite them in the order in which a molecule of urea passes from the renal artery to the outside of the body.

   **tubule   urethra   bladder   glomerulus
   Bowman's capsule   ureter   collecting duct** [7]

9 Match each body structure in column **A** with its role in the defence of the body against disease in column **B**.

A body structures	B roles
tear gland	produces sebum which kills bacteria and fungi
blood	sweep away mucus containing trapped microorganisms and particles
skin	produce hydrochloric acid which kills bacteria
cilia lining the upper respiratory tract	produce the enzyme lysozyme which destroys bacteria
glands in the stomach wall	white cells produce antibodies which destroy antigens

   [5]

4.1 Food and diet

preview

At the end of this section you will:
- understand that different foods contain different amounts of energy
- be able to identify the components of a diet
- know the role of different foods in the body.

Humans as organisms

Nutrients in food

The **nutrients** in food are **carbohydrates**, **fats**, **proteins**, **vitamins** and **minerals**. **Water** and **fibre** are also components of food. Different foods contain nutrients, water and fibre in different proportions. Our **diet** is the food and drink we take in. Remember the sequence:

$$\left.\begin{array}{l}\text{nutrient}\\ +\text{ water}\\ +\text{ fibre}\end{array}\right\} \xrightarrow{\text{components of}} \text{food} \xrightarrow{\text{eaten}} \text{diet}$$

All living things (including us) need food. The nutrients in food are a source of

- **energy** which powers life's activities
- materials for the **growth** and **repair** of bodies
- substances which control the **metabolism** of cells.

On pages 40–1 is a Mind Map for **food and diet**. The checklist of points gives you more information.

Checklist for food and diet

1. ★ The **energy value** of food is measured using an instrument called a bomb calorimeter, shown below.

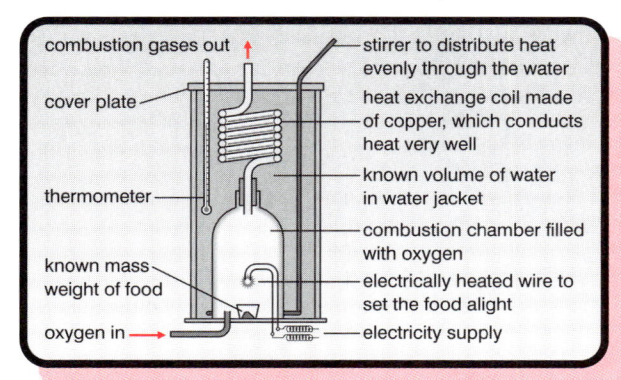

A bomb calorimeter

The burning food heats the surrounding water. The change in temperature of the water is used to work out the energy value of the food:

$$\text{energy released per gram} = \frac{\text{volume of water in water jacket} \times \text{temperature rise}}{\text{mass of food}} \times 4.2$$

   ★ The energy released from food depends on the nutrients it contains.
   - 17.2 kJ/g for carbohydrate
   - 22.2 kJ/g for protein
   - 38.5 kJ/g for fat

   Although protein is an 'energy nutrient', its most important use in the body is for growth and repair.

   ★ People have different energy requirements depending on their
   - **age** – on average young people have greater energy requirements than older people
   - **gender** (male or female) – pregnancy and lactation (milk production) increase the energy requirements of women
   - **activities** – any kind of activity increases a person's energy requirements.

   ★ The rate at which the body uses energy is called the **metabolic rate**. It is lowest (called the **basal metabolic rate**) when the body is at rest.

   ★ If a person eats more food than is necessary for his/her energy needs, the excess is turned into fat. As a result, the person puts on weight.

   ★ To lose weight, a person can
   - take more exercise, which increases energy output
   - eat less high-energy food, decreasing energy input.

2. ★ **Additives** are put into food to
   - make it tastier
   - improve its texture
   - make it more attractive
   - prevent it from spoiling.

   ★ Some additives can make some people unwell.

3. ★ A **balanced diet** is a mixture of foods which together provide sufficient nutrients for healthy living.

   ★ The 'basic four' food groups help us choose a balanced diet.

4. ★ The amount of **alcohol** people consume is measured in units, as shown below.

Units of alcohol

   ★ How much alcohol is too much? It depends on a person's age, size, gender (male or female) and metabolic rate.

5. ★ Vitamin C helps cells to join together. It also controls the use of calcium by bones and teeth.

   ★ Vitamin D helps the body to absorb calcium.

   ★ Deficiency of iron is a common cause of anaemia.

39

4
Life processes and living things

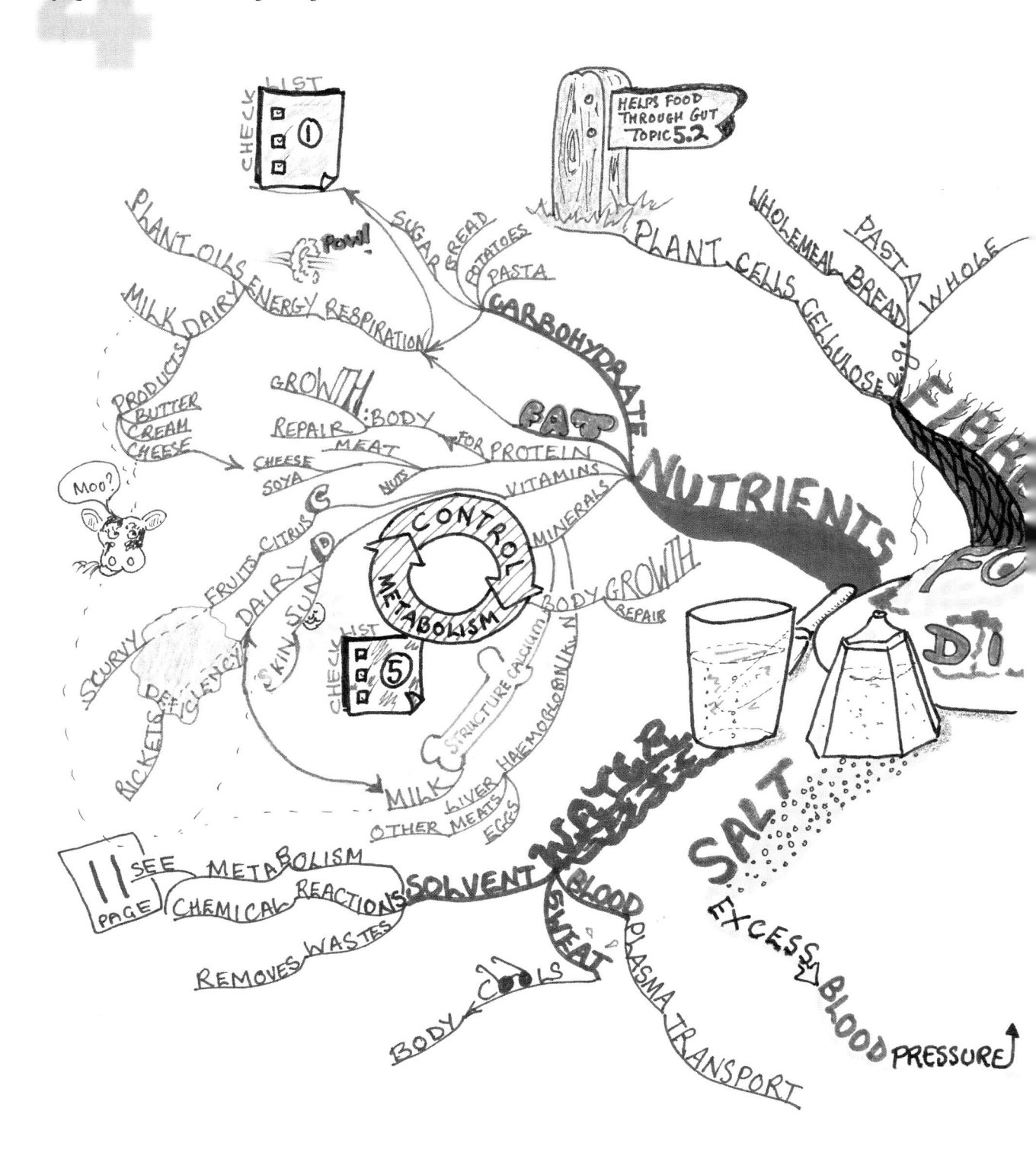

Food and diet

Humans as organisms

GRAIN FOODS

ANTIOXIDANTS
PRESERVATIVES
COLOUR
+FLAVOUR
EMULSIFIER
MIX: OIL WATER

CHECK LIST ②
CHECK LIST ③

VARIETY IS BEST!

FOODS

ADDITIVES

BALANCED GROUPS
daily each choose 4
= HELP HEALTHY EATING

ALCOHOL SENSIBLE
DRINK ? RISK DISEASE
UNITS ♂28 ♀21 per week
CHECK LIST ④

ABUSE DRUNKENNESS
RISK DISEASE
ADDICTION + LIVER DISEASE

FAT EXCESS OVERWEIGHT RISK ☹
BLOOD CHOLESTEROL: SATURATED RISK ☹ ANIMAL
+UNSATURATED RISK ☺ PLANT
CHOLESTEROL DISEASE
SEE PAGE 34

SUGAR EXCESS OVERWEIGHT
+TOOTH DECAY
OUCH! ENAMEL DENTINE PULP CAVITY

↗ RISK DISEASE

↘ = decreased risk
↗ = increased risk

Life processes and living things

4.2 The digestive system

preview

At the end of this section you will:
- know that the digestive system is a muscular tube through which food moves
- understand that as food moves through the digestive system it is processed (digested) into substances which the cells of the body can absorb and use
- be able to identify enzymes responsible for digesting food.

Testing your understanding
The terms:

gut
intestine } all refer to the digestive system.
alimentary canal

Digesting food

Food is processed through the digestive system in the following sequence:

ingestion
food is taken
into the mouth

↓

digestion
large molecules of
food are broken down
into smaller molecules

↓

absorption
the small molecules
of digested food
pass into the body

↓

egestion
undigested food is
removed from the body
through the anus

The digestive system is a muscular tube through which food moves. It processes food.

★ **Mechanical processes** break up food and mix it with digestive juices.

★ **Chemical processes** digest food using different enzymes in the digestive juices. The body cannot absorb the large molecules of carbohydrate, protein and fat in food. They are broken down into smaller molecules which the body can absorb.

On pages 44–5 is the concept map for **the digestive system**. The **liver** and **pancreas** are connected by ducts to the digestive system. They play an important role in the digestion of food. The numbers on the concept map refer to the checklist below.

Checklist for the digestive system

(M) = mechanical processes of digestion

(C) = chemical processes of digestion

1 ★ **(M) Teeth** chew food, breaking it into small pieces.

As a result, the surface area of food exposed to the action of digestive enzymes is increased.

As a result, food is digested more quickly.

2 ★ **(C) Saliva**, produced by the salivary glands, contains the enzyme **amylase**.

As a result, the digestion of starch begins in the mouth.

★ **(M)** Saliva moistens the food.

As a result, the food is made slippery for easy swallowing.

3 ★ **(M)** Muscles of the **stomach** wall and small intestine mix food thoroughly with different juices containing digestive enzymes.

As a result, a liquid paste called **chyme** is formed.

As a result, food and digestive enzymes are brought into intimate contact.

★ **(C)** Gastric juice, produced by **pits** in the stomach wall, contains **hydrochloric acid** and the enzymes **pepsin** and **renin**.

Hydrochloric acid
- increases the acidity of the stomach contents.

As a result, bacteria in the food are killed.

As a result, the action of salivary amylase is stopped.

Pepsin
- begins the digestion of protein.

Renin
- clots milk, making it semi-solid.

As a result, milk stays in the gut long enough to be digested.

4 ★ **(C) Bile**, produced by the **liver**, is a green alkaline liquid which is stored in the gall bladder before release into the small intestine through the bile duct. It
- neutralises acid from the stomach
- breaks fat into small droplets (**emulsification**).

As a result, the surface area of fat exposed to the action of the enzyme **lipase** is increased.

As a result, fat is digested more quickly.

5 ★ **(C) Pancreatic juice**, produced by the **pancreas**, is released into the small intestine through the pancreatic duct. It contains
- **sodium carbonat**e which neutralises stomach acid
- **carbohydrases**, **proteases** and **lipases** (see table below) which digest carbohydrate, protein and fat.

6 ★ **(C) Intestinal juice**, produced by glands in the wall of the **duodenum** and **ileum**, contains
- **carbohydrases** and **lipases** that complete the digestion of carbohydrates and fats.

Chemistry of digestion

Digestive enzymes catalyse the breakdown of food by **hydrolysis**. Water splits large molecules of food into smaller molecules which are suitable for absorption into the body. The table below summarises the process.

What happens to digested food?

Digested food is carried away from the ileum in the blood of the hepatic portal vein and in the fluid of the lymph vessels.

★ Blood transports water, sugars, glycerol and amino acids to the liver.

★ Lymph transports fats and fat-soluble vitamins to a vein in the neck where the substances enter the bloodstream.

The **liver** plays a major role in the metabolism of food substances after they have been absorbed into the body.

★ Glucose may be converted to **glycogen** and stored in the liver. Glycogen may be hydrolysed to glucose and released back into the blood in response to the body's needs.

★ Iron, obtained from destroyed red blood cells, is stored in the liver.

★ Amino acids in excess of the body's needs are broken down (a process called **deamination**) in the liver. Urea is formed and excreted in urine.

★ Amino acids are converted from one type into another in the liver (a process called **transamination**) according to the body's needs.

enzyme group	example	where found	food component	after digestion
carbohydrases (catalyse the digestion of carbohydrates)	amylase	mouth	starch	maltose
	maltase	small intestine	maltose	glucose
proteases (catalyse the digestion of proteins)	pepsin	stomach	protein	polypeptides
	chymotrypsin dipeptidase	small intestine	polypeptides dipeptides	dipeptides amino acids
lipases (catalyse the digestion of fats)	lipase	small intestine	fat	fatty acids + glycerol

Enzymes that digest carbohydrates, proteins and fats

Life processes and living things

MOVING FOOD (throughout the gut)

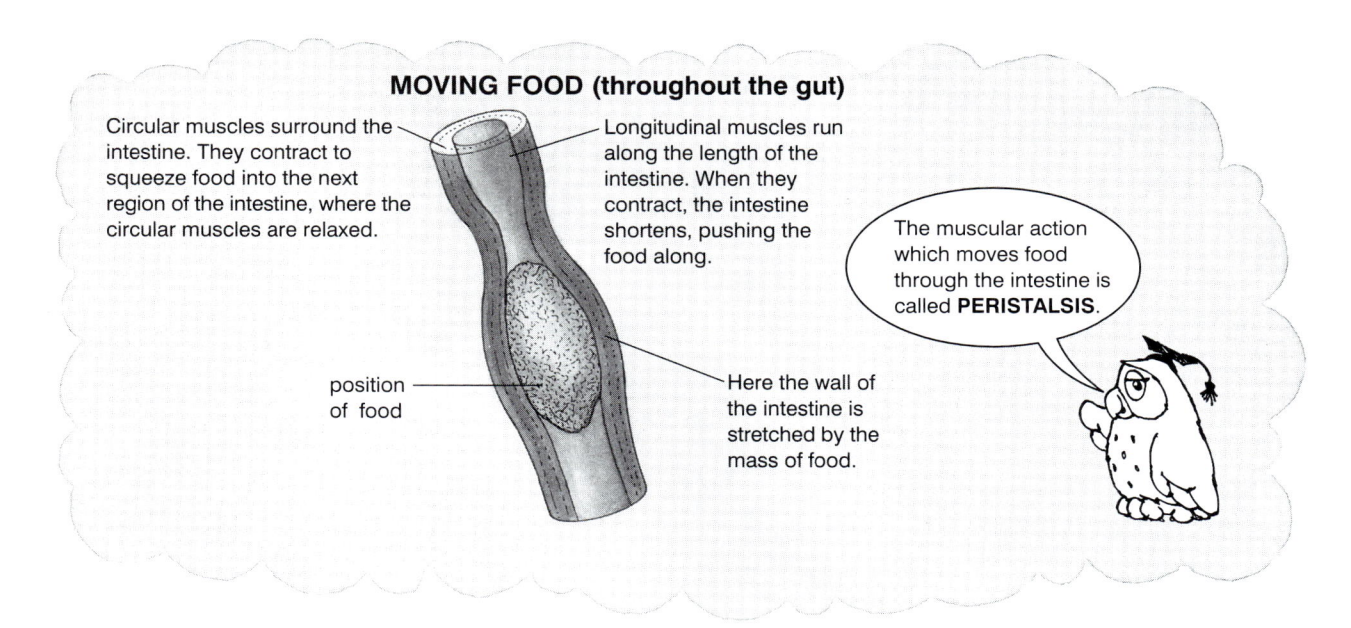

Circular muscles surround the intestine. They contract to squeeze food into the next region of the intestine, where the circular muscles are relaxed.

Longitudinal muscles run along the length of the intestine. When they contract, the intestine shortens, pushing the food along.

position of food

Here the wall of the intestine is stretched by the mass of food.

The muscular action which moves food through the intestine is called **PERISTALSIS**.

ABSORPTION (ileum and colon)

- outer layer
- longitudinal muscles
- circular muscles
- villi

MAGNIFIED ×50

microvilli – tiny projections from each cell of the villus surface

MAGNIFIED ×10 000

The ileum is adapted for the absorption of food by having an increased surface area.

- The intestine is **folded** and packed into the abdominal cavity.
- **Villi** project from the lining of the ileum.
- **Microvilli** project from the surface of each cell lining the villus.

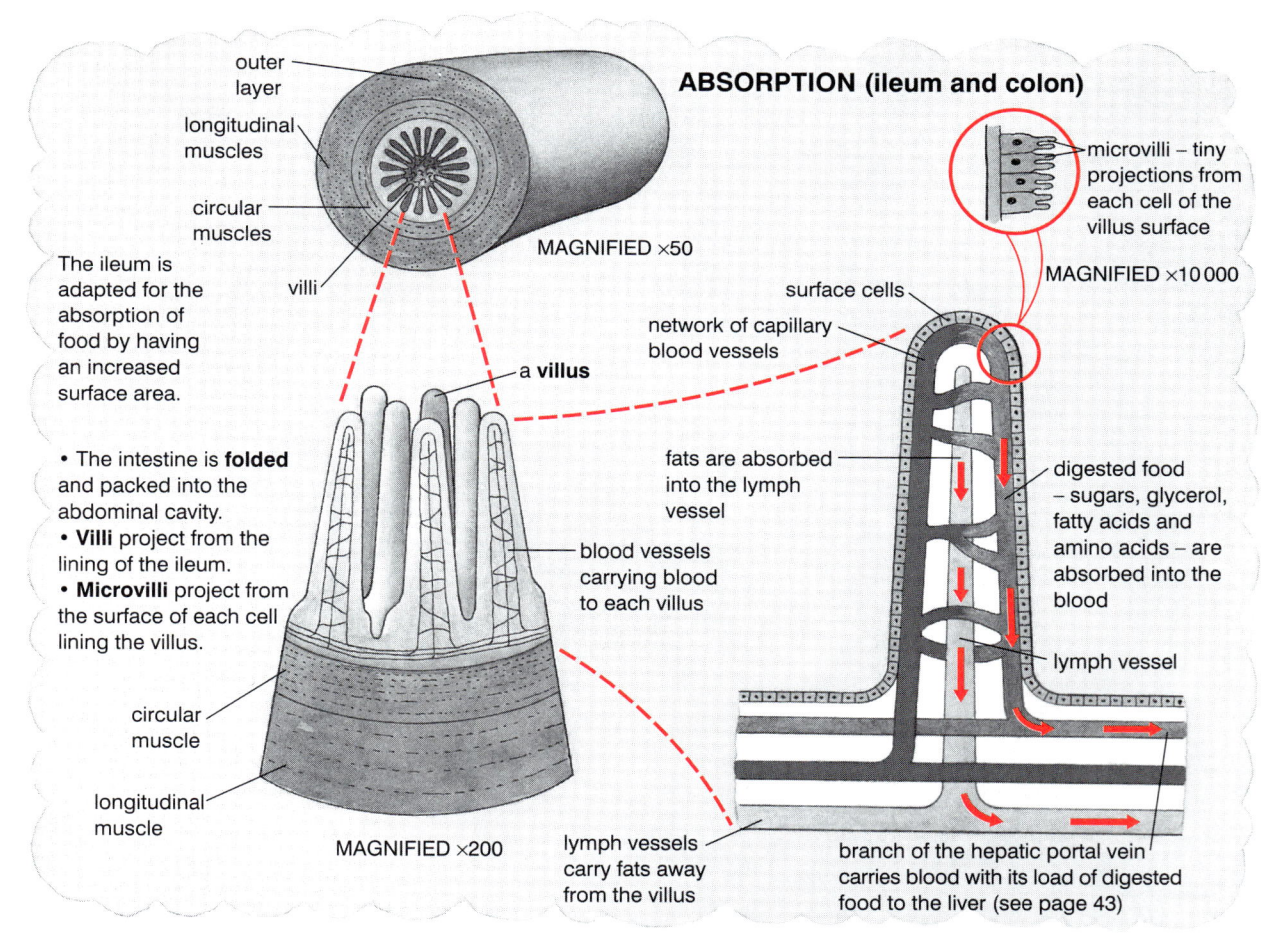

a **villus**

- surface cells
- network of capillary blood vessels
- fats are absorbed into the lymph vessel
- blood vessels carrying blood to each villus
- circular muscle
- longitudinal muscle

MAGNIFIED ×200

lymph vessels carry fats away from the villus

digested food – sugars, glycerol, fatty acids and amino acids – are absorbed into the blood

lymph vessel

branch of the hepatic portal vein carries blood with its load of digested food to the liver (see page 43)

The digestive system – its structure and functions (checklist on pages 42–3)

Humans as organisms

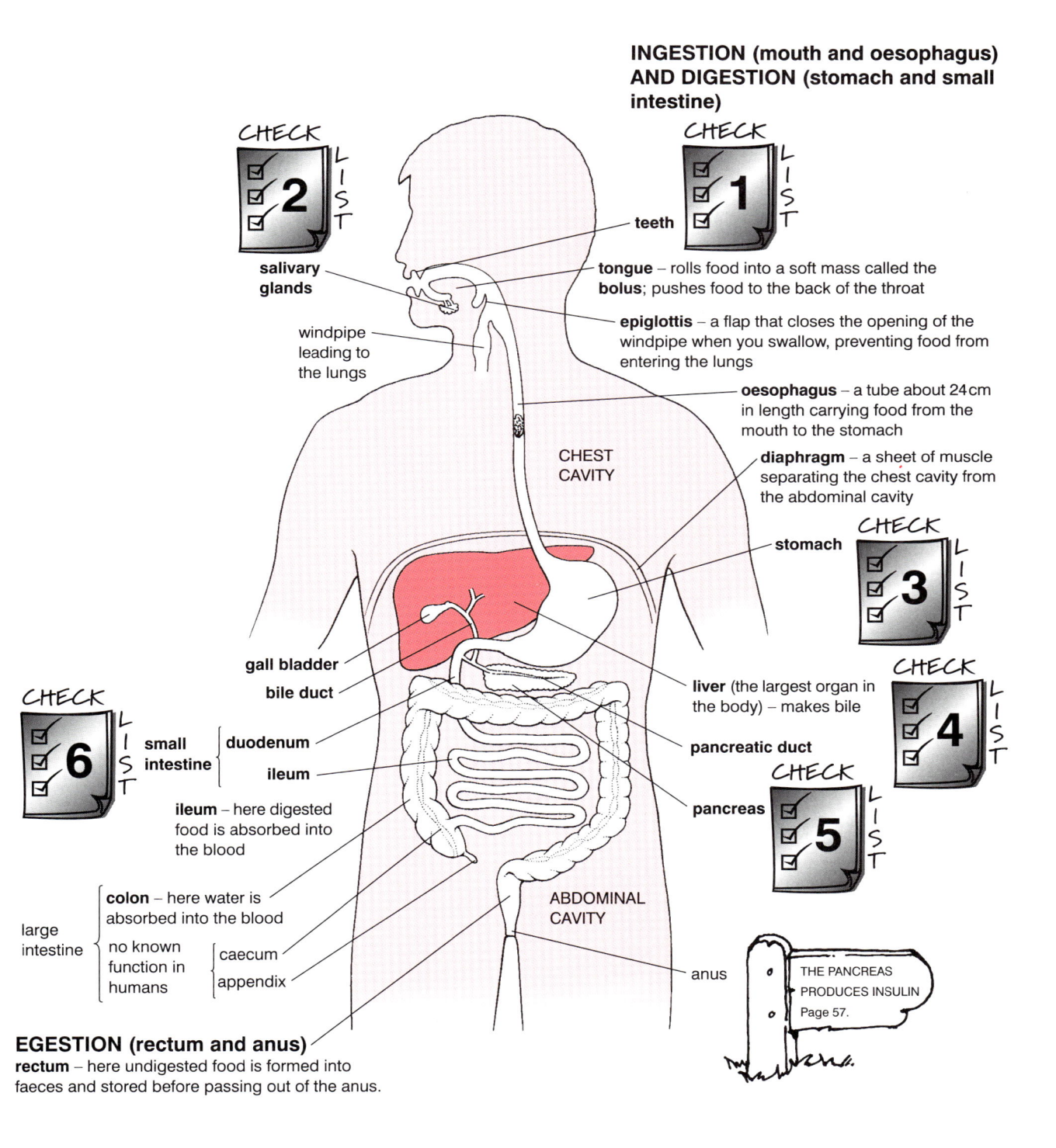

INGESTION (mouth and oesophagus) AND DIGESTION (stomach and small intestine)

CHECK LIST 1

CHECK LIST 2

- **teeth**
- **tongue** – rolls food into a soft mass called the **bolus**; pushes food to the back of the throat
- **salivary glands**
- **windpipe** leading to the lungs
- **epiglottis** – a flap that closes the opening of the windpipe when you swallow, preventing food from entering the lungs
- **oesophagus** – a tube about 24 cm in length carrying food from the mouth to the stomach
- CHEST CAVITY
- **diaphragm** – a sheet of muscle separating the chest cavity from the abdominal cavity

CHECK LIST 3

- **stomach**

CHECK LIST 4

- **gall bladder**
- **bile duct**
- **liver** (the largest organ in the body) – makes bile
- **pancreatic duct**

CHECK LIST 5

- **pancreas**

CHECK LIST 6

- **small intestine**
  - **duodenum**
  - **ileum**
- **ileum** – here digested food is absorbed into the blood
- **large intestine**
  - **colon** – here water is absorbed into the blood
  - **caecum** — no known function in humans
  - **appendix** — no known function in humans
- ABDOMINAL CAVITY
- **anus**

THE PANCREAS PRODUCES INSULIN Page 57.

EGESTION (rectum and anus)

rectum – here undigested food is formed into faeces and stored before passing out of the anus.

45

Life processes and living things

4.3 Blood

preview

At the end of this section you will:
- be able to identify the different components of blood
- understand how different factors (diet, exercise and stress) affect the circulatory system.

Fact file

★ The **heart** is a pump.

★ **Blood** is a liquid containing different cells.

★ **Arteries**, **veins** and **capillaries** are tube-like vessels through which blood flows.

```
         pumps         through
heart ──────────→ blood ──────────→ blood vessels
```

Blood

Blood carries oxygen, digested food, hormones and other substances *to* the tissues and organs of the body that need them. Blood also carries carbon dioxide and other waste substances produced by the metabolism of cells *from* the tissues and organs of the body. On the opposite page is the concept map for **blood**. The number on the concept map refers to the checklist below.

Checklist for blood

1 ★ **Red blood cells** are made in the **marrow** of the limb bones, ribs and vertebrae.

★ Old red blood cells are destroyed in the liver.

LIVER
Page 43.

★ **White blood cells** originate in the **bone marrow** and **spleen**.

★ **Antibodies** produced against a particular **antigen** will attack only that antigen. The antibody is said to be **specific** to that antigen.

Disorders of the blood

★ **Leukaemia** is the overproduction of abnormal white blood cells.

As a result, there are too few red blood cells.

Treatment is with drugs that slow the production of white blood cells, and radiotherapy which kills the abnormal cells.

★ **Haemophilia** is a genetic disease which runs in families. The blood does not clot properly because factor VIII, one of the substances in the blood needed for blood clots to form, is missing.

As a result, **haemophiliacs** (people suffering from haemophilia) lose a lot of blood if they injure themselves.

Treatment is by injections of factor VIII.

GENETIC DISEASES
Page 59.

AIDS

AIDS (**A**cquired **I**mmune **D**eficiency **S**yndrome) is caused by the **H**uman **I**mmunodeficiency **V**irus (**HIV**). The virus attacks a particular type of lymphocyte (see page 59).

As a result, a person infected with HIV has reduced protection from disease-causing microorganisms.

Once HIV has destroyed a number of lymphocytes, the diseases of AIDS develop. Common diseases include:

- pneumonia – a disease of the lungs
- thrush – a fungal infection
- Kaposi's sarcoma – a skin cancer.

Humans as organisms

BLOOD

The sample of human blood has been spun in a centrifuge. The plug of blood cells is examined under a microscope.

balancing tube

plug smeared on to a slide

Plasma – transports heat released by metabolism in the liver, muscles and body fat. Plasma consists of 90% water with 10% of materials dissolved in it:
- **blood proteins** including antibodies that defend the body against disease, fibrinogen which helps stop bleeding, and enzymes
- **foods, vitamins** and **enzymes**
- **wastes**
- **hormones** which help co-ordinate different bodily functions.

types of white cells: phagocyte, lymphocyte
red cells
platelets

CHECK LIST 1

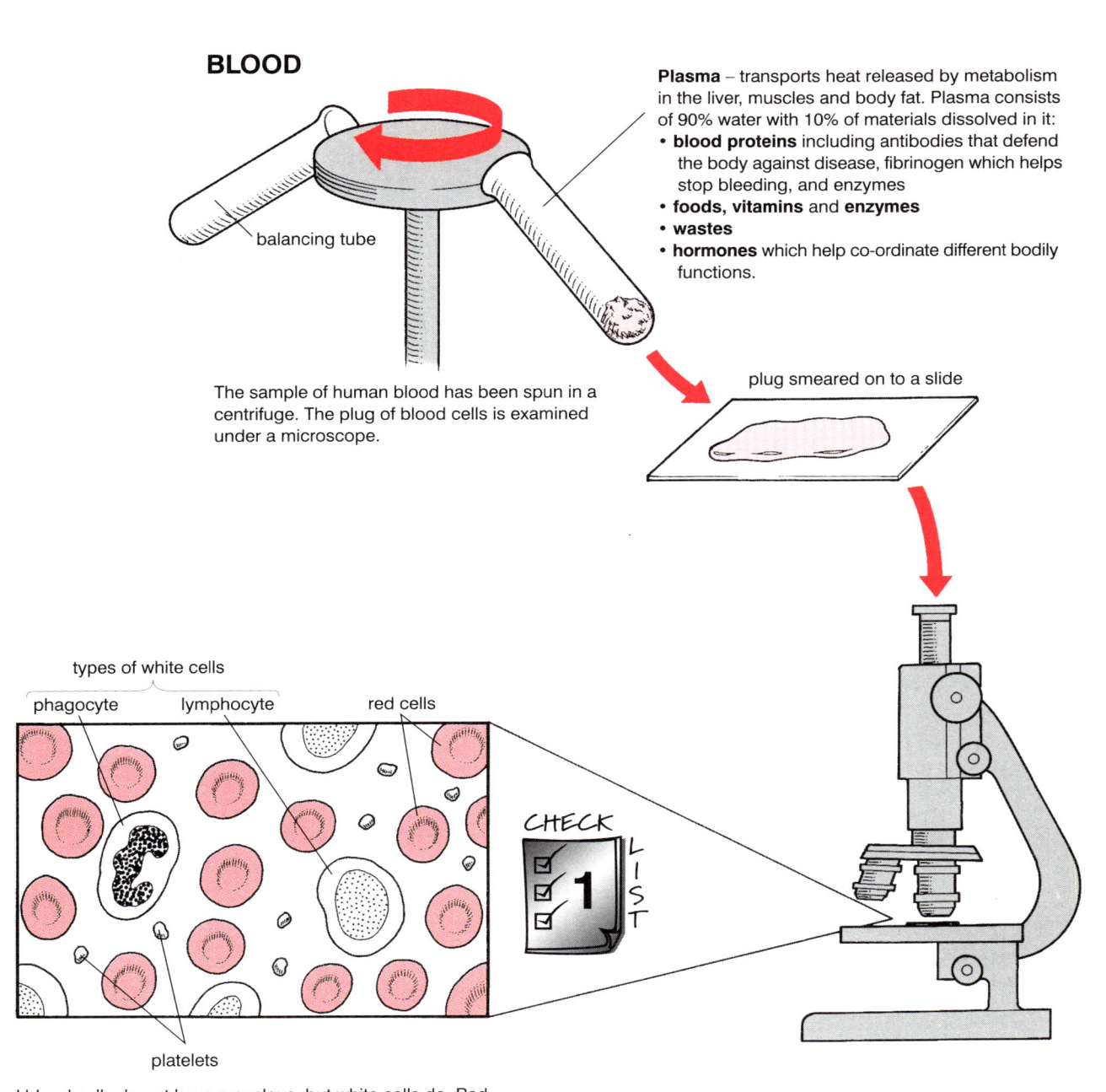

Red blood cells do not have a nucleus, but white cells do. Red cells are packed with the pigment haemoglobin which gives cells their red colour. Notice the characteristic shapes of the nuclei of phagocytes and lymphocytes. Platelets look like fragments of red cells.

Blood

4 Life processes and living things

4.4 Senses and the nervous system

preview

At the end of this section you will know that:
- stimuli are converted by receptors into signals called nerve impulses, to which the body can respond
- neurones (nerve cells) conduct nerve impulses to muscles, which respond by contracting
- muscles are called effectors
- nerves are formed from bundles of neurones and are the link between stimulus and response.

The process runs:

stimulus → receptor → nerves → effector → response

Stimulus and response

A **stimulus** is a change in the environment which causes a living organism to take action. A **response** is the action that the living organism takes. The **nervous system** links stimuli and responses. This is the sequence of events:

★ **Sensory receptor cells** detect stimuli and convert them into **nerve impulses**, to which the body can respond.

★ Nerve impulses are minute electrical disturbances.

★ **Neurones** (nerve cells) conduct nerve impulses to **effectors** (muscles or glands). Muscles respond to nerve impulses by contracting; glands respond by secreting substances. For example, the adrenal glands respond to nerve impulses by producing the hormone adrenaline, which helps the body cope with sudden stress.

HORMONES Pages 54–8.

The nervous system

On pages 50–1 is the concept map for **the nervous system**. The numbers on the concept map refer to the checklist.

Checklist for the nervous system

1 ★ Each **nerve** of the nervous system consists of a bundle of **neurones**.

★ Each neurone transmits nerve impulses to an **effector** (muscle or gland).

★ Nerve impulses are minute electrical disturbances which carry information about stimuli.

★ Nerve impulses stimulate effectors to respond to stimuli in a useful way.

★ A nerve impulse takes just milliseconds to travel along a neurone.

2 ★ **Neurotransmitter** is a chemical substance released from the end of a neurone into the **synapse**.

★ Neurotransmitter is produced only from the end of the neurone before the synapse.

As a result, nerve impulses always travel *from* the receptor *to* the effector.

3 ★ **Reflex responses** happen before the brain has had time to process the nerve impulses carrying the information about the stimulus.

★ When the brain catches up with events, it brings about the next set of reactions – such as a shout of pain.

★ **Ascending fibres** form synapses with sensory neurones. The ascending fibres carry nerve impulses to the brain.

As a result, the brain receives information about the stimulus causing the reflex response.

★ Nerve impulses from the brain are transmitted to effectors by the **descending fibres**, which synapse with motor neurones.

As a result, the reflex response is brought under conscious control.

4 ★ The human brain weighs approximately 1.3 kg and occupies a volume of about 1500 cm^3.

★ Around 6 million neurones make up 1 cm^3 of brain matter.

★ Memory and learning are under the brain's control.

★ Different drugs affect the brain. For example, ethanol (the alcohol in beers, wines and spirits) depresses the activity of the cerebral cortex, affecting judgement and the control of movement.

Humans as organisms

4.5 Sense organs

preview

At the end of this section you will know that:
- **the sense organs consist of sensory cells which are adapted to detect a particular type of stimulus.**

Handy hint
The sensory cells of the

- **S**kin detect heat and cold, touch and pain
- **N**ose detect chemicals
- **E**ye detect light
- **E**ar detect sound
- **T**ongue detect chemicals.

Thinking of the mnemonic **SNEET** will help you remember the major sense organs of the body.

Sensing the surroundings

On pages 52–3 is the concept map for **sense organs**. The numbers refer to the checklist below.

Checklist for sense organs

1 ★ **Tears** lubricate the surface of the eye. They contain the enzyme **lysozyme** which kills bacteria.

★ The **iris** of the eye is usually coloured brown, blue or green.

★ A pair of human eyes contains around 130 million **rods** and 7 million **cones**.

★ **Cone** cells are packed most densely in the region of the **fovea** and respond to bright light.

As a result, objects are seen most clearly if looked at straight on.

★ **Rod** cells occur mostly near the edges of the retina and respond to dim light.

As a result, objects are seen less clearly out of the corner of the eye.

2 ★ Loudness is measured in **decibels**. The faintest sound that the ear can hear is defined as zero decibels.

★ The response of the ear to different levels of loudness varies with frequency. The ear is most sensitive to frequencies around 3000 Hz, and can detect the softest sounds. It is completely insensitive to sounds over 18 000 Hz and cannot detect them.

★ The walls of the ear tube produce wax, which keeps the eardrum soft and supple.

3 ★ The nerve impulses from **temperature receptors** are interpreted by the brain, enabling us to feel whether our surroundings are hot or cold.

★ Sensitivity to **touch** depends on which part of the body is stimulated. The tip of the tongue and the fingertips can distinguish between two pin pricks 1.0 mm apart. Two pinpricks on the thigh may have to be more than 60 mm apart before they are detected as separate stimuli.

4 ★ **Taste buds** help us to decide whether food is safe. A bitter taste is usually a warning signal not to swallow.

★ **Smell** is defined as the detection of substances carried in the air.

★ To be detected, substances which are tasted or smelt must first be dissolved in the watery environment covering the receptor cells.

Check the vibrations

In the concept map, notice the different structures in the ear vibrating in response to sound waves striking the eardrum. The sequence reads:

- eardrum
- bones of the middle ear
- oval window
- fluid in the cochlea
- basilar membrane
- stimulated hair cells (receptors) fire off nerve impulses to the brain along the auditory nerve.

Fact file

★ The ear becomes less and less sensitive if it is regularly exposed to very loud sounds. At noisy discos, you can protect your ears by plugging them with cotton wool.

★ In most humans the ear lobe (pinna) is fixed. Cats and dogs, however, can adjust the pinna and turn it towards sources of sound.

★ A cat's tongue contains very few taste receptors which respond to sugar. Cats, therefore, are among the few animals that do not prefer substances with a sweet taste.

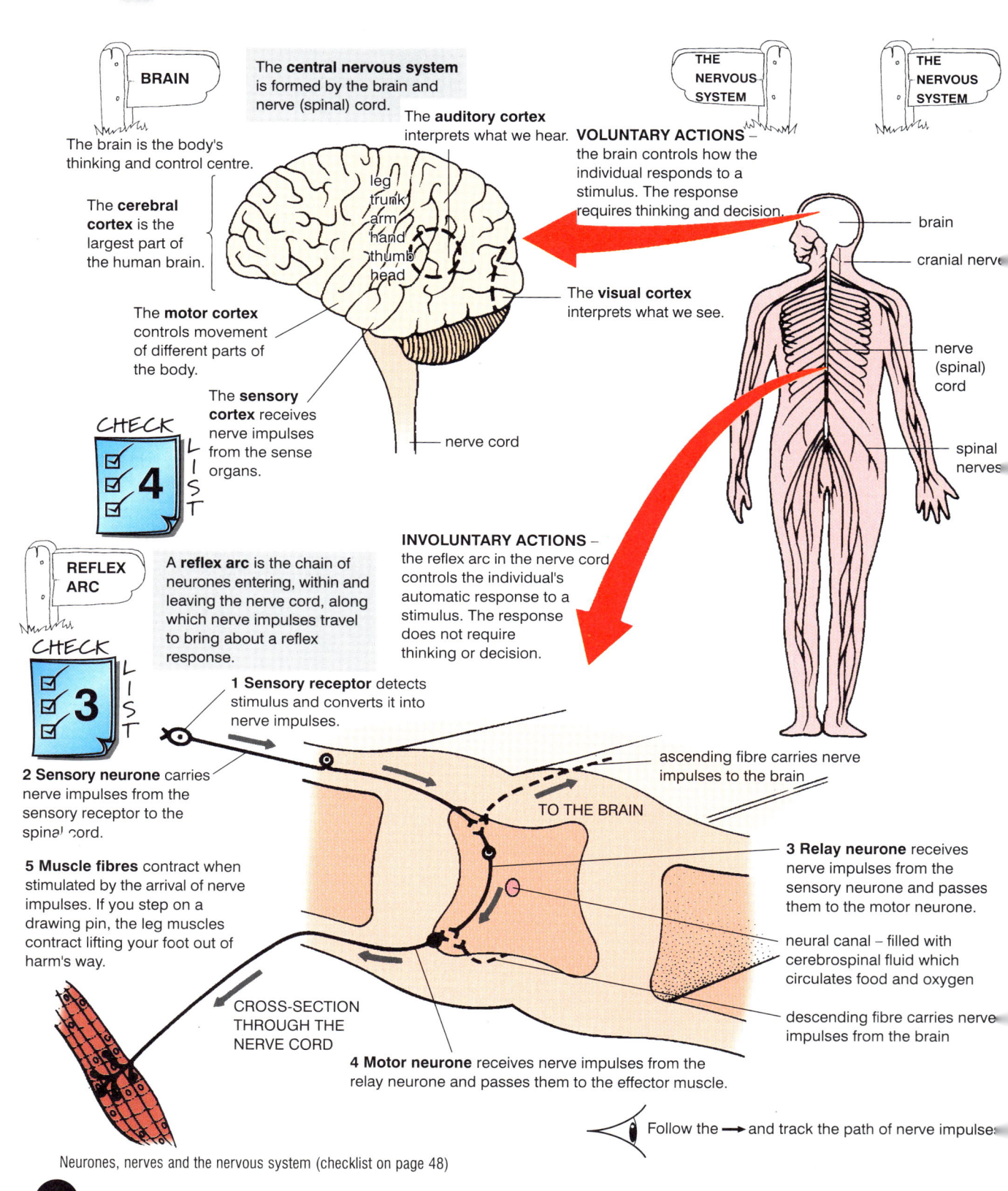

Life processes and living things

THE NERVOUS SYSTEM

BRAIN

The **central nervous system** is formed by the brain and nerve (spinal) cord.

The brain is the body's thinking and control centre.

The **cerebral cortex** is the largest part of the human brain.

The **motor cortex** controls movement of different parts of the body.

The **sensory cortex** receives nerve impulses from the sense organs.

The **auditory cortex** interprets what we hear.

The **visual cortex** interprets what we see.

(labels on brain: leg, trunk, arm, hand, thumb, head)

nerve cord

VOLUNTARY ACTIONS – the brain controls how the individual responds to a stimulus. The response requires thinking and decision.

INVOLUNTARY ACTIONS – the reflex arc in the nerve cord controls the individual's automatic response to a stimulus. The response does not require thinking or decision.

(body diagram labels: brain, cranial nerve, nerve (spinal) cord, spinal nerves)

REFLEX ARC

A **reflex arc** is the chain of neurones entering, within and leaving the nerve cord, along which nerve impulses travel to bring about a reflex response.

CHECK LIST 4

CHECK LIST 3

1 Sensory receptor detects stimulus and converts it into nerve impulses.

2 Sensory neurone carries nerve impulses from the sensory receptor to the spinal cord.

3 Relay neurone receives nerve impulses from the sensory neurone and passes them to the motor neurone.

4 Motor neurone receives nerve impulses from the relay neurone and passes them to the effector muscle.

5 Muscle fibres contract when stimulated by the arrival of nerve impulses. If you step on a drawing pin, the leg muscles contract lifting your foot out of harm's way.

ascending fibre carries nerve impulses to the brain

TO THE BRAIN

neural canal – filled with cerebrospinal fluid which circulates food and oxygen

descending fibre carries nerve impulses from the brain

CROSS-SECTION THROUGH THE NERVE CORD

Follow the → and track the path of nerve impulses

Neurones, nerves and the nervous system (checklist on page 48)

Humans as organisms

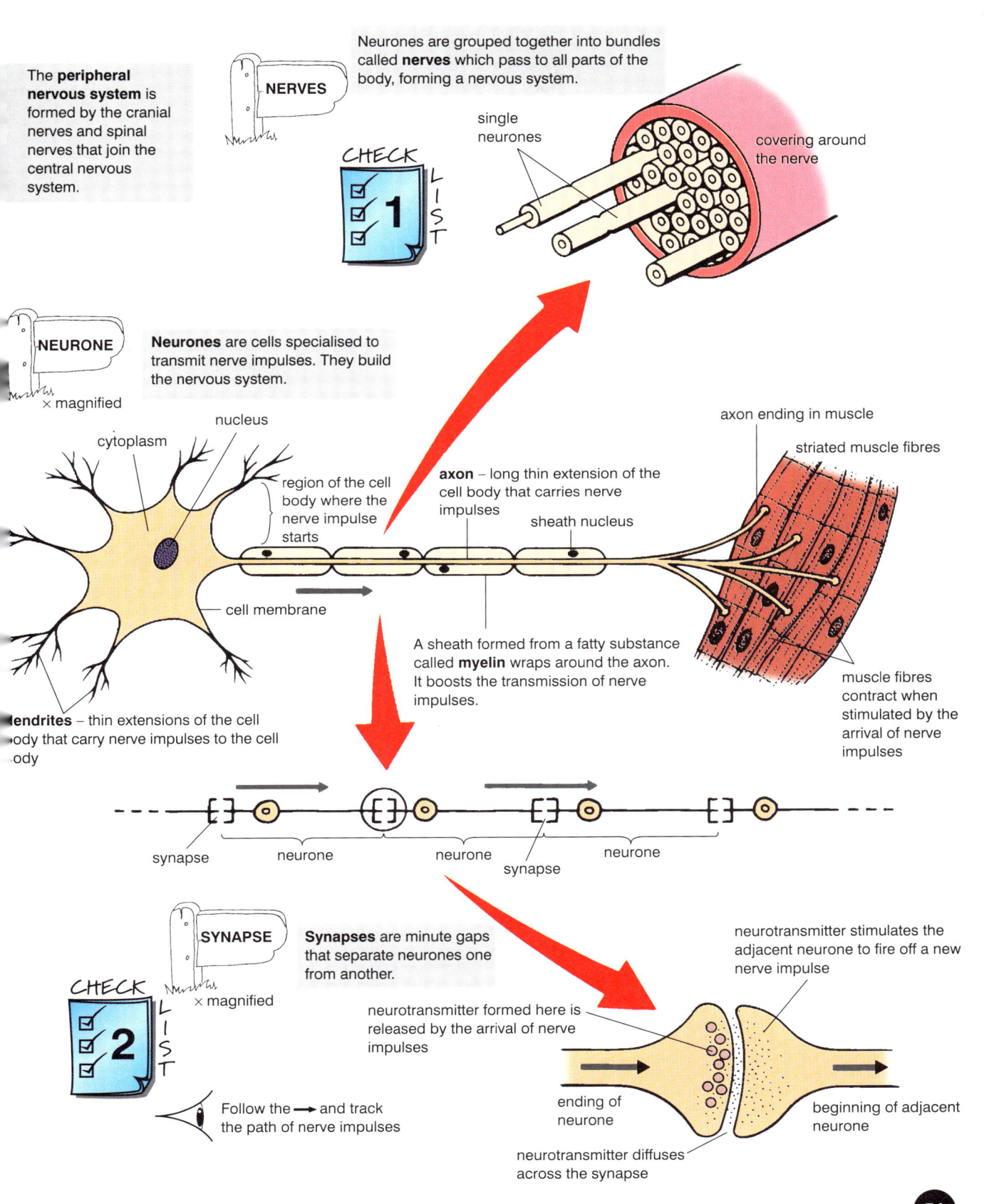

The **peripheral nervous system** is formed by the cranial nerves and spinal nerves that join the central nervous system.

NERVES

Neurones are grouped together into bundles called **nerves** which pass to all parts of the body, forming a nervous system.

- single neurones
- covering around the nerve

CHECK LIST 1

NEURONE × magnified

Neurones are cells specialised to transmit nerve impulses. They build the nervous system.

- cytoplasm
- nucleus
- region of the cell body where the nerve impulse starts
- **axon** – long thin extension of the cell body that carries nerve impulses
- sheath nucleus
- axon ending in muscle
- striated muscle fibres
- cell membrane
- A sheath formed from a fatty substance called **myelin** wraps around the axon. It boosts the transmission of nerve impulses.
- muscle fibres contract when stimulated by the arrival of nerve impulses
- **dendrites** – thin extensions of the cell body that carry nerve impulses to the cell body

synapse — neurone — synapse — neurone — neurone

SYNAPSE × magnified

Synapses are minute gaps that separate neurones one from another.

CHECK LIST 2

Follow the ➝ and track the path of nerve impulses

- neurotransmitter formed here is released by the arrival of nerve impulses
- neurotransmitter stimulates the adjacent neurone to fire off a new nerve impulse
- ending of neurone
- beginning of adjacent neurone
- neurotransmitter diffuses across the synapse

4 Life processes and living things

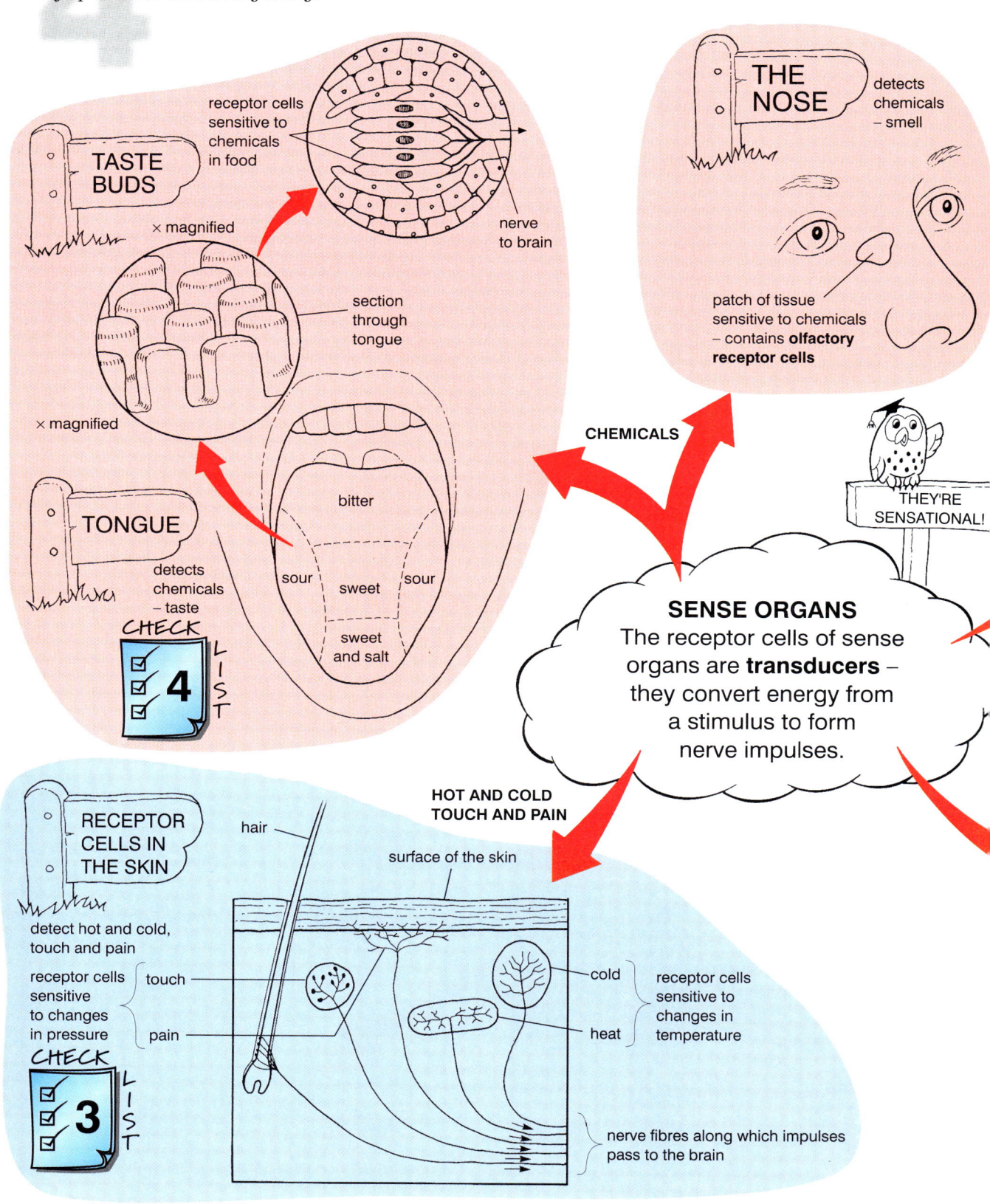

TASTE BUDS
receptor cells sensitive to chemicals in food
× magnified
nerve to brain
section through tongue

TONGUE
detects chemicals – taste

bitter
sour — sweet — sour
sweet and salt

CHECK LIST 4

THE NOSE
detects chemicals – smell

patch of tissue sensitive to chemicals – contains **olfactory receptor cells**

CHEMICALS

THEY'RE SENSATIONAL!

SENSE ORGANS
The receptor cells of sense organs are **transducers** – they convert energy from a stimulus to form nerve impulses.

HOT AND COLD TOUCH AND PAIN

RECEPTOR CELLS IN THE SKIN
detect hot and cold, touch and pain

receptor cells sensitive to changes in pressure { touch, pain }

hair
surface of the skin
cold
heat
receptor cells sensitive to changes in temperature

nerve fibres along which impulses pass to the brain

CHECK LIST 3

Sense organs (checklist on page 49)

Humans as organisms

THE EYE
detects light

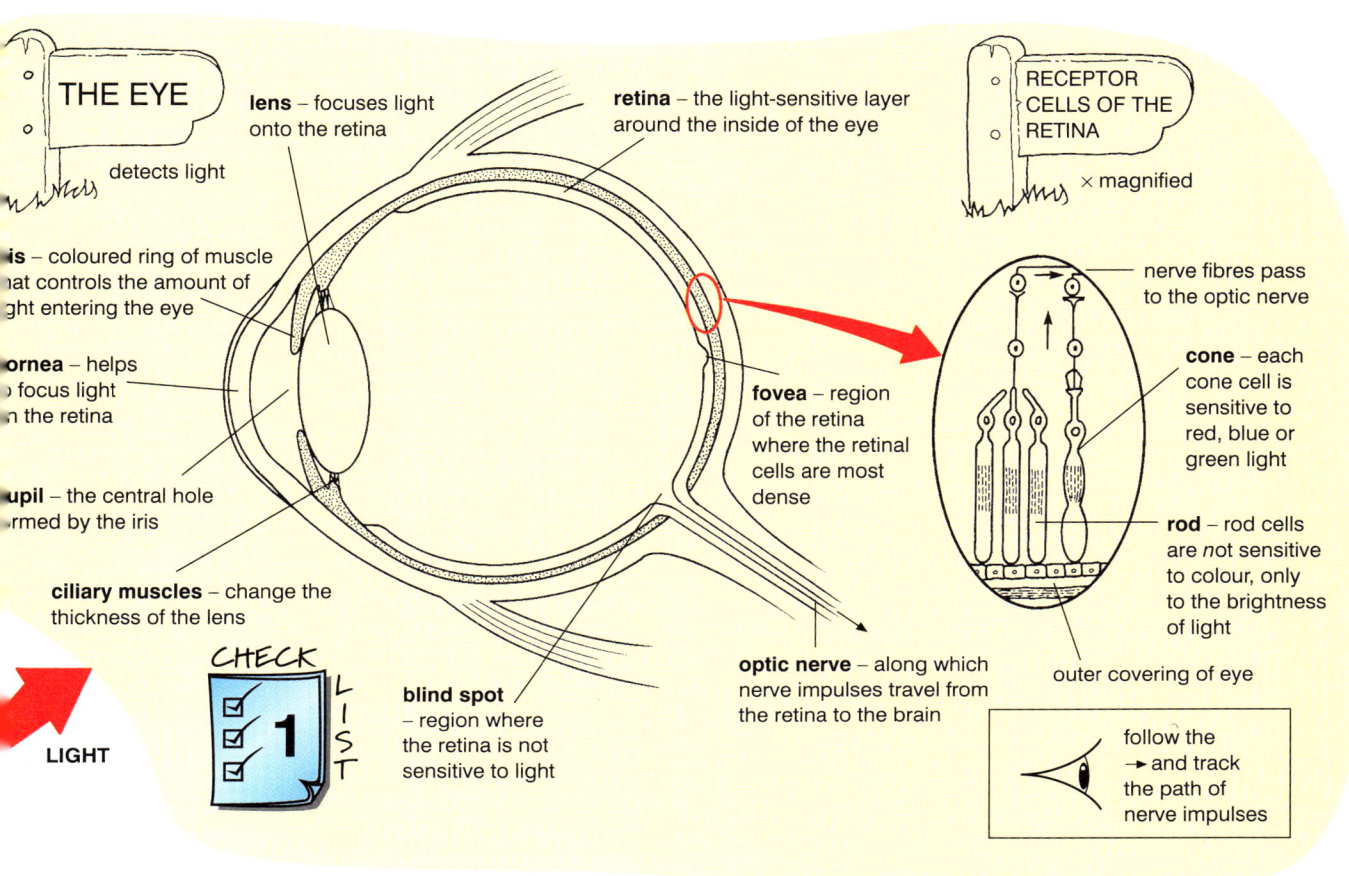

- **lens** – focuses light onto the retina
- **retina** – the light-sensitive layer around the inside of the eye
- **iris** – coloured ring of muscle that controls the amount of light entering the eye
- **cornea** – helps to focus light on the retina
- **pupil** – the central hole formed by the iris
- **ciliary muscles** – change the thickness of the lens
- **blind spot** – region where the retina is not sensitive to light
- **fovea** – region of the retina where the retinal cells are most dense
- **optic nerve** – along which nerve impulses travel from the retina to the brain

LIGHT

CHECK LIST 1

RECEPTOR CELLS OF THE RETINA
× magnified

- nerve fibres pass to the optic nerve
- **cone** – each cone cell is sensitive to red, blue or green light
- **rod** – rod cells are *not* sensitive to colour, only to the brightness of light
- outer covering of eye

follow the → and track the path of nerve impulses

THE EAR
detects sound

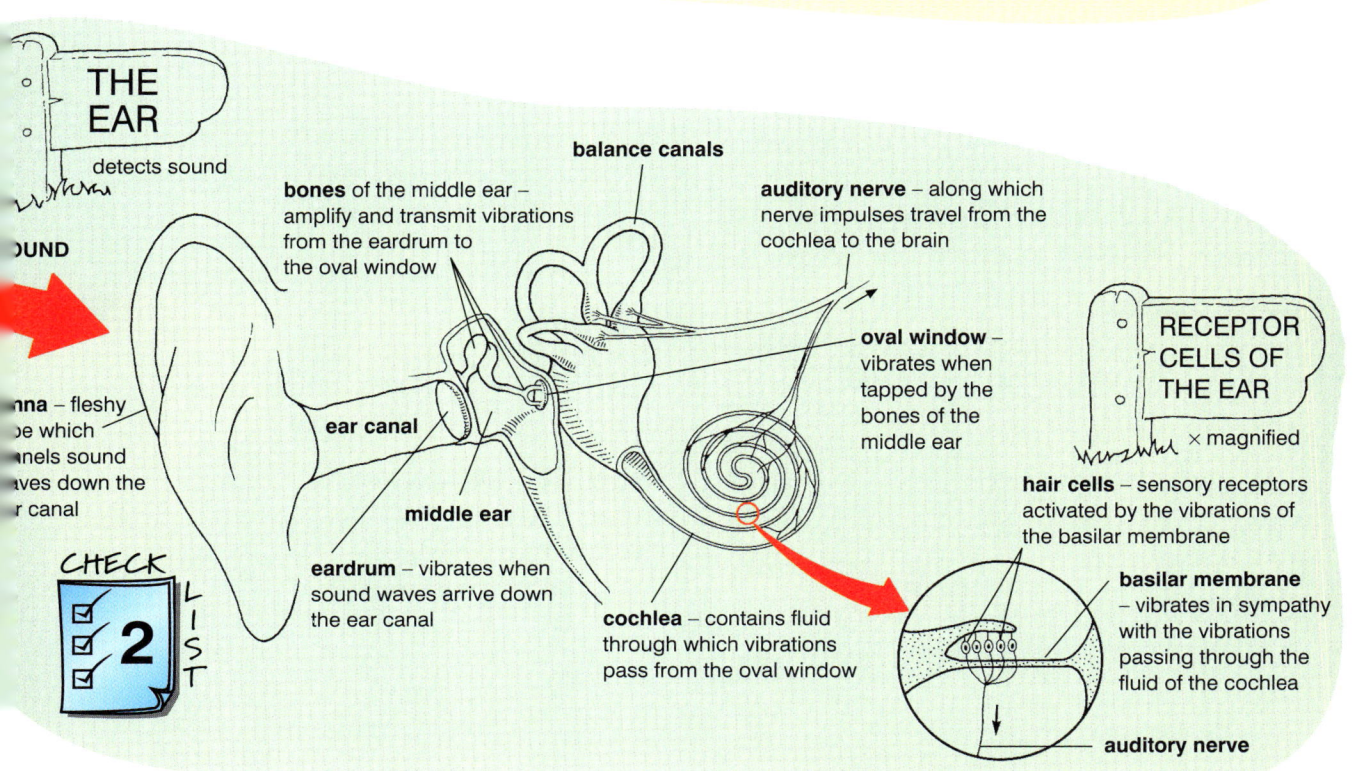

SOUND

- **bones** of the middle ear – amplify and transmit vibrations from the eardrum to the oval window
- **balance canals**
- **auditory nerve** – along which nerve impulses travel from the cochlea to the brain
- **oval window** – vibrates when tapped by the bones of the middle ear
- **pinna** – fleshy lobe which channels sound waves down the ear canal
- **ear canal**
- **middle ear**
- **eardrum** – vibrates when sound waves arrive down the ear canal
- **cochlea** – contains fluid through which vibrations pass from the oval window

CHECK LIST 2

RECEPTOR CELLS OF THE EAR
× magnified

- **hair cells** – sensory receptors activated by the vibrations of the basilar membrane
- **basilar membrane** – vibrates in sympathy with the vibrations passing through the fluid of the cochlea
- **auditory nerve**

53

Life processes and living things

The eye at work

Look up from this page and gaze out of the window at some distant object. Your eye lens becomes thinner to keep your vision in focus. This change in lens shape to keep a nearby object and then a distant object in focus is called **accommodation**.

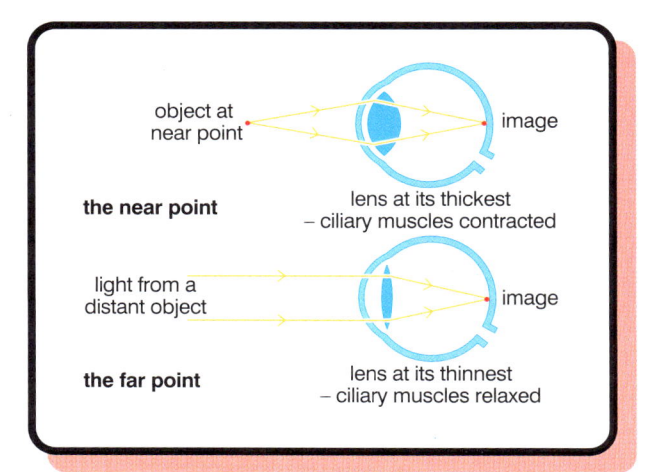

Accommodation keeps objects in focus

Fact file

★ Human eyes are damaged by ultraviolet light. However, insects' eyes can see in ultraviolet light.

★ A normal eye can see clearly any object from far away (at the **far point**) to 25 cm from the eye (the **near point**).

★ The image of an object on the retina is inverted, but the brain interprets it so you see it the right way up.

Light control

The **iris** controls the amount of light entering the eye. Bright light causes a **reflex response**:

★ The muscle of the iris contracts.

   As a result, the pupil narrows.

   As a result, the amount of light entering the eye is reduced.

In dim light:

★ the muscle of the iris relaxes.

   As a result, the pupil widens.

   As a result, the amount of light entering the eye is increased.

4.6 Hormones

preview

At the end of this section you will know that:

- chemicals called hormones regulate the activities of the body
- hormones are produced in the tissues of endocrine glands
- endocrine glands are ductless glands – they release their hormones directly into the bloodstream
- hormones circulate in the blood and cause specific effects on the body
- the tissue on which a particular hormone or group of hormones acts is called a target tissue.

The hormonal system

The blood system is the link between a hormone and its **target tissue**. The sequence reads:

$$\text{endocrine gland} \xrightarrow{\text{produces}} \text{hormone} \xrightarrow{\text{circulates}} \text{blood} \xrightarrow{\text{affects}} \text{target tissue}$$

Hormones affect many of the body's activities. For example, the hormones **insulin** and **glucagon** help regulate the level of glucose in the blood and cope with the surge of glucose at mealtimes and when you eat a snack, such as a bar of chocolate.

Fact file

Most hormones produce their effects rather slowly. They bring about long-term changes in the body such as growth and sexual development.

How hormones work

On pages 56–7 is the concept map which revises **hormones**. The numbers on the concept map refer to the checklist opposite.

Humans as organisms

Checklist for hormones at work

1. ★ If the pancreas does not produce enough insulin, a condition called **diabetes mellitus** occurs.

   As a result, the glucose level in the blood becomes dangerously high and can cause kidney failure and blindness.

   ★ People suffering from diabetes (**diabetics**) are taught to inject themselves regularly with insulin to lower their blood glucose level.

   ★ Glycogen is a polysaccharide whose molecules consist of hundreds of glucose units.

2. ★ The human female usually produces one mature egg each month from the onset of **puberty** (age 11–14 years) to the approach of the **menopause** (age about 45 years). Egg production becomes more irregular and then stops at the menopause (average age around 51 years).

   ★ The contraceptive pill contains one or both of the hormones oestrogen and progesterone. The hormones stop the ovaries from producing eggs.

3. ★ **Diuresis** is the flow of urine from the body. Antidiuretic hormone counteracts diuresis.

   As a result, the flow of urine from the body is reduced.

   ★ Ethanol (the alcohol in beer, wine and spirits) increases diuresis.

4. ★ Unlike most hormones, adrenaline produces its effect very quickly.

   As a result, the body is able to respond to sudden shock or danger.

Fact file – guys and gals

Secondary sexual characteristics are the physical features which distinguish boys from girls. Testosterone helps develop and maintain the secondary sexual characteristics of boys. Oestrogen and progesterone help develop and maintain the secondary sexual characteristics of girls.

guys	gals
pubic hair develops	pubic hair develops
penis gets larger	breasts develop and fat is laid down in the thighs
voice breaks	menstruation starts
hair grows on armpits, chest, face and legs	hair grows on armpits

Secondary sexual characteristics

4.7 Maintaining the internal environment

preview

At the end of this section you will:
- understand that for cells to work efficiently, the composition of the tissue fluid which surrounds them should be kept fairly constant
- know about the important systems which maintain a constant environment in the body: the pancreas and liver (blood glucose), the kidneys (water content) and the skin (temperature).

Conditions in the body

The cells of the body work efficiently when they are

- at an appropriate temperature
- supplied with an appropriate mixture and concentration of substances
- supplied with sufficient water
- at an appropriate acidity/alkalinity (pH).

These conditions are part of the body's **internal environment**. Different mechanisms help regulate the body, keeping its internal environment fairly constant. Keeping conditions constant is called **homeostasis**.

★ The **skin** regulates the body's temperature.

★ The **kidneys** regulate the concentration of salts in the blood, and the water content of the body.

(LIVER AND PANCREAS Pages 56–7.)

★ The **liver** and **pancreas** regulate the concentration of sugar in the blood.

Homeostasis

Homeostasis depends on **negative feedback** mechanisms, which enable different processes to correct themselves when they change. In other words, the processes of life are **self-adjusting**. A level of a chemical or a temperature that deviates from a **set point** (a normal value) is returned to

55

Life processes and living things

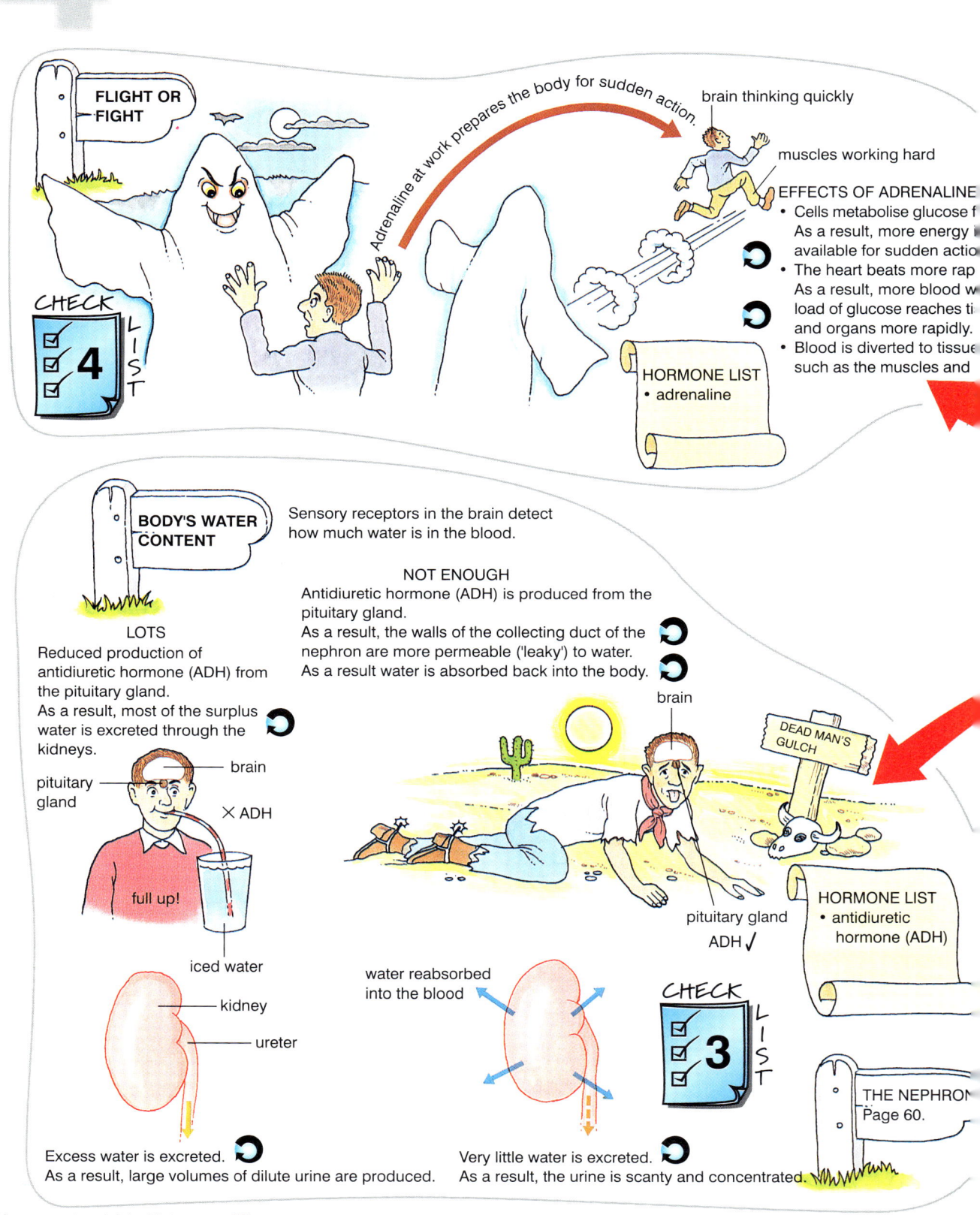

FLIGHT OR FIGHT

Adrenaline at work prepares the body for sudden action.

- brain thinking quickly
- muscles working hard

EFFECTS OF ADRENALINE
- Cells metabolise glucose f[aster]. As a result, more energy [is] available for sudden actio[n].
- The heart beats more rap[idly]. As a result, more blood w[ith its] load of glucose reaches ti[ssues] and organs more rapidly.
- Blood is diverted to tissue[s] such as the muscles and [...]

CHECK LIST 4

HORMONE LIST
- adrenaline

BODY'S WATER CONTENT

Sensory receptors in the brain detect how much water is in the blood.

NOT ENOUGH
Antidiuretic hormone (ADH) is produced from the pituitary gland.
As a result, the walls of the collecting duct of the nephron are more permeable ('leaky') to water.
As a result water is absorbed back into the body.

- brain
- pituitary gland
- ADH ✓

DEAD MAN'S GULCH

water reabsorbed into the blood

Very little water is excreted.
As a result, the urine is scanty and concentrated.

CHECK LIST 3

HORMONE LIST
- antidiuretic hormone (ADH)

THE NEPHRO[N] Page 60.

LOTS
Reduced production of antidiuretic hormone (ADH) from the pituitary gland.
As a result, most of the surplus water is excreted through the kidneys.

- brain
- pituitary gland
- ✗ ADH
- full up!
- iced water
- kidney
- ureter

Excess water is excreted.
As a result, large volumes of dilute urine are produced.

Hormones at work (checklist on page 55)

Humans as organisms

BLOOD GLUCOSE

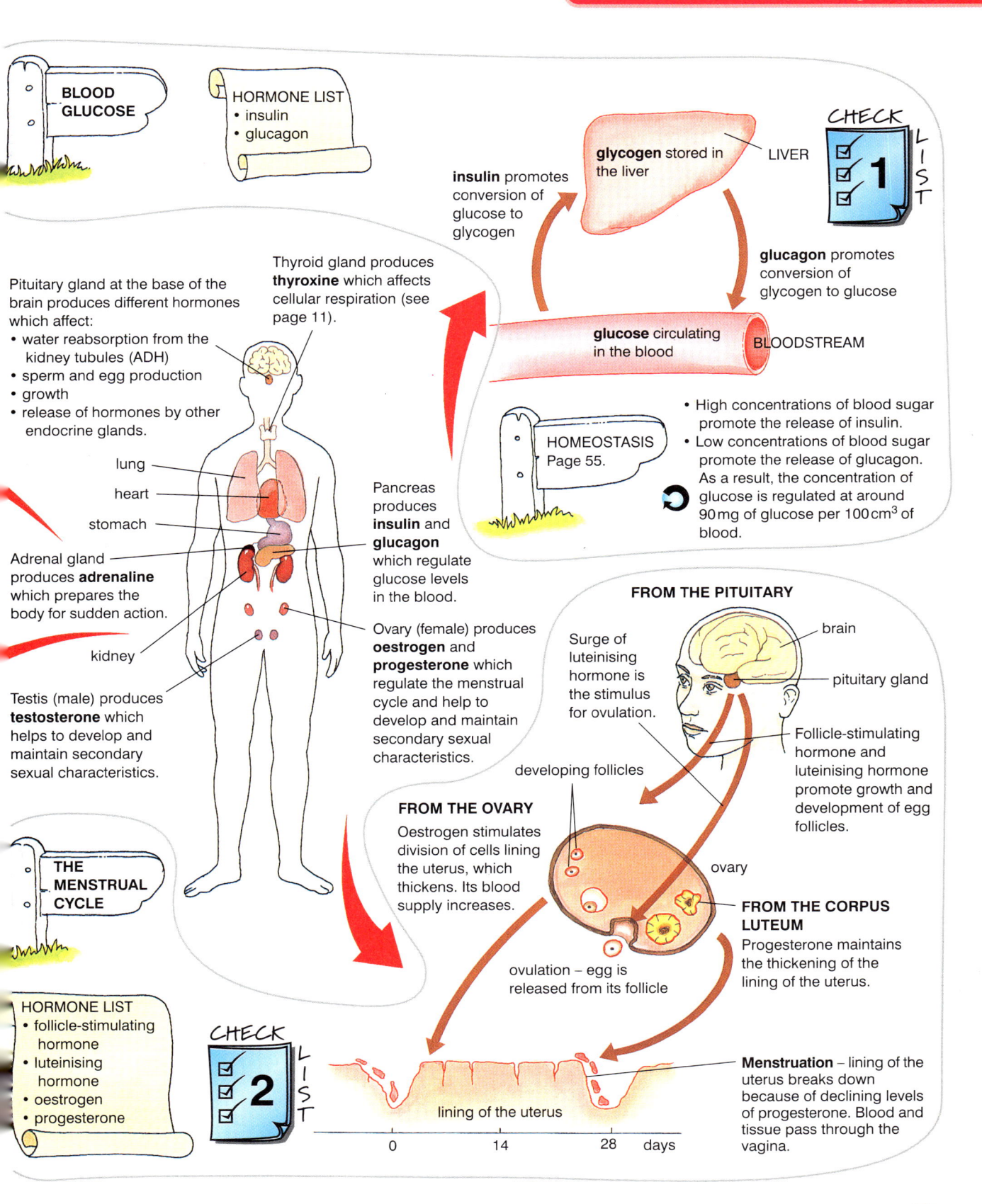

HORMONE LIST
- insulin
- glucagon

CHECK LIST 1

insulin promotes conversion of glucose to glycogen

glycogen stored in the liver — LIVER

glucagon promotes conversion of glycogen to glucose

glucose circulating in the blood — BLOODSTREAM

HOMEOSTASIS Page 55.

- High concentrations of blood sugar promote the release of insulin.
- Low concentrations of blood sugar promote the release of glucagon. As a result, the concentration of glucose is regulated at around 90 mg of glucose per 100 cm^3 of blood.

Pituitary gland at the base of the brain produces different hormones which affect:
- water reabsorption from the kidney tubules (ADH)
- sperm and egg production
- growth
- release of hormones by other endocrine glands.

Thyroid gland produces **thyroxine** which affects cellular respiration (see page 11).

- lung
- heart
- stomach

Adrenal gland produces **adrenaline** which prepares the body for sudden action.

- kidney

Testis (male) produces **testosterone** which helps to develop and maintain secondary sexual characteristics.

Pancreas produces **insulin** and **glucagon** which regulate glucose levels in the blood.

Ovary (female) produces **oestrogen** and **progesterone** which regulate the menstrual cycle and help to develop and maintain secondary sexual characteristics.

THE MENSTRUAL CYCLE

HORMONE LIST
- follicle-stimulating hormone
- luteinising hormone
- oestrogen
- progesterone

CHECK LIST 2

FROM THE PITUITARY

Surge of luteinising hormone is the stimulus for ovulation.

- brain
- pituitary gland

Follicle-stimulating hormone and luteinising hormone promote growth and development of egg follicles.

developing follicles

ovary

FROM THE OVARY
Oestrogen stimulates division of cells lining the uterus, which thickens. Its blood supply increases.

FROM THE CORPUS LUTEUM
Progesterone maintains the thickening of the lining of the uterus.

ovulation – egg is released from its follicle

Menstruation – lining of the uterus breaks down because of declining levels of progesterone. Blood and tissue pass through the vagina.

lining of the uterus

0   14   28   days

57

Life processes and living things

that set point. The menstrual cycle pictured on page 57 illustrates the principles. Rising levels of follicle-stimulating hormone and luteinising hormone stimulate the ovaries to produce the hormone oestrogen. Increasing levels of oestrogen feed back negatively, inhibiting further release of follicle-stimulating hormone. The level of the hormone returns to normal, its role of promoting the growth of egg follicles complete.

On pages 60–1 is the concept map for **homeostasis**. The numbers on the concept map refer to the checklist of points below. Study the concept map and its checklist carefully.

Checklist for homeostasis

1 ★ Each kidney consists of about one million tiny tubules called **nephrons**.

★ The nephron is the working unit of the kidney. It is the structure that brings about homeostatic control of the:
- concentration of salts in the blood
- water content of the body.

The kidney tubules are also responsible for the excretion of urea and other wastes from the body.

2 ★ Hair is made of the protein keratin.

★ **Goose pimples** are bumps on the skin formed when empty hair follicles contract in response to cold.

Fact file

★ Liver metabolism releases a lot of heat energy, which is distributed all over the body by the blood. Humans (and other mammals and birds) have a high metabolic rate, which releases a large amount of heat. This is why mammals and birds are **warm blooded**.

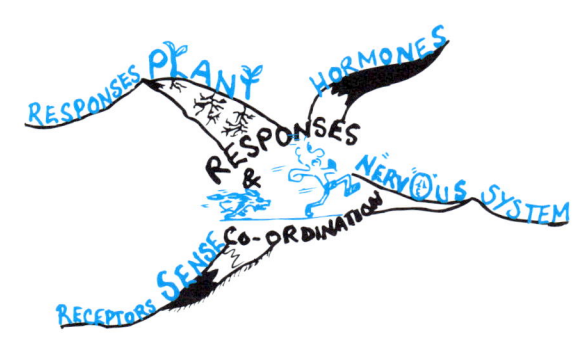

Copy and complete this Mind Map to consolidate your revision of co-ordination in humans and plants.

4.8 Health and disease

preview

At the end of this section you will:
- be able to distinguish between different categories of disease
- know about the defence mechanisms of the body
- understand the harmful effects of smoking
- understand the effects of drug abuse and solvent abuse on the body.

What is disease?

There are several categories of disease.

Infectious diseases are caused by a range of organisms:

- **bacteria**, for example cholera, typhoid fever, tuberculosis, syphilis, gonorrhoea
- **viruses**, for example AIDS, 'flu, poliomyelitis, German measles
- **fungi**, for example thrush, athlete's foot, ringworm
- **protists**, for example malaria, sleeping sickness.

Non-infectious diseases develop because the body is not working properly:

- **cancer** – the uncontrolled division of cells leads to the development of a cancerous growth (**tumour**)
- **degenerative illnesses** – organs and tissues work less well with wear and tear, for example, joints become arthritic and sight and hearing deteriorate with age
- **allergies** – reactions to substances which are normally harmless, for example sensitivity to pollen and dust causes **hay fever**
- **deficiency** – a poor diet may deprive the body of vitamins and other essential substances, for example scurvy (deficiency of vitamin C), rickets (deficiency of vitamin D), kwashiorkor (deficiency of protein).

Genetic diseases result from genetic defects and may be inherited. There are around 4000 genetic diseases in humans. Genetic make-up also influences our vulnerability to other diseases such as diabetes and heart disease.

- **Down's syndrome** is caused by an extra copy of chromosome 21.
- **Sickle-cell anaemia** is caused by a mutation of the gene (**allele**) controlling the synthesis of the blood pigment haemoglobin.

  MUTATION Page 37.

- **Cystic fibrosis** is caused by the mutation of an allele on chromosome 7. The allele controls the production of a polypeptide important for the transport of chloride ions (Cl^-) across the cell membrane.

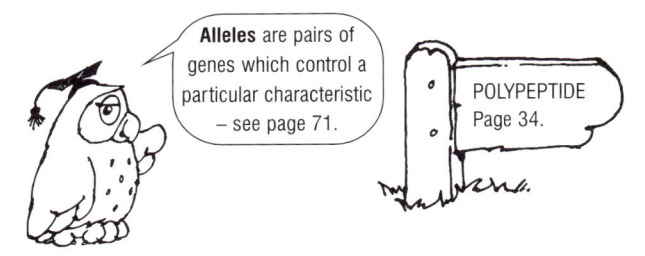

  Alleles are pairs of genes which control a particular characteristic – see page 71.

  POLYPEPTIDE Page 34.

- **Haemophilia** is caused by the mutation of an allele on the X chromosome, as described below.

The allele on the X chromosome normally controls production of **factor VIII**, a substance required for the blood to clot. The defective allele is recessive. The Y chromosome does not carry a dominant allele to mask the effect of the defective recessive allele on the X chromosome. Therefore a man with the defective allele produces no factor VIII, and suffers from haemophilia. For a woman to suffer from haemophilia, she would have to receive the recessive allele from both her father and her mother – a rare occurrence. A woman who has the defective allele on *one* of the X chromosomes is called a **carrier**. She does not suffer from haemophilia because the normal allele on the other X chromosome is dominant.

Muscular dystrophy is another genetic disease linked to the X chromosome.

Humans as organisms

Fighting disease

The body's natural defences against disease are shown below. **Physical** barriers and **chemical** barriers keep us healthy for most of our lives.

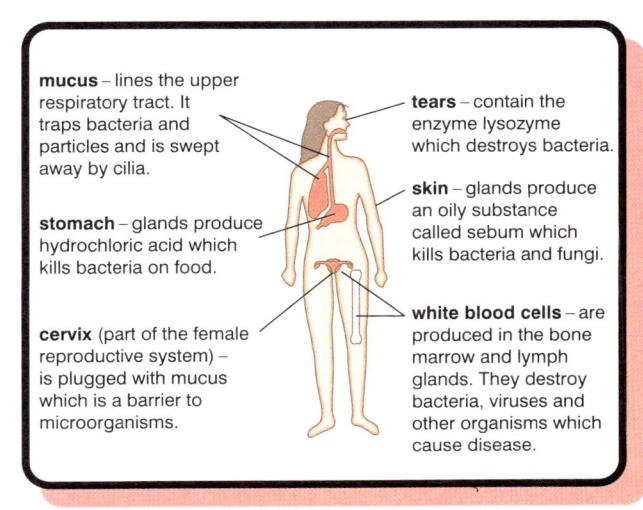

mucus – lines the upper respiratory tract. It traps bacteria and particles and is swept away by cilia.

tears – contain the enzyme lysozyme which destroys bacteria.

stomach – glands produce hydrochloric acid which kills bacteria on food.

skin – glands produce an oily substance called sebum which kills bacteria and fungi.

cervix (part of the female reproductive system) – is plugged with mucus which is a barrier to microorganisms.

white blood cells – are produced in the bone marrow and lymph glands. They destroy bacteria, viruses and other organisms which cause disease.

The body's natural defences against disease

White blood cells

Bacteria, viruses and other microorganisms may infect the blood and tissues of the body and cause disease. Two types of white blood cell, **lymphocytes** and **phagocytes**, protect the body. They work quickly to destroy bacteria, viruses or other cells or substances which the body does not recognise as its own. Such materials 'foreign' to the body are called **antigens**.

There are two types of lymphocyte.

★ **B-lymphocytes** produce **antibodies** which are proteins that attack antigens.

★ **T-lymphocytes** do not produce antibodies. Instead they bind with an antigen and destroy it.

Phagocytes in the blood engulf and destroy antigens. Some phagocytes pass through the walls of blood vessels and migrate through tissues to attack antigens that have entered the body through cuts or scratches. Their action causes an **inflammatory response** – swelling, redness and heat as the phagocytes destroy the invading antigens at the site of the infection. The diagram on page 62 shows B-lymphocytes and phagocytes at work in the blood.

Life processes and living things

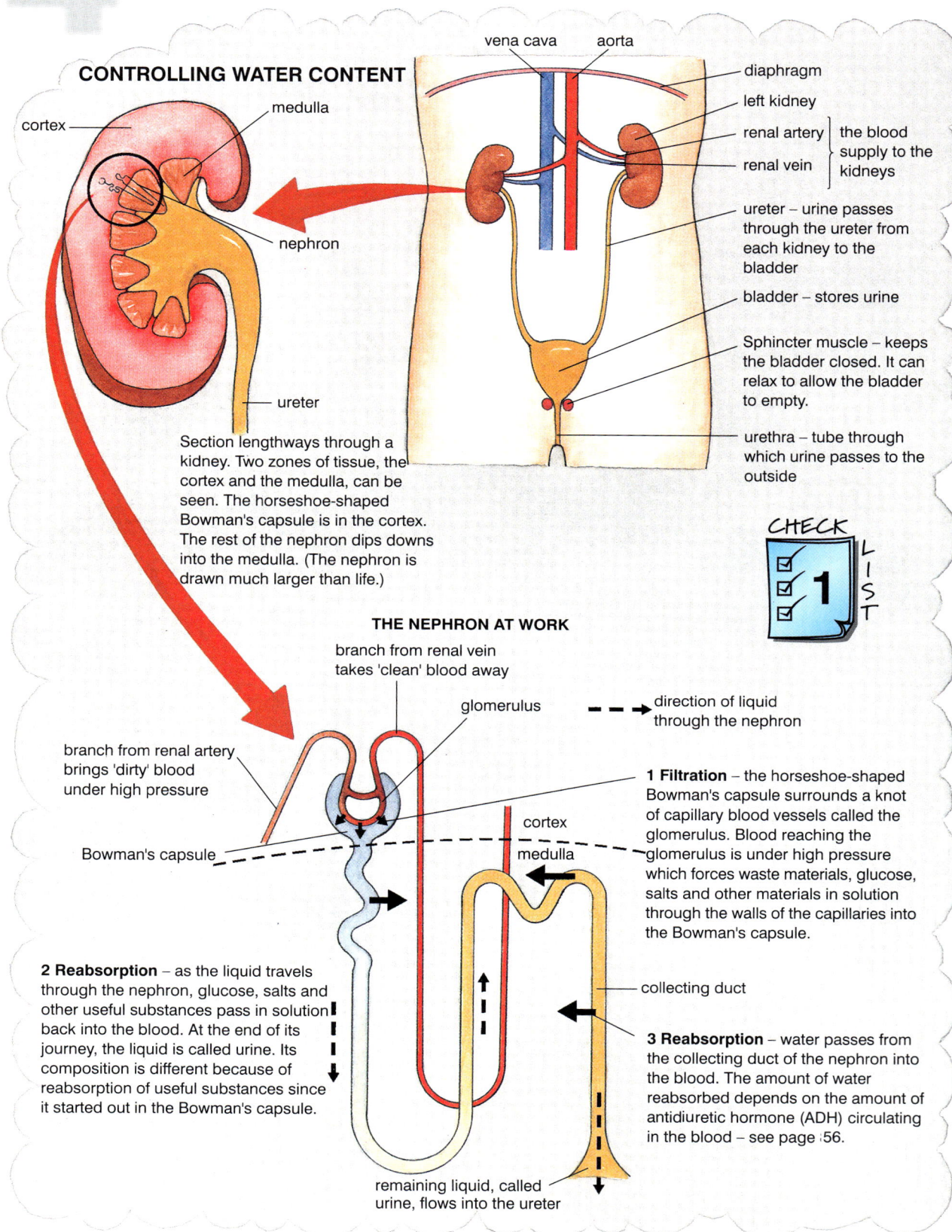

CONTROLLING WATER CONTENT

Labels on kidney cross-section: cortex, medulla, nephron, ureter

Labels on body diagram: vena cava, aorta, diaphragm, left kidney, renal artery, renal vein — the blood supply to the kidneys; ureter – urine passes through the ureter from each kidney to the bladder; bladder – stores urine; Sphincter muscle – keeps the bladder closed. It can relax to allow the bladder to empty; urethra – tube through which urine passes to the outside

Section lengthways through a kidney. Two zones of tissue, the cortex and the medulla, can be seen. The horseshoe-shaped Bowman's capsule is in the cortex. The rest of the nephron dips downs into the medulla. (The nephron is drawn much larger than life.)

CHECK LIST 1

THE NEPHRON AT WORK

Labels: branch from renal vein takes 'clean' blood away; glomerulus; direction of liquid through the nephron; branch from renal artery brings 'dirty' blood under high pressure; Bowman's capsule; cortex; medulla; collecting duct; remaining liquid, called urine, flows into the ureter

1 Filtration – the horseshoe-shaped Bowman's capsule surrounds a knot of capillary blood vessels called the glomerulus. Blood reaching the glomerulus is under high pressure which forces waste materials, glucose, salts and other materials in solution through the walls of the capillaries into the Bowman's capsule.

2 Reabsorption – as the liquid travels through the nephron, glucose, salts and other useful substances pass in solution back into the blood. At the end of its journey, the liquid is called urine. Its composition is different because of reabsorption of useful substances since it started out in the Bowman's capsule.

3 Reabsorption – water passes from the collecting duct of the nephron into the blood. The amount of water reabsorbed depends on the amount of antidiuretic hormone (ADH) circulating in the blood – see page 56.

Homeostasis (checklist on page 58)

Humans as organisms

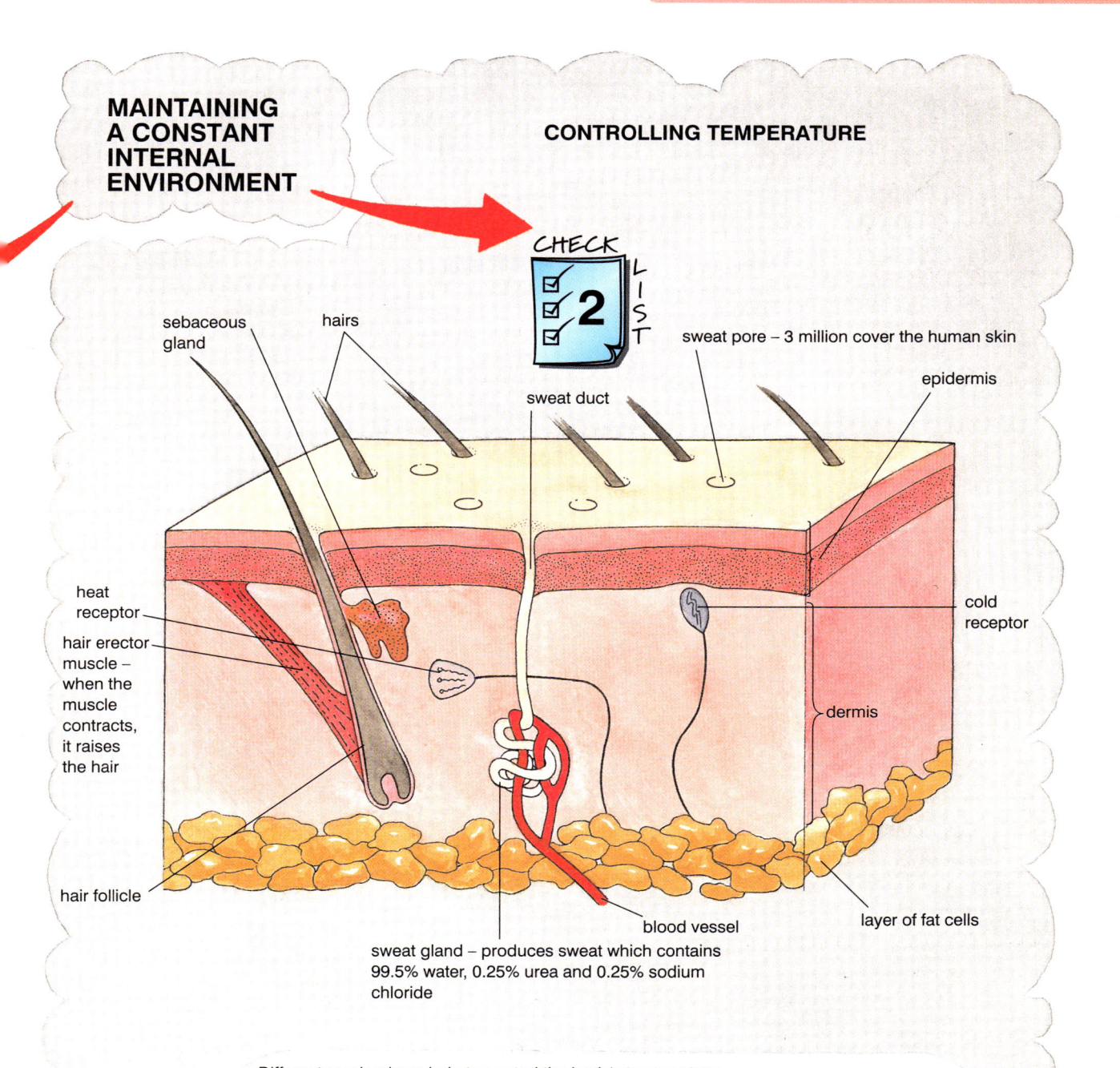

MAINTAINING A CONSTANT INTERNAL ENVIRONMENT

CONTROLLING TEMPERATURE

Diagram labels:
- sebaceous gland
- hairs
- sweat duct
- sweat pore – 3 million cover the human skin
- epidermis
- heat receptor
- hair erector muscle – when the muscle contracts, it raises the hair
- cold receptor
- dermis
- hair follicle
- blood vessel
- layer of fat cells
- sweat gland – produces sweat which contains 99.5% water, 0.25% urea and 0.25% sodium chloride

Different mechanisms help to control the body's temperature:
- Hairs raised by erector muscles trap a layer of air which insulates the body in cold weather (air is a poor conductor of heat). In warm weather, the hair is lowered and no air is trapped.
- Fat insulates the body and reduces heat loss.
- Sweat cools the body because it carries heat energy away from the body as it evaporates.
- Millions of temperature-sensitive sense receptors cover the skin. Nerves connect them to the brain which controls the body's response to changes in temperature in the environment.
- When it is warm, blood vessels in the skin dilate (**vasodilation**). More blood flows through the vessels in the skin and loses heat to the environment. In cold weather, the blood vessels in the skin constrict (**vasoconstriction**) and less heat is lost to the environment.

Life processes and living things

Lymphocytes recognise antigens on the surface of bacteria as 'foreign' and produce antibodies against them.

key
- antibody
- antigen
- immune complex

bacteria → later → Antibodies stick to antigens, forming immune complexes on the surface of the bacteria. This makes the bacteria clump together.

Extensions of the phagocyte cell body flow round the bacteria.

The bacteria are engulfed and enclosed in a vacuole where they are destroyed.

phagocyte

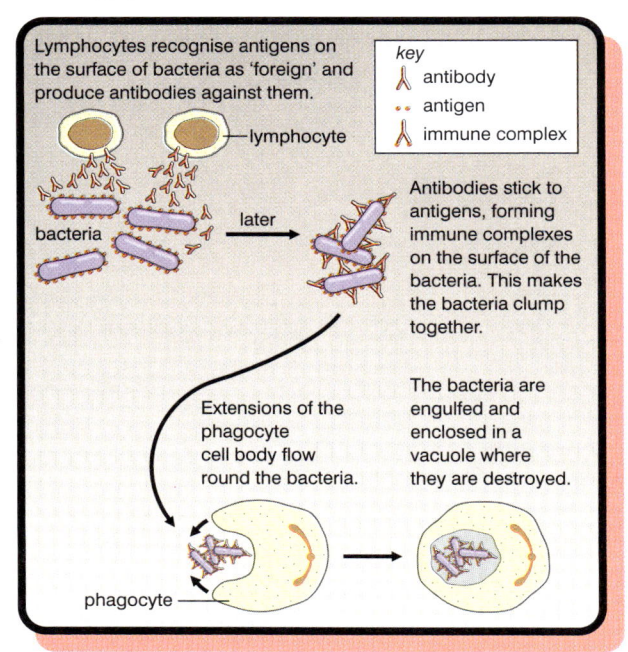

B-lymphocytes produce antibodies which damage bacteria 'foreign' to the body (antigens). Phagocytes engulf the bacteria.

Diseases of the upper respiratory tract and lungs

Despite its filtering and cleaning mechanisms, the upper respiratory tract may become infected by disease-causing microorganisms. Infection of the

- throat (pharynx) is called **pharyngitis**
- voicebox (larynx) is called **laryngitis**
- windpipe (trachea) is called **tracheitis**
- bronchi and bronchioles is called **bronchitis**.

Pneumonia is an infection of the lungs caused by a particular type of bacterium. In pneumonia,

- Fluid collects in the lungs.

As a result, the surface area available for the absorption of oxygen is reduced.

As a result, the patient becomes breathless.

Pleurisy is an infection of the pleural membranes caused by a particular type of bacterium. In pleurisy,

- Infection makes the membranes rough.

As a result, there is pain when the membranes rub together.

Antibiotic drugs are used to treat pneumonia and pleurisy.

Smoking

Smoking cigarettes is a major cause of lung cancer and heart disease. Cigarette smoke is acidic and contains various substances harmful to health.

★ **Nicotine** is a powerful poison which increases the heart rate and blood pressure.

★ **Carbon monoxide** is a poisonous gas which combines 300 times more readily with haemoglobin than oxygen does.

As a result, the level of oxygen in the blood is reduced.

★ **Tar** is a mixture of many compounds, some of which cause cancer (are **carcinogens**).

Some substances in cigarette smoke irritate the membrane lining the upper respiratory tract.

As a result, extra mucus (phlegm) forms in the trachea and bronchi.

As a result, the person may develop 'smoker's cough' in an attempt to remove the excess phlegm.

Other substances in cigarette smoke stop the cilia from beating.

As a result, particles and microorganisms enter the lungs.

As a result, the risk of infection is increased.

Emphysema is caused by repeated coughing, which destroys the walls of the alveoli.

As a result, the surface area available for the absorption of oxygen is reduced.

As a result, the person becomes breathless.

Lung cancer is caused by the carcinogens in tar. Abnormal cell division in lung tissue leads to the development of tumours (growths) which may be difficult to cure. Cancer cells may break away from the tumours and circulate in the blood to start **secondary** growths elsewhere in the body.

The smoking habit

Smoking cigarettes was fashionable in the early 1900s, and many people became smokers. Scientists soon suspected a link between smoking cigarettes and lung cancer.

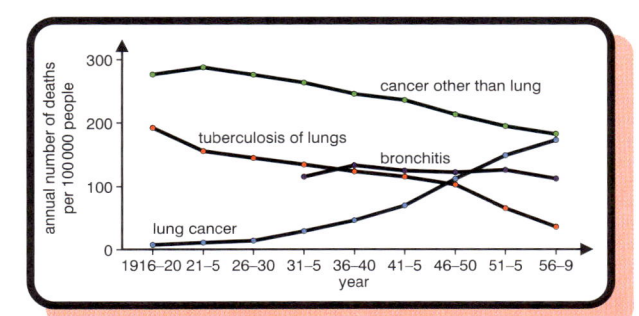

Deaths from lung cancer increased sharply in England and Wales from 1916 to 1960, which was the period when more and more people were smoking cigarettes. Other forms of lung disease were declining.

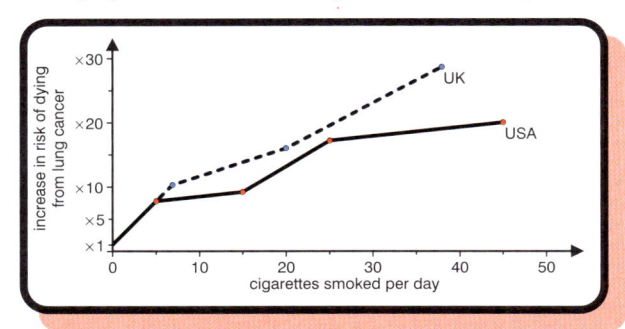

Studies have shown that the more cigarettes smoked, the greater is the risk of dying from lung cancer.

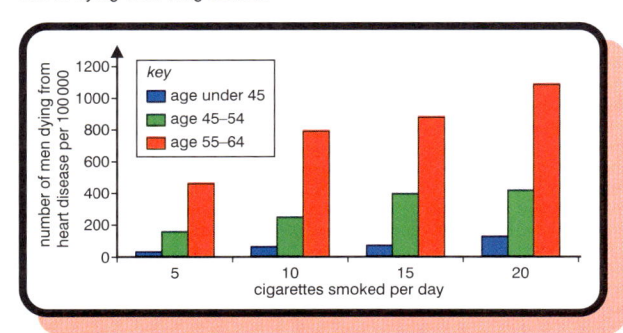

Studies have shown that the more cigarettes smoked, the greater is the risk of dying from heart disease.

Today there are fewer smokers than non-smokers in the United Kingdom. However, of the people who do smoke, there are many young people (especially girls). SMOKING IS A MUG'S GAME – DO NOT START!

REMEMBER – IF YOU DO SMOKE YOU CAN GIVE IT UP. Advice and help are available.

Drugs

Drugs are used to help in the fight against disease. For example,

★ **Antibiotics** are used to attack the different types of bacteria that cause disease.

★ **Analgesics** are drugs that reduce pain (painkillers).

Some drugs are highly **addictive** and may be **abused**. This means they are used for non-medical purposes.

Alcohol

Ethanol (the alcohol in beers, wine and spirits) depresses the activity of the nervous system. Small amounts affect the **cortex** of the brain which controls judgement. Large quantities affect the **motor cortex** which controls movement. Even more impairs memory. Drinking increasing amounts of alcohol affects other areas of the brain until it reaches brain centres that keep us alive. Death may follow.

Solvents

Glues, paints, nail varnish and cleaning fluids (dry cleaners) contain volatile solvents such as esters and ethanol. These are liquids in which other substances dissolve, and which readily produce a vapour at room temperature. Breathing them in gives a warm sense of well-being, but also produces dangerous disorientation. Long-term solvent abuse can damage the brain, kidneys and liver.

BRAIN Page 50.

Life processes and living things

round-up

How much have you improved?
Work out your improvement index on pages 83–4.

1. Simple tests identify the nutrients in different foods. Match the nutrient in column **A** with the test result that identifies the nutrient in column **B**.

A nutrients	B test results
starch	forms a milky emulsion when mixed with warm dilute ethanol
glucose	produces a violet/purple colour when mixed with dilute sodium hydroxide and a few drops of copper sulphate solution
fat	produces a blue/black colour when mixed with a few drops of iodine solution
protein	produces an orange colour when heated with Benedict's solution

   [4]

2. Match each enzyme in column **A** with its role in digestion in column **B**.

A enzymes	B roles
amylase	digests maltose to glucose
pepsin	digests fat to fatty acids and glycerol
lipase	digests starch to maltose
maltase	digests protein to polypeptides

   [4]

3. Distinguish between the following pairs of terms.
   a) antibody and antigen [5]
   b) HIV and AIDS [3]
   c) haemoglobin and haemophilia [5]

4. The different parts of a motor nerve cell are listed in column **A**. Match each part with its description in column **B**.

A parts of a cell	B descriptions
axon	minute electrical disturbance
dendrite	boosts the transmission of nerve impulses
sheath	transmits nerve impulses from the cell body
nerve impulse	carries nerve impulses to the cell body

   [4]

5. Explain the differences between the following pairs of terms.
   a) blind spot and fovea
   b) pupil and iris
   c) cornea and retina [6]

6. How do endocrine glands differ from other glands in the body? [2]

7. Briefly explain how antidiuretic hormone (ADH) keeps the water content of the body steady. [2]

8. Briefly explain
   a) why raised body hair helps us keep warm [3]
   b) why sweating helps us keep cool. [2]

9. Identify the cause of each disease in the list by writing either **B** (for bacterium) or **V** (for virus) next to each one.
   cholera   AIDS   syphilis   'flu   pneumonia [5]

10. Identify the substances in cigarette smoke which are harmful to health. Briefly explain why they are harmful. [6]

Well done if you've improved. Don't worry if you haven't. Take a break and try again.

Inheritance and evolution

5

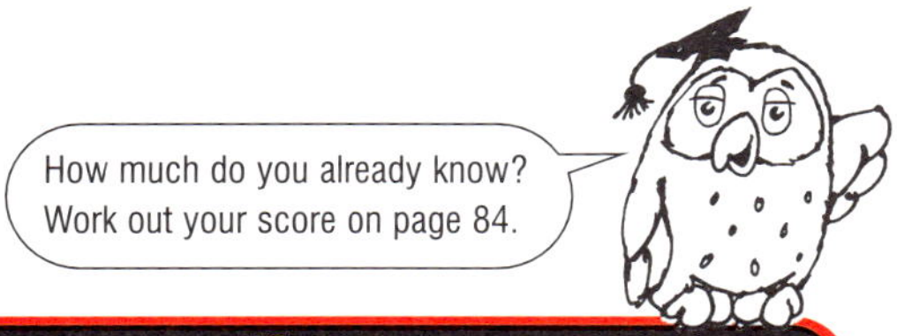

How much do you already know? Work out your score on page 84.

Test yourself

1 The diagram shows the reproductive system of a man. Name parts A–E. [5]

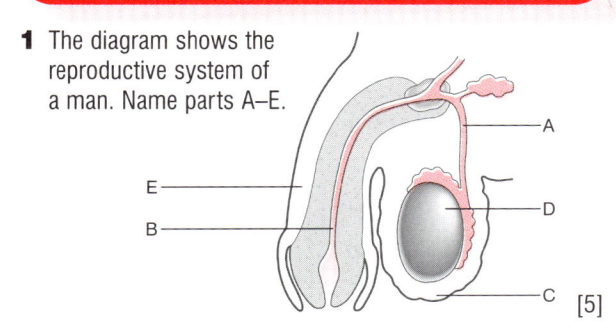

2 Match each structure in column **A** with its correct description in column **B**.

A structures	B descriptions
corm	a horizontal stem running above ground
runner	a short, swollen underground stem
tuber	a large underground bud
bulb	a swelling at the end of a rhizome [4]

3 In humans, the gene for brown eyes (**B**) is dominant to the gene for blue eyes (**b**).
   a) Using the symbols **B** and **b**, state the genotypes of the children that could be born from a marriage between a heterozygous father and a blue-eyed mother. [2]
   b) State whether the children are brown eyed or blue eyed. [2]

4 Distinguish between the following.
   a) restriction enzyme and ligase (splicing enzyme) [7]
   b) biotechnology and genetic engineering [5]
   c) batch culture and continuous culture [7]

5 Why are acquired characteristics not inherited? [3]

6 List the different sources of variation in living things. [6]

7 Why does sexual reproduction produce much more genetic variation than asexual reproduction? [5]

8 Distinguish between the following terms.
   a) ancestors and descendants [1]
   b) adaptation and extinction [2]
   c) evolution and natural selection [3]

9 How are fossils formed? [4]

5.1 Reproduction

preview

At the end of this section you will:
- know that reproduction gives rise to offspring
- understand that sexual reproduction gives rise to variation in offspring and that asexual reproduction gives rise to identical offspring
- be able to identify the components of the human reproductive system
- know how sexual reproduction occurs in humans and in flowering plants.

Sexual or asexual?

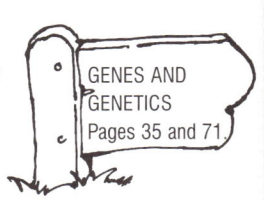

Reproduction passes genetic material on from parents to their offspring. There are two types of reproduction.

GENES AND GENETICS
Pages 35 and 71.

In **sexual reproduction**, *two* parents (male and female) produce sex cells called **gametes**. Gametes are formed by **meiosis**. The male gametes are **sperm**. The female gametes are **eggs**. The sperm and egg fuse – this is called **fertilisation**. The fertilised egg cell is called a **zygote**. The zygote divides repeatedly, producing a ball of cells called an **embryo** which develops into the new individual. The offspring formed by sexual reproduction inherit genes from each parent, and are genetically *different* from one another and from their parents. In other words, they show **variation**.

Dear Student

IMPORTANT ANNOUNCEMENT
Topic 3.2. about meiosis and mitosis is **REALLY REALLY** important to your understanding of sexual and asexual reproduction.

Luv Owl

65

Life processes and living things

In **asexual reproduction**, *one* parent divides by **mitosis** to produce daughter cells which form new individuals. These offspring are genetically *identical* to one another and to their parent because DNA replicates exact copies of itself during mitosis.

Sexual reproduction in humans and flowering plants

How much do you recall about the structure of the reproductive organs in flowering plants and humans? Remember that **flowers** are shoots which are specialised for reproduction. The **genitalia** are the visible parts of the human reproductive system. On the opposite page is the Mind Map for reproduction. The numbers on the Mind Map refer to the checklist below.

Checklist for reproduction

1. ★ The testes hang down between the legs.

   As a result, the testes are protected from injury.

   ★ The position of the testes keeps them about 3°C lower than body temperature.

   As a result, sperm develop properly in the slightly cooler conditions.

   ★ A woman's genitalia cover and protect the opening to the rest of the reproductive system inside her body.

   MENSTRUAL CYCLE Page 57.

2. ★ A fertilised egg is called a **zygote**. It develops into a new individual. The sequence reads:

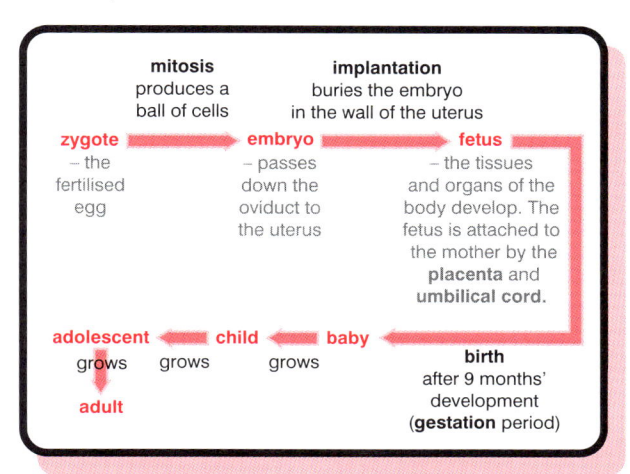

   ```
   mitosis               implantation
   produces a            buries the embryo
   ball of cells         in the wall of the uterus

   zygote     →   embryo      →    fetus
   – the          – passes         – the tissues
   fertilised     down the         and organs of the
   egg            oviduct to       body develop. The
                  the uterus       fetus is attached to
                                   the mother by the
                                   placenta and
                                   umbilical cord.

   adolescent ← child ← baby
   grows       grows   grows       birth
                                   after 9 months'
   adult                           development
                                   (gestation period)
   ```

   The development of the zygote

★ In humans, pregnancy usually results in the birth of only one baby. However, sometimes **twins** are born.

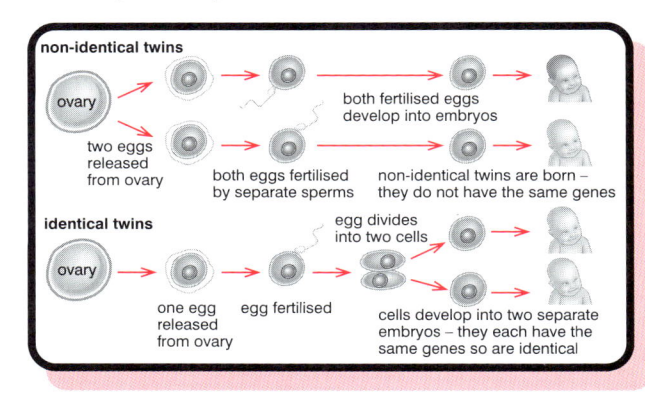

non-identical twins
ovary → two eggs released from ovary → both eggs fertilised by separate sperms → both fertilised eggs develop into embryos → non-identical twins are born – they do not have the same genes

identical twins
ovary → one egg released from ovary → egg fertilised → egg divides into two cells → cells develop into two separate embryos – they each have the same genes so are identical

Producing twins

3. ★ **Contraception** aims to prevent pregnancy by
   - preventing sperm from reaching the egg, or
   - preventing eggs from being produced, or
   - preventing the fertilised egg from developing in the uterus.

4. ★ In flowering plants, sexual reproduction involves **pollination**, **fertilisation** and the formation of **fruits** and **seeds**. The sequence reads:

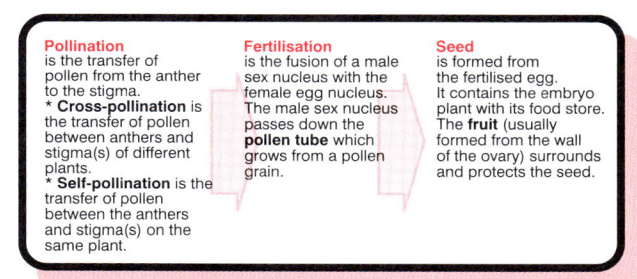

   Pollination is the transfer of pollen from the anther to the stigma.
   * **Cross-pollination** is the transfer of pollen between anthers and stigma(s) of different plants.
   * **Self-pollination** is the transfer of pollen between the anthers and stigma(s) on the same plant.

   Fertilisation is the fusion of a male sex nucleus with the female egg nucleus. The male sex nucleus passes down the **pollen tube** which grows from a pollen grain.

   Seed is formed from the fertilised egg. It contains the embryo plant with its food store. The **fruit** (usually formed from the wall of the ovary) surrounds and protects the seed.

★ Flowers are adapted for pollination.
   - **Insect-pollinated** flowers are brightly coloured and produce nectar and scent to attract insect visitors.
   - **Wind-pollinated** flowers are often a dull colour and are adapted to distribute large quantities of pollen far and wide.

★ Fruits and seeds are adapted for distribution by either animals or wind.
   - **Spines** and **hooks** attach the fruit to passing animals.
   - Animals are attracted to feed on **brightly coloured** fruits. The seeds are protected from the digestive juices in the animal's intestine, and eventually pass out in the animal's faeces.
   - **Parachutes** and **wings** increase the surface area of fruits, helping them travel in the wind.

Inheritance and evolution

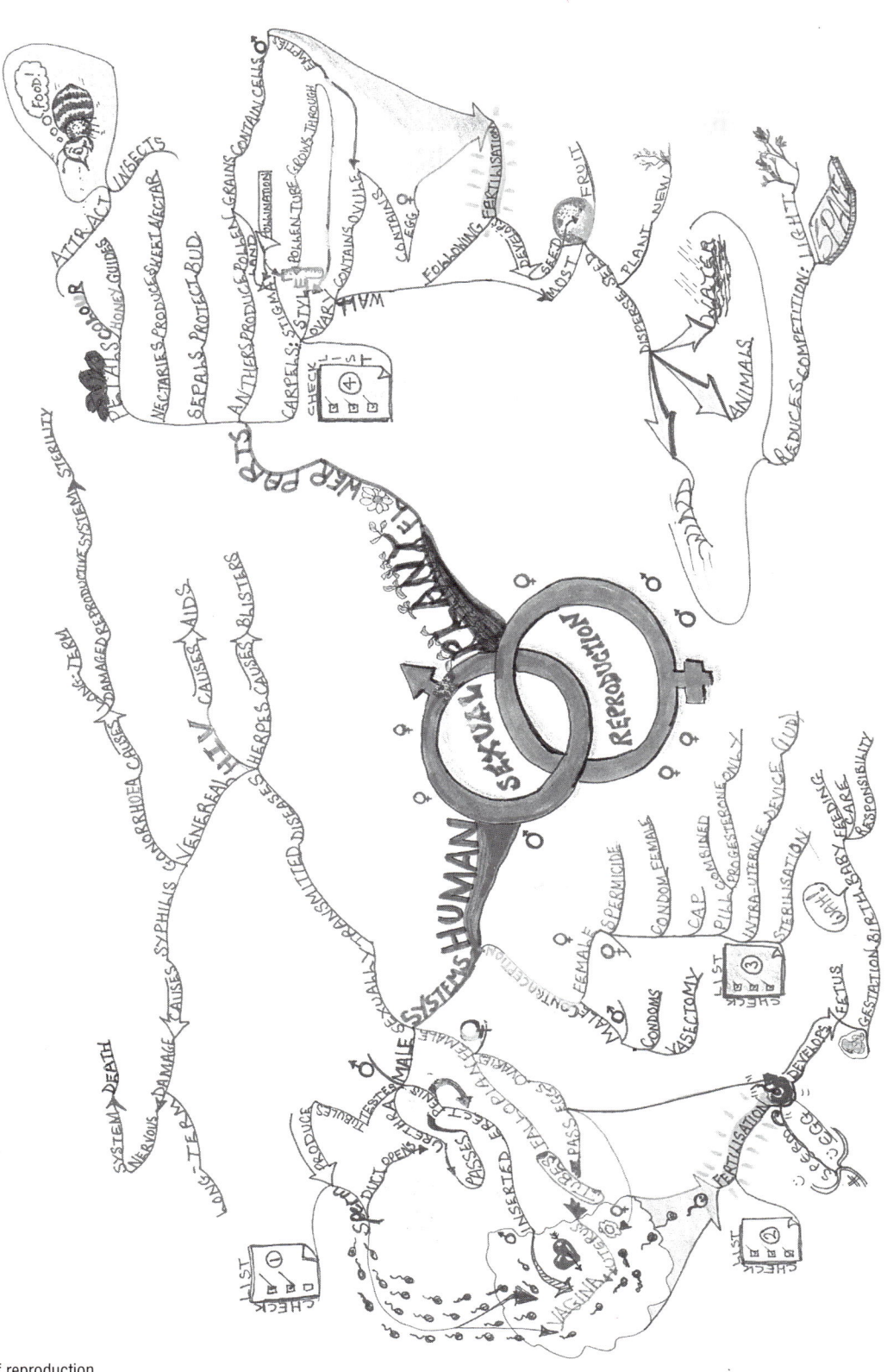

Mind Map of reproduction

Life processes and living things

5.2 Asexual reproduction in plants

preview

At the end of this section you will:
- be able to identify the organs of asexual reproduction in flowering plants
- know that cuttings, graftings and micropropagation are used by farmers and gardeners to produce many identical plants
- understand that asexual reproduction preserves desirable characteristics and so guarantees plant quality.

Remember that asexual reproduction gives rise to **genetically identical** individuals, because DNA replicates during mitosis. This process passes on exact copies of the parent's genetic material to the daughter cells.

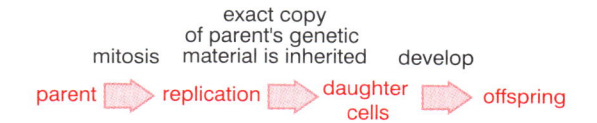

parent ⇒ replication ⇒ daughter cells (exact copy of parent's genetic material is inherited) ⇒ offspring develop
(mitosis)

Remember
★ Genetically identical individuals are called **clones** (see page 25).

Vegetative reproduction

Different parts of flowering plants can reproduce asexually. They are called the **vegetative parts** and are formed from the **root**, **leaf** or **stem**.

Asexual reproduction in flowering plants is sometimes called **vegetative reproduction**. Since the new plants come from a single parent, they are genetically the same and are therefore **clones**.

The vegetative parts of plants store food. The stored food is used for the development of the new plant(s). We sometimes eat these food storage organs as vegetables, for example, potatoes.

The concept map for **asexual reproduction in plants** is shown on the opposite page. It is your revision guide, so study it carefully.

Artificial vegetative reproduction

Gardeners and farmers need to produce fresh stocks of plants that have desirable characteristics such as disease resistance, colour of fruit or shape of flower. The diagram below shows how they use vegetative propagation.

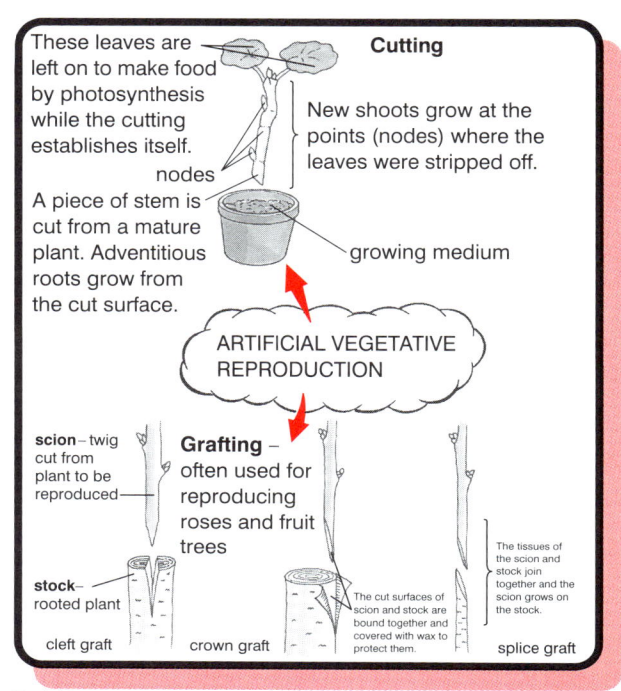

Cutting
- These leaves are left on to make food by photosynthesis while the cutting establishes itself.
- New shoots grow at the points (nodes) where the leaves were stripped off.
- nodes
- A piece of stem is cut from a mature plant. Adventitious roots grow from the cut surface.
- growing medium

ARTIFICIAL VEGETATIVE REPRODUCTION

Grafting – often used for reproducing roses and fruit trees
- **scion** – twig cut from plant to be reproduced
- **stock** – rooted plant
- cleft graft
- crown graft
- The cut surfaces of scion and stock are bound together and covered with wax to protect them.
- The tissues of the scion and stock join together and the scion grows on the stock.
- splice graft

Exploiting vegetative reproduction

Micropropagation is used to grow plants from small pieces, using a technique called **tissue culture**.

★ Small fragments of plant tissue are grown in a liquid or gel that contains all the necessary ingredients.

★ Conditions are sterile.

   As a result, the new plants are free of disease.

★ The temperature is carefully controlled.

All the plants grown from pieces of one parent plant will be genetically identical. They are clones. The advantages are that the plants
- are healthy
- are the same
- retain the desirable characteristics of the parent plant.

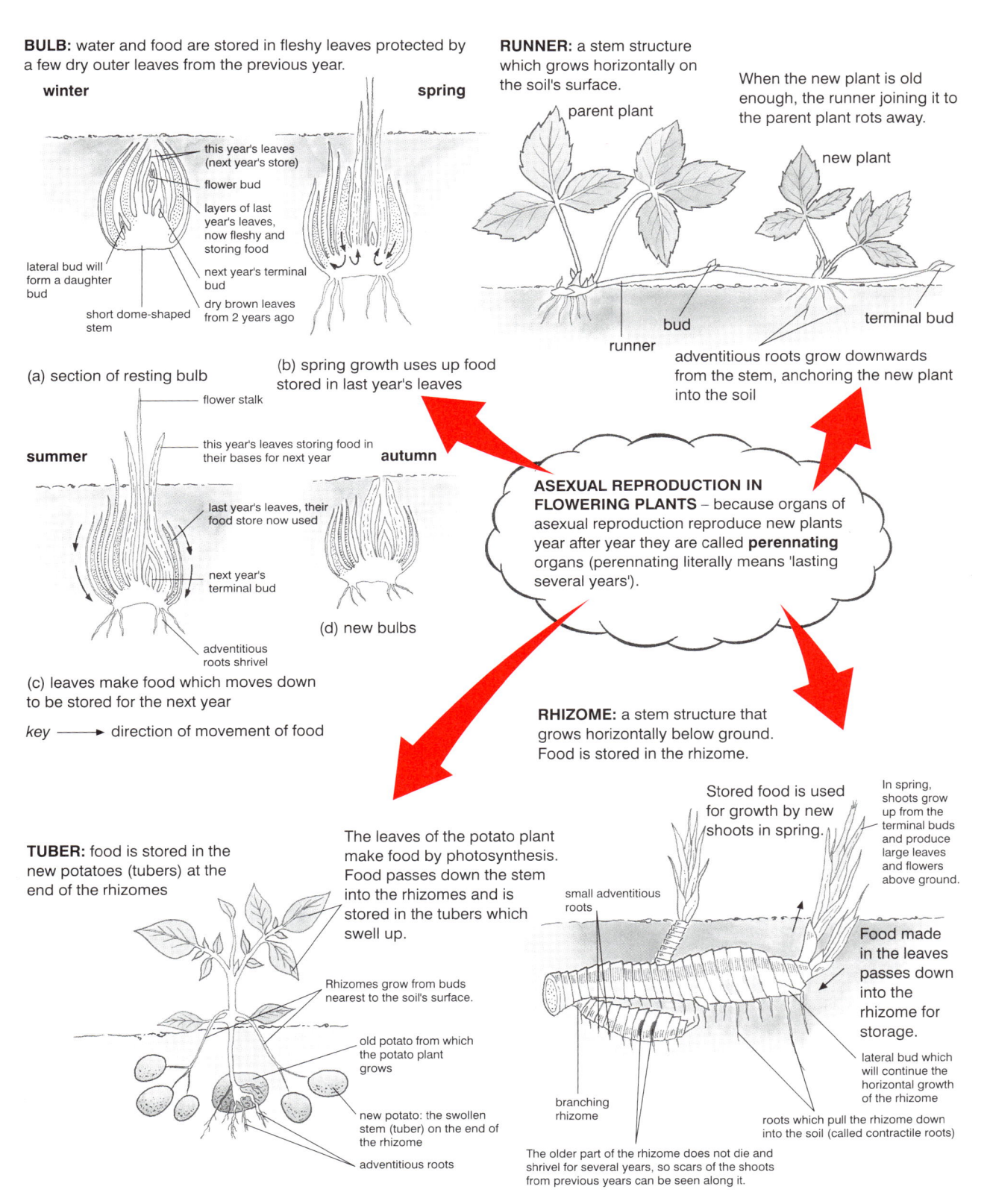

Inheritance and evolution

BULB: water and food are stored in fleshy leaves protected by a few dry outer leaves from the previous year.

winter

- this year's leaves (next year's store)
- flower bud
- layers of last year's leaves, now fleshy and storing food
- next year's terminal bud
- dry brown leaves from 2 years ago
- lateral bud will form a daughter bud
- short dome-shaped stem

(a) section of resting bulb

spring

(b) spring growth uses up food stored in last year's leaves

summer

- flower stalk
- this year's leaves storing food in their bases for next year
- last year's leaves, their food store now used
- next year's terminal bud
- adventitious roots shrivel

(c) leaves make food which moves down to be stored for the next year

autumn

(d) new bulbs

key ⟶ direction of movement of food

RUNNER: a stem structure which grows horizontally on the soil's surface.

- parent plant
- new plant
- bud
- runner
- terminal bud

When the new plant is old enough, the runner joining it to the parent plant rots away.

adventitious roots grow downwards from the stem, anchoring the new plant into the soil

ASEXUAL REPRODUCTION IN FLOWERING PLANTS – because organs of asexual reproduction reproduce new plants year after year they are called **perennating** organs (perennating literally means 'lasting several years').

TUBER: food is stored in the new potatoes (tubers) at the end of the rhizomes

The leaves of the potato plant make food by photosynthesis. Food passes down the stem into the rhizomes and is stored in the tubers which swell up.

- Rhizomes grow from buds nearest to the soil's surface.
- old potato from which the potato plant grows
- new potato: the swollen stem (tuber) on the end of the rhizome
- adventitious roots

RHIZOME: a stem structure that grows horizontally below ground. Food is stored in the rhizome.

Stored food is used for growth by new shoots in spring.

In spring, shoots grow up from the terminal buds and produce large leaves and flowers above ground.

- small adventitious roots
- branching rhizome
- lateral bud which will continue the horizontal growth of the rhizome
- roots which pull the rhizome down into the soil (called contractile roots)

Food made in the leaves passes down into the rhizome for storage.

The older part of the rhizome does not die and shrivel for several years, so scars of the shoots from previous years can be seen along it.

Asexual reproduction in flowering plants

Life processes and living things

5.3 Monohybrid inheritance

preview

At the end of this section you will:
- understand genetic terms
- be able to work out the expected outcome of a monohybrid cross
- understand the inheritance of gender
- understand sex-linked inheritance.

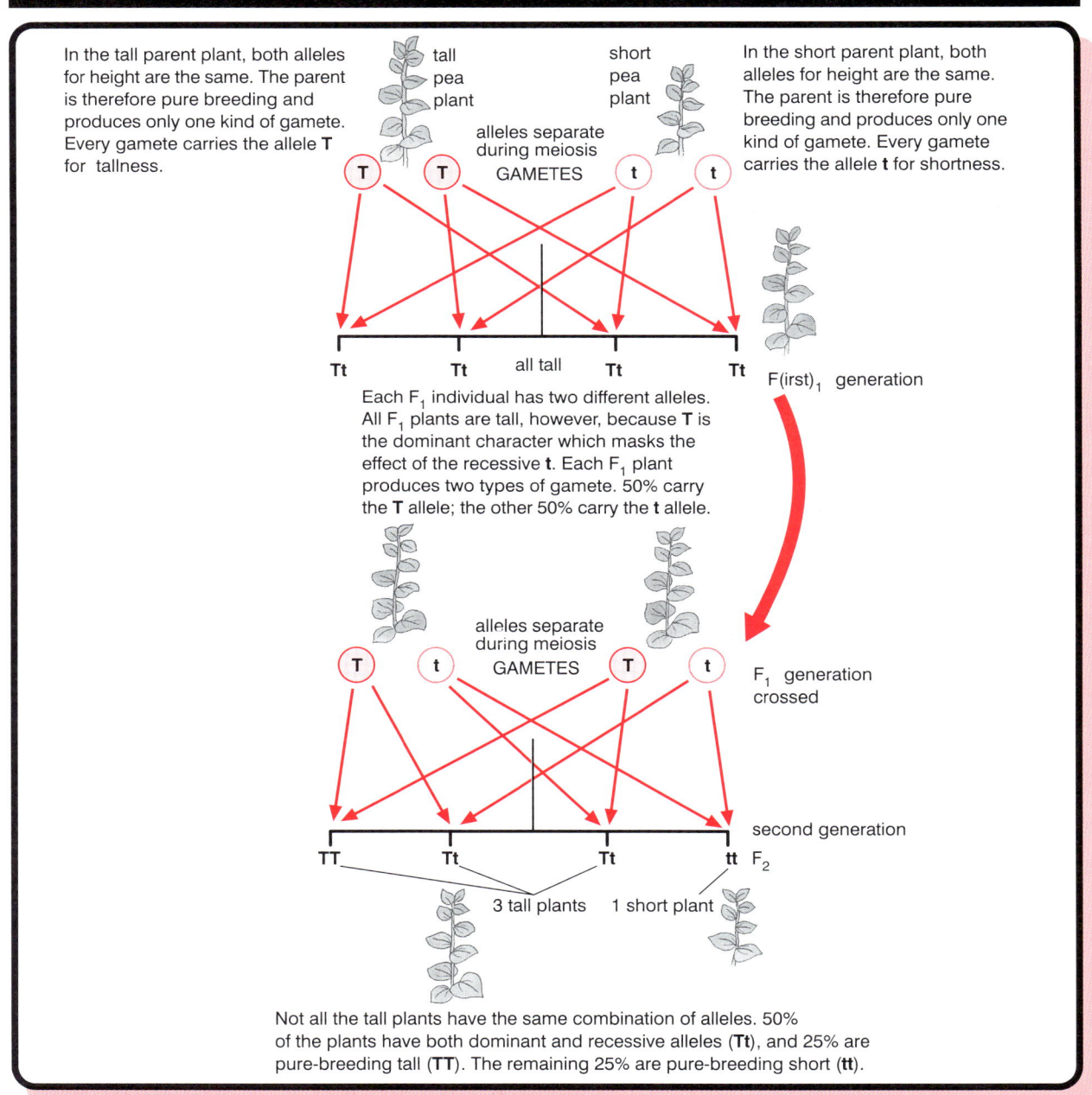

In the tall parent plant, both alleles for height are the same. The parent is therefore pure breeding and produces only one kind of gamete. Every gamete carries the allele **T** for tallness.

tall pea plant   short pea plant

alleles separate during meiosis
GAMETES   **T**   **T**   **t**   **t**

In the short parent plant, both alleles for height are the same. The parent is therefore pure breeding and produces only one kind of gamete. Every gamete carries the allele **t** for shortness.

Tt   Tt   all tall   **Tt   Tt** F_1 generation

Each F_1 individual has two different alleles. All F_1 plants are tall, however, because **T** is the dominant character which masks the effect of the recessive **t**. Each F_1 plant produces two types of gamete. 50% carry the **T** allele; the other 50% carry the **t** allele.

alleles separate during meiosis
GAMETES   **T**   **t**   **T**   **t**

F_1 generation crossed

second generation
TT   Tt   Tt   tt F_2

3 tall plants   1 short plant

Not all the tall plants have the same combination of alleles. 50% of the plants have both dominant and recessive alleles (**Tt**), and 25% are pure-breeding tall (**TT**). The remaining 25% are pure-breeding short (**tt**).

How alleles controlling a characteristic (height) pass from one generation to the next

Fact file

Gregor Mendel was a monk who lived in the Augustinian monastery at the town of Brünn (now Brno in the Czech Republic). He observed the inheritance of different characteristics in the garden pea, and reported the results of his experiments in 1865. The work established the basis of modern genetics.

The vocabulary of genetics

★ **monohybrid inheritance** – the processes by which a single characteristic is passed from parents to offspring, for example flower colour or eye colour

★ **pure breeding** – characteristics that breed true, appearing unchanged generation after generation

★ **parental generation** (symbol **P**) – individuals that are pure breeding for a characteristic

★ **first filial generation** (symbol F_1) – the offspring produced by a parental generation

★ **second filial generation** (symbol F_2) – the offspring produced by crossing members of the first filial generation

★ **gene** – a length of DNA which codes for the whole of one protein

GENES Page 35.

★ **allele** – one of a pair of genes that control a particular characteristic

★ **homozygote** – an individual with identical alleles controlling a particular characteristic. Individuals that are pure breeding for a particular characteristic are **homozygous** for that characteristic

★ **heterozygote** – an individual with different alleles controlling a particular characteristic

★ **expressed** – a gene is expressed when a protein is produced from the activity of the gene

★ **dominant** – any characteristic that appears in the F_1 offspring of a cross between pure-breeding parents with contrasting characteristics, such as tallness and shortness in pea plants, *or* any characteristic expressed by an allele in preference to the form of the characteristic controlled by the allele's partner

★ **recessive** – any characteristic present in the parental generation that misses the F_1 generation but reappears in the F_2 generation, *or* any characteristic of an allele that is not expressed because the form of the characteristic of the allele's partner is expressed in preference, *or* any characteristic of an allele that is only expressed in the absence of the allele's dominant partner

★ **genotype** – the genetic make-up (all of the genes) of an individual

★ **phenotype** – the outward appearance of an individual; the result of those genes of the genotype which are actively expressing characteristics.

Some rules of genetics

★ Paired genes controlling a particular characteristic are called alleles.

★ Letters are used to symbolise alleles.

★ A capital letter is used to symbolise the dominant member of a pair of alleles.

★ A small letter is used to symbolise the recessive member of a pair of alleles.

★ The letter used to symbolise the recessive allele is the same letter as that for the dominant allele.

A monohybrid cross

T is used to symbolise the allele that produces tallness in pea plants, and **t** is used to symbolise the allele that produces shortness. The diagram on the left sets out the results of crosses between tall and short pea plants. Other contrasting characteristics of the pea plant such as seed shape (round or wrinkled), flower colour (purple or white) and pod shape (smooth or wrinkled) are inherited in a similar way.

Life processes and living things

Inheritance of sex

The photograph shows the chromosomes that determine the sex of a person. The larger chromosome is the **X** chromosome; the smaller chromosome is the **Y** chromosome. The body cells of a woman carry two X chromosomes; those of a man carry an X chromosome and a Y chromosome.

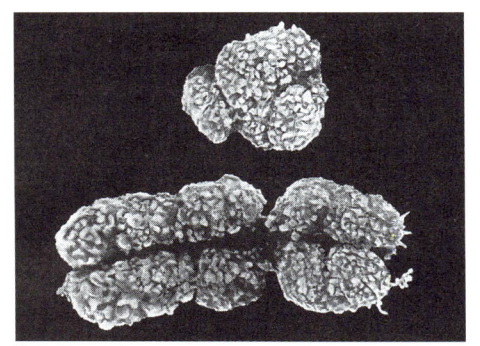

Human sex chromosomes

The diagram below shows how a person's sex is inherited. Notice that

- a baby's sex depends on whether the egg is fertilised by a sperm carrying an X chromosome or one carrying a Y chromosome
- the birth of (almost) equal numbers of girls and boys is governed by the production of equal numbers of X and Y sperms at meiosis.

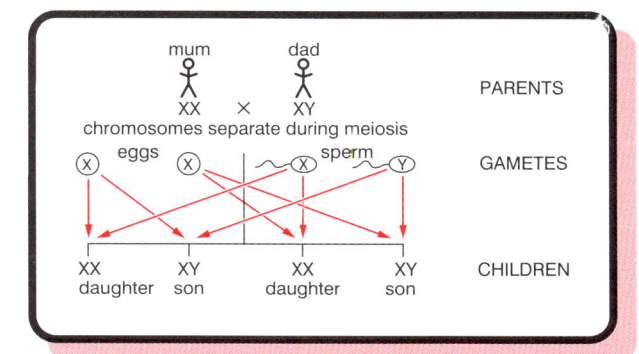

Inheritance of sex in humans

Sex-linked inheritance

Characteristics controlled by alleles situated on the sex chromosomes are said to be **sex-linked** characteristics. The disease **haemophilia** is an example. The diagrams show what happens.

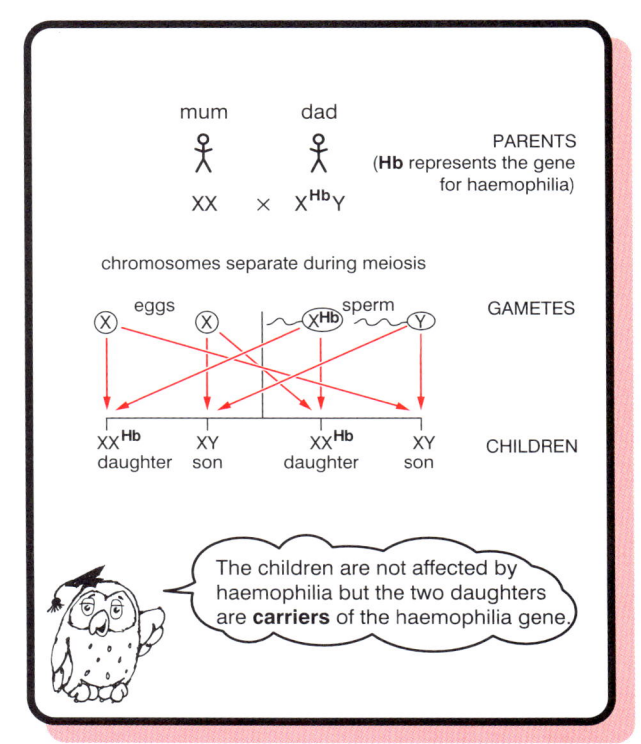

The outcome when a man affected by haemophilia becomes a father

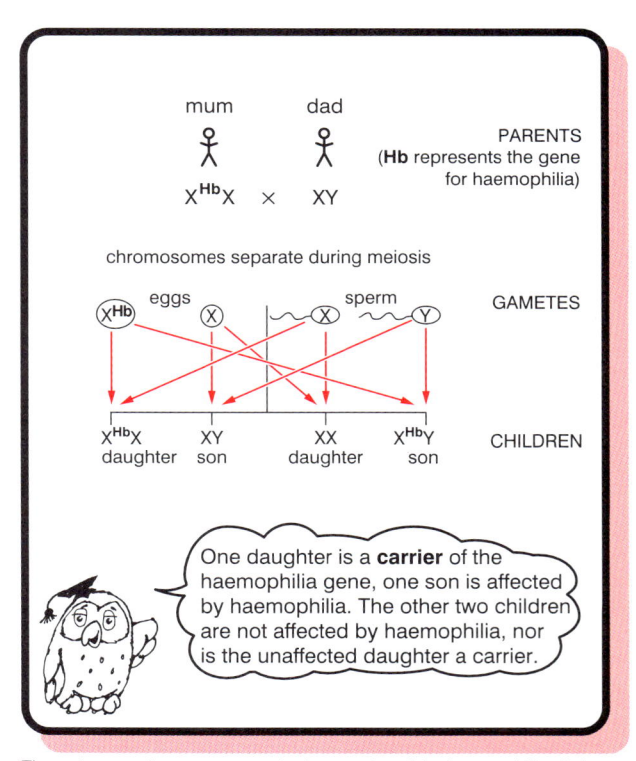

"The children are not affected by haemophilia but the two daughters are **carriers** of the haemophilia gene."

The outcome when a woman who is a carrier of the haemophilia allele becomes a mother

"One daughter is a **carrier** of the haemophilia gene, one son is affected by haemophilia. The other two children are not affected by haemophilia, nor is the unaffected daughter a carrier."

Inheritance and evolution

5.4 Biotechnology

At the end of this section you will:
- know that the processes of biotechnology have a long history in the production of bread and alcoholic drinks
- understand that the techniques of genetic engineering manipulate genes to human advantage
- realise that genetic engineering has transformed biotechnology into a rapidly expanding industry which provides food, medicines and a range of industrial chemicals.

Fact file
★ The word **biotechnology** describes the way we use plant cells, animal cells and microorganisms to produce substances that are useful to us.

Using biotechnology

The history of biotechnology demonstrates the importance of some of the processes of biotechnology.

The traditional: for thousands of years humans have exploited different organisms to make food, using
- **yeast** to make wine, beer and bread
- **moulds** to make cheese
- **bacteria** to make yogurt and vinegar.

The diagram below traces the processes in the production of wine and bread.

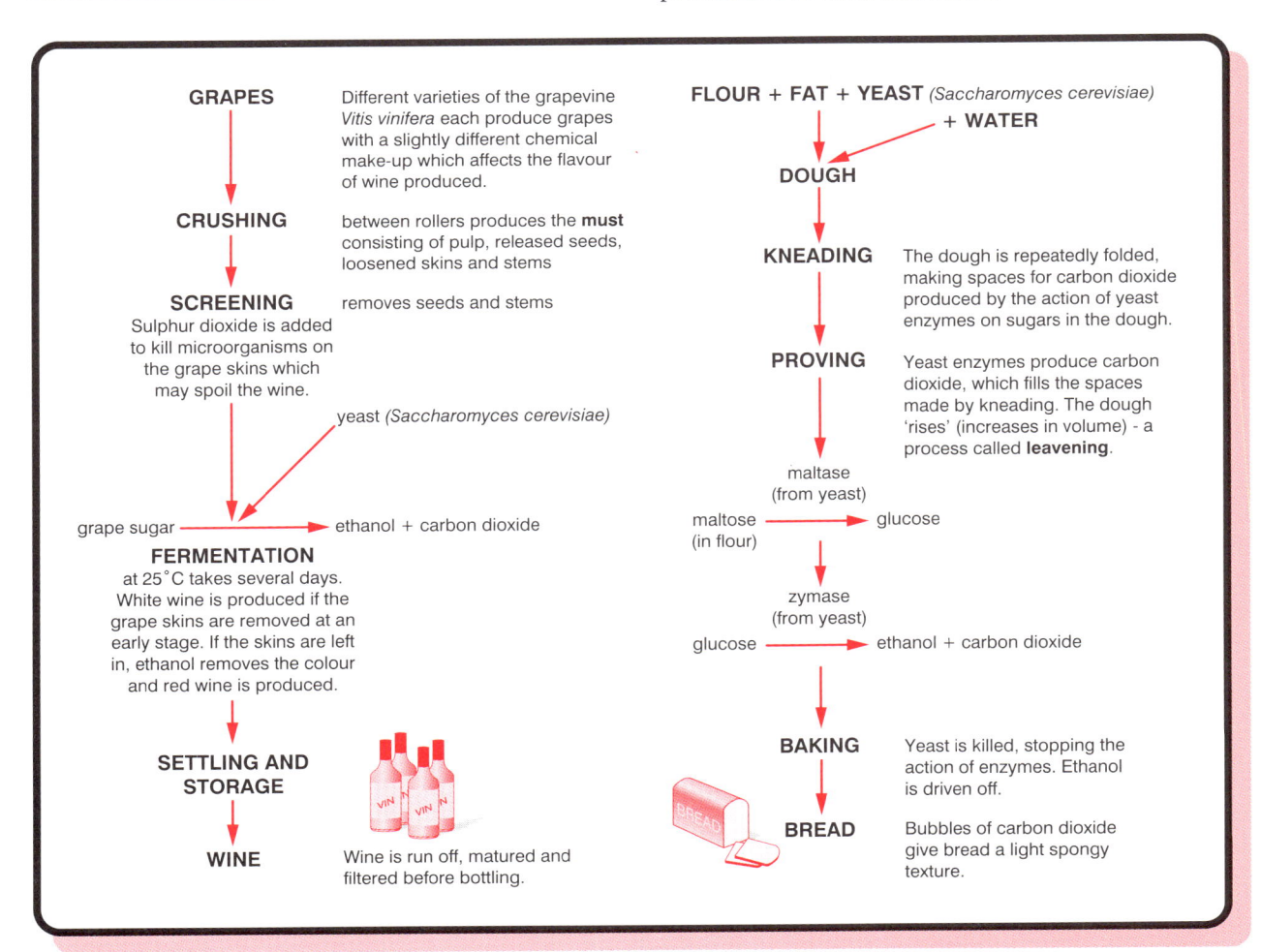

GRAPES — Different varieties of the grapevine *Vitis vinifera* each produce grapes with a slightly different chemical make-up which affects the flavour of wine produced.

↓

CRUSHING — between rollers produces the **must** consisting of pulp, released seeds, loosened skins and stems

↓

SCREENING — removes seeds and stems

Sulphur dioxide is added to kill microorganisms on the grape skins which may spoil the wine.

yeast *(Saccharomyces cerevisiae)*

grape sugar ⟶ ethanol + carbon dioxide

FERMENTATION at 25°C takes several days. White wine is produced if the grape skins are removed at an early stage. If the skins are left in, ethanol removes the colour and red wine is produced.

↓

SETTLING AND STORAGE

↓

WINE — Wine is run off, matured and filtered before bottling.

FLOUR + FAT + YEAST *(Saccharomyces cerevisiae)* + **WATER**

↓

DOUGH

↓

KNEADING — The dough is repeatedly folded, making spaces for carbon dioxide produced by the action of yeast enzymes on sugars in the dough.

↓

PROVING — Yeast enzymes produce carbon dioxide, which fills the spaces made by kneading. The dough 'rises' (increases in volume) - a process called **leavening**.

maltase (from yeast)
maltose (in flour) ⟶ glucose

zymase (from yeast)
glucose ⟶ ethanol + carbon dioxide

↓

BAKING — Yeast is killed, stopping the action of enzymes. Ethanol is driven off.

↓

BREAD — Bubbles of carbon dioxide give bread a light spongy texture.

Making wine and bread

Life processes and living things

Yeast cells use **anaerobic respiration** to convert glucose into **ethanol** ('alcohol' in wines and beers) and **carbon dioxide** (the gas that makes bread rise). The reaction is called **fermentation**. Biotechnology exploits a range of fermentation reactions to produce different substances.

The new: in the 1970s scientists developed the techniques of **genetic engineering**, which introduced the modern era of biotechnology. New methods of manipulating genes became possible because of the discovery of different enzymes in bacteria.

★ **Restriction enzymes** cut DNA into pieces, making it possible to isolate specific genes.

★ **Ligase** (splicing enzyme) allows desirable genes to be inserted into the genetic material of host cells.

Using genetic engineering we can create organisms with specific genetic characteristics, such that they produce substances that we need and want. The microorganisms are cultured in a solution containing all the substances they require for rapid growth and multiplication inside huge containers called **fermenters**. In this way, medicines, foods and industrial chemicals can be made on an industrial scale. The diagram below shows how genetically engineered insulin is made.

INSULIN Page 57.

Remember that the products of biotechnology come from the action of **genes** producing useful substances.

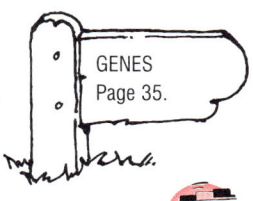

GENES Page 35.

Fact file

★ **Batch culture** produces batches of product in a fermenter. The fermenter is then emptied of the product and the nutrient solution. The fermenter is sterilised with super-heated steam ready for the next batch.

★ **Continuous culture** produces substances as an ongoing process. The product is drawn off the fermenter and nutrients are replaced as they are used.

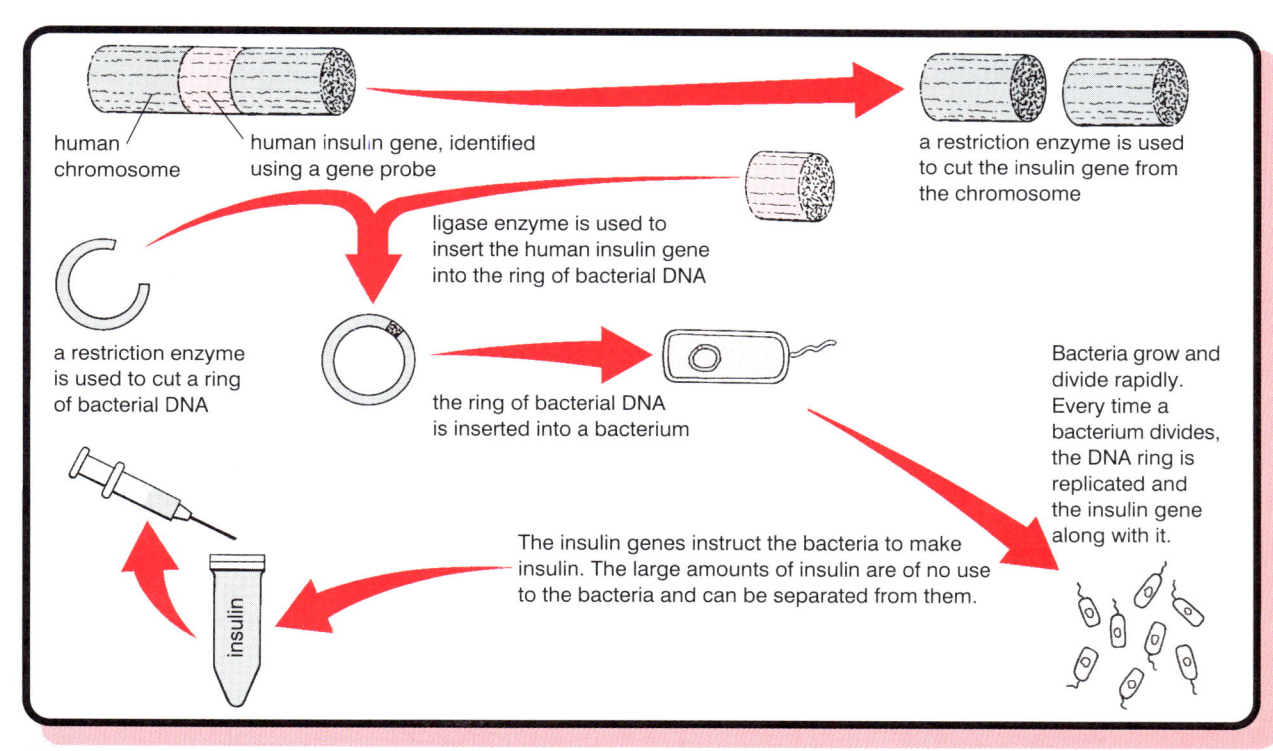

- human chromosome
- human insulin gene, identified using a gene probe
- a restriction enzyme is used to cut the insulin gene from the chromosome
- a restriction enzyme is used to cut a ring of bacterial DNA
- ligase enzyme is used to insert the human insulin gene into the ring of bacterial DNA
- the ring of bacterial DNA is inserted into a bacterium
- Bacteria grow and divide rapidly. Every time a bacterium divides, the DNA ring is replicated and the insulin gene along with it.
- The insulin genes instruct the bacteria to make insulin. The large amounts of insulin are of no use to the bacteria and can be separated from them.
- insulin

Making genetically engineered insulin

5.5 Variation

At the end of this section you will:
- understand the difference between continuous variation and discontinuous variation
- be able to identify the sources of variation
- know that variation is either inherited or acquired.

Genetic and environmental variation

Look closely at your family, friends and classmates. Notice the differently coloured hair and eyes, and the differently shaped faces. We all show **variations** in the different characteristics that make up our physical appearance (**phenotype**).

GENOTYPE and PHENOTYPE Page 71.

Variation arises from **genetic** causes.

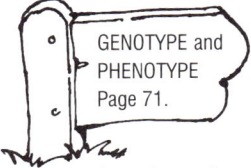

Sexual reproduction (see pages 66–7) involves the fusion of the nucleus of a **sperm** with the nucleus of the **egg**. The fertilisation recombines the genetic material from each parent in new ways within the **zygote**.

Mutations arise as a result of mistakes in the **replication** of DNA (see pages 36–7). Occasionally the wrong base adds to the growing strand of DNA, making the new DNA slightly different from the original. **Ionising radiation** and some **chemicals** increase the probability of gene mutation.

★ Ionising radiation strips electrons from matter exposed to it (ionises the atoms). Emissions from radioactive substances are ionising radiations. They may cause mutations by damaging DNA directly, or by generating highly active components of molecules called **free radicals** which cause the damage indirectly.

★ Chemicals such as the **carcinogens** (substances that cause cancer) in tobacco may lead to mutations of the genes that normally inhibit cell division.

As a result, cell division runs out of control and a cancer develops.

★ **Crossing over** during **meiosis** exchanges a segment of one chromosome (and the genes it carries) with the corresponding segment of its homologous chromosome.

As a result, the sex cells produced by meiosis have a different combination of genes from the parent cell.

Variations that arise from genetic causes are inherited from parents by their offspring, who pass them on to their offspring, and so on from generation to generation. Inherited variation is the raw material on which **natural selection** acts, resulting in **evolution**.

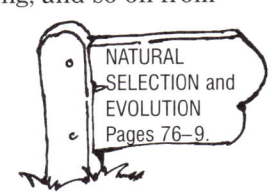

NATURAL SELECTION and EVOLUTION Pages 76–9.

Variation also arises from **environmental** causes. Here, 'environmental' means all the external influences affecting an organism, for example:

★ **Nutrients** in the food we eat and minerals that plants absorb in solution through the roots. In many countries, children are now taller and heavier, age for age, than they were 50 years ago because of improved diet and standards of living.

★ **Drugs**, which may have a serious effect on appearance. **Thalidomide** was given to pregnant women in the 1960s to prevent them feeling sick and help them sleep. The drug can affect the development of the fetus and some women who were prescribed thalidomide gave birth to seriously deformed children.

★ **Temperature** affects the rate of enzyme-controlled chemical reactions. For example, warmth increases the rate of photosynthesis and improves the rate of growth of plants kept under glass.

★ **Physical training** uses muscles more than normal, increasing their size and power. Weightlifters develop bulging muscles as they train for their sport.

Life processes and living things

Variations that arise from environmental causes are *not* inherited, because the sex cells are not affected. Instead the characteristics are said to be **acquired**. The fact that the weightlifter has developed bulging muscles does not mean that his or her children will have bulging muscles – unless they take up weightlifting as well! Because variations as a result of acquired characteristics are not inherited, they do not affect evolution.

Continuous and discontinuous variation

The variations shown by some characteristics are spread over a range of measurements. All intermediate forms of a characteristic are possible between one extreme and the other. We say that the characteristic shows **continuous variation**. The height of a population is an example of continuous variation, as shown.

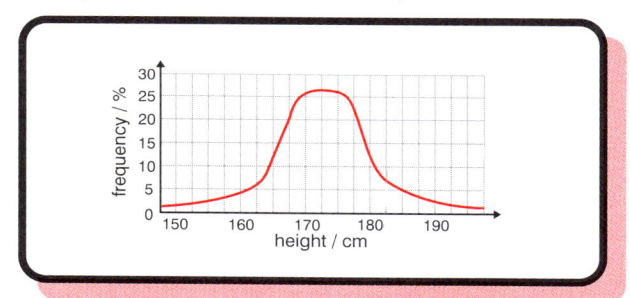

Variation in the height of the adult human population – an example of continuous variation

Other characteristics do not show a continuous trend in variation from one extreme to another. They show categories of the characteristic without any intermediate forms. The ability to roll the tongue is an example – you can either do it or you can't. There are no half-rollers! We say that the characteristic shows **discontinuous variation**.

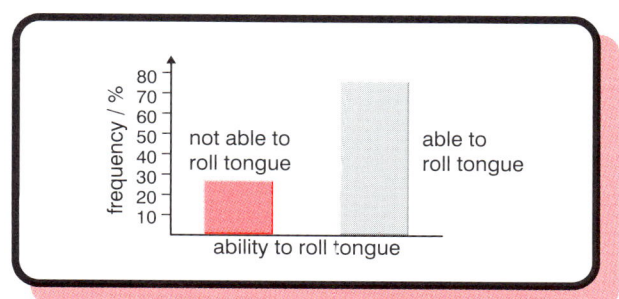

Ability to roll the tongue – an example of discontinuous variation

5.6 Evolution preview

At the end of this section you will:
- know that the British naturalist Charles Darwin was the first person to explain how species can evolve
- understand Darwin's evidence showing that evolution occurs, and that natural selection is the mechanism of evolution
- be able to interpret examples of evolution in action
- know that fossils give a record of organisms that have become extinct.

Fact file – Darwin

★ Charles Darwin (1809–82) was a keen British naturalist who abandoned medicine at Edinburgh and studied theology at Cambridge. His world voyage on HMS *Beagle* (1831–6) provided much of the evidence that
- organisms **evolve** and that
- **natural selection** is the mechanism of evolution.

It was another 20 years before he published these proposals in his book *The Origin of Species*.

The process of evolution

Present-day living things are descended from ancestors that have changed through thousands of generations. The process of change is called **evolution**. The concept map for evolution is shown opposite. It shows that other people's ideas influenced Darwin's thinking on how species can evolve. The numbers on the concept map refer to the checklist of points on page 78. The concept map and its checklist are your revision guide to evolution.

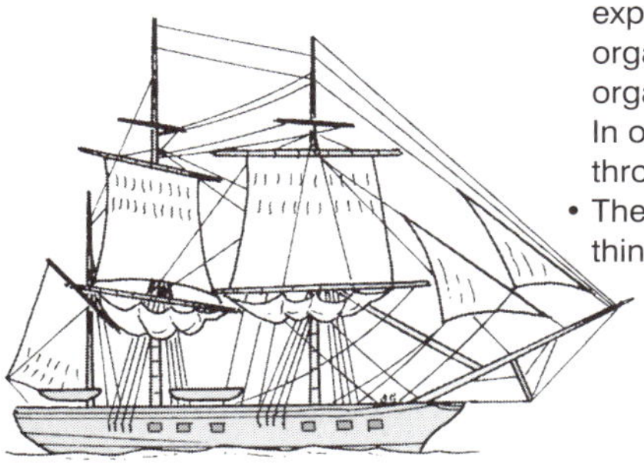

Inheritance and evolution

Evidence
- The fossils that Darwin collected on expeditions inland showed him that organisms today are not the same as organisms that lived a long time ago. In other words, organisms change through time – they evolve.
- There is an enormous variety of living things.

Darwin travelled around the coast of South America on HMS *Beagle*.

CHECKLIST 1

Charles Darwin (1809–82)

Evidence
- Lyell's work showed that the geology of the Earth changed through long periods of time.
- Darwin reasoned that if the geology of Earth had changed then so too could organisms.

Charles Lyell
Darwin and Lyell became friends on Darwin's return to England from the voyage in the *Beagle*. Lyell believed that the Earth was very old.

CHECKLIST 2

THE COMPONENTS OF EVOLUTION

variation + natural selection $\xrightarrow{\text{time}}$ evolution

Evidence
- Artificial selection helped confirm natural selection in Darwin's mind as the mechanism of evolution.

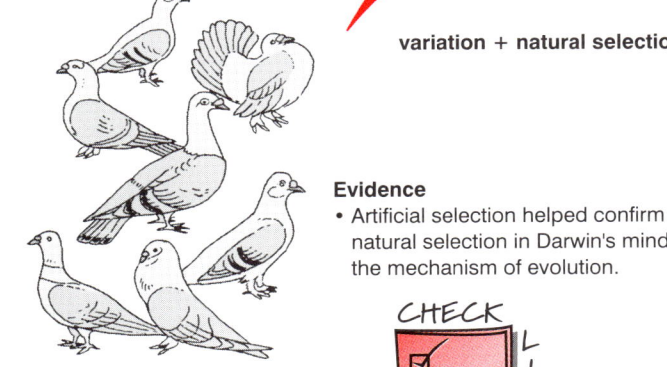

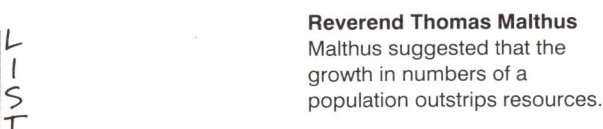

The variety of pigeons bred by 'fanciers' over hundreds of years originated from a 'wild' type common ancestor.

CHECKLIST 4

Evidence
- Darwin reasoned that since the number of individuals in a population does not increase indefinitely, then limiting factors must check the increase in numbers.

Reverend Thomas Malthus
Malthus suggested that the growth in numbers of a population outstrips resources.

CHECKLIST 3

(Checklist overleaf) How Darwin arrived at a theory of evolution through natural selection

Life processes and living things

Checklist for evolution

1. A survey of the South American coast was among the tasks undertaken by the crew of HMS *Beagle* during its world voyage. At that time Darwin took over as the ship's naturalist. He

   - collected **fossils** and specimens of plants and animals on expeditions inland
   - noticed that one type of organism gave way to another as the *Beagle* sailed around the coast of South America
   - observed that the animals along the Pacific coast of South America were different from those along the Atlantic coast
   - compared the wildlife of the Galapagos Islands with the wildlife of the South American mainland, noting the differences between similar species.

   The variety of species that Darwin discovered on his expeditions in South America and the Galapagos Islands convinced him that species change through time; that is, they **evolve**.

2. The famous geologist Charles Lyell (1797–1875) believed that

   - Earth's rocks are very old
   - natural forces produce continuous geological change during the course of Earth's history
   - fossils can be used to date rocks
   - the fossil record was laid down over hundreds of millions of years.

   Darwin read Lyell's books.

   As a result, Darwin reasoned that if rocks have changed slowly over long periods of time, living things might have a similar history.

3. In 1798 the Reverend Thomas Malthus wrote *An Essay on the Principle of Population*. He stated that a population would increase in number indefinitely unless kept in check by shortages of resources such as food and living space. Darwin read the essay in 1838 and reasoned that in nature a 'struggle for existence' must occur. In modern language we say that organisms **compete** for resources in limited supply.

   COMPETITION
   Pages 18–19

4. For centuries we have selected animals and plants for their desirable characteristics, and bred from them. This is called **artificial selection**. For example, dogs have been bred for shape, size and coat colour, resulting in a wide variety of breeds. Darwin investigated the work of breeders of animals and plants, and added to his experience by breeding pigeons. He reasoned that if artificial selection produced change in domestic animals and plants, then natural selection should have the same effect on wildlife.

Fact file – age of the Earth

★ Evidence suggests that Earth was formed about 4500 million years ago and that very simple forms of life first appeared around 4000 million years ago.

The checklist above sets out the different components which were the key to Darwin's understanding of how species evolve.

Variation: Darwin's work during the voyage of HMS *Beagle* and his experience of selectively breeding pigeons provided evidence for the large amount of variation in the characteristics of different species (checklist **1** and **4**).

Natural selection: Malthus' work contributed to Darwin's idea of a 'struggle for existence' (competition for resources). The result is the natural selection of those organisms best suited (**adapted**) to survive (checklist **3**).

Time: Lyell's work showed Darwin that the Earth is very old, giving time for the evolution of species to occur (checklist **2**).

How species evolve – the modern argument summarised

1. Because individuals vary genetically, individuals are slightly different from one another.

2. This variation in a population of individuals is the raw material on which natural selection works, resulting in evolution.

3. Individuals with genes that express characteristics which adapt the individuals to obtain scarce resources are more likely to survive than other less well adapted individuals.

4. The best adapted individuals are more likely to survive and reproduce, and so their offspring will inherit the genes for those favourable characteristics.

Inheritance and evolution

5   In this way organisms accumulate genes for favourable characteristics and change through time; that is, they evolve over many generations.

6   If the environment in which individuals are living changes, then genes for different characteristics might favour survival. Individuals with these characteristics will survive to reproduce and so evolution continues from generation to generation.

> It took Darwin nearly 30 years to develop a theory of evolution through natural selection. The ideas were a revolution in scientific thinking.

Evolution in action

Evolution is still happening. Maintaining the balance between the pale and the dark forms of the peppered moth *Biston betularia* is an example. The diagram below shows what happens.

The fossil record

Fossils are the remains of dead organisms, or impressions made by them. Fossils are usually preserved in sedimentary rocks which are formed layer on layer by the deposition of mud, sand and silt over millions of years. Providing the layers are undisturbed, then the more recent the layer, the nearer it is to the Earth's surface.

As a result, the fossils in each rock layer are a record of life on Earth at the time when the layer was formed.

As a result, a sequence of layers each with its fossils traces the history of life on Earth.

Extinction

Species may die out (become **extinct**) because of the harmful effects of human activities on the environment. Natural extinction also happens over longer periods of time. It makes room for new species to evolve and replace the previous ones. Naturally occurring extinctions are caused by

- competition between species
- changes in the environment.

The mass extinction of whole groups of organisms have occurred at intervals throughout the history of life on Earth. Extinction of the dinosaurs and many other species of reptile about 70 million years ago is a well known example. Their extinction made way for mammals and birds to fill the vacant spaces in the environment.

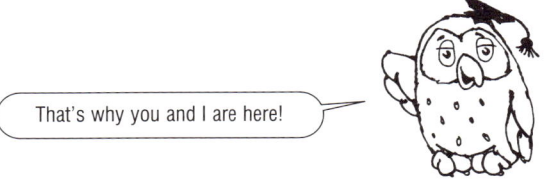

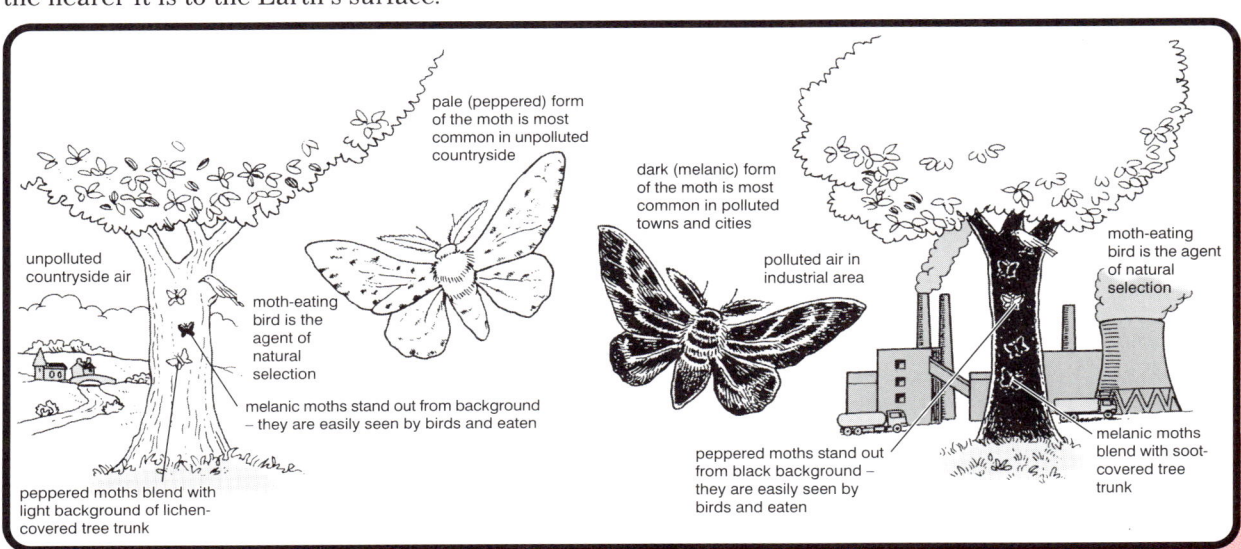

> That's why you and I are here!

---

unpolluted countryside air

pale (peppered) form of the moth is most common in unpolluted countryside

moth-eating bird is the agent of natural selection

melanic moths stand out from background – they are easily seen by birds and eaten

peppered moths blend with light background of lichen-covered tree trunk

dark (melanic) form of the moth is most common in polluted towns and cities

polluted air in industrial area

moth-eating bird is the agent of natural selection

peppered moths stand out from black background – they are easily seen by birds and eaten

melanic moths blend with soot-covered tree trunk

Different forms of *Biston betularia* adapt the moth to survive in different environments

Life processes and living things

round-up

How much have you improved?
Work out your improvement index on pages 84–5.

1. Match each structure in column **A** with its correct description in column **B**.

A structures	B descriptions
seed	structure to which pollen grains attach
ovule	produces a sugar solution
fruit	contains the egg nucleus
stigma	a fertilised ovule
nectary	develops from the ovary after fertilisation

   [5]

2. What are the advantages to growers of reproducing crops asexually? [3]

3. Name the food stored in the organs of asexual reproduction of plants. [1]

4. Briefly explain why the production of clones depends on the process of mitosis. [5]

5. Match each term in column **A** with its correct description in column **B**.

A terms	B descriptions
allele	the processes by which a single characteristic passes from parents to offspring
pure breeding	offspring of the offspring of the parental generation
second filial generation	characteristics that appear unchanged from generation to generation
monohybrid inheritance	one of a pair of genes that control a particular characteristic

   [4]

6. The diagram shows a glass container called a demijohn, in which wine is produced from the fermentation of grape juice by yeast.

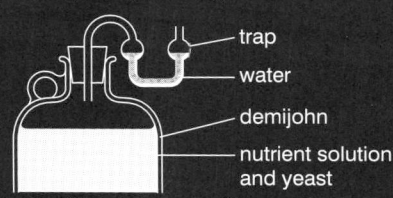

   a) The trap is filled with water. What is the purpose of the trap? [2]
   b) Name the gas bubbling through the water in the trap. [1]
   c) Why is the grape juice called a nutrient solution? [1]
   d) Name the substance in the grape juice fermented by the yeast. [1]

7. In a population of 300 goldfish, variations in two characteristics were measured and the results displayed as charts. Chart A shows variation in the length of the fish; chart B shows variation in their colour.

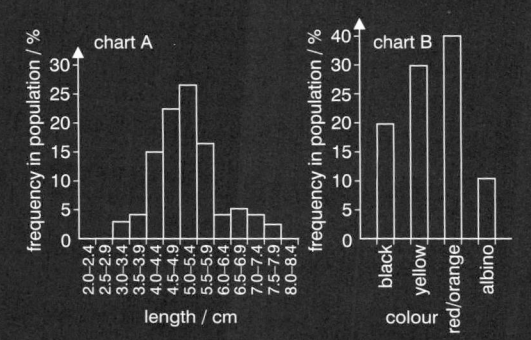

   a) Which chart shows
      (i) continuous variation
      (ii) discontinuous variation?
      (iii) Briefly give reasons for your answers. [6]
   b) Using chart B, calculate the percentage of yellow goldfish in the population. [1]
   c) Albino goldfish are relatively rare. Give a possible genetic explanation for the occurrence of albino goldfish. [1]

8. a) Look at the diagram on page 79. Briefly explain why the population densities of pale peppered moths and dark peppered moths are different in the countryside from in industrial areas. [8]
   b) Why is the moth-eating bird called an agent of natural selection? [2]

9. Briefly explain why genes for characteristics that favour the survival of individuals tend to accumulate from generation to generation. [4]

10. Outline the contributions of the ideas of Charles Lyell and Thomas Malthus to Darwin's development of a theory of evolution through natural selection. [5]

Answers

1 Test yourself (page 10)
Introducing biology
1. a) It would increase (✓). b) It would decrease (✓).
2. a)   b)   c)
   Movement   ✓   ✗
   Respiration   ✓   ✗
   Sensitivity   ✓   ✗
   Growth   ✓   ✗
   Reproduction   ✓   ✗
   Excretion   ✓   ✗
   Nutrition   ✓   ✗   [✓ × 10]
   d) No – plants do not move from place to place (✓).
3. Annual: a plant that grows from seed to maturity and produces new seeds all within one growing season (✓). It then dies (✓). Perennial: a plant that continues to grow and produce seeds for many years (✓).
4. a) To identify different living things by name (✓).
   b) These characteristics vary too much (✓) even between members of the same group of organisms (✓) to be reliable indicators for identification (✓).
5. Soil: is damp (✓); shields organisms from ultraviolet light (✓); maintains a relatively stable temperature compared with air (✓); contains food (✓).

Your score: ☐ out of 24

1 Round-up (page 15)
Introducing biology
1. a) It would boil away (✓).
   b) It would freeze and form ice (✓).
2. a) Oxygen (✓)
   b) Carbon dioxide (✓)
3. a) Respiration releases energy from food (✓). Gaseous exchange takes in oxygen needed for respiration (✓) and removes carbon dioxide produced by respiration (✓).
   b) Excretion removes the waste substances produced by metabolism (✓). Defecation removes the undigested remains of food (✓).
4. The answer should include the idea that although cars move (✓), need fuel (= nutrition) (✓), burn fuel (= respiration) (✓) and produce waste gases (= excretion) (✓) they do not grow (✓) or reproduce (✓) and are not sensitive (✓). Cars therefore do not show all the characteristics associated with living things (✓).

5. A characteristics   B descriptions
   Movement   (✓)   Changing position
   Respiration   (✓)   Releasing energy from food
   Sensitivity   (✓)   Responding to stimuli
   Growth   (✓)   Increasing in size
   Reproduction (✓)   Producing new individuals
   Excretion   (✓)   Removing waste substances produced by cells
   Nutrition   (✓)   Making or obtaining food

6. A animals   B descriptions
   Insect   (✓)   Six legs
   Worm   (✓)   No legs
   Spider   (✓)   Eight legs
   Bird   (✓)   Two legs

7. The unfamiliar specimen is compared with the descriptions in the key (✓).
   The descriptions are followed through (✓) until the description that matches the specimen is found (✓).
   The matching description identifies the specimen (✓).

8. The system gives each living organism a name in two parts (✓). The first is the name of the genus (✓); the second is the species name (✓). The genus and species names identify the organism (✓).

9. Paired statements (✓).

Your score: ☐ out of 37

Your improvement index: $\dfrac{\boxed{}/24}{\boxed{}/37} \times 100\% = \boxed{}\%$

2 Test yourself (page 16)
Organisms in the environment
1. A terms   B descriptions
   Biosphere   (✓)   All the ecosystems of the world
   Community   (✓)   All the organisms that live in a particular ecosystem
   Habitat   (✓)   The place where a group of organisms lives
   Population   (✓)   A group of individuals of the same species

2. Individuals compete for resources (✓) that are in limited supply (✓).
3. Improvements in food production (✓); more jobs (✓); new drugs (accept improvement in medicines/medical care) (✓); improvement in public health (✓).
4. Benefits: more food (✓), reliably produced (✓).
   Costs: loss of wildlife (✓), loss of habitats (✓), pollution from agrochemicals (✓). (Accept other sensible alternatives.)

Your score: ☐ out of 15

81

Life processes and living things

2 Round-up (page 21)

Organisms in the environment

1. Physical *or* abiotic (✓), environment (✓), living *or* biotic (✓), community (✓), habitats (✓), niches (✓).

2. a) Intraspecific competition – competition between individuals of the same species (✓). Interspecific competition – competition between individuals of different species (✓).
   b) Adaptation – an organism is adapted (suited) to survive (✓). Survival – an organism survives (lives) because of its adaptations (✓).
   c) Camouflage – coloration that conceals organisms (✓). Warning coloration – colours that deter predators from attacking prey (✓).

3. a) When prey is scarce predator numbers fall (✓). When prey numbers build up predator numbers follow because there is more prey food (✓). Predator breeds and reproduces more slowly than prey (✓).
   b) The population numbers of each species are stable (✓). (Allow: population numbers of each species fluctuated around a mean (average) number for that species.)
   c) Numbers would increase (✓).
   d) Numbers would decline (✓) to the former level (✓).
   e) Numbers would decline (✓) because of lack of food (✓). (Allow sensible alternative suggestions, e.g. increased mortality due to disease or parasites.)

Your score: ☐ out of 21

Your improvement index: $\dfrac{\boxed{}/21}{\boxed{}/15} \times 100\% = \boxed{}\%$

3 Test yourself (page 24)

Cell activity

1.
A structures		B functions
Mitochondrion	(✓)	Where energy is released from the oxidation of glucose
Cell membrane	(✓)	Partially permeable to substances in solution
Chloroplast	(✓)	Where light energy is captured
Cell wall	(✓)	Fully permeable to substances in solution
Nucleus	(✓)	Contains the chromosomes

2. A group of genetically identical cells (or organisms) (✓).

3. During replication each chromosome (and its DNA) (✓) makes an exact copy of itself (✓).

4. a) Cells die (✓). New cells (✓) which are replicas of the old cells are produced by mitosis (✓).
   b) The daughter cells have the same number of chromosomes as the parent cell (✓). The chromosomes in the daughter cells are identical to those in the parent cells (✓).

5. Haploid cells receive half the diploid number of chromosomes (✓) from their parent cell (✓). Diploid cells receive the full number of chromosomes (✓) from their parent cell (✓).

6. Cells (✓), cells (✓), tissues (✓), an organ (✓), organs (✓), an organ (✓).

7. Cellulose in plant cell walls (✓); chitin in insect exoskeletons (✓).

8. The molecules of unsaturated fats have double bonds between some carbon atoms (✓). Saturated fats have only single bonds between carbon atoms (✓).

9. A nucleotide consists of the sugar ribose (✓) or deoxyribose (✓), one of five different bases (✓) and a phosphate group (✓).

Your score: ☐ out of 31

3 Round-up (page 37)

Cell activity

1. Membrane (✓), cytoplasm (✓), nucleus (✓), mitochondria (✓), chloroplasts (✓), cellulose (✓), vacuole (✓).

2. a) Nucleus (✓), cell membrane (✓), mitochondria (✓), cytoplasm (✓).
   b) Cell wall (✓), large vacuole (✓), chloroplasts (✓).

3. Damaged tissues can be replaced by new cells that are identical to the parent cells (✓).

4. Similarities: replication of each chromosome into chromatids (✓); lining up of the chromosomes on the equator of the cell (✓); separation of the chromatids (✓); chromatids form the new chromosomes in daughter cells (✓); destruction and reformation of the nuclear membrane during the process of cell division (✓).
Differences: chromosomes form homologous pairs in meiosis but not in mitosis (✓); there are two divisions during meiosis but only one division during mitosis (✓); meiosis results in four daughter cells, mitosis in two daughter cells (✓).

5. Cells (✓), tissues (✓), organs (✓), organ systems (✓), organism (✓).

6.
A substances		B functions
Fat	(✓)	Insulates the body
Cellulose	(✓)	A component of the plant cell wall
DNA	(✓)	Carries the genetic code
Polypeptide	(✓)	Made of about 40 amino acids
Glycogen	(✓)	A food substance stored in the liver
Protein	(✓)	Enzymes are made of this substance

7. a) 4 (✓)   b) 4 (✓)

Your score: ☐ out of 36

Your improvement index: $\dfrac{\boxed{}/36}{\boxed{}/31} \times 100\% = \boxed{}\%$

4 Test yourself (page 38)
Humans as organisms

1. a) Carbohydrates (✓), fats (✓), proteins (✓).
   b) Protein (✓)
   c) Fat (✓)
   d) Minerals (✓) and vitamins (✓).

2.
A terms		B descriptions
Ingestion	(✓)	Food is taken into the mouth
Digestion	(✓)	Food is broken down
Absorption	(✓)	Digested food passes into the body
Egestion	(✓)	The removal of undigested food through the anus

3.
A components		B descriptions
Plasma	(✓)	Contains dissolved food substances
Red blood cells	(✓)	Contain haemoglobin
White blood cells	(✓)	Produce antibodies
Platelets	(✓)	Promote the formation of blood clots

4. Receptor (✓), sensory neurone (✓), relay neurone (✓), motor neurone (✓), effector.

5. a) The eardrum vibrates (✓) in response to sound waves (✓).
   b) The bones pass vibrations through the middle ear (✓) and also amplify them (✓).
   c) The pinna funnels sound waves down the ear canal (✓) to the eardrum (✓).
   d) The hair cells are stimulated by the vibrations of the basilar membrane (✓). They fire off nerve impulses to the brain along the auditory nerve (✓).

6. Hormones are chemical substances (✓) which circulate in the blood (✓).

7. Insulin decreases the level of glucose in the blood (✓). Glucagon increases the level of glucose in the blood (✓).

8. Glomerulus (✓), Bowman's capsule (✓), tubule (✓), collecting duct (✓), ureter (✓), bladder (✓), urethra (✓).

9.
A body structures		B roles
Tear gland	(✓)	Produces the enzyme lysozyme which destroys bacteria
Glands in the stomach wall	(✓)	Produce hydrochloric acid which kills bacteria
Skin	(✓)	Produces sebum which kills bacteria and fungi
Cilia lining the upper respiratory tract	(✓)	Sweep away mucus containing trapped microorganisms and particles
Blood	(✓)	White cells produce antibodies which destroy antigens

Your score: [ ] out of 43

4 Round-up (page 64)
Humans as organisms

1.
A nutrients		B test results
Starch	(✓)	Produces a blue/black colour when mixed with a few drops of iodine solution
Glucose	(✓)	Produces an orange colour when heated with Benedict's solution
Fat	(✓)	Forms a milky emulsion when mixed with warm dilute ethanol
Protein	(✓)	Produces a violet/purple colour when mixed with dilute sodium hydroxide and a few drops of copper sulphate solution

2.
A enzymes		B roles
Amylase	(✓)	Digests starch to maltose
Pepsin	(✓)	Digests protein to polypeptides
Lipase	(✓)	Digests fat to fatty acids and glycerol
Maltase	(✓)	Digests maltose to glucose

3. a) Antibodies are proteins (✓) produced by lymphocytes (accept white blood cells) (✓) in response to antigens (✓) which are materials 'foreign' to (accept not recognised by) the body (✓). Antibodies destroy antigens (✓).
   b) HIV is the abbreviation for human immunodeficiency virus (✓) which causes the diseases (✓) that characterise AIDS (✓).
   c) Haemoglobin is the protein (✓) in red blood cells (✓) that absorbs oxygen (✓). Haemophilia is a genetic disease (✓) characterised by the slow clotting time of blood (✓).

4.
A parts of cell		B descriptions
Axon	(✓)	Transmits nerve impulses from the cell body
Dendrite	(✓)	Carries nerve impulses to the cell body
Sheath	(✓)	Boosts the transmission of nerve impulses
Nerve impulse	(✓)	Minute electrical disturbances

5. a) The blind spot is the region of the retina insensitive to light (✓). The fovea is the most sensitive region of the retina, where cone cells are most dense (✓).
   b) The pupil is the central hole formed by the iris (✓). The iris is the coloured ring of muscle that controls the amount of light entering the eye (✓).
   c) The cornea bends light (✓) and helps to focus light onto the retina (✓).

6. Endocrine glands are ductless glands (✓) which release hormones directly into the blood (✓).

7. Antidiuretic hormone promotes reabsorbtion of water into the body (✓) by making the collecting duct of the nephron more permeable to water (✓).

8. a) Raised hairs trap a layer of air (✓) which insulates the body in cold weather (✓). Air is a poor conductor of heat (✓).
   b) Sweat cools the body because it carries heat energy away from the body (✓) as it evaporates (✓).

9. Cholera (B) (✓), AIDS (V) (✓), syphilis (B) (✓), 'flu (V) (✓), pneumonia (B) (✓).

Life processes and living things

10 Nicotine is a poison which increases the heart rate (✓) and blood pressure (✓).
Carbon monoxide combines with haemoglobin (✓) more readily than oxygen (✓).
Tar is a mixture of substances (✓), some of which cause cancer (accept are carcinogens) (✓).

Your score: ☐ out of 51

Your improvement index: $\dfrac{\Box/51}{\Box/43} \times 100\% = \Box\%$

5 Test yourself (page 65)
Inheritance and evolution

1 A sperm duct (✓), B urethra (✓), C scrotal sac (accept scrotum) (✓), D = testis (✓), E = penis (✓).

2
A structures		B descriptions
Corm	(✓)	A short, swollen underground stem
Runner	(✓)	A horizontal stem running above ground
Tuber	(✓)	A swelling at the end of a rhizome
Bulb	(✓)	A large underground bud

3 a) **Bb** (✓) or **bb** (✓).
  b) 50% of the children would be brown eyed (✓); 50% blue eyed (✓).

4 a) Restriction enzyme cleaves (cuts up) lengths of DNA into different fragments (✓) depending on the restriction enzyme used (✓). A particular DNA fragment corresponds to a desired gene (✓). (Accept sensible alternative explanation.) Ligase splices the desired gene from among the fragments of DNA produced by restriction enzyme (✓) into a plasmid vector (✓) which is a loop of bacterial DNA (✓) into which the desired gene is inserted (✓).
  b) Biotechnology uses microorganisms (✓) on a large scale for the production of useful substances (✓).
Genetic engineering manipulates genes (✓) to create organisms (✓) with specific genetic characteristics for producing a range of useful substances (✓).
  c) Batch culture produces batches of substances in a fermenter (✓). The fermenter is then emptied of product and nutrient solution (✓) and sterilised (✓) in preparation for the next batch (✓).
Continuous culture produces substances over an extended period (✓). Product is drawn off and nutrients replaced as they are used (✓) during an ongoing process (✓).

5 Acquired characteristics are those produced in the individual as a result of the influence (effects) of the environment (✓). These characteristics are not the result of genetic influence (✓) and are therefore not inherited (✓).

6 Genetic recombination (✓) as a result of sexual reproduction (✓), mutation (✓), crossing over (✓) during meiosis (✓) and the effects of the environment (✓).

Well done if you mentioned crossing over!

7 During sexual reproduction, genetic material inherited from both parents (✓) recombines in the fertilised egg (✓) producing combinations of genetic material in the offspring different from the combination in each of the parents (✓). During asexual reproduction, offspring inherit identical genetic material from one parent (✓). Mutation is the only source of variation (✓).

8 a) Ancestors are organisms that give rise to offspring, who are their descendants (✓).
  b) Adaptation – an organism with a structure and way of life that best suits it to survive is said to be adapted (✓). Extinction occurs when a species dies out (✓).
  c) Evolution – the change that occurs through many generations of descendants from different ancestors (✓). Natural selection – the process whereby favourable variations survive (✓) so that descendants evolve from ancestors (✓). (Allow: the mechanism of evolution (✓) through the survival of favourable variations (✓).)

9 Fossil formation occurs under the following conditions:
- the replacement of decayed organic material with a permanent alternative (✓)
- the burying of an organism in hardening mud or cooling volcanic ash (✓) followed by the formation of a cast (allow: material that takes on the shape of the original organism) (✓)
- rapid freezing of the organism following its death (✓).

Your score: ☐ out of 56

5 Round-up (page 80)
Inheritance and evolution

1
A structures		B descriptions
Seed	(✓)	A fertilised ovule
Ovule	(✓)	Contains the egg nucleus
Fruit	(✓)	Develops from the ovary after fertilisation
Stigma	(✓)	Structure to which pollen grains attach
Nectary	(✓)	Produces a sugar solution

2 Plants are healthy (✓), the same (accept uniform) (✓), and retain desirable characteristics (✓).

3 Starch (✓)

Answers

4 During mitosis, the DNA of the parent cell replicates (✓) so that daughter cells receive exact copies of the parent cell's genetic material (✓). Daughter cells divide and develop into new individuals which inherit the exact characteristics of the parent (✓). Offspring of the parent are also genetically identical to one another (✓) and are a clone (✓).

5

A terms		B descriptions
Allele	(✓)	One of a pair of genes that control a particular characteristic
Pure breeding	(✓)	Characteristics that appear unchanged from generation to generation
Second filial generation	(✓)	Offspring of the offspring of the parental generation
Monohybrid inheritance	(✓)	The processes by which a single characteristic passes from parents to offspring

6 a) The trap allows gas to escape (✓) and prevents unwanted airborne microorganisms from contaminating the mixture (✓).
b) Carbon dioxide (✓)
c) The grape juice provides the substances yeast cells need to grow and multiply (✓)
d) Sugar (accept glucose) (✓).

7 a) (i) A (✓)
   (ii) B (✓)
   (iii) Chart A shows intermediate lengths of fish (✓) over a range of measurements (✓). Chart B shows categories of colour (✓) without any intermediate forms (✓).
b) 90% (✓)
c) Albino fish occur as a result of a mutation of the alleles controlling colour (✓).

8 a) In unpolluted countryside, pale peppered moths blend with the light background of (are camouflaged on) the lichen-covered tree trunk (✓). Fewer are eaten by moth-eating birds (suffer less predation) (✓) than dark peppered moths (✓) which are more conspicuous (✓). In polluted industrial areas, dark peppered moths are less conspicuous against the soot-covered tree trunks (✓). Fewer are eaten by moth-eating birds (suffer less predation) (✓) than pale peppered moths (✓) which are more conspicuous (✓).
b) The bird eats the moths which are conspicuous (✓) and therefore not adapted to blend with their surroundings (✓).

9 Individuals with genes for characteristics that favour survival are more likely to reproduce (✓). Their offspring inherit the favourable genes (✓) and in turn are more likely to survive and reproduce (✓) so handing on the favourable genes to the next generation, and so on (✓).

10 Charles Lyell stated that the Earth was very old (✓). This suggested to Darwin that there was sufficient time for the process of evolution to occur (✓). Malthus suggested that limited resources regulated population numbers (✓) which would otherwise increase indefinitely (✓). Darwin concluded that there must be a struggle for existence (competition for limited resources) (✓).

Your score: ☐ out of 50

Your improvement index: $\dfrac{\Box/50}{\Box/56} \times 100\% = \Box\%$

#	Section	Page
1	**Matter and the kinetic theory**	**88**
1.1	States of matter	88
1.2	Change of state	88
1.3	Some properties of materials	89
1.4	Composite materials	89
1.5	The kinetic theory	89
1.6	What does the kinetic theory explain?	90
2	**Elements, compounds and equations**	**91**
2.1	Metallic and non-metallic elements	91
2.2	Structures of elements	91
2.3	Compounds	91
2.4	Symbols	92
2.5	Formulas	92
2.6	Equations	94
3	**Separating substances**	**95**
3.1	Mixtures from the Earth	95
3.2	Soluble solid from insoluble solid	95
3.3	Soluble solids by chromatography	96
3.4	Immiscible liquids	96
3.5	Solvent from solute	96
3.6	Miscible liquids	97
4	**The structure of the atom**	**98**
4.1	Protons, neutrons and electrons	98
4.2	Focus on the atom	98
5	**The chemical bond**	**102**
5.1	Bond formation	102
5.2	Ions	102
5.3	Ionic bonding	102
5.4	Covalent bonding	103
5.5	Ionic and covalent substances	104
6	**The periodic table**	**106**
6.1	Classifying elements	106
6.2	A repeating pattern	109
7	**Acids, bases and salts**	**110**
7.1	Acids	110
7.2	Bases	112
7.3	Neutralisation	112
7.4	Indicators	112
7.5	Salts	114
8	**Air**	**115**
8.1	Separating gases from air	115
8.2	Oxygen	115
8.3	Oxidation and reduction	116
8.4	Nitrogen	117
8.5	Carbon dioxide	117
8.6	The noble gases	117
8.7	The problem of pollution	118
9	**Water**	**121**
9.1	The water cycle	121
9.2	Dissolved oxygen	121
9.3	Pure water	122
9.4	Pollution of water	122
10	**Rocks**	**123**
10.1	Types of rock	123
10.2	The landscape	124
10.3	Materials from rocks	124
11	**Metals and alloys**	**126**
11.1	Reactions of metals	126
11.2	Metals in the periodic table	127
11.3	The reactivity series	127
11.4	Extracting metals	127
11.5	Corrosion of metals	128
11.6	Conservation	129
11.7	Uses of metals and alloys	129
12	**Reaction speeds**	**131**
12.1	Particle size	131
12.2	Concentration	132
12.3	Pressure	132
12.4	Temperature	132
12.5	Light	132
12.6	Catalysts	132
13	**Fuels**	**134**
13.1	Fossil fuels	134
13.2	Fuels from petroleum	135
13.3	Alkanes	135
13.4	Energy and chemical reactions	136
13.5	Heat of reaction	136
14	**Alkenes and plastics**	**138**
14.1	Alkenes	138
14.2	Reactions of alkenes	138
14.3	Uses of plastics	139
Answers		**140**
Periodic table		**148**
Mind Maps		**149**
Index		**220**

Materials and their properties

Matter and the kinetic theory

preview

At the end of this topic you will be able to:

- describe the states of matter and changes of state
- apply the kinetic theory of matter to solids, liquids, gases, changes of state, dissolving, diffusion and Brownian motion.

How much do you already know? Work out your score on page 140.

Test yourself

1. Name the three chief states of matter. [3]
2. What can you tell about the purity of a solid from its melting point? [2]
3. What is the difference between evaporation and boiling? [2]
4. How can you tell when a liquid is boiling? [1]
5. Why do vegetables cook faster in a pressure cooker? [2]
6. Why does it take a long time to boil potatoes on a high mountain? [2]
7. What is a) the resemblance b) the difference between a plastic material and an elastic material? [3]
8. Why are crystals shiny? [3]
9. What happens to the heat energy that is supplied to a solid to make it melt? [2]
10. One litre of water forms 1333 litres of steam. Explain the big difference in volume. [2]
11. Explain why a spoonful of salt can flavour a whole pan of soup. [3]

1.1 States of matter

Everything in the Universe is composed of matter. Matter exists in three chief states: the solid, liquid and gaseous states. Their characteristics are shown in the table.

	volume	shape	effect of rise in temperature
solid	fixed	definite	expands slightly
liquid	fixed	flows – changes shape to fit the shape of the container	expands
gas	changes to fit the container	changes to fit the container	expands greatly (gases have much lower densities than solids and liquids)

Characteristics of the solid, liquid and gaseous states

1.2 Change of state

Matter can change from one state into another, as shown in the diagram.

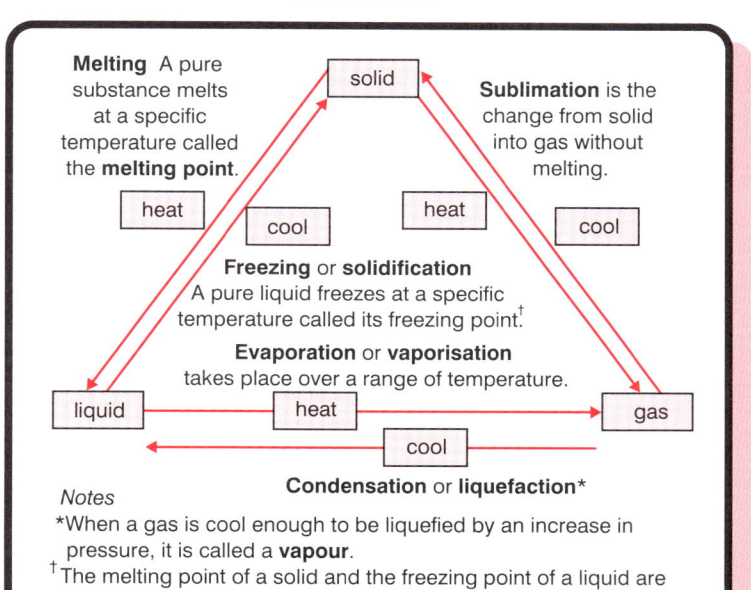

Melting A pure substance melts at a specific temperature called the **melting point**.

Sublimation is the change from solid into gas without melting.

Freezing or **solidification** A pure liquid freezes at a specific temperature called its freezing point.[†]

Evaporation or **vaporisation** takes place over a range of temperature.

Condensation or **liquefaction**[*]

Notes
*When a gas is cool enough to be liquefied by an increase in pressure, it is called a **vapour**.
† The melting point of a solid and the freezing point of a liquid are the same temperature.

1.3 Some properties of materials

★ **Density:** density = $\dfrac{\text{mass}}{\text{volume}}$.

★ **Melting point:** while a pure solid melts, the temperature remains constant at the melting point of the solid.

★ **Boiling point:** while a pure liquid boils, the temperature remains constant at the boiling point of the liquid.

★ **Conductivity** (thermal and electrical): the ability to conduct heat and electricity is a characteristic of metals and alloys.

★ **Solubility:** a solution consists of a **solute** dissolved in a **solvent**. A concentrated solution contains a high proportion of solute; a dilute solution contains a low proportion of solute. A saturated solution contains as much solute as it is possible to dissolve at the stated temperature.

Solubility is the mass of solute that will dissolve in 100 g of solvent at the stated temperature.

Two ways of expressing concentration are:

concentration = $\dfrac{\text{mass of solute}}{\text{volume of solution}}$

concentration = $\dfrac{\text{amount (moles) of solute}}{\text{volume of solution}}$

1.4 Composite materials

A **composite material** is a mixture of two or more materials which combines their properties. Here are some examples.

- Reinforced concrete combines the compressive (crushing) strength of concrete with the tensile (stretching) strength of the reinforcing steel rods.
- Glass-fibre-reinforced plastic combines plasticity with the strength of fibres, which prevent cracking.
- Plasterboard combines plaster, a brittle material, with paper fibres that prevent cracking.

1.5 The kinetic theory

According to the **kinetic theory of matter**, all forms of matter are made up of small particles which are in constant motion. The theory explains the states of matter and changes of state.

In a solid, the particles are close together and attract one another strongly. They are arranged in a regular three-dimensional structure. The particles can vibrate, but they cannot move out of their positions in the structure.

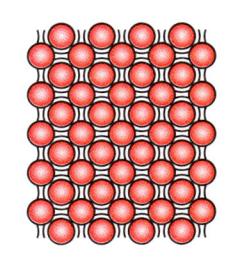

The arrangement of particles in a solid

When the solid is heated, the particles vibrate more energetically. If they gain enough energy, they may break away from the structure and become free to move independently. When this happens, the solid has melted.

In a liquid, the particles are further apart than in a solid. They are free to move about. This is why a liquid flows easily and has no fixed shape. There are forces of attraction between particles. When a liquid is heated, some particles gain enough energy to break away from the other particles and become a gas.

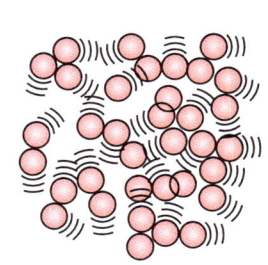

The arrangement of particles in a liquid

Most of a gas is space, through which the particles move at high speed. There are only very small forces of attraction between the particles. When a mass of liquid vaporises, it forms a very much larger volume of gas because the particles are so much further apart in a gas.

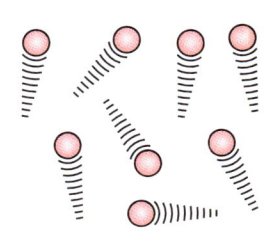

The arrangement of particles in a gas

Collisions between the gas particles and the container create pressure on the container.

Materials and their properties

Crystals

A crystal is a piece of matter with a regular shape and smooth surfaces which reflect light. Viewed through an electron microscope, crystals can be seen to consist of a regular arrangement of particles. The regular arrangement of particles gives the crystal its regular shape.

A beam of X-rays passed through a crystal onto a photographic plate produces a regular pattern of dots called an **X-ray diffraction photograph**. From the pattern of dots, a crystallographer can work out the arrangement of particles in the crystal.

1.6 What does the kinetic theory explain?

Dissolving of a solid

When a solid dissolves, particles of solid separate from the crystal and spread out through the solvent to form a solution.

Diffusion of a gas

When a gas is released into a container, particles of gas move through the container until the gas has spread evenly through all the space available.

Evaporation or vaporisation

Attractive forces exist between the particles in a liquid. Some particles with more energy than the average break away from the attraction of other particles and escape into the vapour phase. The average energy of the particles that remain is lower than before – the liquid has cooled.

Brownian motion

The botanist William Brown used his microscope a century ago to observe grains of pollen suspended in water. He saw that the grains were in constant motion. The explanation is that water molecules collide with a pollen grain and give it a push. The direction of the push changes as different numbers of molecules strike the pollen grain from different sides.

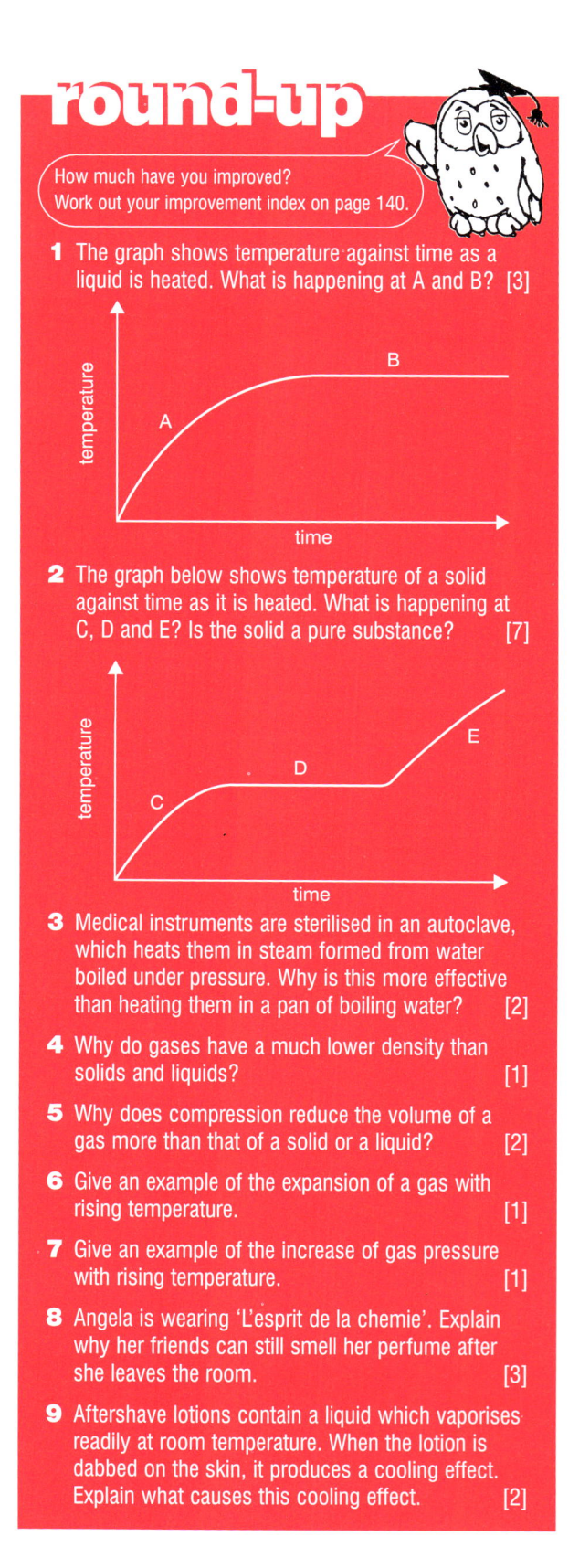

round-up

How much have you improved?
Work out your improvement index on page 140.

1 The graph shows temperature against time as a liquid is heated. What is happening at A and B? [3]

2 The graph below shows temperature of a solid against time as it is heated. What is happening at C, D and E? Is the solid a pure substance? [7]

3 Medical instruments are sterilised in an autoclave, which heats them in steam formed from water boiled under pressure. Why is this more effective than heating them in a pan of boiling water? [2]

4 Why do gases have a much lower density than solids and liquids? [1]

5 Why does compression reduce the volume of a gas more than that of a solid or a liquid? [2]

6 Give an example of the expansion of a gas with rising temperature. [1]

7 Give an example of the increase of gas pressure with rising temperature. [1]

8 Angela is wearing 'L'esprit de la chemie'. Explain why her friends can still smell her perfume after she leaves the room. [3]

9 Aftershave lotions contain a liquid which vaporises readily at room temperature. When the lotion is dabbed on the skin, it produces a cooling effect. Explain what causes this cooling effect. [2]

Elements, compounds and equations

preview

At the end of this topic you will be able to:

- list the differences between metallic and non-metallic elements
- describe the structures of some elements
- distinguish between an element, a compound and a mixture
- write an equation for a chemical reaction.

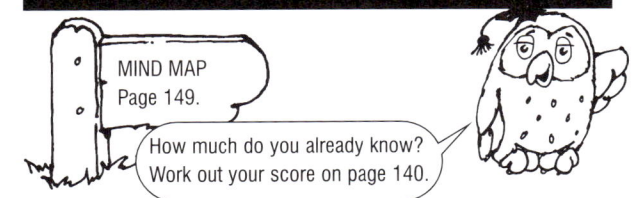

MIND MAP Page 149.

How much do you already know? Work out your score on page 140.

Test yourself

1. Explain what is meant by an element. [3]
2. What chemical properties of zinc classify it as a metallic element? [7]
3. Explain why diamond is hard while graphite is soft. [4]
4. Name two methods that can be used to split a compound into elements. [2]
5. How many atoms are there in $2Al(OH)_3$? [1]
6. Balance the equation and insert state symbols. [8]

    $Na + H_2O \rightarrow NaOH + H_2$

2.1 Metallic and non-metallic elements

Elements are pure substances that cannot be split up into simpler substances. Some elements exist as **allotropes** – forms of the same element which have different crystalline structures. Allotropes of carbon are shown on page 93. Elements are classified as metallic and non-metallic, as shown in the table overleaf.

2.2 Structures of elements

Individual molecules

Some elements consist of small individual molecules with negligible forces of attraction between them, e.g. oxygen O_2 and chlorine Cl_2.

Molecular structures

Some elements consist of molecules held in a crystal structure by weak intermolecular forces. Solid iodine is a structure composed of I_2 molecules; iodine vapour consists of individual I_2 molecules.

Giant molecules

Some elements consist of giant molecules or macromolecules, which are composed of millions of atoms bonded together in a three-dimensional structure, e.g. the allotropes of carbon – diamond, graphite and fullerenes – shown on page 93.

2.3 Compounds

A **compound** is a pure substance that consists of two or more elements which are chemically combined in fixed proportions by mass. Some compounds can be **synthesised** from their elements, e.g. calcium burns in oxygen to form calcium oxide; hot copper combines with chlorine to form copper chloride.

It may be possible to split up a compound into its elements

- by **thermal decomposition**, e.g. silver oxide splits up into silver and oxygen when heated
- by **electrolysis**, e.g. water is electrolysed to hydrogen and oxygen.

Materials and their properties

metallic elements	non-metallic elements
physical properties	*physical properties*
solids except for mercury	solids and gases, except for bromine (which is a liquid)
dense, hard	Most of the solid elements are softer than metals (diamond is exceptional).
A smooth metallic surface is shiny; many metals tarnish in air.	Most non-metallic elements are dull (diamond is exceptional).
The shape can be changed without breaking by the application of force – either compression, as in hammering, or tension, as in stretching, e.g. drawing out into a wire.	Many non-metallic elements are brittle – they break when a force is applied.
conduct heat (although highly polished surfaces reflect heat)	are poor thermal conductors
are good electrical conductors	are poor electrical conductors, except for graphite; some, e.g. silicon, are semiconductors
are sonorous – make a pleasing sound when struck	are not sonorous
chemical properties	*chemical properties*
able to donate electrons	able to accept electrons
many displace hydrogen from dilute acids to form salts	do not react with acids, except for oxidising acids, e.g. concentrated sulphuric acid
The metal is the cation (positive ion) in the salts, e.g. Na^+, Ca^{2+}; some metals also form oxoanions, e.g. ZnO_2^{2-}, AlO_3^-.	form anions (negative ions), e.g. S^{2-}, and oxoanions, e.g. SO_4^{2-}
form basic oxides and hydroxides, e.g. Na_2O, $NaOH$, CaO, $Ca(OH)_2$	form acidic oxides, e.g. CO_2, SO_2, or neutral oxides, e.g. CO, NO
The chlorides are ionic solids, e.g. $MgCl_2$, $AlCl_3$.	The chlorides are covalent volatile liquids, e.g. SCl_2, PCl_3.
Hydrides are formed only by the metals in Groups 1 and 2, and these hydrides are unstable, e.g. NaH.	form stable hydrides, e.g. HBr, H_2S

Characteristics of metallic and non-metallic elements

A compound differs from a mixture of elements as shown in the table on the opposite page.

2.4 Symbols

Every element has its own **symbol**. The symbol is a letter or two letters which stand for one atom of the element, e.g. aluminium Al, iron Fe. See the table on page 101.

2.5 Formulas

Every compound has a **formula**. This is composed of the symbols of the elements present along with numbers which give the ratio in which the atoms are present.

A molecule of sulphuric acid (see below) contains 2 hydrogen atoms, 1 sulphur atom and 4 oxygen atoms, giving the formula H_2SO_4.

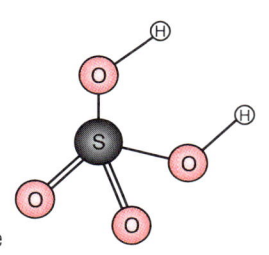

H_2SO_4 – a single molecule

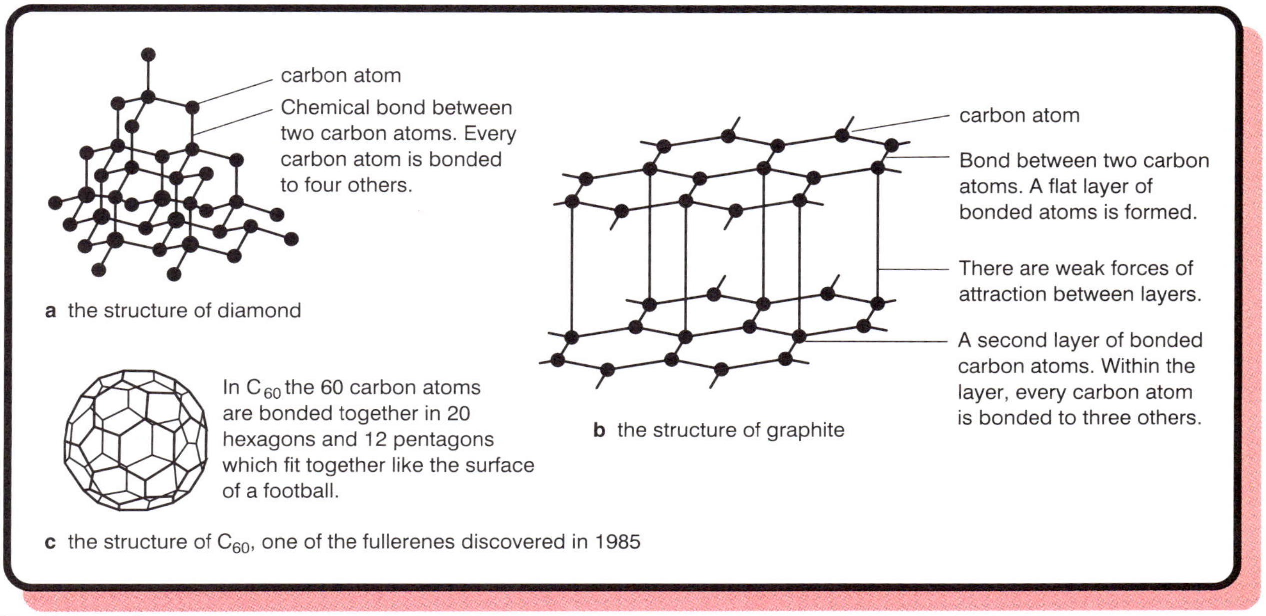

Elements, compounds and equations

a the structure of diamond
- carbon atom
- Chemical bond between two carbon atoms. Every carbon atom is bonded to four others.

b the structure of graphite
- carbon atom
- Bond between two carbon atoms. A flat layer of bonded atoms is formed.
- There are weak forces of attraction between layers.
- A second layer of bonded carbon atoms. Within the layer, every carbon atom is bonded to three others.

c the structure of C_{60}, one of the fullerenes discovered in 1985

In C_{60} the 60 carbon atoms are bonded together in 20 hexagons and 12 pentagons which fit together like the surface of a football.

The allotropes of carbon

mixtures	compounds
No chemical change takes place when a mixture is made.	When a compound is made, a chemical reaction takes place, and heat is often taken in or given out.
A mixture has the same properties as its components.	A compound has a new set of properties; it does not behave in the same way as the components.
A mixture can be separated into its parts by methods such as distillation (see pages 95–7).	A compound can be split into its elements or into simpler compounds only by a chemical reaction.
A mixture can contain its components in any proportions.	A compound contains its elements in fixed proportions by mass, e.g. magnesium oxide always contains 60% by mass of magnesium.

Differences between mixtures and compounds

Silicon(IV) oxide, shown here, consists of macromolecules which contain twice as many oxygen atoms as silicon atoms, giving the formula SiO_2.

The formula of ammonium sulphate is $(NH_4)_2SO_4$. The '2' multiplies the symbols in brackets: there are 2 nitrogen, 8 hydrogen, 1 sulphur and 4 oxygen atoms.

Writing $2Al_2O_3$ means that the numbers below the line each multiply the symbols in front of them, and the 2 on the line multiplies everything that comes after it, giving a total of 4 aluminium and 6 oxygen atoms.

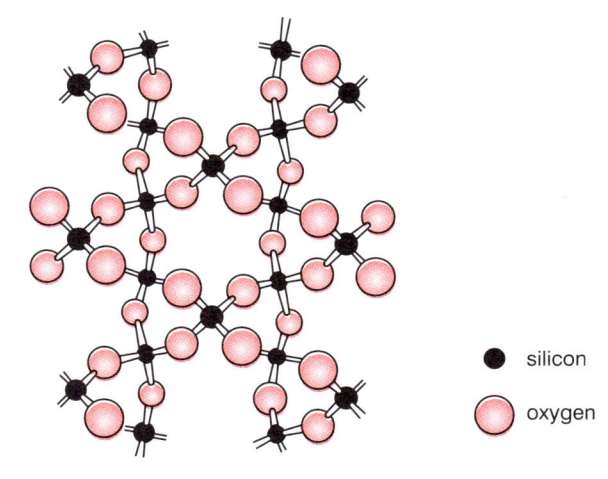

SiO_2 – a macromolecule

- silicon
- oxygen

Materials and their properties

2.6 Equations

To write an equation for a chemical reaction:

1. Write a word equation for the reaction.
2. Put in the symbols for the elements and the formulas for the compounds.
3. Put in the **state symbols** (s) for solid, (l) for liquid, (g) for gas, (aq) for in aqueous solution (in water).
4. **Balance** the equation. This means making the number of atoms of each element on the left-hand side (LHS) equal the number on the right-hand side (RHS). Do this by writing a 2, 3 or other numeral in front of a symbol or a formula to multiply that symbol or formula. **Never try to balance an equation by altering a formula**.

Example

1. calcium + water → hydrogen + calcium hydroxide solution
2. $Ca + H_2O \rightarrow H_2 + Ca(OH)_2$
3. $Ca(s) + H_2O(l) \rightarrow H_2(g) + Ca(OH)_2(aq)$
4. There are 2 hydrogen atoms on the LHS and 4 hydrogen atoms on the RHS. There is 1 oxygen atom on the LHS and 2 oxygen atoms on the RHS. Multiply H_2O by 2:

   $Ca(s) + 2H_2O(l) \rightarrow H_2(g) + Ca(OH)_2(aq)$

The equation is now balanced.

Copy and complete this Mind Map to summarise this topic.

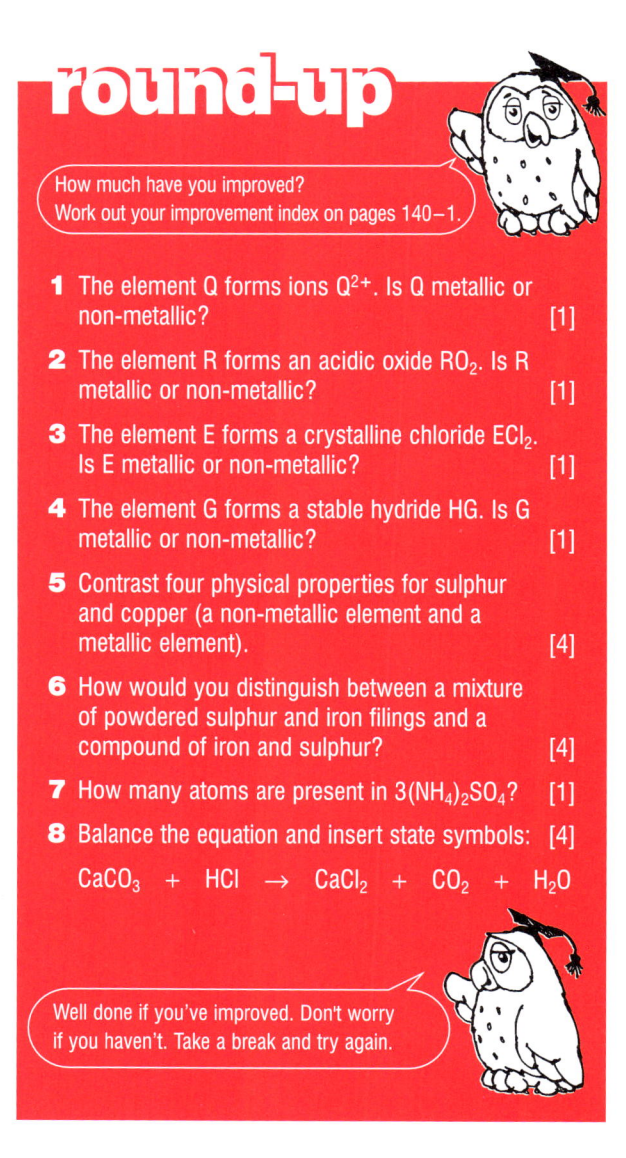

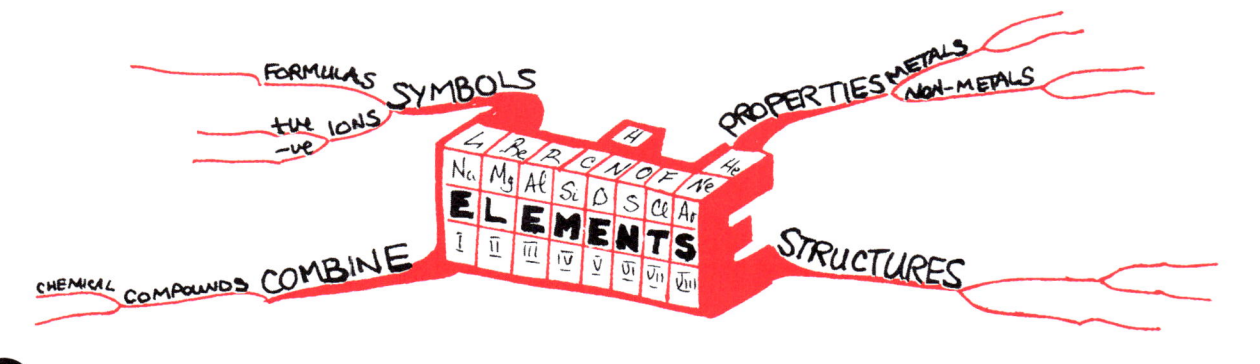

round-up

How much have you improved?
Work out your improvement index on pages 140–1.

1. The element Q forms ions Q^{2+}. Is Q metallic or non-metallic? [1]
2. The element R forms an acidic oxide RO_2. Is R metallic or non-metallic? [1]
3. The element E forms a crystalline chloride ECl_2. Is E metallic or non-metallic? [1]
4. The element G forms a stable hydride HG. Is G metallic or non-metallic? [1]
5. Contrast four physical properties for sulphur and copper (a non-metallic element and a metallic element). [4]
6. How would you distinguish between a mixture of powdered sulphur and iron filings and a compound of iron and sulphur? [4]
7. How many atoms are present in $3(NH_4)_2SO_4$? [1]
8. Balance the equation and insert state symbols: [4]

   $CaCO_3 + HCl \rightarrow CaCl_2 + CO_2 + H_2O$

Well done if you've improved. Don't worry if you haven't. Take a break and try again.

Separating substances

preview

At the end of this topic you will be able to:

- **describe methods for separating the components of mixtures.**

How much do you already know? Work out your score on page 141.

Test yourself

1. Suggest methods for separating
   a) sand and gravel from a mixture of both [1]
   b) blood cells from plasma [1]
   c) salts A and B, where both are soluble in hot water but only B is soluble in cold water [4]
   d) vinegar and olive oil [1]
   e) small diamonds from a mixture of diamonds and salt crystals [2]
   f) ethanol and water. [1]

3.1 Mixtures from the Earth

All the materials we use must come from the Earth's crust and atmosphere. Few of the raw materials we use are found in a pure state in the Earth's crust, and we have to separate the substances we want from a mixture of substances. The table shows some separation methods.

3.2 Soluble solid from insoluble solid

To separate a soluble solid from a mixture with an insoluble solid, add a solvent, e.g. water, and stir to dissolve the soluble solid. Filter as shown in the diagram. The insoluble solid is left on the filter paper. Evaporate the filtrate to obtain the soluble solid.

A faster method of filtration is filtration under reduced pressure.

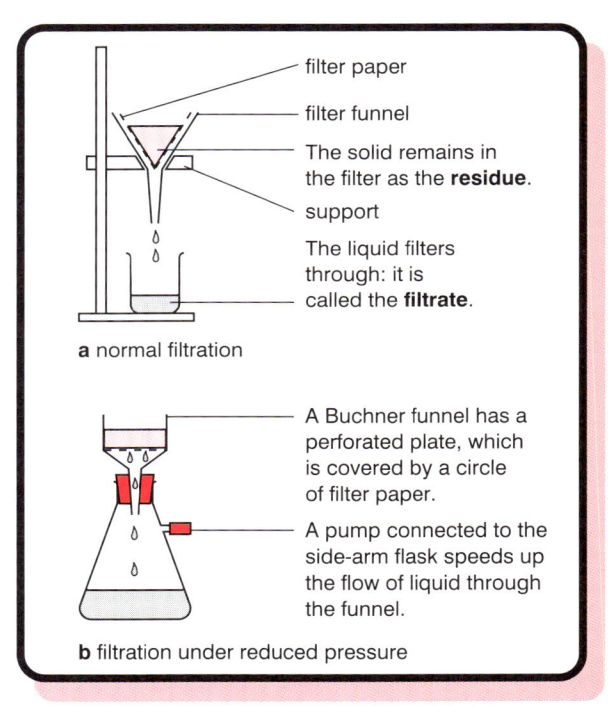

- filter paper
- filter funnel
- The solid remains in the filter as the **residue**.
- support
- The liquid filters through: it is called the **filtrate**.

a normal filtration

- A Buchner funnel has a perforated plate, which is covered by a circle of filter paper.
- A pump connected to the side-arm flask speeds up the flow of liquid through the funnel.

b filtration under reduced pressure

Filtration

mixture	type	method
solid + solid	solid mixture	Utilise a difference in properties, e.g. solubility or magnetic properties.
	in a solution	Use chromatography.
solid + liquid	mixture	Filter or centrifuge.
	solution	Crystallise to obtain the solid; distil to obtain the liquid.
liquid + liquid	miscible (form one layer)	Use fractional distillation.
	immiscible (form two layers)	Use a separating funnel.

Methods of separating pure substances from mixtures

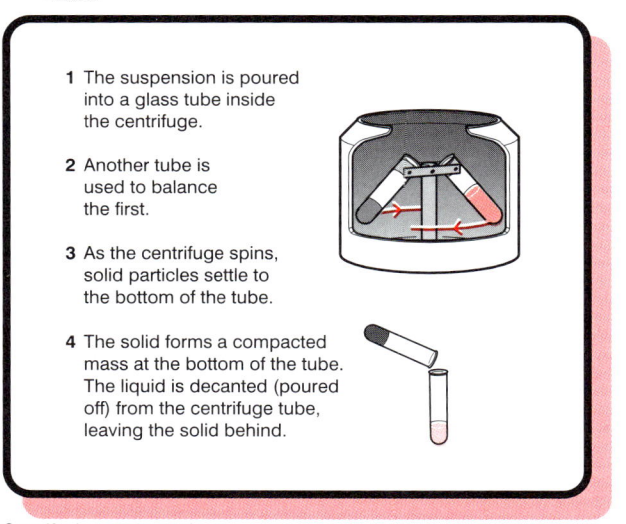

Materials and their properties

Centrifuging a suspension

1. The suspension is poured into a glass tube inside the centrifuge.
2. Another tube is used to balance the first.
3. As the centrifuge spins, solid particles settle to the bottom of the tube.
4. The solid forms a compacted mass at the bottom of the tube. The liquid is decanted (poured off) from the centrifuge tube, leaving the solid behind.

Filtration cannot separate particles which are so small that they pass through the pores in filter paper. An example is bacteria, which form a **suspension** in water. When a suspension of bacteria in liquid is spun at high speed, bacteria settle to the bottom. This method of separation is called **centrifuging** or **centrifugation**.

3.3 Soluble solids by chromatography

The following diagram shows chromatography on a solution of the pigments in green leaves. The solvent, ethanol, carries the pigments through a strip of **chromatography paper**. The pigments separate because they travel at different speeds.

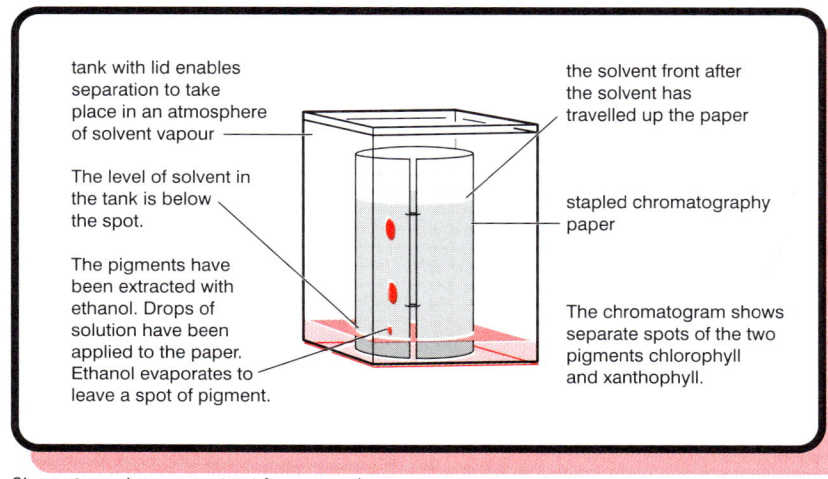

Chromatography on an extract from green leaves

- tank with lid enables separation to take place in an atmosphere of solvent vapour
- The level of solvent in the tank is below the spot.
- The pigments have been extracted with ethanol. Drops of solution have been applied to the paper. Ethanol evaporates to leave a spot of pigment.
- the solvent front after the solvent has travelled up the paper
- stapled chromatography paper
- The chromatogram shows separate spots of the two pigments chlorophyll and xanthophyll.

3.4 Immiscible liquids

The mixture of immiscible liquids, e.g. oil and water, is poured into a **separating funnel**. The mixture settles into two layers. The tap is opened to allow the bottom layer to run into a receiver. Then the tap is closed and the receiver is changed. The top layer is run into the second receiver.

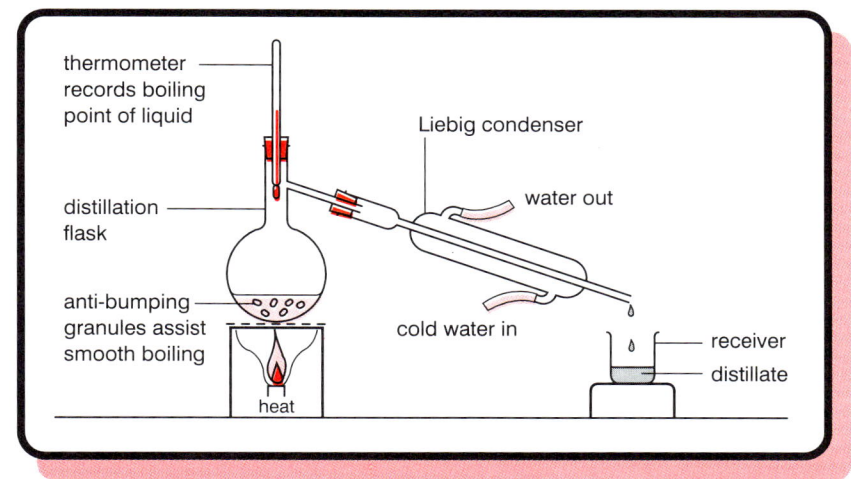

3.5 Solvent from solute

To separate the solvent and solute in a solution, heat the solution in the **distillation** apparatus shown here. The solvent distils over and condenses into the receiver, leaving the solute behind in the distillation flask.

A laboratory distillation apparatus

- thermometer records boiling point of liquid
- distillation flask
- anti-bumping granules assist smooth boiling
- Liebig condenser
- water out
- cold water in
- receiver
- distillate
- heat

3.6 Miscible liquids

Heat the mixture in the **fractional distillation** apparatus shown here. The lower boiling point liquid, e.g. ethanol, b.p. 78 °C, distils over first. Then the temperature rises as the liquid with the higher boiling point, e.g. water, b.p. 100 °C, distils over.

Fractional distillation can be run continuously (non-stop). Continuous fractional distillation is used to separate crude petroleum oil into a number of useful fuels (see pages 134–5).

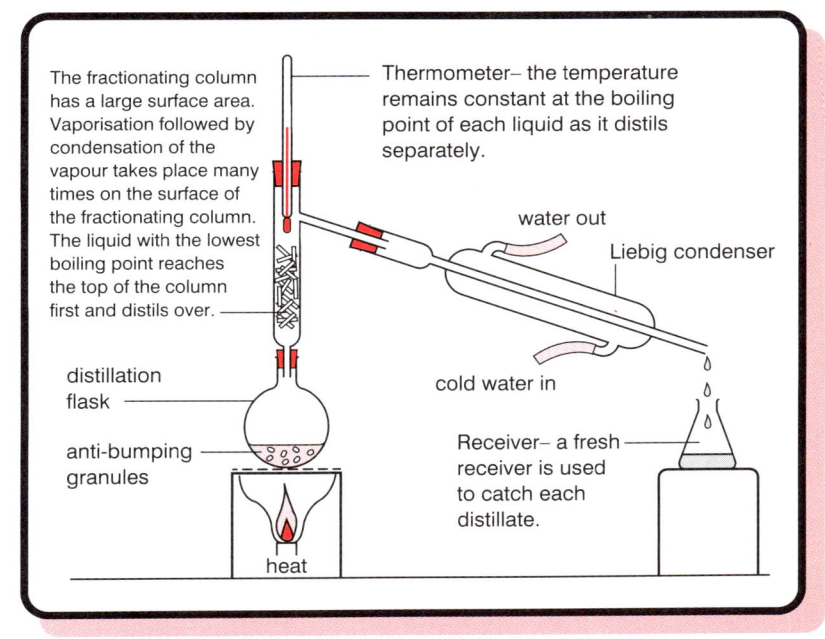

The fractionating column has a large surface area. Vaporisation followed by condensation of the vapour takes place many times on the surface of the fractionating column. The liquid with the lowest boiling point reaches the top of the column first and distils over.

Thermometer– the temperature remains constant at the boiling point of each liquid as it distils separately.

water out
Liebig condenser
cold water in

distillation flask
anti-bumping granules

Receiver– a fresh receiver is used to catch each distillate.

heat

Apparatus for fractional distillation

round-up

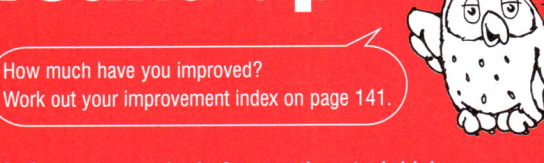

How much have you improved? Work out your improvement index on page 141.

1. Suggest a method of separating steel drink cans from a collection of empty steel cans and aluminium cans. [2]

2. A mixture contains the salts C and D. Neither is soluble in water. C is soluble in ethanol. Suggest a method you could use to separate C and D. Mention any safety precautions. [5]

3. How are gasoline and diesel oil separated from crude oil? Explain why the method works. [3]

4. The manufacturer Colorit has a patent on three pigments A, B and C. The firm suspects that a rival firm which has brought out the pigments P1 and P2 is using Colorit's pigments. The works analytical chemist runs a chromatogram on all five pigments. The results of her analysis are shown in the diagram. What conclusions can you draw? [2]

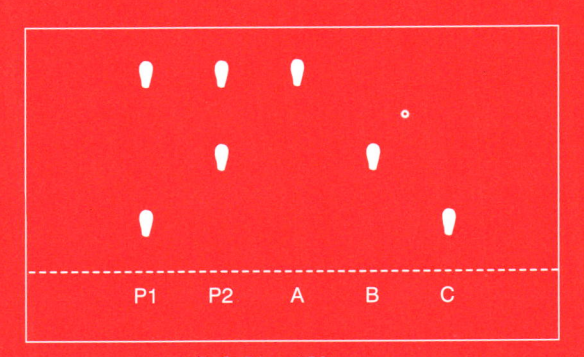

Chromatogram of A, B, C, P1 and P2

5. An oil tanker collides with a rocky promontory and thousands of litres of oil escape to form an oil slick. A salvage ship sucks up a mixture of oil and sea water from the surface. Suggest a method of separating the valuable oil from sea water. [3]

Well done if you've improved. Don't worry if you haven't. Take a break and try again.

The structure of the atom

preview

At the end of this topic you will:

- know the names of the particles of which atoms are composed
- know how particles are arranged in the atom
- understand the terms atomic number, mass number, relative atomic mass, relative molecular mass and isotope.

How much do you already know? Work out your score on page 141.

Test yourself

1. An atom is made of charged particles called protons and electrons. Why is an atom uncharged? [2]

2. An atom of potassium has mass number 39 and atomic number 19. What is **a)** the number of electrons and **b)** the number of neutrons? [2]

3. Why do the isotopes of an element have the same chemical reactions? [2]

4. What is meant by **a)** the atomic number and **b)** the mass number of an element? [3]

5. Write the symbol, with mass number and atomic number, for each of the following isotopes:
   a) phosphorus with atomic number 15 and mass number 31 [2]
   b) potassium with atomic number 19 and mass number 39. [2]

6. An atom of carbon has 6 electrons. Say how the electrons are divided between shells. [2]

4.1 Protons, neutrons and electrons

The concept map opposite gives a summary of the nature of the sub-atomic particles, their masses and charges and some ways of expressing the masses of atoms.

4.2 Focus on the atom

The diagram below shows how protons, neutrons and electrons are arranged in the atom.

The nucleus occupies a tiny volume in the centre of the atom. It consists of protons and neutrons.

The electrons occupy the space surrounding the nucleus. They repel the electrons of neighbouring atoms. The electrons are in constant motion, moving round the nucleus in circular paths called orbitals.

The arrangement of particles in the atom

The electrons moving in orbitals further away from the nucleus have more energy than those close to the nucleus. A group of orbitals of similar energy is called a **shell** (see diagram on page 100). In the outermost shell of any atom, the maximum number of electrons is eight.

The structure of the atom

Mass
Mass of proton
= mass of neutron
= 1 atomic mass unit, a.m.u.
Mass of electron
= 0.0005 a.m.u.

Charge
Negative charge on electron = −1 elementary charge unit.
Positive charge on proton = +1.
Neutrons are uncharged.

The protons and neutrons are located in the **nucleus** of the atom. The electrons are present in the space outside the nucleus (see diagram opposite).

THE ATOM consists of subatomic particles: **protons**, **neutrons** and **electrons**.

Atomic number Z of element
= number of protons in the nucleus of an atom of the element
= number of electrons in the atom.
Mass number A of atom = sum of number of protons + number of neutrons.
Number of neutrons = $A - Z$.

Relative atomic mass A_r = mass of one atom of element ÷ $\frac{1}{12}$ mass of one atom of carbon-12.
Relative molecular mass M_r = mass of one molecule or one formula unit of a compound ÷ $\frac{1}{12}$ mass of one atom of carbon-12.

Electrons occupy orbitals. They are arranged in shells of orbitals, with orbitals of lowest energy filled first (see overleaf). The **electron arrangement** of an atom can be predicted from its atomic number, e.g. Ca with $Z = 20$ has the arrangement 2.8.8.2.

Some elements consist of **isotopes** – forms of the element which have the same number of protons but different numbers of neutrons (the same atomic number but different mass numbers.)

Chlorine consists of two kinds of atoms, one with 17 protons and 18 neutrons, called chlorine-35, and one with 17 protons and 20 neutrons, called chlorine-37. The **isotopes** can be written as

mass number → $^{35}_{17}$Cl ← symbol
atomic number →
and $^{37}_{17}$Cl.

The relative atomic mass of the element is the **weighted average** of the relative atomic masses of its isotopes. There are three chlorine-35 atoms for every chlorine-37 atom. Therefore
$$A_r(Cl) = \frac{(3 \times 35) + (1 \times 37)}{4} = 35.5$$

The isotopes of carbon are $^{12}_{6}$C and $^{14}_{6}$C.
The isotopes of hydrogen are $^{1}_{1}$H, $^{2}_{1}$H and $^{3}_{1}$H.

Concept map: the nature of the atom

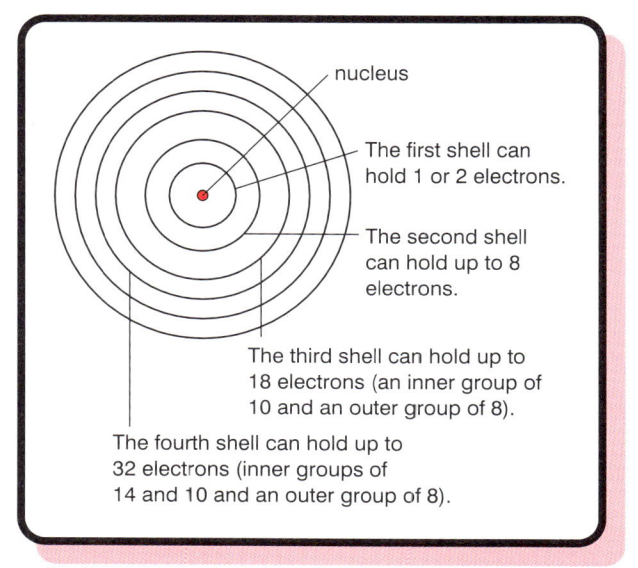

Materials and their properties

energy levels. The arrangements of electrons in an atom of carbon (atomic number 6) and an atom of magnesium (atomic number 12) are shown here.

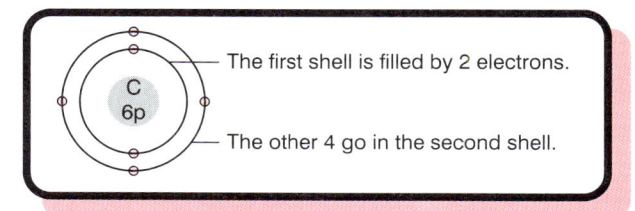

- nucleus
- The first shell can hold 1 or 2 electrons.
- The second shell can hold up to 8 electrons.
- The third shell can hold up to 18 electrons (an inner group of 10 and an outer group of 8).
- The fourth shell can hold up to 32 electrons (inner groups of 14 and 10 and an outer group of 8).

Shells of electrons

C 6p
- The first shell is filled by 2 electrons.
- The other 4 go in the second shell.

The arrangement of electrons in the carbon atom (2.4)

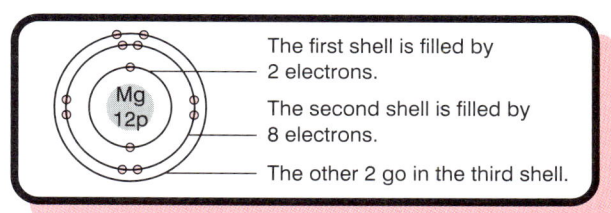

Mg 12p
- The first shell is filled by 2 electrons.
- The second shell is filled by 8 electrons.
- The other 2 go in the third shell.

The arrangement of electrons in the magnesium atom (2.8.2)

If you know the atomic number of an element, you can work out the arrangement of electrons. The lower energy levels are filled before the higher energy levels.

The table opposite gives the electron arrangements of the first 20 elements.

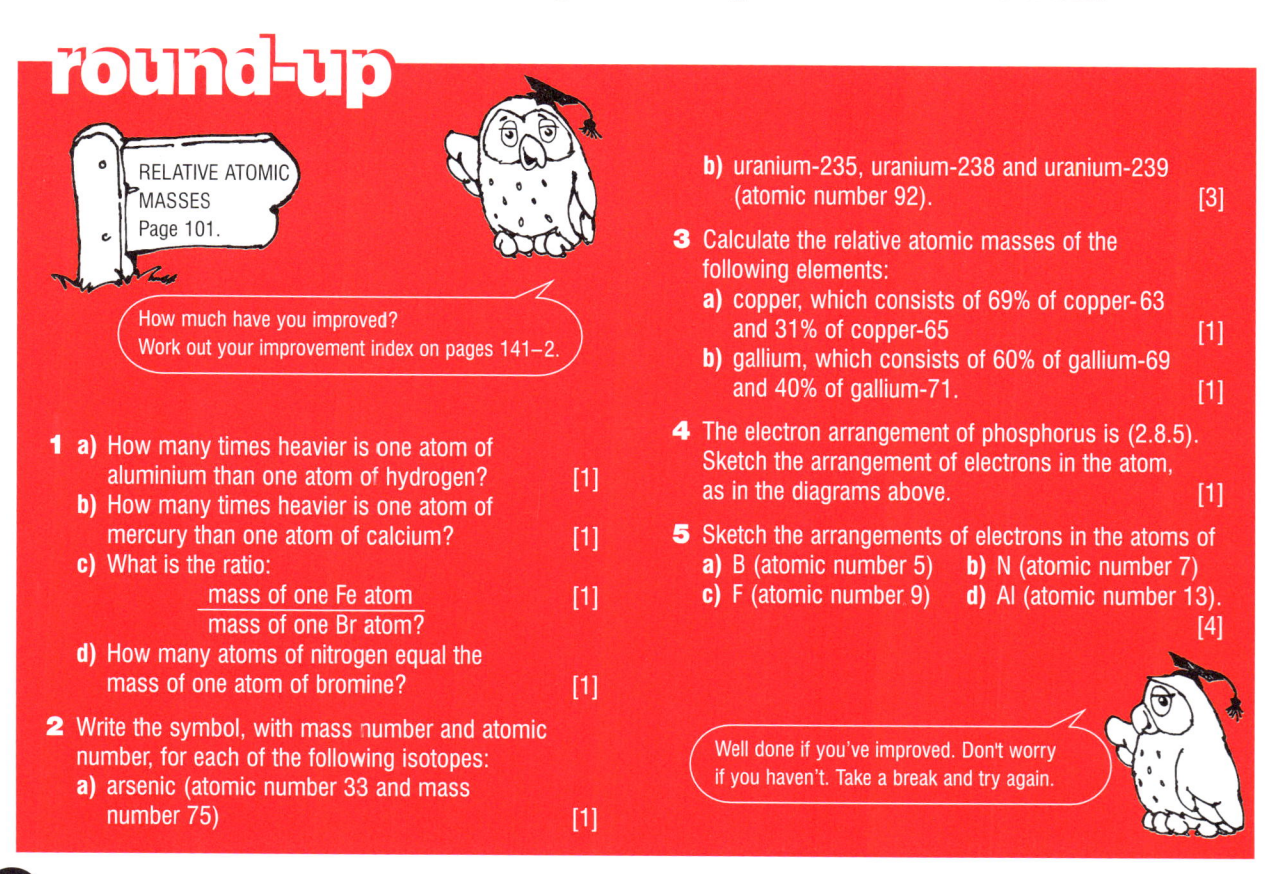

round-up

RELATIVE ATOMIC MASSES
Page 101.

How much have you improved? Work out your improvement index on pages 141–2.

1 a) How many times heavier is one atom of aluminium than one atom of hydrogen? [1]
b) How many times heavier is one atom of mercury than one atom of calcium? [1]
c) What is the ratio:
$$\frac{\text{mass of one Fe atom}}{\text{mass of one Br atom}}?$$ [1]
d) How many atoms of nitrogen equal the mass of one atom of bromine? [1]

2 Write the symbol, with mass number and atomic number, for each of the following isotopes:
a) arsenic (atomic number 33 and mass number 75) [1]
b) uranium-235, uranium-238 and uranium-239 (atomic number 92). [3]

3 Calculate the relative atomic masses of the following elements:
a) copper, which consists of 69% of copper-63 and 31% of copper-65 [1]
b) gallium, which consists of 60% of gallium-69 and 40% of gallium-71. [1]

4 The electron arrangement of phosphorus is (2.8.5). Sketch the arrangement of electrons in the atom, as in the diagrams above. [1]

5 Sketch the arrangements of electrons in the atoms of
a) B (atomic number 5) **b)** N (atomic number 7)
c) F (atomic number 9) **d)** Al (atomic number 13). [4]

Well done if you've improved. Don't worry if you haven't. Take a break and try again.

The structure of the atom

element	symbol	atomic number	number of electrons in				electron arrangement
			1st level	2nd level	3rd level	4th level	
hydrogen	H	1	1				1
helium	He	2	2				2
lithium	Li	3	2	1			2.1
beryllium	Be	4	2	2			2.2
boron	B	5	2	3			2.3
carbon	C	6	2	4			2.4
nitrogen	N	7	2	5			2.5
oxygen	O	8	2	6			2.6
fluorine	F	9	2	7			2.7
neon	Ne	10	2	8			2.8
sodium	Na	11	2	8	1		2.8.1
magnesium	Mg	12	2	8	2		2.8.2
aluminium	Al	13	2	8	3		2.8.3
silicon	Si	14	2	8	4		2.8.4
phosphorus	P	15	2	8	5		2.8.5
sulphur	S	16	2	8	6		2.8.6
chlorine	Cl	17	2	8	7		2.8.7
argon	Ar	18	2	8	8		2.8.8
potassium	K	19	2	8	8	1	2.8.8.1
calcium	Ca	20	2	8	8	2	2.8.8.2

Electron arrangements of the first 20 elements

element	symbol	A_r
aluminium	Al	27
bromine	Br	80
calcium	Ca	40
hydrogen	H	1
iron	Fe	56
mercury	Hg	200
nitrogen	N	14

Table of relative atomic masses

Now draw your own Mind Map of this topic:

The chemical bond 5

preview

At the end of this topic you will:

- understand how atoms combine by forming ionic bonds and covalent bonds
- understand how ionic compounds and covalent compounds differ in properties and structure.

How much do you already know? Work out your score on page 142.

Test yourself

1 Write words in the spaces to complete the sentences.

When an ionic compound is formed, some atoms lose electrons to become _____ ions while other atoms gain electrons to become _____ ions. Ions are held together by _____ attraction in a three-dimensional structure called a _____ . [4]

2 The element E has the electron arrangement E(2.8.2). The element Q has the electron arrangement Q(2.8.7). Explain what happens to atoms of E and Q when they combine to form an ionic compound, and give the formula of the compound. [3]

3 The element T has the electron arrangement T(2.7). Sketch the arrangement of electrons in an atom of T and in the molecule T_2. [2]

5.1 Bond formation

When chemical reactions take place, it is the electrons in the outer shell that are involved in the formation of bonds. The resistance of the noble gases to chemical change is believed to be due to the stability of the full outer shell of eight electrons (two for helium). When atoms react, they gain, lose or share electrons to attain an outer shell of eight electrons. Metallic elements frequently combine with non-metallic elements to form compounds.

5.2 Ions

ATOMIC STRUCTURE Page 98.

How is an ion formed from an atom? Atoms are uncharged. The number of protons in an atom is the same as the number of electrons. If an atom either gains or loses electrons, it will become electrically charged. Metal atoms and hydrogen atoms form positive ions (**cations**) by losing one or more electrons. Atoms of non-metallic elements form negative ions (**anions**) by gaining one or more electrons.

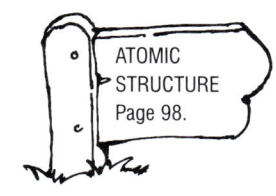

sodium atom Na → electron e^- + sodium ion Na^+
(11 protons,   (11 protons,
11 electrons,   10 electrons,
charge = 0)   charge = +1)

chlorine atom Cl + electron e^- → chloride ion Cl^-
(17 protons,   (17 protons,
17 electrons,   18 electrons,
charge = 0)   charge = –1)

The table below gives the symbols and formulas of some ions.

cations	anions
hydrogen ion H^+	bromide ion Br^-
sodium ion Na^+	chloride ion Cl^-
copper(II) ion Cu^{2+}	iodide ion I^-
lead(II) ion Pb^{2+}	hydroxide ion OH^-
aluminium ion Al^{3+}	nitrate ion NO_3^-
	sulphate ion SO_4^{2-}

5.3 Ionic bonding

Example 1

Sodium burns in chlorine to form sodium chloride. The following diagram shows what happens to the electrons.

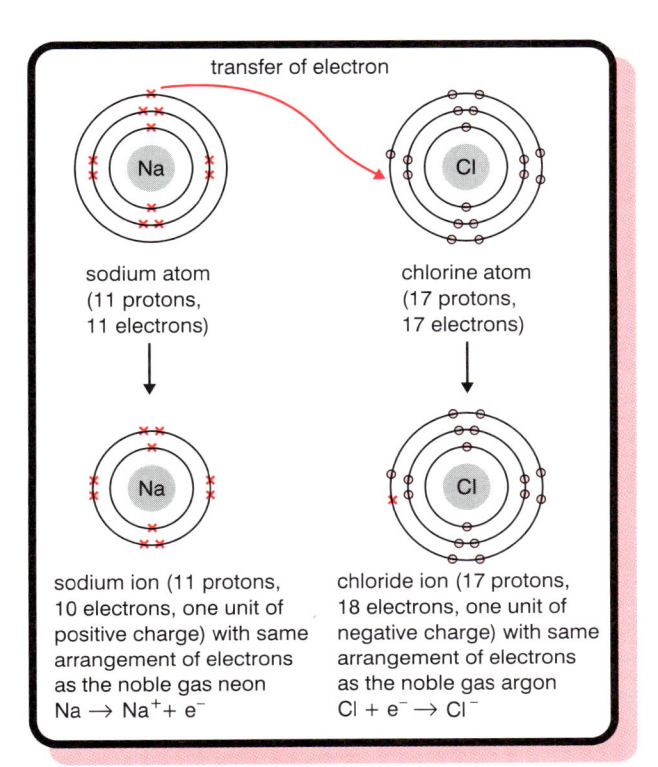

The chemical bond

The formation of sodium chloride

There is an electrostatic force of attraction between oppositely charged ions. This force is called an **ionic bond** or **electrovalent bond**. The ions Na⁺ and Cl⁻ are part of a **giant ionic structure** (a crystal). The ions cannot move out of their positions in the structure, and the crystal cannot conduct electricity. When the solid is melted or dissolved, the ions become free to move and conduct electricity.

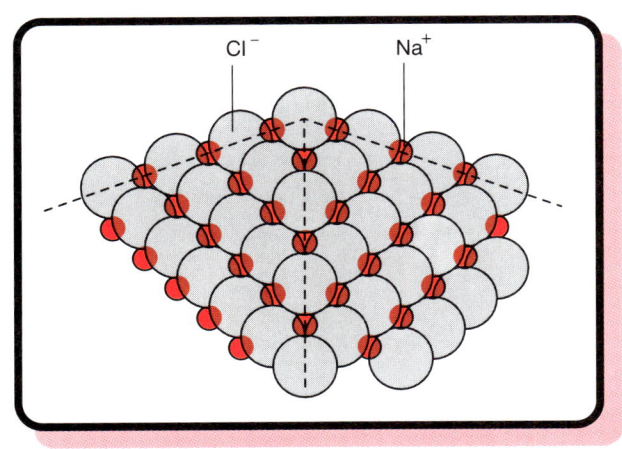

The structure of sodium chloride

Example 2

Magnesium + fluorine → magnesium fluoride

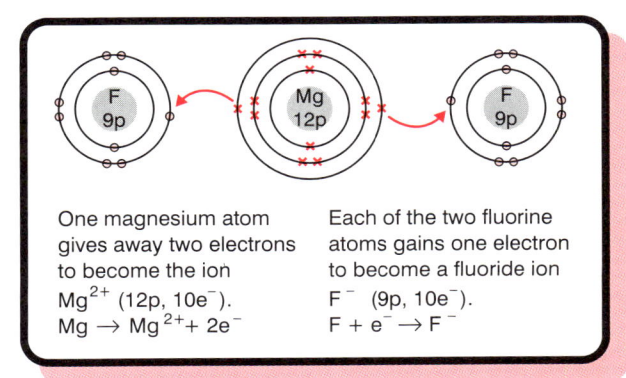

One magnesium atom gives away two electrons to become the ion Mg^{2+} (12p, 10e⁻).
$Mg \rightarrow Mg^{2+} + 2e^-$

Each of the two fluorine atoms gains one electron to become a fluoride ion F^- (9p, 10e⁻).
$F + e^- \rightarrow F^-$

The formation of magnesium fluoride

The formula of magnesium fluoride is $Mg^{2+}2F^-$ or MgF_2.

Example 3

Magnesium + oxygen → magnesium oxide

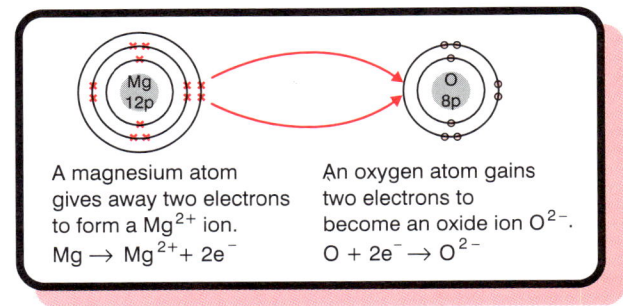

A magnesium atom gives away two electrons to form a Mg^{2+} ion.
$Mg \rightarrow Mg^{2+} + 2e^-$

An oxygen atom gains two electrons to become an oxide ion O^{2-}.
$O + 2e^- \rightarrow O^{2-}$

The formation of magnesium oxide

The formula of magnesium oxide is $Mg^{2+}O^{2-}$ or MgO.

5.4 Covalent bonding

When two non-metallic elements combine, both want to gain electrons; neither wants to form positive ions. They combine by sharing electrons. A shared pair of electrons is a **covalent bond**. If two pairs of electrons are shared, the bond is a **double bond**.

Materials and their properties

Example 1

Hydrogen + fluorine → hydrogen fluoride, HF

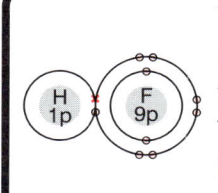

The hydrogen atom shares its electron with the fluorine atom. H has a full shell of two electrons, the same arrangement as helium.

The fluorine atom shares one of its electrons with the hydrogen atom. F has a full shell of eight electrons, the same arrangement as neon.

The formation of hydrogen fluoride

The shared pair of electrons is attracted to the hydrogen nucleus and to the fluorine nucleus, and bonds the two nuclei together.

Example 2

Hydrogen + oxygen → water, H_2O

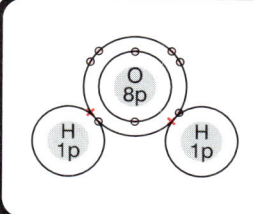

Two hydrogen atoms each share an electron with an oxygen atom. Each hydrogen atom has an outer shell of two electrons, and the oxygen atom has an outer shell of eight electrons.

The formation of water

Example 3

Nitrogen + hydrogen → ammonia, NH_3

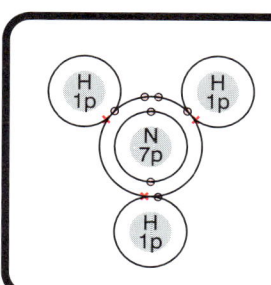

One nitrogen atom shares three electrons, one with each of three hydrogen atoms. The nitrogen atom has eight electrons in its outer shell (like neon), and each hydrogen has two electrons in its outer shell (like helium).

The formation of ammonia

5.5 Ionic and covalent substances

The concept map opposite summarises the types of bonds formed by different substances.

round-up

How much have you improved? Work out your improvement index on page 142.

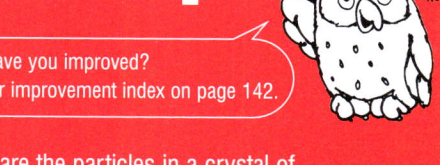

1. **a)** What are the particles in a crystal of sodium chloride? [2]
   b) What holds the particles together? [1]
   c) Describe the arrangement of particles in the crystal. [2]

2. Draw the arrangement of electrons in a molecule of hydrogen chloride. [2]

3. Give an example of a covalent substance which
   a) has individual molecules   **b)** is a molecular solid   **c)** has giant molecules. [3]

4. Name the following compounds:
   a) $Ca(OH)_2$ **b)** Na_2SO_3 **c)** $CuCO_3$
   d) $Mg(HCO_3)_2$ **e)** KNO_3. [5]

Well done if you've improved. Don't worry if you haven't. Take a break and try again.

The chemical bond

IONIC AND COVALENT SUBSTANCES

Ionic bonding
Ionic compounds are formed when a metallic element combines with a non-metallic element. An **ionic bond** is formed by **transfer of electrons** from one atom to another to form ions.

Covalent bonding
Atoms of non-metallic elements combine with other non-metallic elements by **sharing pairs of electrons** in their outer shells. A shared pair of electrons is a **covalent bond**.

There are three **types of covalent substances**.

1. Many covalent substances are composed of small individual molecules with only very small forces of attraction between molecules, e.g. the gases HCl, SO_2, CO_2, CH_4.

2. Some covalent substances consist of small molecules with weak forces of attraction between molecules, e.g. the volatile liquid ethanol, C_2H_5OH, and solid carbon dioxide.

3. Some covalent substances consist of giant molecules, e.g. quartz (silicon(IV) oxide). These substances have high melting and boiling points.

Atoms of **metallic elements** form positive ions (cations). Elements in Groups 1, 2 and 3 of the periodic table form ions with charges +1, +2 and +3, e.g. Na^+, Mg^{2+}, Al^{3+}. Atoms of **non-metallic elements** form negative ions (anions). Elements in Groups 6 and 7 of the periodic table form ions with charges −2 and −1, e.g. O^{2-} and Cl^-.

The maximum number of covalent bonds that an atom can form is equal to the number of electrons in the outer shell. An atom may not use all its outer electrons in bond formation.

Ionic compounds are **electrolytes** – they conduct electricity when molten or in solution and are split up (**electrolysed**) in the process. Covalent compounds are **non-electrolytes**.

The strong electrostatic attraction between ions of opposite charge is an **ionic bond**. An ionic compound is composed of a giant regular structure of ions (see diagram of sodium chloride structure on page 103). This regular structure makes ionic compounds **crystalline**. The strong forces of attraction between ions make it difficult to separate the ions, and ionic compounds therefore have **high melting and boiling points**.

Organic solvents, e.g. ethanol and propanone, have covalent bonds. They dissolve covalent compounds but not ionic compounds.

Concept map: ionic and covalent substances

The periodic table

preview

At the end of this topic you will:

- understand the structure of the periodic table
- know the nature of the elements in Groups 0, 1, 2, 7 and the transition elements.

How much do you already know? Work out your score on page 142.

Test yourself

1 a) What are the noble gases? [2]
  b) In which group of the periodic table are they? [1]
  c) What do the noble gases have in common regarding
   (i) their electron arrangements and
   (ii) their chemical reactions? [2]

2 X is a metallic element. It reacts slowly with water to give a strongly alkaline solution. In which group of the periodic table would you place X? [1]

3 Y is a non-metallic element. It reacts vigorously with sodium to give a salt of formula NaY. In which group of the periodic table would you place Y? [1]

4 Z is a metallic element which reacts rapidly with water to give a flammable gas and an alkaline solution. In which group of the periodic table would you place Z? [1]

5 a) Name the halogens. [4]
  b) In which group of the periodic table are they? [1]
  c) Does the chemical reactivity of the halogens increase or decrease with atomic number? [1]
  d) Give the formulas of the products of the reactions of
   (i) sodium (ii) iron with each of the halogens. [8]

6 a) What is a transition metal? [1]
  b) Name two transition metals. [1]

6.1 Classifying elements

Topic 2 dealt with the classification of elements as metallic and non-metallic elements. A major advance was made by John Newlands in 1866 and Dmitri Mendeleev in 1871 when they originated the periodic table. The modern periodic table is based on arranging the elements in order of increasing atomic number. A vertical row of elements is called a **group** and a horizontal row is called a **period**.

The following patterns can be seen in the arrangement of the elements in the periodic table.

1. The reactive metals are at the left-hand side of the table, less reactive metallic elements in the middle block and non-metallic elements at the right-hand side.

2. The differences between the metals in Group 1, those in Group 2 and the transition metals are summarised in the table at the top of page 108.

3. Silicon and germanium are on the borderline between metals and non-metals. These elements are semiconductors, intermediate between metals, which are electrical conductors, and non-metals, which are non-conductors of electricity. Semiconductors are vital to the computer industry.

4. Group 7 is a set of very reactive non-metallic elements called the **halogens**. They react with metals to form salts; see the table on page 108.

5. When Mendeleev drew up his periodic table in 1871, only 55 elements were known. He left gaps in the table and predicted that new elements would be discovered which would fit the gaps. When the noble gases were discovered, one by one, their atomic numbers placed them in between Groups 1 and 7, and a new Group 0 had to be created for them.

The periodic table

Group	1	2												3	4	5	6	7	0
	H																		He
	Li	Be												B	C	N	O	F	Ne
	Na	Mg												Al	Si	P	S	Cl	Ar
	K	Ca	Sc	Ti	V	Cr	Mn	Fe	Co	Ni	Cu	Zn	Ga	Ge	As	Se	Br	Kr
	Rb	Sr	Y	Zr	Nb	Mo	Tc	Ru	Rh	Pd	Ag	Cd	In	Sn	Sb	Te	I	Xe
	Cs	Ba	La	Hf	Ta	W	Re	Os	Ir	Pt	Au	Hg	Tl	Pb	Bi	Po	At	Rn

metals — transition metals — less reactive metals

reactive metals

The reactivity of metals increases **down** each group. →

non-metals

The reactivity of non-metals increases **up** each group. ←

Elements on or near this line are **metalloids**: they have some metallic characteristics and some non-metallic characteristics.

non-metals

The periodic table

107

Materials and their properties

metal	reaction with air	reaction with water	reaction with dilute hydrochloric acid	trend
Group 1 the alkali metals				
lithium sodium potassium rubidium caesium	Burn vigorously to form the strongly basic oxide M_2O which dissolves in water to give the strong alkali MOH.	React vigorously to form hydrogen and a solution of the strong alkali MOH.	The reaction is dangerously violent.	The vigour of all these reactions increases down the group.
Group 2 the alkaline earths				
beryllium magnesium calcium strontium barium	Burn to form the strongly basic oxides MO, which are sparingly soluble or insoluble.	Reacts very slowly. Burns in steam. React readily to form hydrogen and the alkali $M(OH)_2$.	React readily to give hydrogen and a salt, e.g. MCl_2.	The vigour of all these reactions increases down the group. Group 2 elements are less reactive than Group 1.
Transition metals				
iron zinc copper	When heated, form oxides without burning. The oxides and hydroxides are weaker bases than those of Groups 1 and 2 and are insoluble.	Iron rusts slowly. Iron and zinc react with steam to form hydrogen and the oxide. Copper does not react.	Iron and zinc react to give hydrogen and a salt. Copper does not react.	Transition metals are less reactive than Groups 1 and 2. In general, their compounds are coloured; they are used as catalysts.

Some reactions of metals

Note
M stands for the symbol of a metallic element. Dilute sulphuric acid reacts with metals in the same way as dilute hydrochloric acid. Dilute nitric acid is an oxidising agent and attacks metals, e.g. copper, which are not sufficiently reactive to react with other dilute acids.

OXIDISING AGENT
Pages 116–17.

halogen	state at room temperature	reaction with sodium	reaction with iron	trend
fluorine	gas	explosive	explosive	The vigour of these reactions decreases down the group.
chlorine	gas	Heated sodium burns in chlorine to form sodium chloride.	Reacts vigorously with hot iron to form iron(III) chloride.	
bromine	liquid	Reacts less vigorously to form sodium bromide.	Reacts less vigorously to form iron(III) bromide.	
iodine	solid	Reacts less vigorously than bromine to form sodium iodide.	Reacts less vigorously than bromine to form iron(II) iodide.	

Some reactions of the halogens

6.2 A repeating pattern

You can see that the arrangement opposite has the following features:

★ The elements are listed in order of increasing atomic number.

★ Elements which have the same number of electrons in the outermost shell fall into the same **group** (vertical column) of the periodic table.

★ The noble gases are in Group 0. For the rest of the elements, the group number is the number of electrons in the outermost shell.

★ The first **period** (horizontal row) contains only hydrogen and helium. The second period contains the elements lithium to neon. The third period contains the elements sodium to argon.

	Group 1	Group 2	Group 3	Group 4	Group 5	Group 6	Group 7	Group 0
Period 1	H (1)							He (2)
Period 2	Li (2.1)	Be (2.2)	B (2.3)	C (2.4)	N (2.5)	O (2.6)	F (2.7)	Ne (2.8)
Period 3	Na (2.8.1)	Mg (2.8.2)	Al (2.8.3)	Si (2.8.4)	P (2.8.5)	S (2.8.6)	Cl (2.8.7)	Ar (2.8.8)
Period 4	K (2.8.8.1)	Ca (2.8.8.2)						

A section of the periodic table

round-up

How much have you improved?
Work out your improvement index on page 143.

1 Magnesium chloride, MgCl₂, is a solid of high melting point, and tetrachloromethane, CCl₄, is a volatile liquid. Explain how differences in chemical bonding account for these differences. [4]

2 Choose from the elements: Na, Mg, Al, Si, P, S, Cl, Ar.
  a) List the elements that react readily with cold water to form alkaline solutions. [2]
  b) List the elements that form sulphates. [3]
  c) Name the elements which exist as molecules containing (i) one atom (ii) two atoms. [2]
  d) Which element has both metallic and non-metallic properties? [1]

3 Give the formulas of the oxides of sodium, magnesium, aluminium and silicon. [4]

4 What have the following compounds in common? the sulphate of chlorine, the carbonate of silicon and the hydride of argon [1]

5 The elements sodium and potassium have the electron arrangements Na(2.8.1) and K(2.8.8.1). How does this explain the similarity in their reactions? [2]

6 Radium, Ra, is a radioactive element of atomic number 88 which falls below barium in Group 2. What can you predict about
  a) the nature of radium oxide [3]
  b) the reaction of radium with water [3]
  c) the reaction of radium with dilute hydrochloric acid? [4]
Give the physical state and type of bonding in any compounds you mention. Include the names and formulas of any compounds formed.

7 Astatine, At, is a radioactive element of atomic number 85 which follows fluorine in Group 7. What can you predict about
  a) the nature of its compound with hydrogen [3]
  b) the reaction of astatine with sodium? [4]
Give the physical state and type of bonding in any compounds you mention. Include the names and formulas of any compounds formed.

Well done if you've improved. Don't worry if you haven't. Take a break and try again.

Acids, bases and salts

7

preview

At the end of this topic you will:

- be able to define the terms 'acid', 'base' and 'alkali'
- know the typical reactions of acids and bases
- know how to prepare salts and know the uses of some important salts.

MIND MAP Page 150.

How much do you already know? Work out your score on page 143.

Test yourself

1 Say whether the substances listed are strongly acidic (SA), weakly acidic (WA), strongly basic (SB), weakly basic (WB) or neutral (N).
   a) battery acid, pH 0 [1]
   b) rainwater, pH 6.5 [1]
   c) blood, pH 7.4 [1]
   d) sea water, pH 8.5 [1]
   e) cabbage juice, pH 5.0 [1]
   f) saliva, pH 7.0 [1]
   g) washing soda, pH 11.5 [1]

2 You are given two bottles labelled 'acid 1' and 'acid 2'. One is a weak acid and the other is a strong acid. Describe two tests you could do to find out which is which. [3]

3 Name
   a) a strong acid present in your stomach [1]
   b) a base present in indigestion tablets [1]
   c) a weak acid present in fruits [1]
   d) a weak base used as a domestic cleaning fluid. [1]

4 Kleenit is an oven spray for cleaning greasy ovens. It contains a concentrated solution of sodium hydroxide.
   a) Why does sodium hydroxide remove grease? [1]
   b) Why does sodium hydroxide work better than ammonia? [1]
   c) What two safety precautions should you take when using Kleenit? [2]
   d) Why does Moppit, a fluid used for cleaning floors, contain ammonia rather than sodium hydroxide? [1]
   e) Why do soap manufacturers use sodium hydroxide, not ammonia? [1]

7.1 Acids

Where are acids found?

The following are strong acids:

- Hydrochloric acid occurs in the stomach, where it aids digestion.
- Nitric acid is used in the production of fertilisers and explosives.
- Sulphuric acid is used car batteries and in the production of fertilisers.

The following are weak acids:

- Carbonic acid is used in fizzy drinks.
- Citric acid occurs in lemons and other citrus fruits.
- Ethanoic acid occurs in vinegar.
- Lactic acid is present in sour milk.

What do acids do?

Acids are compounds that release hydrogen ions when dissolved in water. The hydrogen ions are responsible for the typical reactions of acids. Strong acids are completely ionised; for example, hydrochloric acid solution consists of the ions H^+ and Cl^- and water molecules. There are no molecules of HCl in the solution. Weak acids consist chiefly of molecules, but a small fraction of the molecules are ionised. Weak acids therefore have a low concentration of hydrogen ions in solution and react less readily than strong acids.

The concept map opposite gives a summary of the properties of acids.

Acids, bases and salts

- Wear **safety glasses** when working with acids.

- Acids have a **sour taste**, e.g. citric acid in lemons, ethanoic acid in vinegar.

- Acids change the colours of **indicators**:
  - blue litmus turns red
  - methyl orange turns red
  - universal indicator turns red.

ACIDS

- Solutions of acids may be **electrolysed**. Hydrogen ions accept electrons to become hydrogen atoms. Then hydrogen atoms combine to form hydrogen molecules.
  $H^+(aq) + e^- \rightarrow H(g)$
  $2H(g) \rightarrow H_2(g)$

- The **definition of an acid** given by Arrhenius is: an acid is a substance that releases **hydrogen ions** when dissolved in water.

- Acids react with many **metals** to give hydrogen and a salt of the metal.

  Some metals, e.g. Cu, react very slowly. Some metals, e.g. Na, react dangerously fast. Some, e.g. Mg, Zn, Fe, react at moderate **speed**.
  (**Test** for H_2: introduce a lighted splint. There is an explosive 'pop' as hydrogen burns in air.)

- Acids neutralise **bases**, e.g. MgO, to form a salt and water. Acids neutralise **alkalis**, e.g. NaOH, to form a salt and water.

- Acids react with **carbonates** and **hydrogencarbonates** to give carbon dioxide + a salt + water. (**Test** for CO_2: turns limewater, $Ca(OH)_2(aq)$, cloudy.)

Concept map: The properties of acids

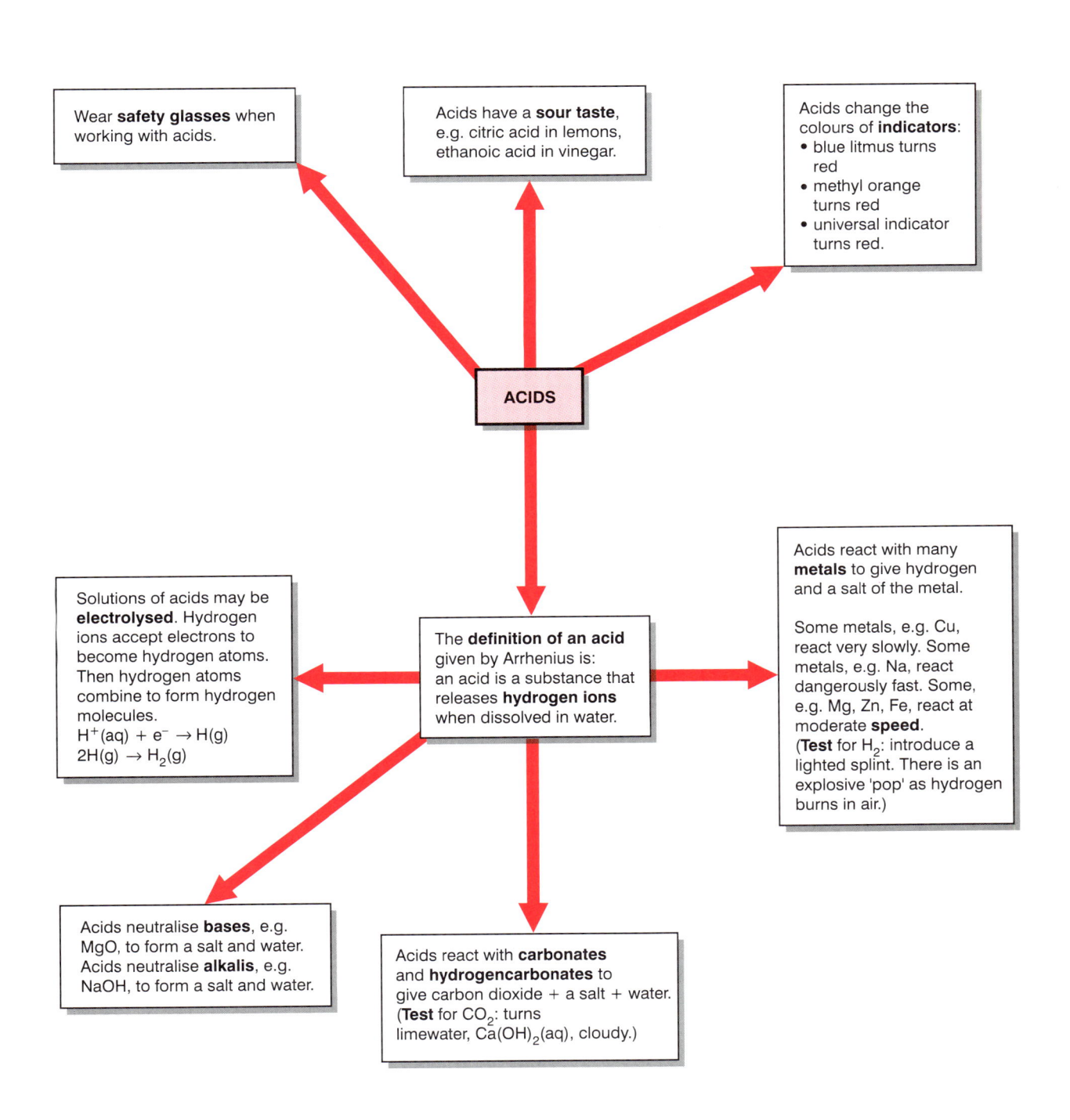

Materials and their properties

7.2 Bases

Where do you find bases?

The following are strong bases:

- Calcium hydroxide is used to treat soil which is too acidic.
- Calcium oxide is used in the manufacture of cement and concrete.
- Magnesium hydroxide is used in anti-acid indigestion tablets.
- Sodium hydroxide is used in soap manufacture and as a degreasing agent.
- The weak base ammonia is used in cleaning fluids, as a degreasing agent and in the manufacture of fertilisers.

What do bases do?

A **base** is a substance that reacts with an acid to form a salt and water as the only products. A soluble base is called an **alkali**. Sodium hydroxide, NaOH, is a strong base and a strong alkali. It is completely ionised in solution as Na^+ and OH^- ions. Ammonia is only slightly ionised and the concentration of hydroxide ions in the solution is small. Ammonia is therefore a weak base.

The concept map opposite gives a summary of the properties of bases.

7.3 Neutralisation

Neutralisation is the combination of hydrogen ions (from an acid) and hydroxide ions (from an alkali) or oxide ions (from an insoluble base) to form water. In the process a salt is formed. For example, with an alkali:

hydrochloric acid + sodium hydroxide → sodium chloride + water

$$HCl(aq) + NaOH(aq) \rightarrow NaCl(aq) + H_2O(l)$$

acid + alkali → salt + water

The hydrogen ions and hydroxide ions combine to form water molecules.

$$H^+(aq) + OH^-(aq) \rightarrow H_2O(l)$$

Sodium ions and chloride ions remain in the solution, which becomes a solution of sodium chloride.

With a base:

sulphuric acid + copper(II) oxide → copper(II) sulphate + water

$$H_2SO_4(aq) + CuO(s) \rightarrow CuSO_4(aq) + H_2O(l)$$

acid + base → salt + water

Hydrogen ions and oxide ions combine to form water:

$$2H^+(aq) + O^{2-}(s) \rightarrow H_2O(l)$$

Copper(II) ions and sulphate ions remain in the solution, which becomes a solution of copper(II) sulphate.

7.4 Indicators

indicator	acidic colour	neutral colour	alkaline colour
litmus	red	purple	blue
phenolphthalein	colourless	colourless	red
methyl orange	red	orange	yellow

Universal indicator can distinguish between strong and weak bases, as shown in the diagram below.

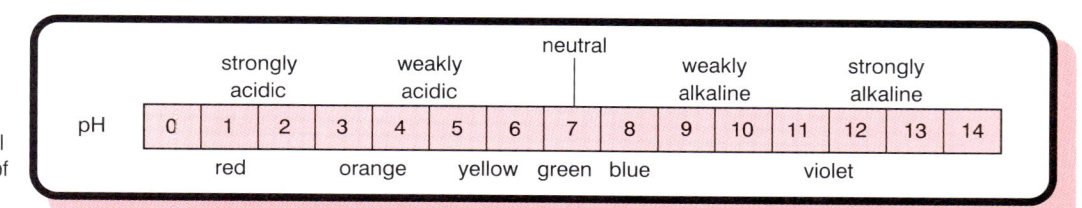

	strongly acidic	weakly acidic	neutral	weakly alkaline	strongly alkaline
pH	0 1 2	3 4 5 6	7	8 9 10	11 12 13 14
	red	orange yellow	green blue		violet

The colour of universal indicator in solutions of different pH

Acids, bases and salts

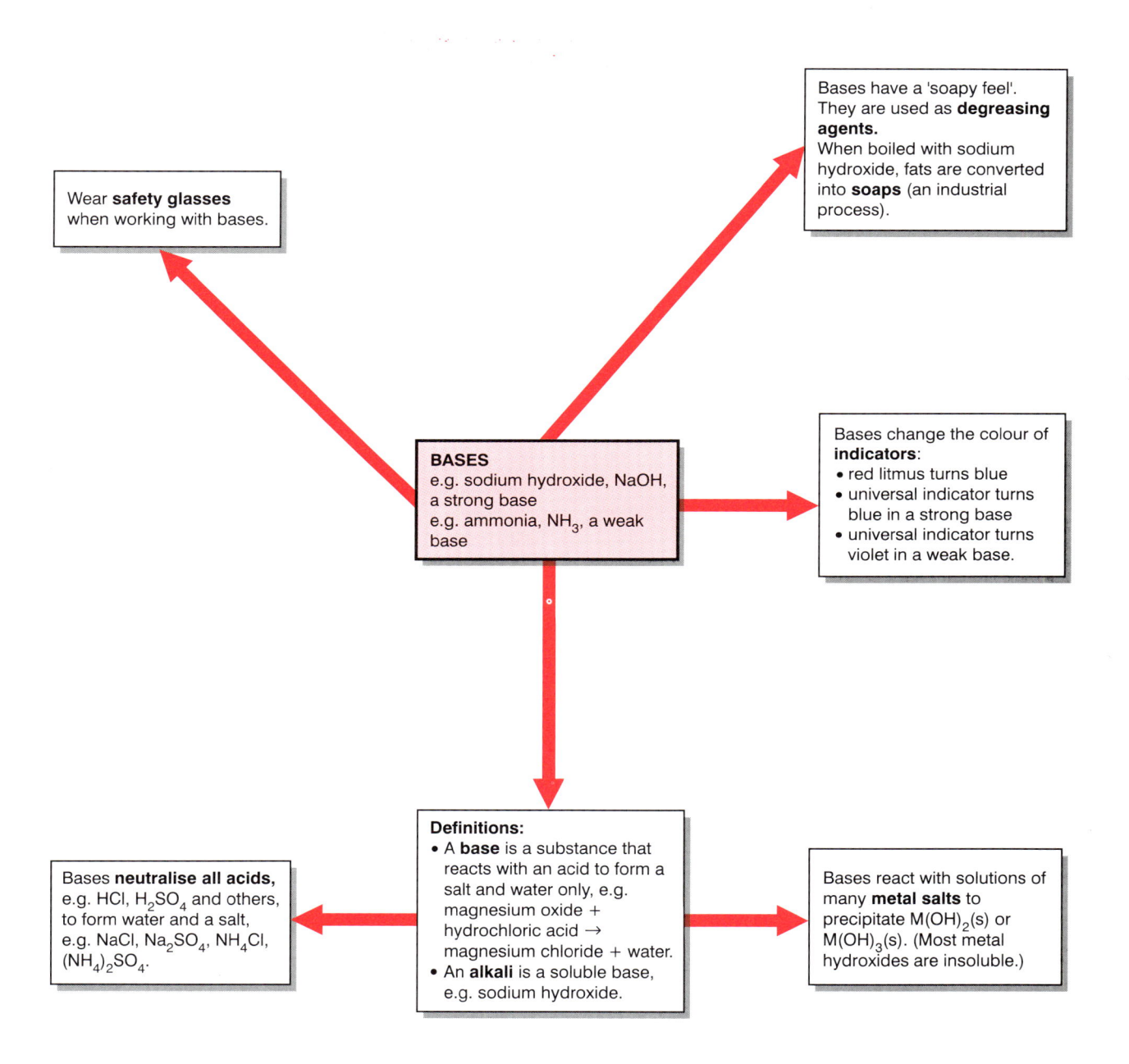

BASES
e.g. sodium hydroxide, NaOH, a strong base
e.g. ammonia, NH_3, a weak base

Wear **safety glasses** when working with bases.

Bases have a 'soapy feel'. They are used as **degreasing agents**.
When boiled with sodium hydroxide, fats are converted into **soaps** (an industrial process).

Bases change the colour of **indicators**:
- red litmus turns blue
- universal indicator turns blue in a strong base
- universal indicator turns violet in a weak base.

Definitions:
- A **base** is a substance that reacts with an acid to form a salt and water only, e.g. magnesium oxide + hydrochloric acid → magnesium chloride + water.
- An **alkali** is a soluble base, e.g. sodium hydroxide.

Bases **neutralise all acids**, e.g. HCl, H_2SO_4 and others, to form water and a salt, e.g. NaCl, Na_2SO_4, NH_4Cl, $(NH_4)_2SO_4$.

Bases react with solutions of many **metal salts** to precipitate $M(OH)_2(s)$ or $M(OH)_3(s)$. (Most metal hydroxides are insoluble.)

Concept map: The properties of bases

7 Materials and their properties

7.5 Salts

Some useful salts

★ **Common salt, sodium chloride**, NaCl, is used for seasoning and preserving food. Sodium chloride is also used in the manufacture of:
- chlorine (disinfectant and bleach)
- hydrogen (fuel and reducing agent)
- sodium hydroxide (used to make paper, soap, etc.)
- sodium carbonate (used to make glass).

★ **Sodium carbonate-10-water**, $Na_2CO_3.10H_2O$, 'washing soda', is used as a water softener, an ingredient of washing powders and bath salts.

★ **Sodium hydrogencarbonate**, $NaHCO_3$, 'baking soda', is added to self-raising flour. It decomposes at oven temperature to give carbon dioxide and steam, which make bread and cakes rise.

★ **Calcium sulphate-$\frac{1}{2}$-water**, $CaSO_4.\frac{1}{2}H_2O$, is plaster of Paris. When mixed with water it combines and sets to form a strong 'plaster cast'. It is also used for plastering walls.

★ **Silver bromide**, AgBr, is used in black-and-white photographic film.

★ **Iron(II) sulphate-7-water**, $FeSO_4.7H_2O$, is used in some kinds of 'iron tablets' which people take for anaemia.

★ **Barium sulphate**, $BaSO_4$, is used in 'barium meals' because barium ions show up well on X-rays and reveal the position of a stomach ulcer (see page 194).

★ **Copper(II) sulphate**, $CuSO_4$, is used as a fungicide for spraying grapes, potatoes and other crops.

★ **Calcium fluoride**, CaF_2, is added to toothpastes. Tooth enamel reacts with fluorides to form a harder enamel which is better at resisting attack by mouth acids. Many water companies add a small amount of calcium fluoride to drinking water.

★ **NPK fertilisers** contain ammonium nitrate, NH_4NO_3, and ammonium sulphate, $(NH_4)_2SO_4$, as sources of nitrogen; calcium phosphate, $Ca_3(PO_4)_2$, as a source of phosphorus; and potassium chloride, KCl, as a source of potassium.

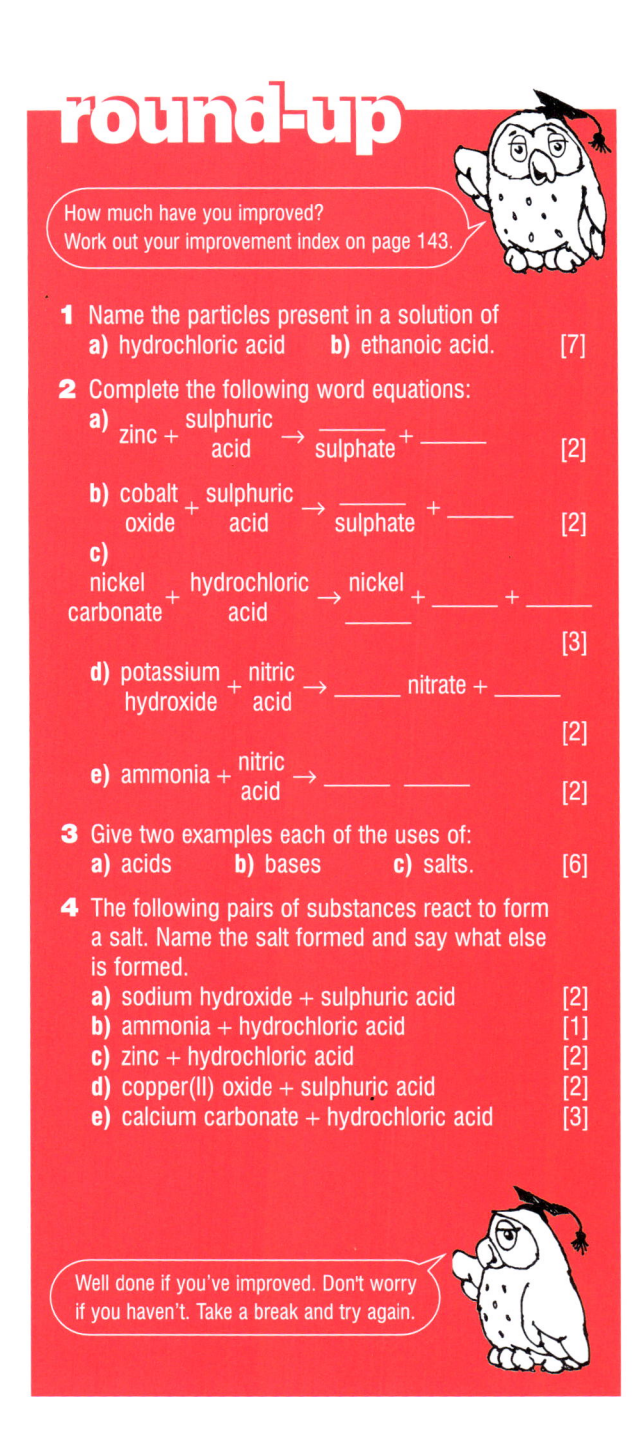

round-up

How much have you improved? Work out your improvement index on page 143.

1. Name the particles present in a solution of
   a) hydrochloric acid   b) ethanoic acid.   [7]

2. Complete the following word equations:
   a) zinc + sulphuric acid → _____ sulphate + _____   [2]
   b) cobalt oxide + sulphuric acid → _____ sulphate + _____   [2]
   c) nickel carbonate + hydrochloric acid → nickel _____ + _____ + _____   [3]
   d) potassium hydroxide + nitric acid → _____ nitrate + _____   [2]
   e) ammonia + nitric acid → _____ _____   [2]

3. Give two examples each of the uses of:
   a) acids   b) bases   c) salts.   [6]

4. The following pairs of substances react to form a salt. Name the salt formed and say what else is formed.
   a) sodium hydroxide + sulphuric acid   [2]
   b) ammonia + hydrochloric acid   [1]
   c) zinc + hydrochloric acid   [2]
   d) copper(II) oxide + sulphuric acid   [2]
   e) calcium carbonate + hydrochloric acid   [3]

Well done if you've improved. Don't worry if you haven't. Take a break and try again.

Air

preview

At the end of this topic you will:

- know the composition of Earth's atmosphere
- know the reactions and importance of oxygen
- understand oxidation–reduction reactions
- appreciate the effects of pollutants in the atmosphere.

MIND MAP Page 151.

How much do you already know? Work out your score on page 143.

Test yourself

1. Give the percentage by volume in pure dry air of oxygen and nitrogen. [2]
2. Give two industrial uses for oxygen. [2]
3. What is the name for an oxidation reaction in which energy is released? [1]
4. Describe a test for oxygen. [1]
5. Complete the sentence.

   Oxidation is the _____ of oxygen or the _____ of hydrogen or the _____ of electrons. [3]
6. How would you test an invisible gas to find out if it is carbon dioxide? [2]
7. Name four atmospheric pollutants and state one source of each. [8]

8.1 Separating gases from air

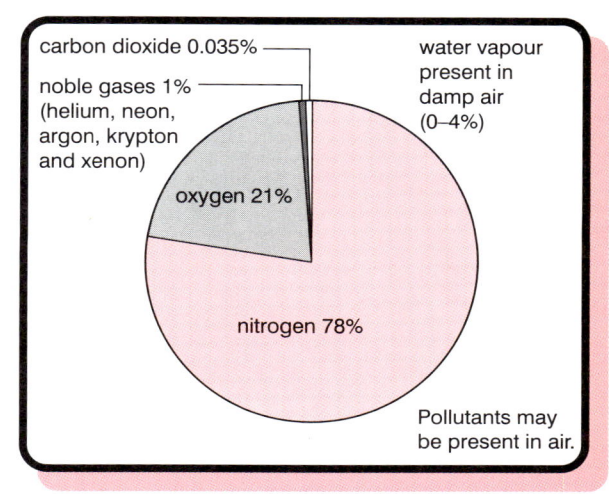

- carbon dioxide 0.035%
- noble gases 1% (helium, neon, argon, krypton and xenon)
- water vapour present in damp air (0–4%)
- oxygen 21%
- nitrogen 78%
- Pollutants may be present in air.

The composition of pure, dry air in percentage by volume

Oxygen, nitrogen and argon are obtained by fractional distillation of liquid air. Liquid air at $-190\,°C$ is fed into an insulated fractionation column. Nitrogen (boiling point $-196\,°C$) vaporises at the top of the column, argon (boiling point $-186\,°C$) vaporises from the middle of the column, and oxygen (boiling point $-183\,°C$) is left at the bottom of the column.

8.2 Oxygen

Plants and animals need oxygen for respiration. Aquatic plants and animals depend on the oxygen dissolved in water. Pollutants such as excess decaying organic matter use up dissolved oxygen and put aquatic animals and plants at risk.

Uses of pure oxygen

★ Aeroplanes which fly at high altitude, and all space flights, carry oxygen.

★ Deep-sea divers carry cylinders which contain a mixture of oxygen and helium.

★ An oxyacetylene torch (which burns ethyne, C_2H_2, in oxygen) has a very hot flame, about $4000\,°C$, and is used for welding and cutting metals.

Materials and their properties

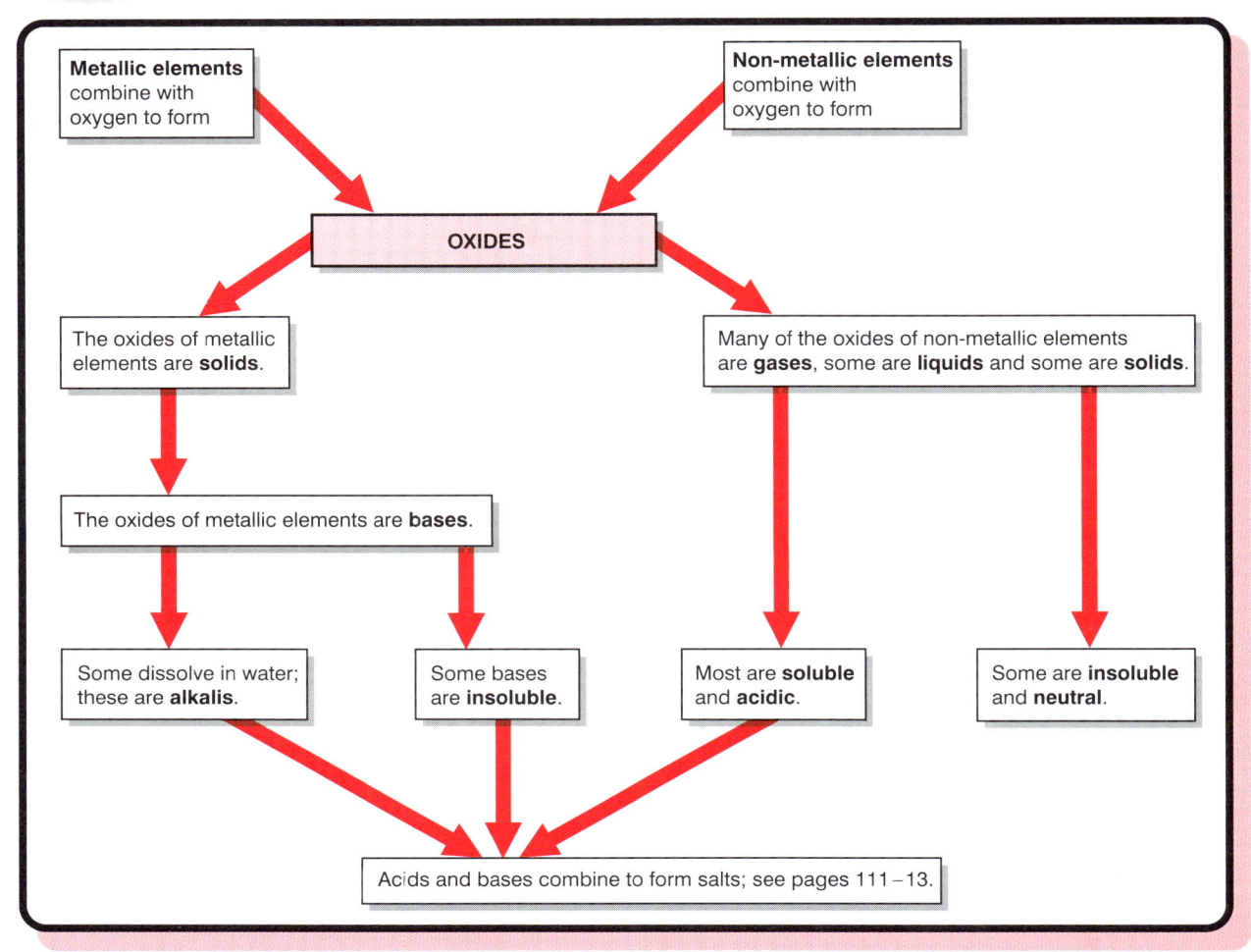

```
                Metallic elements                  Non-metallic elements
                combine with                       combine with
                oxygen to form                     oxygen to form
                              ↓                  ↓
                                    OXIDES
                        ↓                              ↓
        The oxides of metallic              Many of the oxides of non-metallic elements
        elements are solids.                are gases, some are liquids and some are solids.
                ↓                                          ↓
        The oxides of metallic elements are bases.
            ↓               ↓                      ↓                    ↓
    Some dissolve in water;  Some bases       Most are soluble      Some are insoluble
    these are alkalis.       are insoluble.   and acidic.           and neutral.
            ↓               ↓                      ↓
            Acids and bases combine to form salts; see pages 111–13.
```

Concept map: properties of oxides

★ Cast iron contains carbon, which is burnt off in a stream of oxygen to make steel.

★ Oxygen is pumped into polluted rivers and lakes.

Reactions of oxygen

Oxygen is colourless, odourless and slightly soluble in water. Many elements react with oxygen to form oxides.

★ Combination with oxygen is called **oxidation**.

★ Oxidation in which energy is given out is called **combustion**.

★ Combustion accompanied by a flame is called **burning**.

★ Substances which undergo combustion to give out a lot of energy are called **fuels**.

★ Many substances burn in oxygen, and all substances burn more rapidly in oxygen than in air.

★ **Test for oxygen:**
a glowing wooden splint lowered into oxygen starts to burn brightly.

The concept map above shows the properties of oxides.

8.3 Oxidation and reduction

Fact file

★ **Oxidation** = gain of oxygen or loss of hydrogen

★ **Reduction** = loss of oxygen or gain of hydrogen

★ An **oxidising agent** gives oxygen or takes hydrogen.

★ A **reducing agent** takes oxygen or gives hydrogen.

★ Oxidation and reduction occur together in **oxidation–reduction reactions** or **redox reactions**.

Here is an example of a redox reaction:

lead(II) oxide + hydrogen → lead + water

$PbO(s) + H_2(g) \rightarrow Pb(s) + H_2O(l)$

In this reaction,

- hydrogen has gained oxygen: hydrogen has been oxidised
- lead(II) oxide has lost oxygen: lead(II) oxide has been reduced
- hydrogen has taken oxygen from another substance: hydrogen is a reducing agent
- lead(II) oxide has given oxygen to another substance: lead(II) oxide is an oxidising agent
- oxidation and reduction are occurring together.

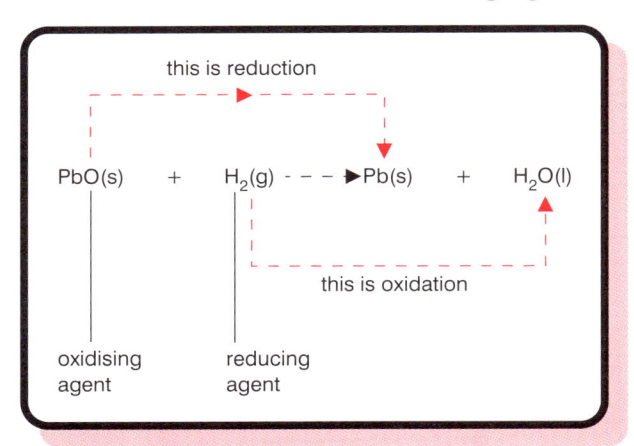

```
                this is reduction
            ┌──────────────────────┐
            ▼                      │
PbO(s)  +  H_2(g)  - - - ▶ Pb(s)  +  H_2O(l)
   │                                   ▲
   └───────────────────────────────────┘
                this is oxidation

oxidising      reducing
agent          agent
```

You can also think of oxidation and reduction in terms of electron transfer:

Oxidation	**R**eduction
Is	**I**s
Loss	**G**ain
of electrons	of electrons

8.4 Nitrogen

Nitrogen is a gas which does not take part in many chemical reactions. It combines with hydrogen to form ammonia. This reaction is the basis of the fertiliser industry. Many uses of nitrogen arise from its lack of reactivity.

★ Liquid nitrogen is used in the fast-freezing of foods.

★ Many foods are packed in an atmosphere of nitrogen to prevent oils and fats in the foods from being oxidised to rancid products.

★ Oil tankers, road tankers and grain silos are flushed out with nitrogen as a precaution against fire.

8.5 Carbon dioxide

Uses of carbon dioxide

★ Soft drinks are made by dissolving carbon dioxide in water under pressure and adding sugar and flavourings.

★ Solid carbon dioxide sublimes (turns into a vapour on warming). It is used as the refrigerant 'dry ice'.

★ Carbon dioxide is used in fire extinguishers because it does not support combustion and is denser than air.

Test for carbon dioxide

Carbon dioxide reacts with a solution of calcium hydroxide (limewater) to form a white precipitate of calcium carbonate.

carbon dioxide + calcium hydroxide → calcium carbonate + water

$CO_2(g) + Ca(OH)_2(aq) \rightarrow CaCO_3(s) + H_2O(l)$

8.6 The noble gases

Helium, neon, argon, krypton and xenon are the noble gases.

GROUPS OF THE PERIODIC TABLE Page 106.

★ Helium is used in airships because of its low density.

★ Neon and other noble gases are used in illuminated signs.

★ Argon is used to fill light bulbs.

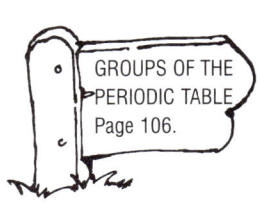

Materials and their properties

8.7 The problem of pollution

Carbon monoxide

Source: most of the carbon monoxide in the air comes from vehicle engines, where it is formed by the incomplete combustion of petrol. Soil organisms remove carbon monoxide from the air. However, in cities, where the concentration of carbon monoxide is high, there is little soil to remove it.

Effects: carbon monoxide combines with haemoglobin, the red pigment in the blood, and prevents haemoglobin from combining with oxygen. At a level of 1%, carbon monoxide will kill quickly; at lower levels, it causes headaches and dizziness and affects reaction times. Being colourless and odourless, carbon monoxide gives no warning of its presence.

A solution to the problem may come from fitting vehicles with catalytic converters.

Sulphur dioxide

Sources: major sources of the sulphur dioxide in the air are

- the extraction of metals from sulphide ores
- the burning of coal, which contains 0.5–5% sulphur, mostly in electricity power stations
- oil-burning power stations, because fuel oil contains sulphur compounds.

Effects: sulphur dioxide is a colourless gas with a very penetrating and irritating smell. Atmospheric sulphur dioxide is thought to contribute to bronchitis and lung diseases. It is a cause of acid rain.

Solutions to the problem: see below.

Acid rain

Rain is naturally weakly acidic because it dissolves carbon dioxide from the air. The pH of natural rainwater is 5.2. Rain with a pH below this is described as **acid rain**.

There are many effects of acid rain:

- damage to lakes and the fish and plants in them; see diagram below

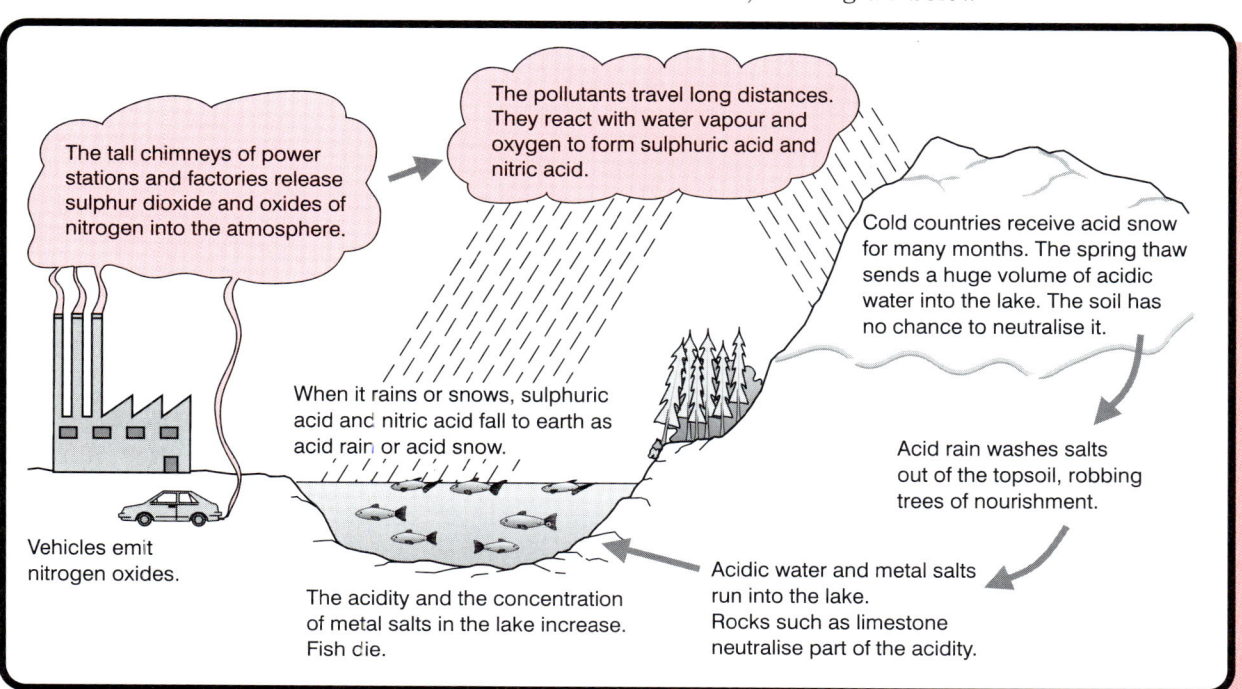

- The tall chimneys of power stations and factories release sulphur dioxide and oxides of nitrogen into the atmosphere.
- The pollutants travel long distances. They react with water vapour and oxygen to form sulphuric acid and nitric acid.
- When it rains or snows, sulphuric acid and nitric acid fall to earth as acid rain or acid snow.
- Vehicles emit nitrogen oxides.
- The acidity and the concentration of metal salts in the lake increase. Fish die.
- Cold countries receive acid snow for many months. The spring thaw sends a huge volume of acidic water into the lake. The soil has no chance to neutralise it.
- Acid rain washes salts out of the topsoil, robbing trees of nourishment.
- Acidic water and metal salts run into the lake. Rocks such as limestone neutralise part of the acidity.

Acid rain; its source and its effect on lake water

- washing of nutrients out of topsoil, resulting in poor crops and damage to trees
- costly damage to building materials, e.g. limestone, concrete, cement and metal.

What can be done?

Members of the European Community (EC) have agreed to make a 60% to 70% cut in their emissions of sulphur dioxide by 2003. Power stations must make a big contribution to solving the problem. Some lines of attack are:

1 Coal can be crushed and washed with a solvent to remove much of the sulphur content.

2 Fuel oil can be purified at the refinery – at a cost.

3 Sulphur dioxide can be removed from the exhaust gases of power stations. In **flue gas desulphurisation** (**FGD**), jets of wet powdered limestone neutralise acidic gases as they pass up the chimney of the power station.

4 In a **pulverised fluidised bed combustion** (**PFBC**) furnace, the coal is pulverised (broken into small pieces) and burnt on a bed of powdered limestone, which is 'fluidised' (kept in motion by an upward flow of air). As the coal burns, sulphur dioxide reacts with the limestone.

5 Nuclear power stations do not send pollutants into the air. However, they create the problem of storing radioactive waste.

RADIOACTIVITY Pages 179–184.

Smoke, dust and grit

Particles enter the air from natural sources such as dust storms, forest fires and volcanic eruptions. Coal-burning power stations, incinerators, industries and vehicles add to the pollution. When smoke particles mix with fog, **smog** is formed. Smog contains sulphuric acid, which has been formed from sulphur dioxide in the smoke. Breathing smog makes the lungs produce mucus, making it more difficult to breathe.

Methods of removing particles include:

- using sprays of water to wash out particles from waste gases
- passing exhaust gases through filters
- using electrostatic precipitators which attract particles to charged plates.

The exhaust gases of vehicles are not treated by any of these methods.

Oxides of nitrogen

Source: when fuels are burned in air, the temperature rises. Some of the nitrogen and oxygen in the air combine to form nitrogen monoxide, NO, and nitrogen dioxide, NO_2. This mixture (shown as NO_x) is emitted by power stations, factories and vehicles.

Effects: nitrogen monoxide is soon converted into nitrogen dioxide which is highly toxic, and which contributes to the formation of acid rain (see previous page).

Solution to the problem: the presence of a catalyst (platinum) brings about the reaction:

nitrogen monoxide + carbon monoxide → nitrogen + carbon dioxide

$$2NO(g) + 2CO(g) \rightarrow N_2(g) + 2CO_2(g)$$

The **catalytic converters** which are now fitted in the exhausts of cars reduce the emission of oxides of nitrogen in this way. Unleaded petrol must be used because lead compounds in the exhaust gases would stop the catalyst working.

Hydrocarbons

Sources: the hydrocarbons in the air come from natural sources, such as the decay of plant material (85%), and from vehicles (15%).

Effects: in sunlight, hydrocarbons react with oxygen and oxides of nitrogen to form **photochemical smog**. This contains irritating and toxic compounds.

Solutions to the problem: if the air supply in a vehicle engine is increased, the petrol burns completely. However, at the same time, the formation of NO_x increases. A solution may be

Materials and their properties

found by running the engine at a lower temperature and employing a catalyst to promote combustion.

Lead

Sources: lead compounds enter the air from the combustion of coal, the roasting of metal ores and from vehicle engines. Since the introduction of unleaded petrol, the level of lead in the atmosphere has fallen.

Effects: lead causes depression, tiredness, irritability and headaches. Higher levels of lead cause damage to the brain, liver and kidneys.

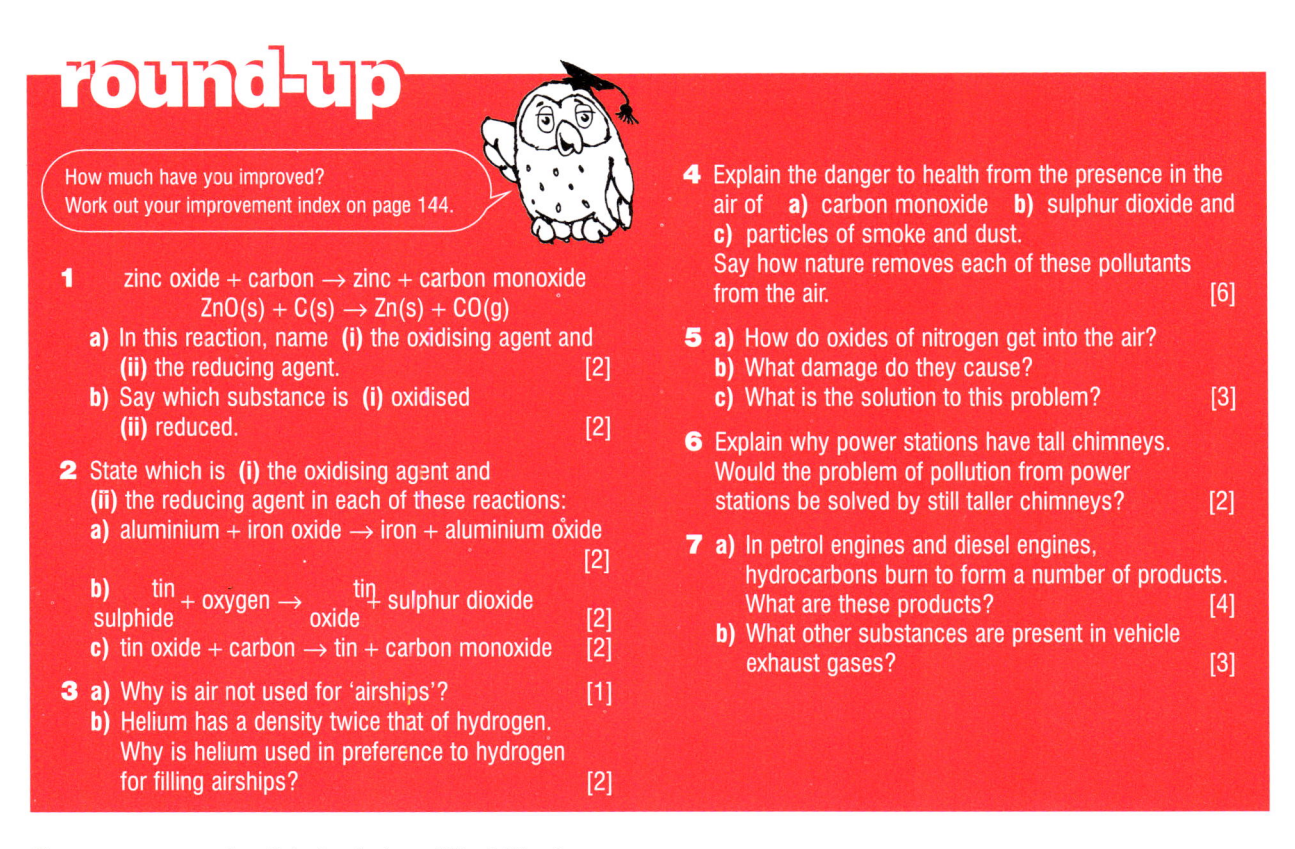

round-up

How much have you improved? Work out your improvement index on page 144.

1 zinc oxide + carbon → zinc + carbon monoxide
$ZnO(s) + C(s) \rightarrow Zn(s) + CO(g)$
  a) In this reaction, name **(i)** the oxidising agent and **(ii)** the reducing agent. [2]
  b) Say which substance is **(i)** oxidised **(ii)** reduced. [2]

2 State which is **(i)** the oxidising agent and **(ii)** the reducing agent in each of these reactions:
  a) aluminium + iron oxide → iron + aluminium oxide [2]
  b) tin sulphide + oxygen → tin oxide + sulphur dioxide [2]
  c) tin oxide + carbon → tin + carbon monoxide [2]

3 a) Why is air not used for 'airships'? [1]
  b) Helium has a density twice that of hydrogen. Why is helium used in preference to hydrogen for filling airships? [2]

4 Explain the danger to health from the presence in the air of **a)** carbon monoxide **b)** sulphur dioxide and **c)** particles of smoke and dust.
Say how nature removes each of these pollutants from the air. [6]

5 a) How do oxides of nitrogen get into the air?
  b) What damage do they cause?
  c) What is the solution to this problem? [3]

6 Explain why power stations have tall chimneys. Would the problem of pollution from power stations be solved by still taller chimneys? [2]

7 a) In petrol engines and diesel engines, hydrocarbons burn to form a number of products. What are these products? [4]
  b) What other substances are present in vehicle exhaust gases? [3]

Can you summarise this topic in a Mind Map?
To start you off ...

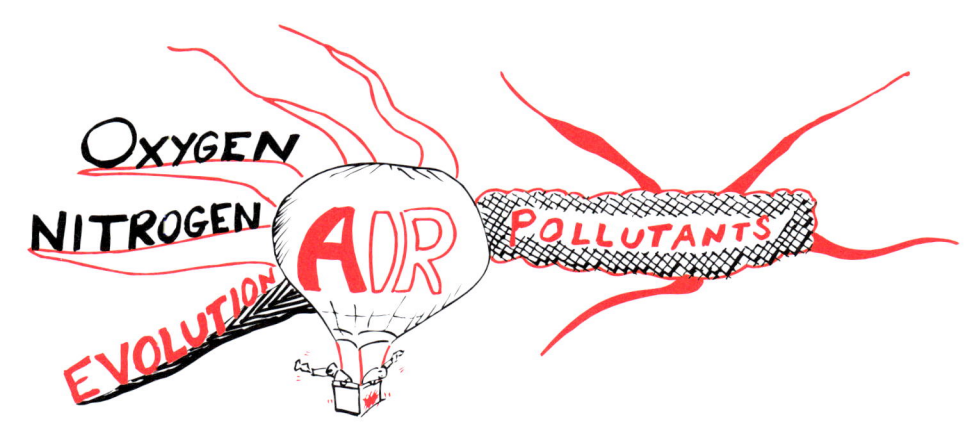

OXYGEN   NITROGEN   AIR   POLLUTANTS   EVOLUTION

Water

preview

At the end of this topic you will:

- appreciate the importance of the water cycle
- know how to purify water and how to test for water
- appreciate the dangers of water pollution.

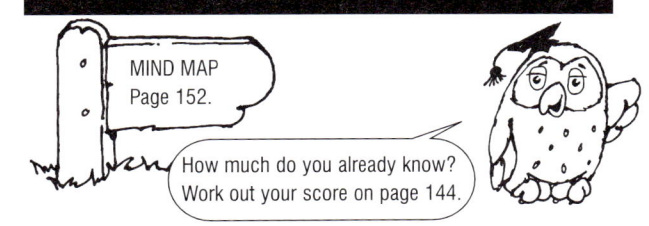

MIND MAP Page 152.

How much do you already know? Work out your score on page 144.

Test yourself

1 Name three processes which send water vapour into the atmosphere. [3]
2 Explain why rainwater is weakly acidic. [1]
3 State **a)** a test to find out whether a liquid contains water **b)** a test to show whether a liquid is pure water. [3]
4 Name three types of living things for which dissolved oxygen is important. [3]

9.1 The water cycle

The water cycle is shown in the diagram below.

9.2 Dissolved oxygen

The solubility of oxygen in water is 10 p.p.m. (parts per million), only about 10 g oxygen per tonne of

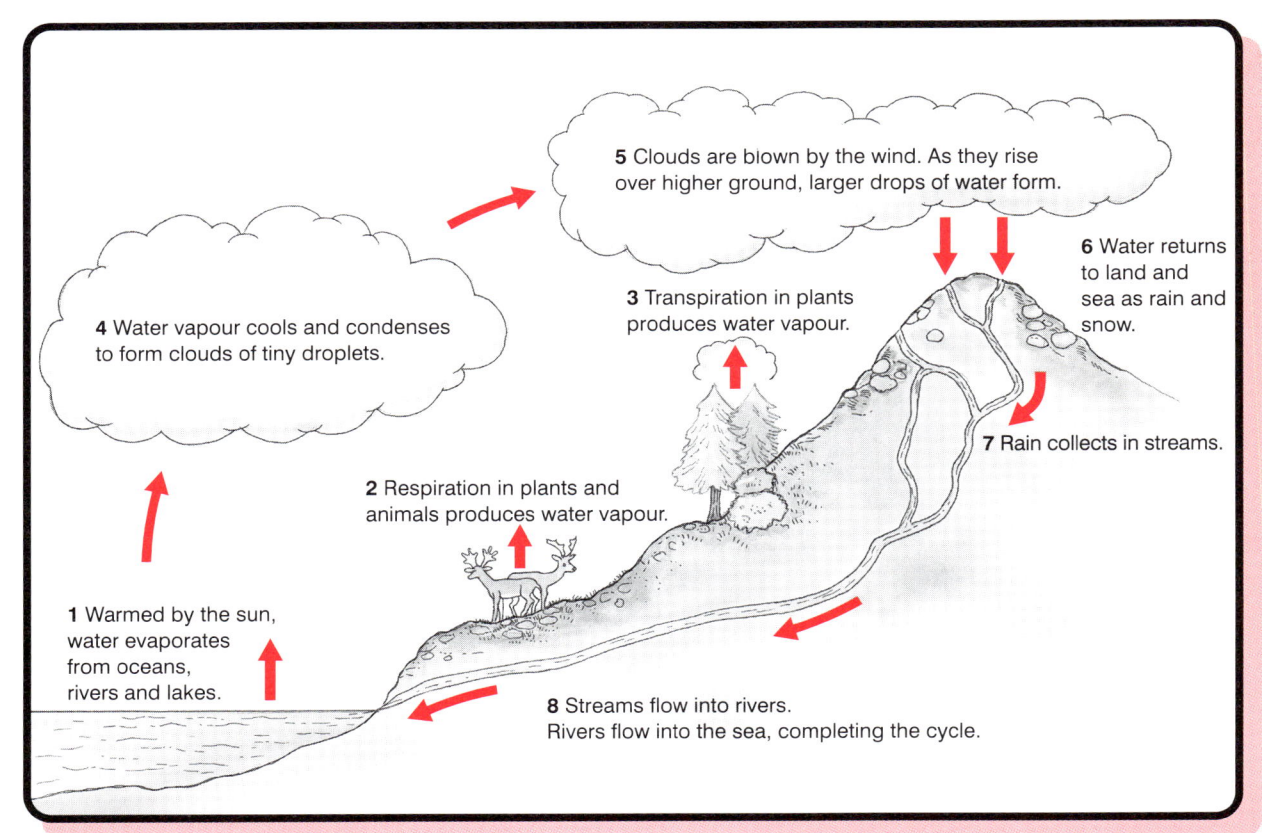

5 Clouds are blown by the wind. As they rise over higher ground, larger drops of water form.

6 Water returns to land and sea as rain and snow.

3 Transpiration in plants produces water vapour.

4 Water vapour cools and condenses to form clouds of tiny droplets.

7 Rain collects in streams.

2 Respiration in plants and animals produces water vapour.

1 Warmed by the sun, water evaporates from oceans, rivers and lakes.

8 Streams flow into rivers. Rivers flow into the sea, completing the cycle.

The water cycle

Materials and their properties

water. Fish and other water-living animals and plants depend on this dissolved oxygen. **Aerobic** bacteria which feed on plant and animal debris in the water also depend on the dissolved oxygen. If the oxygen is used up, for example to oxidise untreated sewage, the aerobic bacteria die and **anaerobic** bacteria take over. They digest biomass to produce unpleasant-smelling decay products.

9.3 Pure water

Test for water

or for any liquid that contains water:

Water turns white anhydrous copper(II) sulphate blue:

copper(II) sulphate + water → copper(II) sulphate-5-water

$CuSO_4(s) + 5H_2O(l) \rightarrow CuSO_4.5H_2O$

The water in copper(II) sulphate-5-water is combined as **water of crystallisation**. It gives the hydrate its crystalline form and colour.

Tests for pure water

1 The boiling point is 100°C at 1 atm.
2 The freezing point is 0°C at 1 atm.

9.4 Pollution of water

Pollution by industry

Many industrial firms have their factories on the banks of rivers and estuaries and discharge waste into the water. The National Rivers Authority was set up in 1989 to watch over the quality of rivers and prosecute polluters. It does not watch over tidal waters, and much sewage and industrial waste is poured into coastal waters and estuaries.

Pollution by sewage

Much sewage is discharged into rivers and estuaries without being treated. This gives swimmers at some of Britain's bathing beaches some nasty surprises. Dozens of British beaches fail to meet European Community standards because they have too high a level of coliform bacteria and faecal bacteria in the water.

Pollution by agriculture

Fertilisers: when an excess of fertiliser is used, some of it is not absorbed by the crop. Rain washes it out of the soil, and it accumulates in groundwater. The water industry uses groundwater as a source of drinking water. There is concern that nitrates in drinking water can lead to the formation of nitrosoamines, compounds which cause cancer.

Fertiliser which plants fail to absorb may be carried into the water of a lake, where it nourishes the growth of algae and water plants. This accidental enrichment of the water causes algae to form a thick mat of **algal bloom**, and weeds flourish. When algae die and decay, they use up dissolved oxygen. The fish in the lake are deprived of oxygen and die. The lake becomes a 'dead lake'. This process is called **eutrophication**.

Pesticides: these may enter lakes and become part of a food chain.

Pollution by oil

If a tanker has an accident at sea, oil is spilt, and a huge oil slick floats on the surface of the ocean. It is very slowly oxidised by air and decomposed by bacteria. While the oil slick remains, it poisons fish and glues the feathers of sea birds together so that they cannot fly. When the oil slick washes ashore, it fouls beaches.

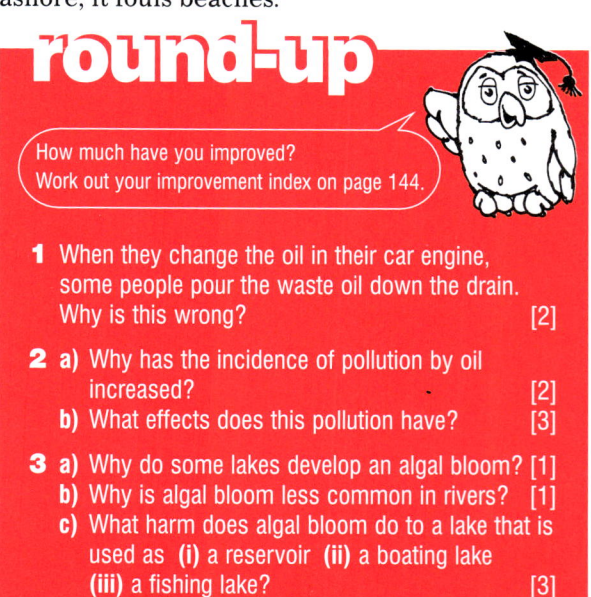

round-up

How much have you improved?
Work out your improvement index on page 144.

1 When they change the oil in their car engine, some people pour the waste oil down the drain. Why is this wrong? [2]

2 a) Why has the incidence of pollution by oil increased? [2]
   b) What effects does this pollution have? [3]

3 a) Why do some lakes develop an algal bloom? [1]
   b) Why is algal bloom less common in rivers? [1]
   c) What harm does algal bloom do to a lake that is used as (i) a reservoir (ii) a boating lake (iii) a fishing lake? [3]

Rocks

preview

At the end of this topic you will:

- know about the different types of rock
- know how useful materials are obtained from rocks.

How much do you already know? Work out your score on page 144.

Test yourself

1. Name
   a) the type of rock which is formed when lava solidifies
   b) the type of rock which is formed by compressing deposits of solid particles
   c) the type of rock formed by the action of heat and pressure on types **a** and **b**. [3]

2. Of which type of rock was the original crust of Earth made? [1]

3. Name three weathering agents which act on rocks and shape the landscape. [3]

4. State three uses for limestone. [3]

5. Name two materials that can be made from silica (sand). [2]

10.1 Types of rock

Igneous rocks

Molten rock beneath Earth's crust is called **magma**. Magma tends to rise, and, when cracks appear in the Earth's crust, magma is forced out from the mantle as lava. It erupts on to the surface of the Earth as a volcano. When volcanic lava cools, it crystallises to form **extrusive igneous rocks**. The faster the rate of cooling, the smaller the crystals that are formed. When magma crystallises below Earth's surface, **intrusive igneous rocks** are formed. Igneous rocks include

- basalt, an extrusive igneous rock formed by free-flowing mobile lava
- granite, an intrusive igneous rock
- pumice, formed from a foam of lava and volcanic gases.

Sedimentary rocks

The rocks on Earth's surface are worn down by weathering and by erosion. The fragments that are worn away are carried by winds, ice and rivers and eventually deposited as a **sediment**. A bed of sediment may form on a sea shore, on an ocean floor or in a desert. As more material is deposited on top, the pressure makes the sediment **lithify** – form a sedimentary rock. Sedimentary rocks may contain fossils – imprints of dead plants or animals which were included in the rocks as they formed. Fossils are used to date rocks. If a rock contains the marks of creatures known to have been alive 250 million years ago, the rock must be 250 million years old. Sedimentary rocks include

- limestone, formed from the shells of dead animals
- coal, formed from the remains of dead plants
- sandstone, compacted grains of sand.

Metamorphic rocks

Metamorphic rocks are formed from igneous and sedimentary rocks at high temperature or high pressure. Included among metamorphic rocks are

- marble, formed from limestone at high temperature
- slate, formed from clay, mud and shale at high pressure.

Earth's crust is composed of 8% sedimentary rocks, 65% igneous rocks and 27% metamorphic rocks.

10 Materials and their properties

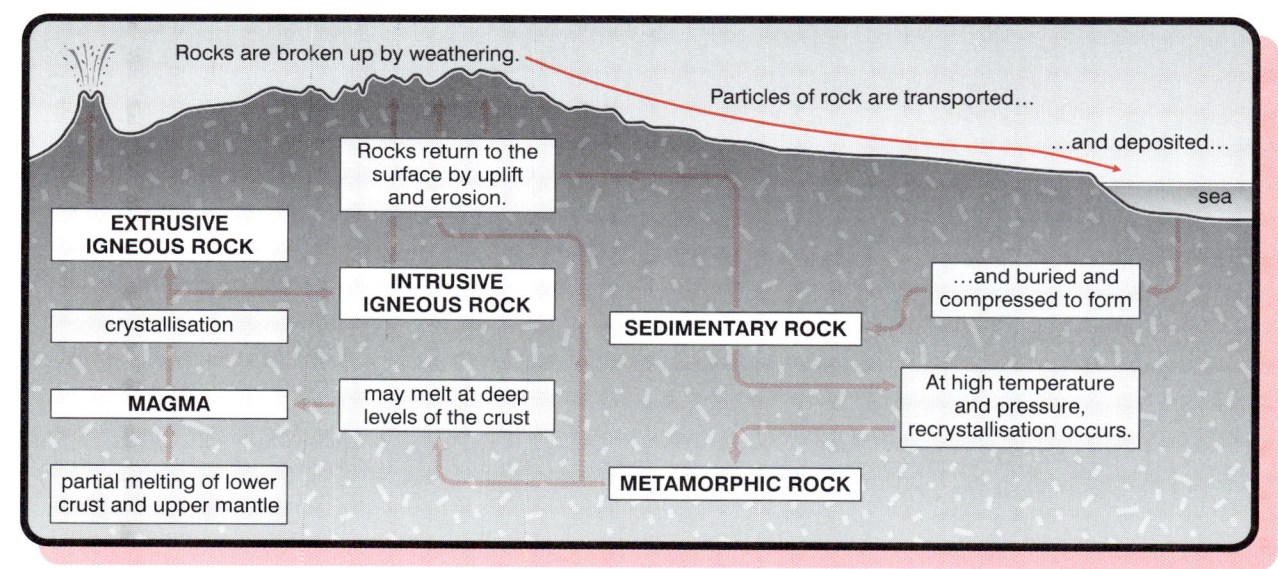

The rock cycle

The rock cycle

The interconversion between igneous rocks, sedimentary rocks and metamorphic rocks is called the **rock cycle** (see diagram above).

10.2 The landscape

Rocks are constantly being slowly broken down into smaller particles by **physical forces**, such as the wind, and **chemical reactions** which attack rocks. These processes are called **weathering**. When rocks are broken down and the particles are carried away by an agent such as water or wind, the process is called **erosion**. Weathering and erosion shape the landscape. The following agents shape the landscape:

- rainwater enters cracks in a rock, freezes, expands and opens the cracks wider
- rivers and streams carry material in solution and in suspension
- erosion happens when minerals dissolve slightly in water
- chemical reactions occur, e.g. between acidic water and limestone rocks
- glaciers move slowly over a landscape, wearing down rocks
- wind has a landscaping effect which is strongest in desert areas.

10.3 Materials from rocks

Many useful materials are obtained from rocks. Metals are extracted from compounds which occur in rocks; see page 127. Limestone and silica are important rocks. The concept map opposite shows the uses of limestone.

Silicon(IV) oxide (silica), SiO_2, is a source of silicon for silicon chips. Glass is made by melting silica with limestone and sodium carbonate.

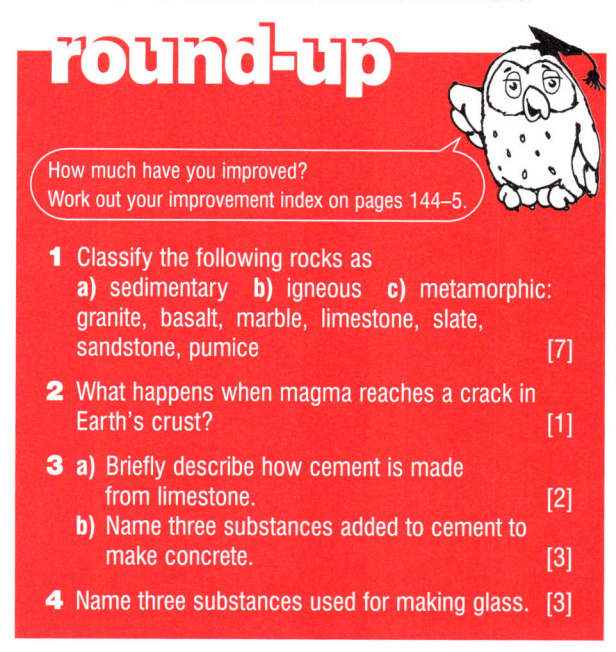

round-up

How much have you improved?
Work out your improvement index on pages 144–5.

1. Classify the following rocks as
   a) sedimentary **b)** igneous **c)** metamorphic:
   granite, basalt, marble, limestone, slate, sandstone, pumice [7]

2. What happens when magma reaches a crack in Earth's crust? [1]

3. **a)** Briefly describe how cement is made from limestone. [2]
   b) Name three substances added to cement to make concrete. [3]

4. Name three substances used for making glass. [3]

Rocks

LIMESTONE
calcium carbonate, $CaCO_3$

- Used in the manufacture of iron in the blast furnace; see page 127.
- melted with sand and sodium carbonate; see page 124. → glass
- Widely used as a building material; marble is another form of calcium carbonate.
- Powdered limestone is used to neutralise acidity in lakes and soils.
- Heated in a lime kiln forms calcium oxide (quicklime); see below.
  - add water → Calcium hydroxide (slaked lime) is
    - used to reduce excessive acidity of soils
    - mixed with sand to form mortar, used to hold bricks together.
- powdered limestone or chalk ($CaCO_3$) + clay or shale (SiO_2)
  - roast in a rotary kiln → cement (mainly calcium silicate)
  - Add calcium sulphate to prevent cement from setting too quickly. Add water, sand and crushed rock. A slow chemical reaction occurs. → concrete – a versatile building material → reinforced concrete

Concept map: materials from limestone

A lime kiln

1. Limestone and coke are fed in. The two cones lower to let the load fall in.
2. A draught of air enters. Coke burns in it.
3. Calcium carbonate decomposes. Calcium oxide (quicklime) is removed at the bottom of the kiln.
4. Air and carbon dioxide are swept out. Carbon dioxide can be removed from the stream of gas and sold.

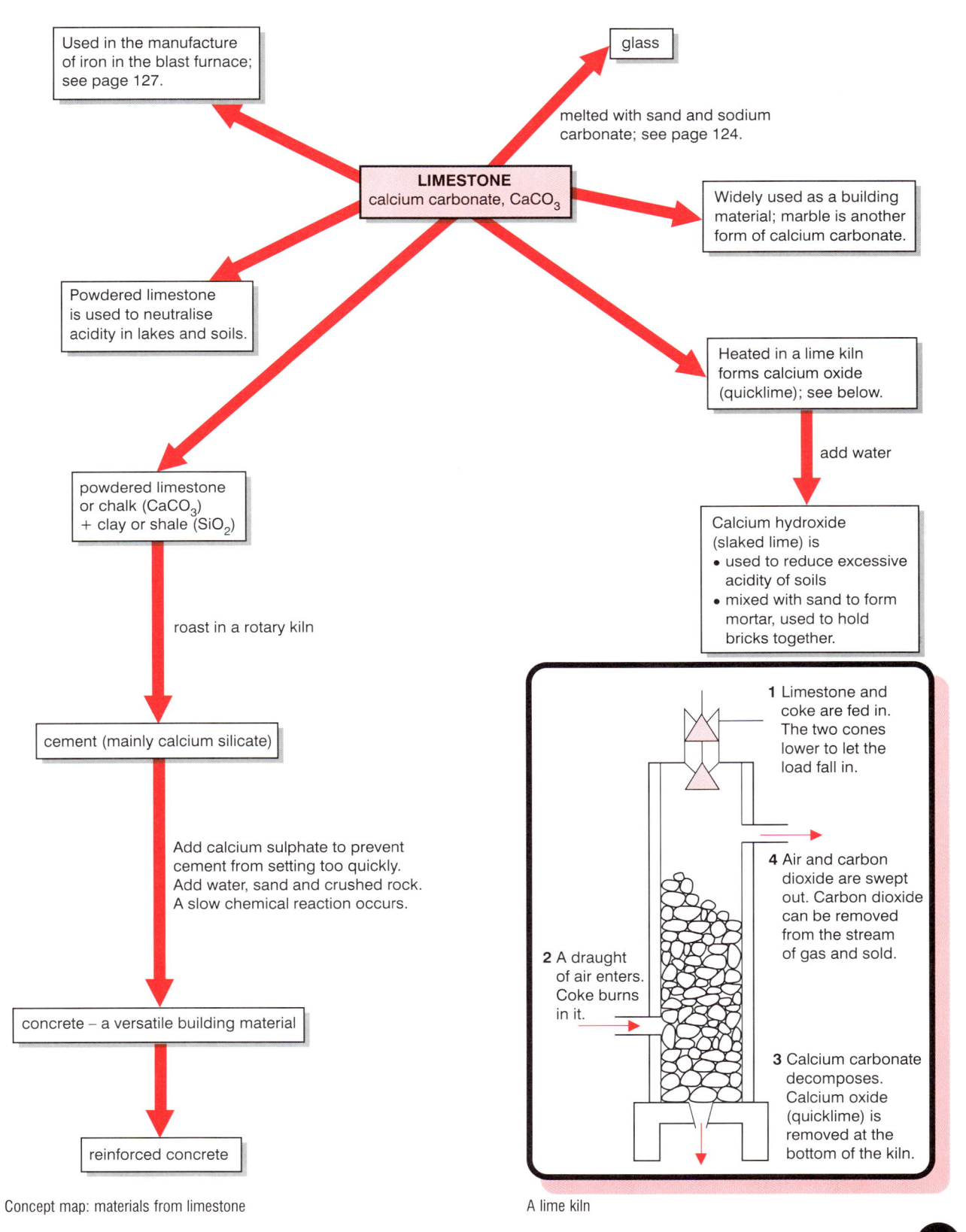

Metals and alloys

preview

At the end of this topic you will:

- be familiar with the chemical reactions of metals
- understand the reactivity series
- know methods of preventing the rusting of iron.

MIND MAP Page 153.

How much do you already know? Work out your score on page 145.

Test yourself

1. List three characteristics of metals. [3]
2. Name three metals that burn in air to form oxides. [3]
3. Name two metals that do not react when heated in air. [2]
4. Name three metals that react with cold water and say what products are formed. [5]
5. What is formed when a metal reacts with hydrochloric acid? [2]
6. In which groups of the periodic table do you find
   a) sodium b) magnesium c) transition metals? [3]
7. What method is used to extract very reactive metals from their ores? [2]
8. How is iron extracted from its ore? [3]
9. Name two metals which become coated with a film of oxide on exposure to the air. [2]

11.1 Reactions of metals

Most metals react slowly with air to form a surface film of metal oxide. This reaction is called **tarnishing**. Gold and platinum do not tarnish in air. Aluminium rapidly forms a surface layer of aluminium oxide and only shows its true reactivity if this layer is removed. The table below shows some of the reactions of metals.

metal	reaction when heated in oxygen	reaction with cold water	reaction with dilute hydrochloric acid
potassium sodium lithium calcium magnesium aluminium zinc iron	burn to form the oxides	displace hydrogen; form alkaline hydroxides.	react dangerously fast to form hydrogen and the metal chloride
		reacts slowly	displace hydrogen; form metal chlorides
		do not react, except for slow rusting of iron; all react with steam	
tin lead copper silver gold platinum	slowly form oxides without burning	do not react even with steam	react very slowly to form hydrogen and the metal chloride
	do not react		do not react

Reactions of metals

The metals can be placed in an order of reactivity which is called the **reactivity series**:

potassium	K
sodium	Na
lithium	Li
calcium	Ca
magnesium	Mg
aluminium	Al
zinc	Zn
iron	Fe
tin	Sn
lead	Pb
copper	Cu
silver	Ag
gold	Au
platinum	Pt

↑ increase in reactivity
↑ increase in the ease with which metals react to form ions
↑ increase in the ease of decomposition of compounds by heat and electrolysis

Part of the reactivity series of metals

11.2 Metals in the periodic table

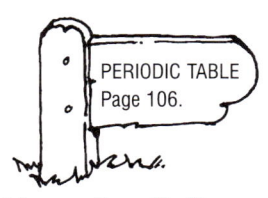

PERIODIC TABLE Page 106.

In Group 1 of the periodic table are the **alkali metals**, and in Group 2 are the **alkaline earths**. Aluminium is in Group 3. The less reactive metals tin and lead are in Group 4. The metals in the block between Group 2 and Group 3 are called the **transition metals**, e.g. iron, nickel, copper and zinc. For the differences between the physical and chemical properties of metallic and non-metallic elements, see page 92.

11.3 The reactivity series

Competition between metals to form ions

Metals high in the reactivity series form ions with ease. A metal which is higher in the reactivity series will displace a metal which is lower in the reactivity series from a salt, for example:

zinc + copper(II) sulphate → copper + zinc sulphate
(blue solution) (reddish brown solid) (colourless solution)

$$Zn(s) + CuSO_4(aq) \rightarrow Cu(s) + ZnSO_4(aq)$$

Compounds and the reactivity series

The higher a metal is in the reactivity series,
- the more readily it forms compounds
- the more difficult it is to split up its compounds.

Oxides

★ Hydrogen will reduce the oxides of metals which are low in the reactivity series, e.g.

copper(II) oxide + hydrogen $\xrightarrow{heat}$ copper + water

$$CuO(s) + H_2(g) \rightarrow Cu(s) + H_2O(l)$$

★ Carbon, when heated, will reduce the oxides of metals which are low in the reactivity series, e.g.

lead(II) oxide + carbon $\xrightarrow{heat}$ lead + carbon monoxide

$$PbO(s) + C(s) \rightarrow Pb(s) + CO(g)$$

★ Carbon monoxide is used to reduce hot iron oxide to iron.

iron(III) oxide + carbon monoxide $\xrightarrow{heat}$ iron + carbon dioxide

$$Fe_2O_3(s) + 3CO(g) \rightarrow 2Fe(s) + 3CO_2(g)$$

★ The oxides of metals which are high in the reactivity series, e.g. aluminium, are not reduced by hydrogen or carbon or carbon monoxide.

★ Silver and mercury are very low in the reactivity series. Their oxides decompose when heated.

11.4 Extracting metals

The method chosen for extracting a metal from its ore depends on the position of the metal in the reactivity series; see table overleaf.

Iron

The chief ores of iron are haematite, Fe_2O_3, magnetite, Fe_3O_4, and iron pyrites, FeS_2. The sulphide ore is roasted in air to convert it into an oxide. The oxide ores are reduced to iron in a blast furnace. The blast furnace is run continuously. The low cost of extraction and the plentiful raw materials make iron cheaper than other metals.

Materials and their properties

potassium, sodium, calcium, magnesium	Anhydrous chloride is melted and electrolysed.
aluminium	Molten anhydrous oxide is electrolysed.
zinc, iron, lead	Sulphides are roasted to give oxides which are reduced with carbon; oxides are reduced with carbon.
copper	Sulphide ore is heated with a controlled volume of air.
silver, gold	Found 'native' (as the free metals).

Methods used for the extraction of metals from their ores

11.5 Corrosion of metals

★ **Copper**: the green roofs you see on some buildings are of copper, which has corroded in the air to copper carbonate hydroxide, $Cu(OH)_2.CuCO_3$.

★ **Aluminium**: as soon as a fresh surface of aluminium meets the air, it is corroded to form a thin film of the oxide, which prevents air from reaching the metal below.

★ **Chromium** forms a protective oxide layer in the same way as aluminium. Stainless steel cutlery is made of a chromium–steel alloy (mixture).

★ **Nickel** forms a protective oxide layer as soon as a fresh surface of nickel meets the air. Nickel-plated steels are very useful.

★ **Lead** water pipes were used for centuries. However, water attacks lead slowly to form soluble lead compounds.

★ **Zinc** corrodes quickly in air to form a film of zinc carbonate. This protects the zinc beneath from further attack. Iron can be coated with zinc (**galvanised**) to protect it from rusting.

Rusting of iron and steel

The corrosion of iron and steel is called rusting. Rust has the formula $Fe_2O_3.nH_2O$, where n, the number of water molecules in the formula, varies.

The combination of reagents that attacks iron is water, air and acid. The carbon dioxide in the air provides the acidity. If the water contains salts, the speed of rusting is increased. In a warm climate, rusting is more rapid than at lower temperatures.

The rusting of iron is an expensive problem. The table below lists some of the methods used to protect iron and steel against rusting.

method	where used	comment
1 a coat of paint	large objects, e.g. ships and bridges	If the paint is scratched, the iron beneath it starts to rust.
2 a film oil or grease	moving parts of machinery	The protective film must be renewed.
3 a coat of metal		
a) chromium plating	trim on cars, cycle handlebars, taps	Applied by electroplating, decorative as well as protective.
b) galvanising (zinc plating)	galvanised steel girders are used in buildings	Even if the layer of zinc is scratched, the iron underneath does not rust. Zinc cannot be used for food cans because zinc and its compounds are poisonous.
c) tin plating	food cans	If the layer of tin is scratched, the iron beneath it rusts.
4 stainless steel	cutlery, car accessories	Steels containing chromium (10–25%) or nickel (10–20%) do not rust.
5 sacrificial protection	ships	Bars of zinc attached to the hull of a ship corrode and protect the ship from rusting.
	underground pipes	Bags of magnesium scrap attached to underground iron pipes corrode in preference to the pipes. The scrap must be replaced from time to time.

Rust prevention

11.6 Conservation

The Earth's resources of metals are limited. It makes sense to collect scrap metals and recycle them. In addition, there is a saving in fuel resources because less energy is needed for recycling than for extracting metals from their ores. There is another reason for conserving metals: the impact which mining has on the environment. Before recycling, scrap metals must be collected, sorted and stored until there is enough to process.

11.7 Uses of metals and alloys

The strengths of metals and **alloys** (mixtures of metals) find them thousands of uses; the table below lists just some of these.

metal/alloy	characteristics	uses
aluminium	low density good electrical conductor good thermal conductor reflector of light non-toxic resistant to corrosion	aircraft manufacture (Duralumin) overhead electrical cable saucepans, etc. car headlamps food packaging door frames, window frames, etc.
brass, an alloy of copper and zinc	golden colour, harder than copper, resists corrosion	ships' propellers, taps, screws, electrical fittings
bronze, an alloy of copper and tin	golden colour, hard, sonorous, resistant to corrosion	coins, medals, statues, springs, church bells
copper	good electrical conductor not corroded	electrical circuits water pipes and tanks
Duralumin, an alloy of aluminium	low density, stronger than aluminium	aircraft and spacecraft
gold	beautiful colour never tarnishes	jewellery, dentistry, electrical contacts
iron	hard, strong, inexpensive, rusts	construction, transport
lead	dense, unreactive, soft, not very strong	car batteries, divers' weights, roofing
magnesium	bright flame	flares and flash bulbs
mercury	liquid at room temperature	thermometers, dental amalgam for filling teeth
nickel	resists corrosion, strong, tough, hard	stainless steel
silver	beautiful colour and shine good electrical conductor good reflector of light	jewellery, silverware contacts in computers, etc. mirrors, dental amalgam
solder, alloy of tin and lead	low melting point	joining metals in an electrical circuit
steel, an iron alloy	strong	buildings, machinery, transport
tin	low in reactivity series	coating 'tin cans'
titanium	low in density, strong, very resistant to corrosion	high-altitude planes, nose-cones of spacecraft
zinc	high in reactivity series	protection of iron and steel by galvanising

The uses of some metals and alloys

11 Materials and their properties

round-up

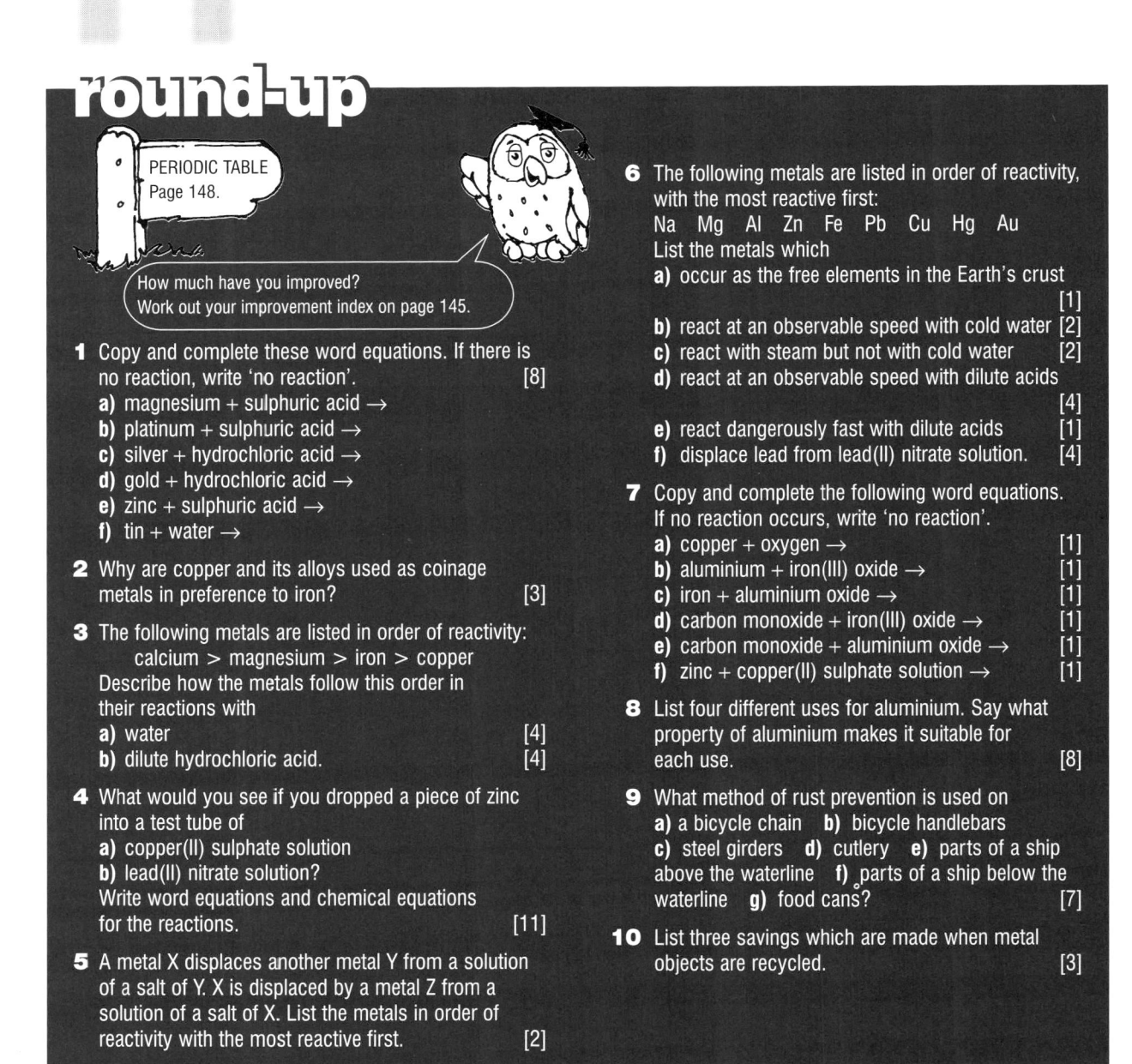

PERIODIC TABLE Page 148.

How much have you improved? Work out your improvement index on page 145.

1. Copy and complete these word equations. If there is no reaction, write 'no reaction'. [8]
   a) magnesium + sulphuric acid →
   b) platinum + sulphuric acid →
   c) silver + hydrochloric acid →
   d) gold + hydrochloric acid →
   e) zinc + sulphuric acid →
   f) tin + water →

2. Why are copper and its alloys used as coinage metals in preference to iron? [3]

3. The following metals are listed in order of reactivity:
   calcium > magnesium > iron > copper
   Describe how the metals follow this order in their reactions with
   a) water [4]
   b) dilute hydrochloric acid. [4]

4. What would you see if you dropped a piece of zinc into a test tube of
   a) copper(II) sulphate solution
   b) lead(II) nitrate solution?
   Write word equations and chemical equations for the reactions. [11]

5. A metal X displaces another metal Y from a solution of a salt of Y. X is displaced by a metal Z from a solution of a salt of X. List the metals in order of reactivity with the most reactive first. [2]

6. The following metals are listed in order of reactivity, with the most reactive first:
   Na Mg Al Zn Fe Pb Cu Hg Au
   List the metals which
   a) occur as the free elements in the Earth's crust [1]
   b) react at an observable speed with cold water [2]
   c) react with steam but not with cold water [2]
   d) react at an observable speed with dilute acids [4]
   e) react dangerously fast with dilute acids [1]
   f) displace lead from lead(II) nitrate solution. [4]

7. Copy and complete the following word equations. If no reaction occurs, write 'no reaction'.
   a) copper + oxygen → [1]
   b) aluminium + iron(III) oxide → [1]
   c) iron + aluminium oxide → [1]
   d) carbon monoxide + iron(III) oxide → [1]
   e) carbon monoxide + aluminium oxide → [1]
   f) zinc + copper(II) sulphate solution → [1]

8. List four different uses for aluminium. Say what property of aluminium makes it suitable for each use. [8]

9. What method of rust prevention is used on
   a) a bicycle chain   b) bicycle handlebars
   c) steel girders   d) cutlery   e) parts of a ship above the waterline   f) parts of a ship below the waterline   g) food cans? [7]

10. List three savings which are made when metal objects are recycled. [3]

Make your own Mind Map! This is only a starting point. The rest is up to you!

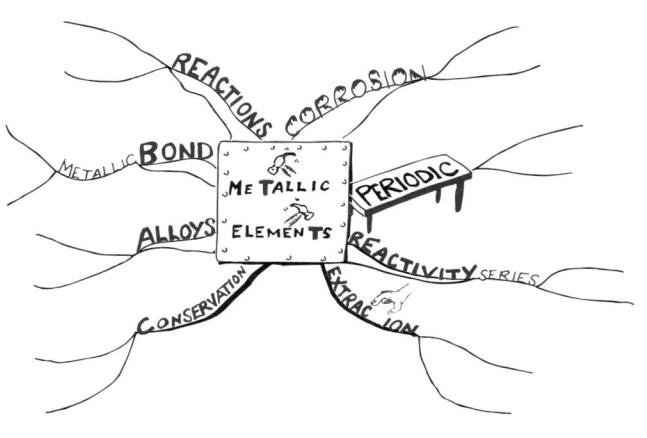

Reaction speeds

preview

At the end of this topic you will:

- understand the factors which can change the speed of a chemical reaction.

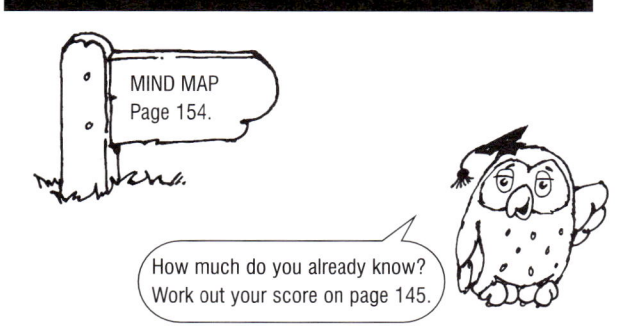

MIND MAP Page 154.

How much do you already know? Work out your score on page 145.

Test yourself

1. Which act faster to cure acid indigestion, indigestion tablets or indigestion powders? Explain your answer. [2]

2. a) Suggest three ways in which you could speed up the reaction between zinc and dilute sulphuric acid:

   $Zn(s) + H_2SO_4(aq) \rightarrow H_2(g) + ZnSO_4(aq)$ [3]

   b) Explain why each of these methods increases the speed of the reaction. [4]

3. Sketch an apparatus in which you could collect a gaseous product of a reaction and measure the rate at which it was formed. [5]

4. What is a catalyst? [2]

5. Why are catalysts important in industry? [2]

6. Name two reactions which depend on the absorption of light energy. [2]

12.1 Particle size

The reaction between a solid and a liquid is speeded up by using smaller particles of the solid reactant. The reason is that it is the atoms or ions at the surface of the solid that react, and the ratio of surface area:mass is greater for small particles than for large particles.

The diagram below shows an apparatus which you may have used to investigate the effect of particle size on the reaction:

calcium carbonate + hydrochloric acid → carbon dioxide + calcium chloride + water

$CaCO_3(s) + 2HCl(aq) \rightarrow CO_2(g) + CaCl_2(aq) + H_2O(l)$

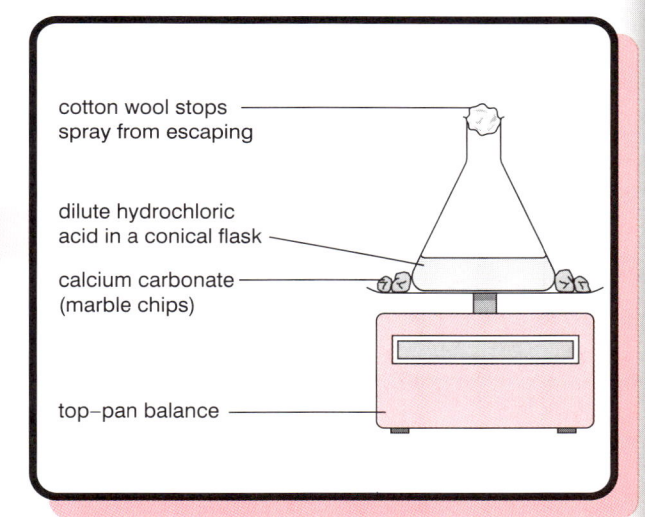

- cotton wool stops spray from escaping
- dilute hydrochloric acid in a conical flask
- calcium carbonate (marble chips)
- top–pan balance

The effect of particle size on the speed of a reaction

As the reaction happens, carbon dioxide is given off and the mass of the reacting mixture decreases.

1. Note the mass of flask + acid + marble chips.

2. Add the marble chips to the acid, and start a stopwatch.

3. Note the mass after 10 seconds and then every 30 seconds for 5–10 minutes.

4. Plot the mass against time since the start of the reaction.

5. Repeat with the same mass of smaller chips.

Materials and their properties

12

12.2 Concentration

A precipitate of sulphur is formed in the reaction:

sodium thiosulphate + hydrochloric acid → sulphur + sulphur dioxide + sodium chloride + water

$$Na_2S_2O_3(aq) + 2HCl(aq) \rightarrow S(s) + SO_2(g) + 2NaCl(aq) + H_2O(l)$$

1. Watch the precipitate of sulphur appear.
2. Note the time when the precipitate is thick enough to block your view of a cross on a piece of paper.
3. Repeat for various concentrations of acid and for various concentrations of thiosulphate.

The experiment shows that, for this reaction,

- rate of reaction is proportional to concentration of thiosulphate
- rate of reaction is proportional to concentration of acid.

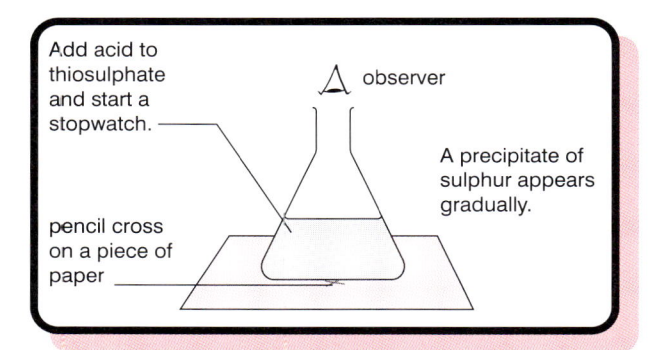

The time needed to complete the reaction decreases with increasing temperature.

The speed of the reaction increases with increasing temperature.

The effect of temperature on the speed of a reaction

The effect of concentration on the speed of a reaction

12.3 Pressure

An increase in pressure increases the rates of reactions between gases. As the molecules are pushed more closely together, they react more rapidly.

12.4 Temperature

The reaction between thiosulphate and acid can be used to study the effect of temperature on the rate of a reaction, as shown in the following graphs. This reaction goes twice as fast at 30°C as it does at 20°C. At higher temperatures, ions have more kinetic energy and collide more often and more vigorously, giving them a greater chance of reacting.

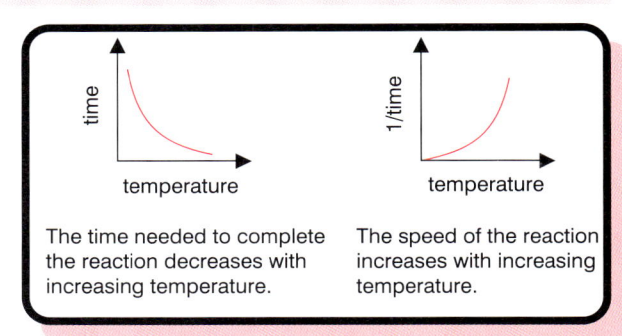

12.5 Light

Heat is not the only form of energy that speeds up chemical reactions. Light energy enables many reactions to take place, e.g. photosynthesis and photography.

12.6 Catalysts

Hydrogen peroxide decomposes to form oxygen and water:

hydrogen peroxide → oxygen + water

$$2H_2O_2(aq) \rightarrow O_2(g) + 2H_2O(l)$$

The decomposition takes place very slowly unless a **catalyst**, e.g. manganese(IV) oxide, is present. The rate at which the reaction takes place can be found by collecting the oxygen formed and measuring its volume at certain times after the start of the reaction, as shown in the diagram.

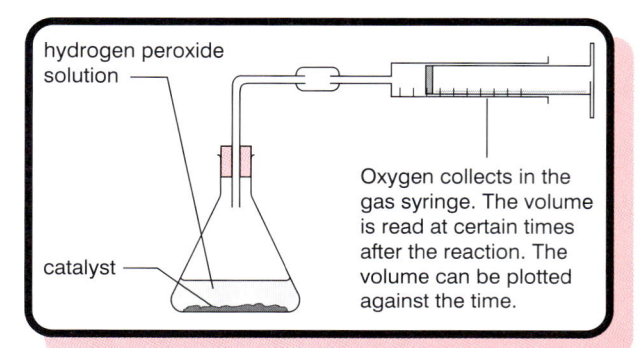

Collecting and measuring a gas

Reaction speeds

★ A catalyst is a substance which increases the rate of a chemical reaction without being used up in the reaction.

★ A catalyst will catalyse a certain reaction or group of reactions. Platinum catalyses certain oxidation reactions, and nickel catalyses some hydrogenation reactions.

★ Catalysts are very important in industry. They enable a manufacturer to make a product more rapidly or at a lower temperature.

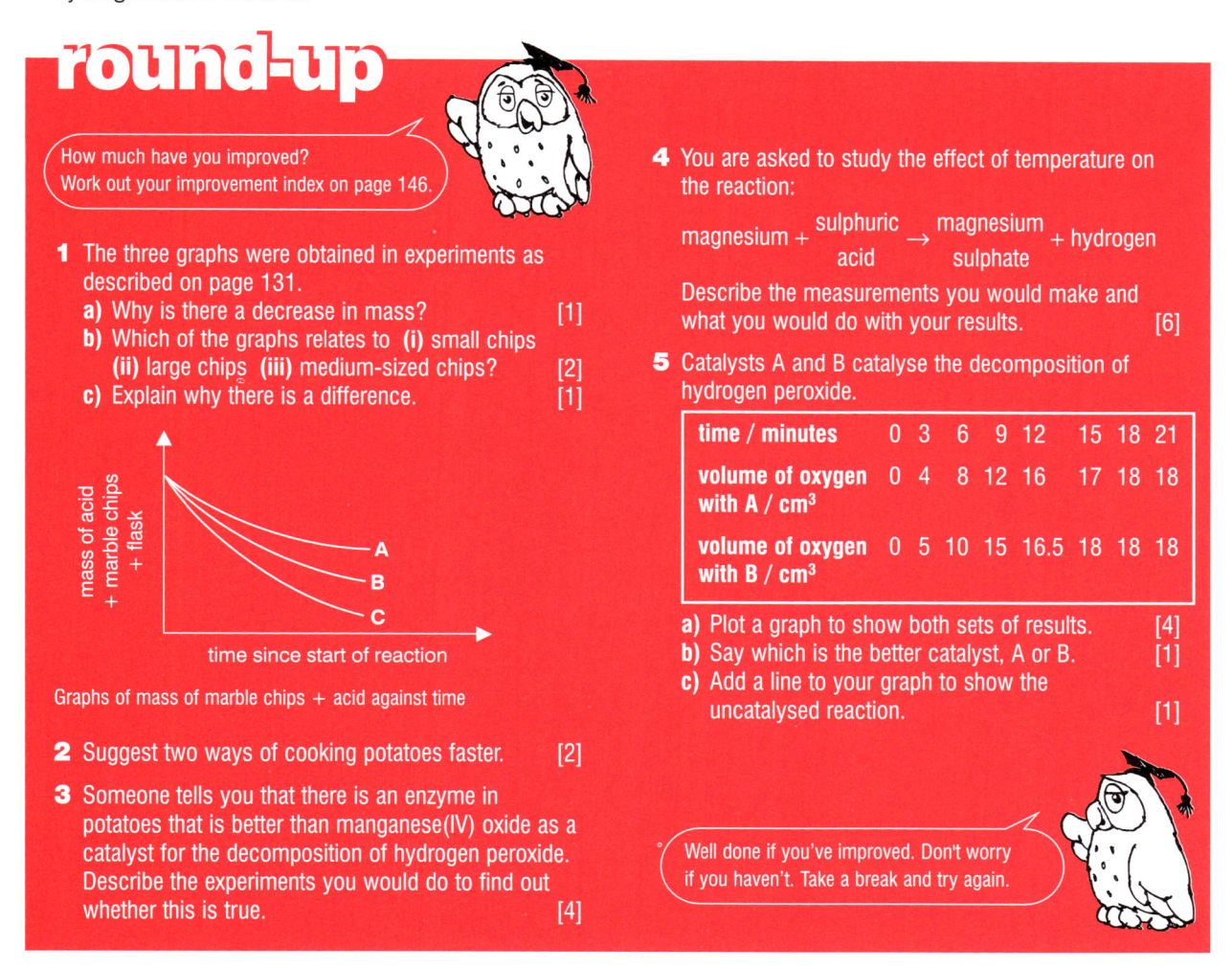

round-up

How much have you improved? Work out your improvement index on page 146.

1 The three graphs were obtained in experiments as described on page 131.
  a) Why is there a decrease in mass? [1]
  b) Which of the graphs relates to (i) small chips (ii) large chips (iii) medium-sized chips? [2]
  c) Explain why there is a difference. [1]

Graphs of mass of marble chips + acid against time
(y-axis: mass of acid + marble chips + flask; x-axis: time since start of reaction; curves labelled A, B, C)

2 Suggest two ways of cooking potatoes faster. [2]

3 Someone tells you that there is an enzyme in potatoes that is better than manganese(IV) oxide as a catalyst for the decomposition of hydrogen peroxide. Describe the experiments you would do to find out whether this is true. [4]

4 You are asked to study the effect of temperature on the reaction:

magnesium + sulphuric acid → magnesium sulphate + hydrogen

Describe the measurements you would make and what you would do with your results. [6]

5 Catalysts A and B catalyse the decomposition of hydrogen peroxide.

time / minutes	0	3	6	9	12	15	18	21
volume of oxygen with A / cm^3	0	4	8	12	16	17	18	18
volume of oxygen with B / cm^3	0	5	10	15	16.5	18	18	18

  a) Plot a graph to show both sets of results. [4]
  b) Say which is the better catalyst, A or B. [1]
  c) Add a line to your graph to show the uncatalysed reaction. [1]

Well done if you've improved. Don't worry if you haven't. Take a break and try again.

Can you summarise this topic in a Mind Map?
To start you off …

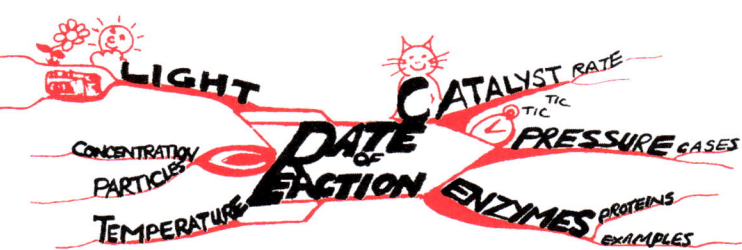

13 Fuels

preview

At the end of this topic you will:

- know about fossil fuels: coal, oil and natural gas
- know about the alkane hydrocarbons
- understand energy diagrams and heat of reaction.

MIND MAP Page 155.

How much do you already know? Work out your score on page 146.

Test yourself

1. Why are coal and oil called 'fossil fuels'? [3]
2. What is most of the world's coal used for? [1]
3. Crude oil can be separated into useful fuels and other substances.
   a) Name the process which is used. [1]
   b) Name four fuels obtained from crude oil. [4]
   c) Name two other useful substances separated from crude oil. [2]
4. Name the compounds with formulas a) CH_4 b) C_2H_6 c) C_3H_8 d) and name the series to which they belong. [4]
5. Explain what is meant by 'cracking'. [4]
6. Divide the following list of reactions into
   a) exothermic reactions b) endothermic reactions: [4]
   photosynthesis, combustion, cracking of hydrocarbons, respiration.

13.1 Fossil fuels

Coal

Coal is one of the fuels we describe as **fossil fuels**. It was formed from dead plant material decaying slowly over millions of years under the pressure of deposits of mud and sand. Coal is a complicated mixture of carbon, hydrocarbons and other compounds. Much of the coal used in the world is burned in power stations. The main combustion products are carbon dioxide and water.

COMBUSTION Page 116.

Petroleum oil and natural gas

Petroleum oil (usually called simply oil) and natural gas are fossil fuels: they are the remains of sea animals which lived millions of years ago. Decaying slowly under the pressure of layers of mud and silt, the organic part of the creatures' bodies turned into a mixture of hydrocarbons: petroleum oil. The sediment on top of the decaying matter became compressed to form rock, so oil is held in porous oil-bearing rock. Natural gas is always formed in the same deposits as oil.

The economic importance of oil

Industrialised countries depend on fossil fuels for transport, for power stations and for manufacturing industries. The petrochemicals industry makes a vast number of important chemicals from oil including fertilisers, herbicides, insecticides and the raw materials needed by the pharmaceutical industry. When we have used the Earth's deposits of coal, oil and gas, there will be no more forthcoming. The economies of all industrial countries will depend on alternative energy sources.

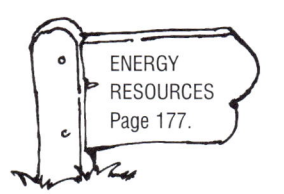

ENERGY RESOURCES Page 177.

13.2 Fuels from petroleum

Fractional distillation

FRACTIONAL DISTILLATION Page 97.

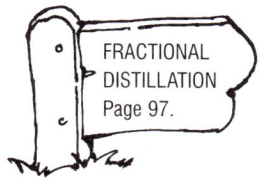

Crude oil is separated by fractional distillation into a number of important fuels. Each fraction is collected over a certain boiling point range. Each fraction is a mixture of hydrocarbons (compounds which consist of hydrogen and carbon only).

Petroleum gases (below 25 °C) are liquefied under pressure, and sold in cylinders as 'bottled gas' for use in gas cookers.

Petrol (gasoline) (40–75 °C) vaporises easily at the temperature of vehicle engines.

Naphtha (75–150 °C) is used in the manufacture of plastics, fabrics, medicines, agricultural chemicals, etc.

Kerosene (150–260 °C) needs a higher temperature for combustion. It is used as aviation fuel.

Diesel oil (260–340 °C) is used in the diesel engine which has a special fuel injection system to allow this fuel to burn. It is used in buses, lorries, etc.

Lubricating oil (340–500 °C) is used as a lubricant to reduce engine wear.

Fuel oil (>500 °C) is a viscous liquid with a high ignition temperature. It is used in ships, heating plants and power stations. To help it to ignite, fuel oil must be sprayed into the combustion chambers as a fine mist.

Bitumen is left as a residue at the bottom of the distillation column. It is used to waterproof roofs and pipes and to tar roads.

Petroleum fractions and their uses

The use that is made of each fraction depends on these factors, all of which increase with the size of the molecules:

- its boiling point range: the higher the boiling point range, the more difficult it is to vaporise in a vehicle engine.
- its viscosity: the more viscous a fraction is, the less easily it flows.
- its ignition temperature: the less easily a fraction ignites, the less flammable it is.

Cracking

We use more naphtha, petrol and kerosene than heavy fuel oil. The technique called **cracking** is used to convert the high boiling point range fractions into the lower boiling point range fractions petrol and kerosene.

vapour of hydrocarbon with large molecules and high boiling point $\xrightarrow[\text{e.g. } Al_2O_3 \text{ or } SiO_2]{\textit{cracking} \text{ passed over a heated catalyst}}$ mixture of hydrocarbons with smaller molecules and low boiling point, and hydrogen. The mixture is separated by fractional distillation.

13.3 Alkanes

Most of the hydrocarbons in crude oil belong to the **homologous series** called **alkanes**; they are shown in the table. A homologous series is a set of compounds with similar chemical properties in which one member of the series differs from the next by a $-CH_2-$ group. Physical properties such as boiling point vary gradually as the size of the molecules increases.

The alkanes	
name	formula
methane	CH_4
ethane	C_2H_6
propane	C_3H_8
butane	C_4H_{10}
pentane	C_5H_{12}
hexane	C_6H_{14}
general formula	C_nH_{2n+2}

Materials and their properties

Here are the structural formulas for the first three alkenes:

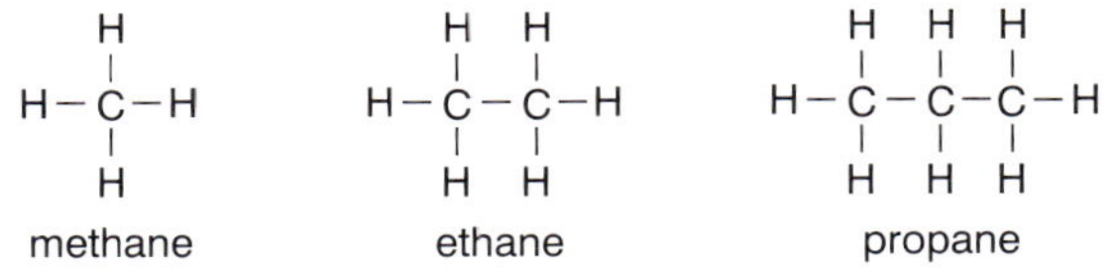

methane, ethane, propane

Alkanes do not take part in many chemical reactions. Their important reaction is combustion.

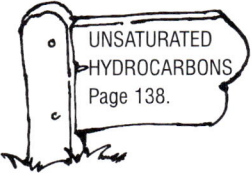

Alkanes contain only single bonds between carbon atoms. Such hydrocarbons are called **saturated hydrocarbons**. This is in contrast to the alkenes, which contain double bonds and are **unsaturated hydrocarbons**.

UNSATURATED HYDROCARBONS Page 138.

13.4 Energy and chemical reactions

Exothermic reactions

1. **Combustion**: the combustion of hydrocarbons is an exothermic reaction – heat is given out.

   methane + oxygen → carbon dioxide + water; heat is given out

   $CH_4(g) + 2O_2(g) \rightarrow CO_2(g) + 2H_2O(l)$

   octane + oxygen → carbon dioxide + water; heat is given out

   ★ An oxidation reaction in which heat is given out is **combustion**.
   ★ Combustion accompanied by a flame is **burning**.
   ★ A substance which is oxidised with the release of energy is a **fuel**.

2. **Respiration**: our bodies obtain energy from the oxidation of foods, e.g. glucose, in cells. This process is called **cellular respiration**.

   glucose + oxygen → carbon dioxide + water; energy is given out

   $C_6H_{12}O_6(aq) + 6O_2(g) \rightarrow 6CO_2(g) + 6H_2O(l)$

3. **Neutralisation**

   hydrogen ion + hydroxide ion → water; heat is given out

   $H^+(aq) + OH^-(aq) \rightarrow H_2O(l)$

Endothermic reactions

1. **Photosynthesis**: plants convert carbon dioxide and water into sugars in the process of photosynthesis.

   catalysed by chlorophyll
   carbon dioxide + water → glucose + oxygen; energy of sunlight is taken in

   $6CO_2(g) + 6H_2O(l) \rightarrow C_6H_{12}O_6(aq) + 6O_2(g)$

2. **Thermal decomposition**; for example the cracking of hydrocarbons and the decomposition of calcium carbonate:

   calcium carbonate $\xrightarrow{heat}$ calcium oxide + carbon dioxide; heat is taken in

   $CaCO_3(s) \rightarrow CaO(s) + CO_2(g)$

13.5 Heat of reaction

The atoms, ions or molecules in a substance are held together by chemical bonds. Energy must be supplied if these chemical bonds are to be broken. When bonds are created, energy is given out. The reactants and the products possess different amounts of energy because they have different chemical bonds; see diagram below.

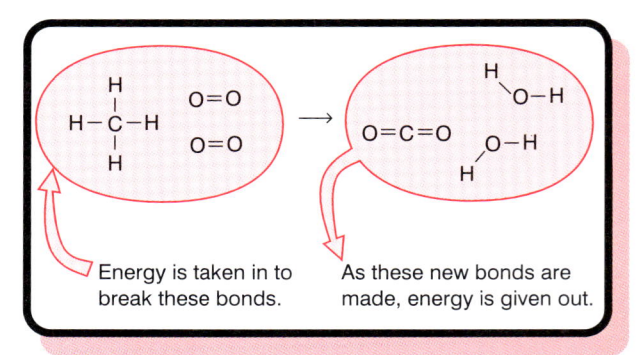

Energy is taken in to break these bonds. As these new bonds are made, energy is given out.

Bonds broken and made when methane burns

In the reaction shown, the energy taken in is less than the energy given out: this reaction is exothermic.

The graphs below are energy diagrams, in which:

- H = energy content of a substance
- ΔH = heat of reaction = heat taken in or given out during a reaction
- ΔH = energy of products – energy of reactants
- In an **exothermic reaction**, the products of the reaction contain less energy than the reactants. When the reactants change into the products, they get rid of their extra energy by giving out heat to the surroundings.
- In an **endothermic reaction**, the reactants have to climb to a higher energy level to change into the products. To do this, they take energy from the surroundings: they cool the surroundings.

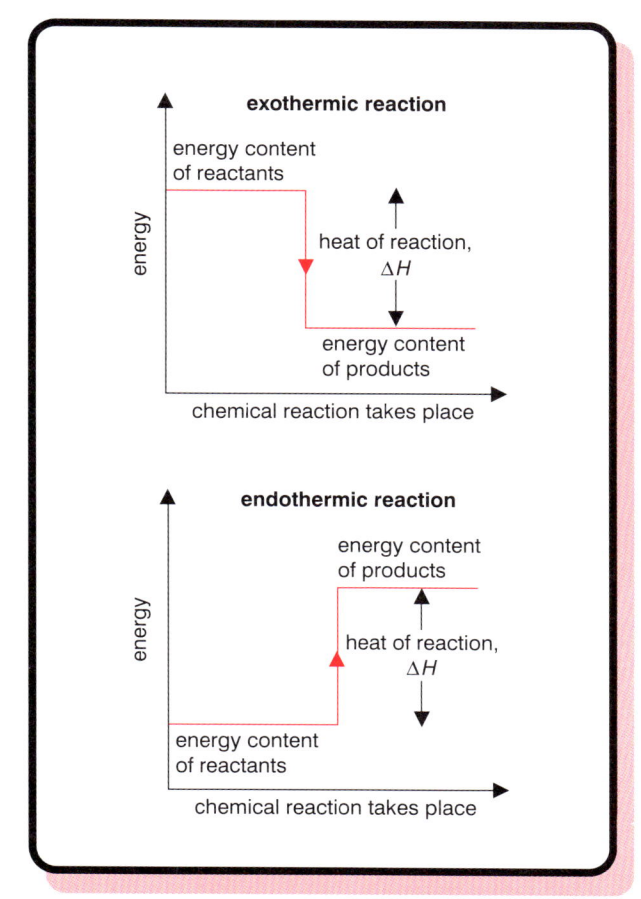

Energy diagrams for an exothermic reaction and an endothermic reaction

round-up

How much have you improved?
Work out your improvement index on page 146.

1. Explain **a)** what is meant by a 'fossil fuel' [4]
   b) why the Earth's reserves of fossil fuels are running out. [2]

2. **a)** Briefly explain how crude oil is separated into natural gas, gasoline, naphtha, kerosene, diesel oil and fuel oil. [2]
   b) State one use for each of the fractions. [6]
   c) Give three differences in properties between gasoline and fuel oil. [3]
   d) A barrel of oil yields less gasoline than fuel oil. The demand for gasoline is, however, greater than the demand for fuel oil. Explain why fuel oil cannot be used in car engines. [2]
   e) Briefly explain why an increase in the price of oil has a great impact worldwide. [4]

3. Draw an energy diagram for the combustion of petrol to form carbon dioxide and water. Mark ΔH on your diagram, and state whether the reaction is exothermic or endothermic. [3]

4. Draw an energy diagram for the cracking of heavy fuel oil to form kerosene. Mark ΔH on your diagram, and state whether the reaction is exothermic or endothermic. [3]

Well done if you've improved. Don't worry if you haven't. Take a break and try again.

Alkenes and plastics

14

preview

At the end of this topic you will:

- know the general formula and reactions of alkenes
- understand the differences between thermoplastic and thermosetting plastics
- know the names and uses of some poly(alkenes).

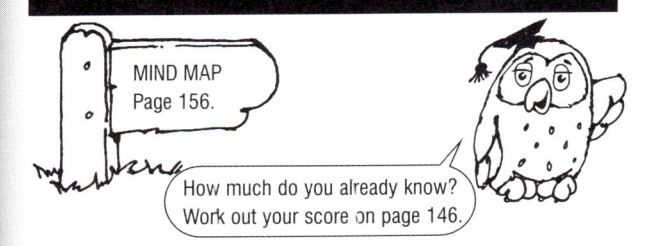

MIND MAP Page 156.

How much do you already know? Work out your score on page 146.

Test yourself

1. Draw the functional group of an alkene. Say in what type of reactions this functional group takes part. [2]
2. Unlike alkanes, alkenes are not used as fuels. Why is this? [2]
3. Explain what is meant by addition polymerisation. [2]
4. Name two sets of plastics which differ in their reaction to heat. Describe the difference in behaviour. [4]
5. By what types of process are the two different kinds of plastics moulded? [2]

14.1 Alkenes

The alkenes are a homologous series of hydrocarbons, as shown in the following table.

The alkenes	
name	formula
ethene	C_2H_4
propene	C_3H_6
butene	C_4H_8
general formula	C_nH_{2n}

The double bond (see page 103) between the carbon atoms is the **functional group** of alkenes, and is responsible for their reactions. Alkenes are described as **unsaturated hydrocarbons**. They will react with hydrogen in an **addition reaction** to form saturated hydrocarbons (alkanes).

ethene + hydrogen → ethane

14.2 Reactions of alkenes

Alkenes are not used as fuels because they are an important source of other compounds. The double bond makes them chemically reactive, and they are starting materials in the manufacture of plastics, fibres, solvents and other chemicals.

Addition polymerisation: in this reaction, many molecules of the **monomer**, e.g. ethene, join together (**polymerise**) to form the **polymer**, e.g. poly(ethene). The polymers are plastics.

The conditions needed are:

ethene $\xrightarrow{\text{pass at high pressure over a heated catalyst}}$ poly(ethene)

$n\text{CH}_2\text{=CH}_2 \longrightarrow (-\text{CH}_2-\text{CH}_2-)_n$

In poly(ethene), n is between 30 000 and 40 000. Poly(ethene) is used for making plastic bags, for kitchenware (buckets, bowls, etc.), for laboratory tubing and for toys. It is flexible and difficult to break. Polymers of alkenes are called poly(alkenes).

Alkenes and plastics

14.3 Uses of plastics

Plastics are
- strong
- low in density
- good insulators of heat and electricity
- resistant to attack by chemicals
- smooth
- able to be moulded into different shapes.

There are two kinds of plastics, **thermoplastics** and **thermosetting plastics**. The difference is shown in the diagram below.

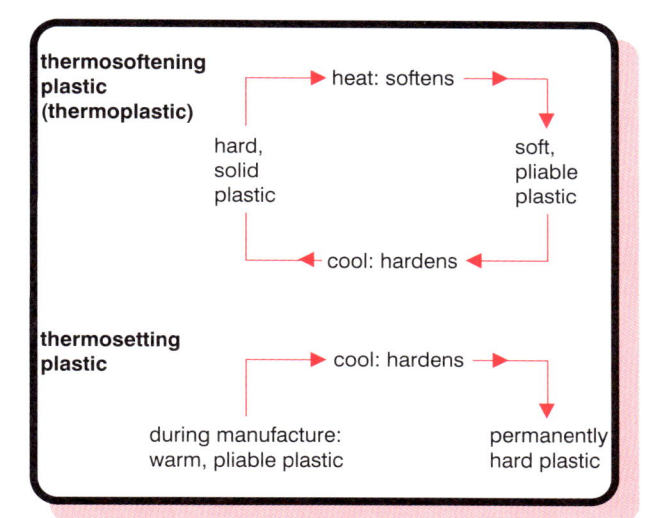

```
thermosoftening
plastic              → heat: softens →
(thermoplastic)
                hard,                    soft,
                solid                    pliable
                plastic                  plastic
                     ← cool: hardens ←


thermosetting
plastic              → cool: hardens →

             during manufacture:         permanently
             warm, pliable plastic       hard plastic
```

The reason for the difference in behaviour is a difference in structure, as shown.

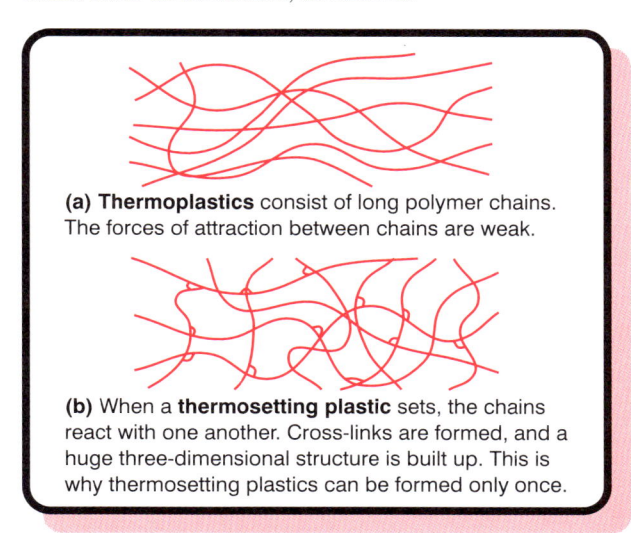

(a) Thermoplastics consist of long polymer chains. The forces of attraction between chains are weak.

(b) When a **thermosetting plastic** sets, the chains react with one another. Cross-links are formed, and a huge three-dimensional structure is built up. This is why thermosetting plastics can be formed only once.

The structure of **(a)** a thermosoftening plastic
(b) a thermosetting plastic

Moulding of thermoplastics can be a **continuous process**: solid granules of the plastic are fed into one end of the moulding machine, softened by heat and then moulded to come out of the other end in the shape of tubes, sheets or rods. It is easy to manufacture coloured articles by adding a pigment to the plastic.

The moulding of thermosetting plastics is a **batch process**. The monomer is poured into the mould and heated. As it polymerises, the plastic solidifies and a press forms it into the required shape while it is setting.

Both types of plastic have their advantages. A material used for electrical fittings and counter tops must be able to withstand high temperatures without softening. 'Thermosets' are used.

round-up

How much have you improved?
Work out your improvement index on page 147.

1. **a)** Write **(i)** the molecular formulas **(ii)** the structural formulas of ethane and ethene. [4]
   b) State the difference between the chemical bonding in the two compounds. [4]

2. State the advantage that plastic has
   a) over china for making cups and saucers and dolls [1]
   b) over lead for making toy farmyard animals and soldiers [1]
   c) over glass for making motorbike windscreens. [1]

3. The formula of propenamide is:
   $$\begin{array}{c} H-C-CONH_2 \\ \| \\ H-C-H \end{array}$$
   Draw the formula of the polymer poly(propenamide). [1]

4. **a)** What does the word 'plastic' mean? [2]
   b) There are two big classes of plastics, which behave differently when heated. Name the two classes. Describe the difference in behaviour. Say how this difference is related to the molecular nature of the plastics. [5]

5. **a)** What is meant by the statement that plastics are non-biodegradable? [1]
   b) Why is this a disadvantage? [1]
   c) What is wrong with burning plastic waste? [2]
   d) Suggest an alternative to burning plastic waste. [1]

Answers

1 Test yourself (page 88)

Matter and the kinetic theory

1. solid (✓), liquid (✓), gas (✓).
2. A pure solid melts at a fixed temperature (✓); an impure solid melts over a range of temperature (✓).
3. Evaporation takes place over a range of temperature (✓). Boiling takes place at a certain temperature (✓).
4. Bubbles of vapour appear in the body of the liquid (✓).
5. In a pressure cooker, water boils at a temperature above 100°C (✓) and foods cook faster at higher temperature (✓).
6. On a high mountain, air pressure is lower than at sea level (✓), and water boils below 100°C (✓).
7. a) Both change shape when a force is applied (✓).
   b) When the force ceases, a plastic material retains its new shape (✓), but an elastic material returns to its previous shape (✓).
8. Crystals consist of a regular arrangement of particles (✓). As a result the surfaces are smooth (✓) and reflect light (✓).
9. The particles that make up the solid gain enough energy to break free from the attractive forces (✓) between particles which maintain the solid structure, and the particles move independently (✓).
10. In a gas, e.g. steam, the molecules are very much further apart (✓) than in a liquid (✓).
11. Particles (✓) of salt dissolve (✓) and spread out (✓) through the soup.

Your score: ☐ out of 25

1 Round-up (page 90)

Matter and the kinetic theory

1. At A, the temperature of the liquid is rising (✓). At B, the temperature stays constant because the liquid is boiling (✓) and all the heat is being used to convert liquid into gas (✓).
2. At C, the temperature of the solid is rising as it is heated (✓). At D the solid starts to melt (✓), and the temperature stays constant at the melting point (✓) while heat is used in the conversion of solid into liquid (✓). At E all the solid has melted (✓), and the temperature of the liquid rises as it is heated (✓). The sharp melting point shows that the solid is a pure substance (✓).
3. Under pressure, water boils at a temperature above 100°C (✓) and the hotter steam kills more bacteria than steam at 100°C (✓).
4. Most of a gas is space; the molecules are far apart (✓).
5. There is so much space between the molecules of a gas (✓) that it is easy for them to move closer together (✓) when the pressure is increased.
6. One example, e.g. heating a lump of bread dough, e.g. air in a hot air balloon expands and is less dense than the air outside the balloon (✓).
7. One example, e.g. increase in the pressure of air in car tyres, e.g. removing a dent from a table tennis ball by warming, e.g. a balloon filled with gas bursts if it is heated (✓).
8. The liquid vaporises (✓). A gas diffuses (✓) to occupy the whole of its container, i.e. the whole of the room (✓).
9. Liquids need energy to vaporise (see page 90) (✓). Aftershave lotion takes this energy from the skin (✓).

Your score: ☐ out of 22

Your improvement index: $\dfrac{\boxed{}/22}{\boxed{}/25} \times 100\% = \boxed{}\%$

2 Test yourself (page 91)

Elements, compounds and equations

1. An element is a pure substance (✓) that cannot be split up (✓) into simpler substances (✓).
2. Zinc reacts with dilute acids (✓) to form hydrogen (✓) and a salt (✓). It forms the cation Zn^{2+} (✓). The oxide and hydroxide are basic (✓) (and amphoteric). The chloride is a solid salt (✓). It forms no hydride (✓).
3. In diamond every carbon atom is covalently bonded to four other carbon atoms (✓). In graphite carbon atoms are covalently bonded together in layers (✓). The layers are joined by weak forces (✓), so one layer can slide over another (✓).
4. Thermal decomposition (✓), electrolysis (✓).
5. 14 (✓)
6. $2Na(s) + 2H_2O(l) \rightarrow 2NaOH(aq) + H_2(g)$
   (✓✓✓✓ for state symbols, ✓✓✓✓ for balancing)

Your score: ☐ out of 25

2 Round-up (page 94)

Elements, compounds and equations

1. Metallic (✓)
2. Non-metallic (✓)
3. Metallic (✓)
4. Non-metallic (✓)

140

Answers

5 For example:
   a) Appearance: sulphur is dull, whereas copper is shiny (✓).
   b) Sulphur is shattered by hammering, whereas copper can be hammered into shape (✓).
   c) Sulphur does not conduct heat or electricity, whereas copper is a good thermal and electrical conductor (✓).
   d) Sulphur is not sonorous; copper is sonorous (✓).

6 The appearance of the mixture (speckled yellow and grey) is different from that of the compound (dark grey throughout) (✓). The iron in the mixture reacts with dilute acids to give hydrogen (✓). The compound, iron(II) sulphide, reacts with acids to give hydrogen sulphide (✓), with a characteristic smell. The iron in the mixture is attracted to a magnet (✓).

7 45 (✓)

8 $CaCO_3(s) + 2HCl(aq) \rightarrow CaCl_2(aq) + CO_2(g) + H_2O(l)$
(✓✓✓ for state symbols, ✓ for factor 2)

Your score: ☐ out of 17

Your improvement index: $\frac{\boxed{}/17}{\boxed{}/25} \times 100\% = \boxed{}\%$

3 Test yourself (page 95)

Separating substances

1 a) Use a coarse seive to hold back the gravel and let sand through (✓).
   b) Centrifuge (✓)
   c) Dissolve the mixture of A and B in hot water (✓). Cool (✓). Filter to obtain A (✓). Evaporate the solution to obtain B (✓).
   d) Use a separating funnel (✓). Olive oil forms a layer on top of vinegar.
   e) Stir with warm water to dissolve the salt (✓). Filter to obtain the diamonds (✓).
   f) Fractional distillation (✓)

Your score: ☐ out of 10

3 Round-up (page 97)

Separating substances

1 Use a magnet or a magnetic field (✓) to attract the steel cans but not the aluminium cans (✓).

2 Stir the mixture of C and D with ethanol (✓). Filter to obtain D (✓). Evaporate the solution to obtain C (✓). Ethanol is flammable (✓): evaporate over a water bath (✓).

3 By fractional distillation (✓) (see page 97). Fractions with low boiling points are collected from the top of the distillation column (✓), while fractions with high boiling points are collected from the bottom of the column (✓).

4 The chromatogram shows that P1 contains A and C (✓), while P2 contains A and B (✓).

5 Allow to settle in a tank so that the oil forms a layer on top of the water (✓). Then carefully withdraw the oil from the top of the tank (✓) by suction (✓).

Your score: ☐ out of 15

Your improvement index: $\frac{\boxed{}/15}{\boxed{}/10} \times 100\% = \boxed{}\%$

4 Test yourself (page 98)

The structure of the atom

1 The number of protons = number of electrons (✓) and the positive charge on a proton has the same value as the negative charge on an electron (✓).

2 a) 19 (✓)   b) 20 (✓)

3 Their chemical reactions are identical because it is the electrons that determine the chemical behaviour (✓), and isotopes have the same electron arrangement (✓).

4 a) The number of protons (= number of electrons) in an atom of the element (✓).
   b) The number of protons + neutrons in an atom of the element (✓✓).

5 a) $^{31}_{15}P$ (✓✓)   b) $^{39}_{19}K$ (✓✓)

6 Two in the first shell (✓), four in the second shell (✓).

Your score: ☐ out of 15

4 Round-up (page 100)

The structure of the atom

1 a) 27 (✓)   b) 5 (✓)   c) 0.7 (✓)   d) 4 (✓)

2 a) $^{75}_{33}As$ (✓)   b) $^{235}_{92}U$ (✓), $^{238}_{92}U$ (✓), $^{239}_{92}U$ (✓)

3 a) 63.6 (✓)   b) 69.8 (✓)

4
(Diagram of phosphorus atom with P 15p nucleus and electron shells showing 2, 8, 5 arrangement) (✓)

Materials and their properties

5 a) B, 5p b) N, 7p c) F, 9p d) Al, 13p

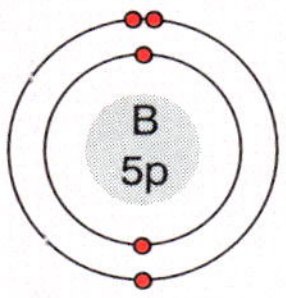

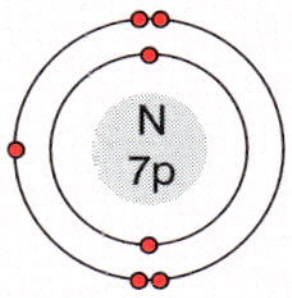

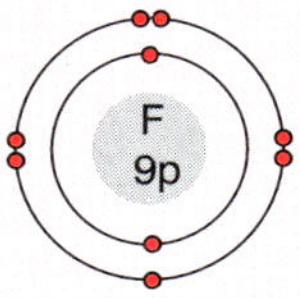

(✓✓✓✓)

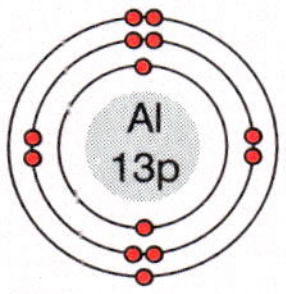

Your score: ☐ out of 15

Your improvement index: $\frac{\Box/15}{\Box/15} \times 100\% = \Box\%$

5 Test yourself (page 102)

The chemical bond

1 Positive (✓), negative (✓), electrostatic (✓), crystal (✓).

2 Each atom of E loses two electrons to become E^{2+} (2.8) (✓). Each atom of Q gains one electron to become Q^- (2.8.8) (✓). The compound EQ_2 is formed (✓).

3 T (✓) T_2 (✓)

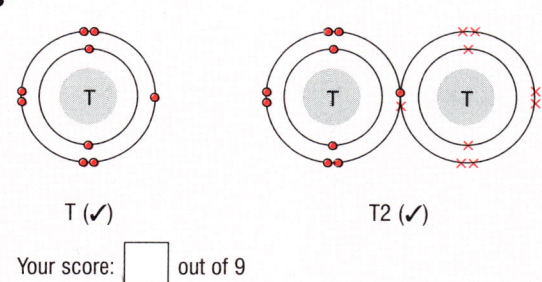

Your score: ☐ out of 9

5 Round-up (page 104)

The chemical bond

1 a) Sodium ions, Na^+ (✓) and chloride ions, Cl^- (✓).
   b) Electrostatic attraction (✓).
   c) A three-dimensional arrangement (✓) of alternate Na^+ ions and Cl^- ions (✓).

2 H—Cl (✓✓)

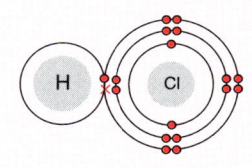

3 For example, one of: a) O_2, CH_4 (✓) b) $I_2(s)$, $CO_2(s)$ (✓)
   c) Diamond, graphite, silicon(IV) oxide (✓).

4 a) Calcium hydroxide (✓)   b) Sodium sulphite (✓)
   c) Copper(II) carbonate (✓)   d) Magnesium hydrogencarbonate (✓)
   e) Potassium nitrate (✓)

Your score: ☐ out of 15

Your improvement index: $\frac{\Box/15}{\Box/9} \times 100\% = \Box\%$

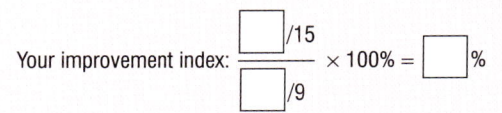

6 Test yourself (page 106)

The periodic table

1 a) He, Ne, Ar, Kr, Xe (✓), a set of very unreactive gases present in air (✓).
   b) Group 0 (✓)
   c) (i) They have a full outer shell of electrons (✓).
      (ii) They are very unreactive (✓). (Some take part in no chemical reactions. Krypton and xenon react with fluorine.)

2 Group 2 (✓)

3 Group 7 (✓)

4 Group 1 (✓)

5 a) Fluorine (✓), chlorine (✓), bromine (✓), iodine (✓).
   b) Group 7 (✓)   c) Decreases (✓)
   d) (i) NaF (✓), NaCl (✓), NaBr (✓), NaI (✓)
      (ii) FeF_3 (✓), $FeCl_3$ (✓), $FeBr_3$ (✓), FeI_2 (✓)

6 a) An element in the block of the periodic table between Groups 2 and 3 (✓).
   b) See pages 107–8 (✓).

Your score: ☐ out of 24

6 Round-up (page 109)

The periodic table

1. Magnesium chloride is a three-dimensional structure of ions (✓) with strong forces of attraction between them (✓). Tetrachloromethane consists of individual covalent molecules (✓) with only weak forces of attraction between them (✓).
2. a) Na (✓), Mg (✓) b) Na (✓), Mg (✓), Al (✓)
   c) (i) Argon (✓)   (ii) Chlorine (✓)   d) Silicon (✓)
3. Na_2O (✓), MgO (✓), Al_2O_3 (✓), SiO_2 (✓)
4. They do not exist (✓).
5. They both have one electron in the outermost shell (✓). It is the electrons in the outermost shell that decide chemical reactions (✓).
6. a) Basic (✓), ionic solid (✓), formula RaO (✓).
   b) Reacts readily to form hydrogen (✓) and the alkali radium hydroxide (✓), $Ra(OH)_2$ (✓).
   c) Reacts readily to form hydrogen (✓) and a solution of the ionic compound (✓) radium chloride (✓), $RaCl_2$ (✓).
7. a) Hydrogen astatide is a gas (✓), a covalent compound (✓) which forms an acidic solution in water (✓).
   b) Astatine reacts slowly with sodium (✓) to form the ionic solid (✓) sodium astatide (✓), NaAt (✓).

Your score: ☐ out of 36

Your improvement index: ☐/36 / ☐/24 × 100% = ☐%

7 Test yourself (page 110)

Acids, bases and salts

1. a) SA (✓) b) WA (✓) c) WB (✓) d) WB (✓)
   e) WA (✓) f) N (✓)   g) SB (✓)
2. You could compare the rates (✓) at which hydrogen is given off (✓) in the reactions of the two acids with magnesium or another metal (✓),
   or the rates (✓) at which carbon dioxide is given off (✓) in the reactions of the acids with a carbonate or hydrogencarbonate (✓).
3. a) Hydrochloric acid (✓) b) For example, magnesium hydroxide (✓) c) Citric acid (✓) d) Ammonia (✓)
4. a) Sodium hydroxide converts grease into soap (✓).
   b) Sodium hydroxide is a stronger base than ammonia (✓).
   c) Wear glasses (✓) and rubber gloves (✓).
   d) Sodium hydroxide would be too dangerous or corrosive (✓).
   e) The saponification of fats by a weak base, e.g. ammonia, is very slow (✓).

Your score: ☐ out of 20

7 Round-up (page 114)

Acids, bases and salts

1. a) H^+ ions (✓), Cl^- ions (✓), H_2O molecules (✓).
   b) H^+ ions (✓), ethanoate ions (✓), ethanoic acid molecules (✓), H_2O molecules (✓).
2. a) Zinc + sulphuric acid → zinc sulphate + hydrogen (✓✓)
   b) Cobalt oxide + sulphuric acid → cobalt sulphate + water (✓✓)
   c) Nickel carbonate + hydrochloric acid → nickel chloride + carbon dioxide + water (✓✓✓)
   d) Potassium hydroxide + nitric acid → potassium nitrate + water (✓✓)
   e) Ammonia + nitric acid → ammonium nitrate (✓✓)
3. a) See page 110 for two examples (✓✓).
   b) See page 112 for two examples (✓✓).
   c) See page 114 for two examples (✓✓).
4. a) Sodium sulphate + water (✓✓).
   b) Ammonium chloride, no other product (✓).
   c) Zinc chloride + hydrogen (✓✓).
   d) Copper(II) sulphate + water (✓✓).
   e) Calcium chloride + carbon dioxide + water (✓✓✓).

Your score: ☐ out of 34

Your improvement index: ☐/34 / ☐/20 × 100% = ☐%

8 Test yourself (page 115)

Air

1. 21% O_2 (✓), 78% N_2 (✓)
2. Two from, for example, oxyacetylene flame, steel-making, sewage treatment, combatting pollution (✓✓).
3. Combustion (✓)
4. It makes a glowing splint burn more brightly (✓).
5. Gain (✓), loss (✓), loss (✓).
6. Pass through limewater, $Ca(OH)_2(aq)$ (✓). A white precipitate shows that the gas is carbon dioxide (✓).
7. Four from, for example, carbon monoxide – vehicle engines; sulphur dioxide – combustion of fuels; hydrocarbons – combustion of fuels; NO_x – vehicle engines; dust – combustion of fuels, mining, factories; lead compounds – vehicle engines (✓✓✓✓✓✓✓).

Your score: ☐ out of 19

Materials and their properties

8 Round-up (page 120)
Air
1. a) (i) Zinc oxide (✓) (ii) Carbon (✓)
   b) (i) Carbon (✓) (ii) Zinc oxide (✓)
2. a) (i) Iron oxide (✓) (ii) Aluminium (✓)
   b) (i) Oxygen (✓) (ii) Tin sulphide (✓)
   c) (i) Tin oxide (✓) (ii) Carbon (✓)
3. a) Airships need to be lighter than air (✓).
   b) Helium is a noble gas (✓); hydrogen forms an explosive mixture with air (✓).
4. a) Poisonous (✓); removed by soil bacteria (✓).
   b) Causes respiratory difficulties (✓); acid rain (✓).
   c) Causes respiratory difficulties (✓); washed out in rain (✓).
5. a) From vehicle exhausts, power stations, factories (✓).
   b) One of the causes of acid rain (✓).
   c) Catalytic converters (✓).
6. Tall chimneys carry pollutants away from the area of the power station (✓). Taller chimneys do not prevent acid rain (✓).
7. a) Carbon dioxide (✓), carbon monoxide (✓), carbon (✓), water (✓).
   b) Oxides of nitrogen (✓), hydrocarbons (✓), sulphur dioxide (✓).

Your score: ☐ out of 31

Your improvement index: $\dfrac{\Box/31}{\Box/19} \times 100\% = \Box\%$

9 Test yourself (page 121)
Water
1. Evaporation (✓), respiration (✓), transpiration (✓).
2. Carbon dioxide dissolves in rainwater (✓).
3. a) Water turns anhydrous copper(II) sulphate (✓) from white to blue (✓) (or anhydrous cobalt(II) chloride from blue to pink).
   b) Pure water boils at 100°C (or freezes at 0°C) (✓).
4. For example, aquatic plants (✓), fish (✓), aerobic bacteria (✓).

Your score: ☐ out of 10

9 Round-up (page 122)
Water
1. Oil is discharged from sewers into waterways (✓). The oxidation of hydrocarbons in the oil uses up dissolved oxygen in the water (✓).
2. a) Modern tankers are very large (✓). Any accident that happens involves a large loss of oil (✓).
   b) Poisons fish (✓), glues feathers of sea birds (✓), fouls beaches (✓).
3. a) Eutrophication leads to an increase in the growth of algae (✓).
   b) Fertilisers do not accumulate as much in running water (✓).
   c) (i) You cannot drink water full of algae (✓).
      (ii) Propellers get entangled in algae (✓).
      (iii) Fish die because decaying algae use up all the dissolved oxygen (✓).

Your score: ☐ out of 12

Your improvement index: $\dfrac{\Box/12}{\Box/10} \times 100\% = \Box\%$

10 Test yourself (page 123)
Rocks
1. a) Igneous (✓) b) Sedimentary (✓)
   c) Metamorphic (✓)
2. Igneous (✓)
3. Three from, for example, rain, rivers, glaciers, wind (✓✓✓).
4. Three from, for example, to neutralise acidity in lakes and soils; used as a building material; in the manufacture of cement, quicklime, glass and iron (✓✓✓).
5. For example, silicon, glass (✓✓).

Your score: ☐ out of 12

10 Round-up (page 124)
Rocks
1. a) Limestone (✓), sandstone (✓).
   b) Basalt (✓), granite (✓), pumice (✓).
   c) Marble (✓), slate (✓).
2. a) A volcanic eruption (✓).
3. a) Powdered limestone is mixed with clay or shale (✓) in a rotary kiln (✓).
   b) Three from water, sand, crushed rock, calcium sulphate (✓✓✓).

Answers

4 Silicon(IV) oxide (silica), calcium carbonate, sodium carbonate (✓✓✓).

Your score: ☐ out of 16

Your improvement index: $\frac{\boxed{}/16}{\boxed{}/12} \times 100\% = \boxed{}\%$

11 Test yourself (page 126)
Metals and alloys

1. Metals can change shape without breaking (✓), conduct heat (✓), conduct electricity (✓).

2. Three from, for example, potassium, sodium, lithium, calcium, magnesium, aluminium, zinc, iron (✓✓✓).

3. Two from, for example, silver, gold, platinum (✓✓).

4. Three from, for example, lithium, sodium, potassium, calcium, magnesium (slowly) (✓✓✓). Products are hydrogen (✓) and the metal hydroxide (✓).

5. Hydrogen (✓) and the metal chloride (✓).

6. a) Group 1 (✓)   b) Group 2 (✓)
   c) Between Group 2 and Group 3 (✓).

7. Electrolysis (✓) of the molten anhydrous chloride or oxide (✓).

8. The ore is heated with limestone and coke in a blast furnace (✓✓✓).

9. Two from, for example, aluminium, chromium, nickel (✓✓).

Your score: ☐ out of 25

11 Round-up (page 130)
Metals and alloys

1. a) Magnesium sulphate and hydrogen (✓✓).
   e) Zinc sulphate and hydrogen (✓✓).
   b), c), d) and f) No reaction (✓✓✓✓).

2. Copper alloys do not rust (✓). They are softer than iron (✓) and easier to mint (✓).

3. a) With water, calcium reacts steadily (✓), magnesium over several days (✓), iron rusts over a period of weeks (✓), and copper does not react (✓).
   b) With dilute hydrochloric acid, calcium reacts extremely vigorously (✓), magnesium reacts in minutes (✓), iron reacts at moderate speed with warm acid (✓), and copper does not react (✓).

4. a) The blue colour of the solution fades (✓) and a reddish brown solid is precipitated (✓).
   Zinc + copper(II) sulphate → copper + zinc sulphate (✓✓)
   $Zn(s) + CuSO_4(aq) \rightarrow Cu(s) + ZnSO_4(aq)$ (✓✓)
   b) Grey crystals appear (✓).
   Zinc + lead(II) nitrate → lead + zinc nitrate (✓✓)
   $Zn(s) + Pb(NO_3)_2(aq) \rightarrow Pb(s) + Zn(NO_3)_2(aq)$ (✓✓)

5. Z > X > Y (✓✓)

6. a) Au (✓)   b) Na (✓), Mg (✓)   c) Zn (✓), Fe (✓)
   d) Na (✓), Mg (✓), Zn (✓), Fe (✓)   e) Na (✓)
   f) Mg (✓), Al (✓), Zn (✓), Fe (✓) (Na reacts with water instead of with Pb^{2+}).

7. a) Copper(II) oxide (✓)   b) Aluminium oxide + iron (✓)
   d) Carbon dioxide + iron (✓)   f) Copper + zinc sulphate solution (✓)   c) and e) No reaction (✓✓).

8. For uses of aluminium related to properties, see table on page 129. (✓✓✓✓ for four uses, ✓✓✓✓ for four properties.)

9. a) Oiling (✓)   b) Chromium-plating (✓)
   c) Galvanising (coating with zinc) (✓)
   d) Stainless steel (✓)   e) Painting (✓)
   f) Sacrificial protection by e.g. zinc (✓)
   g) Tin-plating (✓)

10. Saving of Earth's resources (✓), saving of energy used in extracting the metal, (✓) limiting damage to the environment through mining (✓).

Your score: ☐ out of 70

Your improvement index: $\frac{\boxed{}/70}{\boxed{}/25} \times 100\% = \boxed{}\%$

12 Test yourself (page 131)
Reaction speeds

1. Indigestion powders (✓) because the ratio surface area : mass is greater (✓).

2. a) Use smaller pieces of zinc (✓), use a more concentrated solution of acid (✓), raise the temperature (✓).
   b) In smaller particles, the ratio surface area : mass is larger (✓). At a higher concentration, collisions take place more frequently between hydrogen ions and zinc (✓). At a higher temperature, the hydrogen ions have higher energy (✓), and collide more frequently with the particles of zinc (✓).

3. An apparatus with a gas syringe, see page 132, and a clock (✓✓✓✓✓).

4. A catalyst is a substance which increases the rate of a chemical reaction without being used up in the reaction (✓✓).

5. Industrial manufacturers can make their product more rapidly or at a lower temperature with the use of a catalyst (✓✓).

6. Photosynthesis, photography (✓✓).

Your score: ☐ out of 20

145

Materials and their properties

12 Round-up (page 133)
Reaction speeds
1. a) Carbon dioxide is given off (✓).
   b) (i) C (ii) A (iii) B (✓✓).
   c) The ratio of surface area : volume differs (✓).
2. Cut them into smaller pieces (✓). Use a higher temperature by using a pressure cooker (✓).
3. Use an apparatus such as that shown on page 132 (bottom) (✓). Using potato, measure the volume of oxygen formed at certain times after the start of the reaction (✓). Plot volume against time (✓). Repeat the measurement using manganese(IV) oxide. Compare the two graphs (✓).
4. You could take pieces of magnesium ribbon of the same length and therefore approximately the same mass (✓). You could find out how long it took (✓) for a piece of magnesium ribbon to react completely with a certain volume of acid (✓) of a certain concentration (✓) at different temperatures (✓). You could plot time against temperature or 1/time (rate) against temperature (✓).
5. a) Axes labelled correctly and units shown (✓), points plotted correctly (✓), points covering at least half of each scale (✓), smooth lines drawn through the points (✓).
   b) B (✓)
   c) Your line should should show very slow evolution of oxygen (✓).

Your score: ☐ out of 22

Your improvement index: $\dfrac{\Box/22}{\Box/20} \times 100\% = \Box\%$

13 Test yourself (page 134)
Fuels
1. Coal and oil were formed from the remains of plants and trees (coal) (✓) and sea animals and plants (oil) (✓) which lived millions of years ago (✓).
2. It is burnt in power stations (✓).
3. a) Fractional distillation (✓).
   b) Four from: petroleum gas, gasoline, kerosene, diesel oil, fuel oil (✓✓✓✓).
   c) Two from: lubricating oil, bitumen, naphtha (✓✓).
4. a) Methane (✓) b) Ethane (✓) c) Propane (✓)
   d) The alkane series (✓).
5. Converting hydrocarbons with large molecules (✓) and high boiling points (✓) into hydrocarbons with smaller molecules (✓) and lower boiling points (✓).
6. a) Combustion (✓), respiration (✓).
   b) Photosynthesis (✓), cracking of hydrocarbons (✓).

Your score: ☐ out of 23

13 Round-up (page 137)
Fuels
1. a) Fossil fuels are formed by the decay (✓) of the remains of plants (✓) and animals (✓) over long periods of time (✓).
   b) Fossil fuels took millions of years to form (✓) and we are using them up much more quickly (✓).
2. a) Fractional distillation (✓) separates the fractions on the basis of their different boiling point ranges (✓).
   b) For uses see the diagram on page 135 (✓✓✓✓✓).
   c) Gasoline has a lower boiling point (✓), lower ignition temperature (✓) and lower viscosity than fuel oil (✓).
   d) It does not vaporise (✓) and does not ignite (✓).
   e) Fuels from petroleum oil are important in transport (✓), industry (✓) and power generation (✓). Oil is a source of valuable petrochemicals (✓).
3. As for exothermic energy diagram on page 137 (✓✓), exothermic (✓).
4. As for endothermic energy diagram on page 137 (✓✓), endothermic (✓).

Your score: ☐ out of 29

Your improvement index: $\dfrac{\Box/29}{\Box/23} \times 100\% = \Box\%$

14 Test yourself (page 138)
Alkenes and plastics
1. $>\!C\!=\!C\!<$ (✓), addition reactions (✓).
2. Alkenes are reactive (✓) and are therefore the starting materials for the manufacture of many other compounds (✓).
3. The addition of many identical small molecules to form a large molecule (✓). The substance with small molecules is the monomer; the substance with large molecules is the polymer (✓).
4. Thermosetting plastics can be softened by heat and hardened by cooling (✓) many times (✓). Thermosetting plastics are softened by heat (✓) only during manufacture (✓).
5. For thermosoftening plastics a continuous process is used (✓). For thermosetting plastics, a batch process is used (✓).

Your score: ☐ out of 12

Answers

14 Round-up (page 139)

Alkenes and plastics

1 a) (i) Ethane C_2H_6 (✓), ethene C_2H_4 (✓)

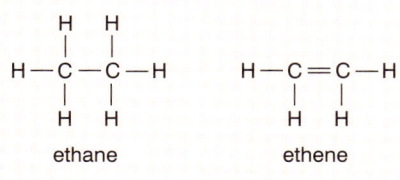

(ii)

```
      H   H                    
      |   |                    
  H — C — C — H       H — C = C — H
      |   |               |   |
      H   H               H   H
      ethane              ethene
```
(✓✓)

b) Ethane has only single bonds (✓); it is a saturated compound (✓). Ethene has a carbon–carbon double bond (✓); it is an unsaturated compound (✓).

2 a) Less breakable (✓).
b) Cheaper, less breakable, non-toxic (✓).
c) Much less breakable (✓).

3

```
      H    CONH₂
      |    |
   ─( C  — C )─
      |    |   n
      H    H
```
(✓)

4 a) When deformed, a plastic changes shape (✓) and retains the new shape when the deforming force is removed (✓).

b) Thermoplastic – can be softened by heat (✓) many times (✓).
Thermosetting – can be moulded only once (✓).
Thermoplastic – individual chains can move with respect to one another (✓).
Thermosetting – chains are cross-linked (✓).

5 a) Most plastics cannot be decomposed by natural biological processes (✓).
b) Plastic rubbish accumulates in landfill sites and never decomposes (✓).
c) Some plastics form toxic combustion products (✓). Also, burning them is a waste of Earth's resources (✓).
d) Recycling (✓).

Your score: ☐ out of 24

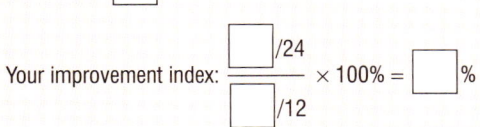

Your improvement index: $\dfrac{\Box/24}{\Box/12} \times 100\% = \Box\%$

Materials and their properties

THE PERIODIC TABLE OF THE ELEMENTS

Group 1	2											3	4	5	6	7	0
						H hydrogen 1											He helium 2
Li lithium 3	Be beryllium 4											B boron 5	C carbon 6	N nitrogen 7	O oxygen 8	F fluorine 9	Ne neon 10
Na sodium 11	Mg magnesium 12											Al aluminium 13	Si silicon 14	P phosphorus 15	S sulphur 16	Cl chlorine 17	Ar argon 18
K potassium 19	Ca calcium 20	Sc scandium 21	Ti titanium 22	V vanadium 23	Cr chromium 24	Mn manganese 25	Fe iron 26	Co cobalt 27	Ni nickel 28	Cu copper 29	Zn zinc 30	Ga gallium 31	Ge germanium 32	As arsenic 33	Se selenium 34	Br bromine 35	Kr krypton 36
Rb rubidium 37	Sr strontium 38	Y yttrium 39	Zr zirconium 40	Nb niobium 41	Mo molybdenum 42	Tc technetium 43	Ru ruthenium 44	Rh rhodium 45	Pd palladium 46	Ag silver 47	Cd cadmium 48	In indium 49	Sn tin 50	Sb antimony 51	Te tellurium 52	I iodine 53	Xe xenon 54
Cs caesium 55	Ba barium 56	La lanthanum 57	Hf hafnium 72	Ta tantalum 73	W tungsten 74	Re rhenium 75	Os osmium 76	Ir iridium 77	Pt platinum 78	Au gold 79	Hg mercury 80	Tl thallium 81	Pb lead 82	Bi bismuth 83	Po polonium 84	At astatine 85	Rn radon 86
Fr francium 87	Ra radium 88	Ac actinium 89															

lanthanum series: elements 58–71
actinium series: elements 90–103

148

Mind Maps: Materials and their properties

Elements, compounds and equations (Topic 2)

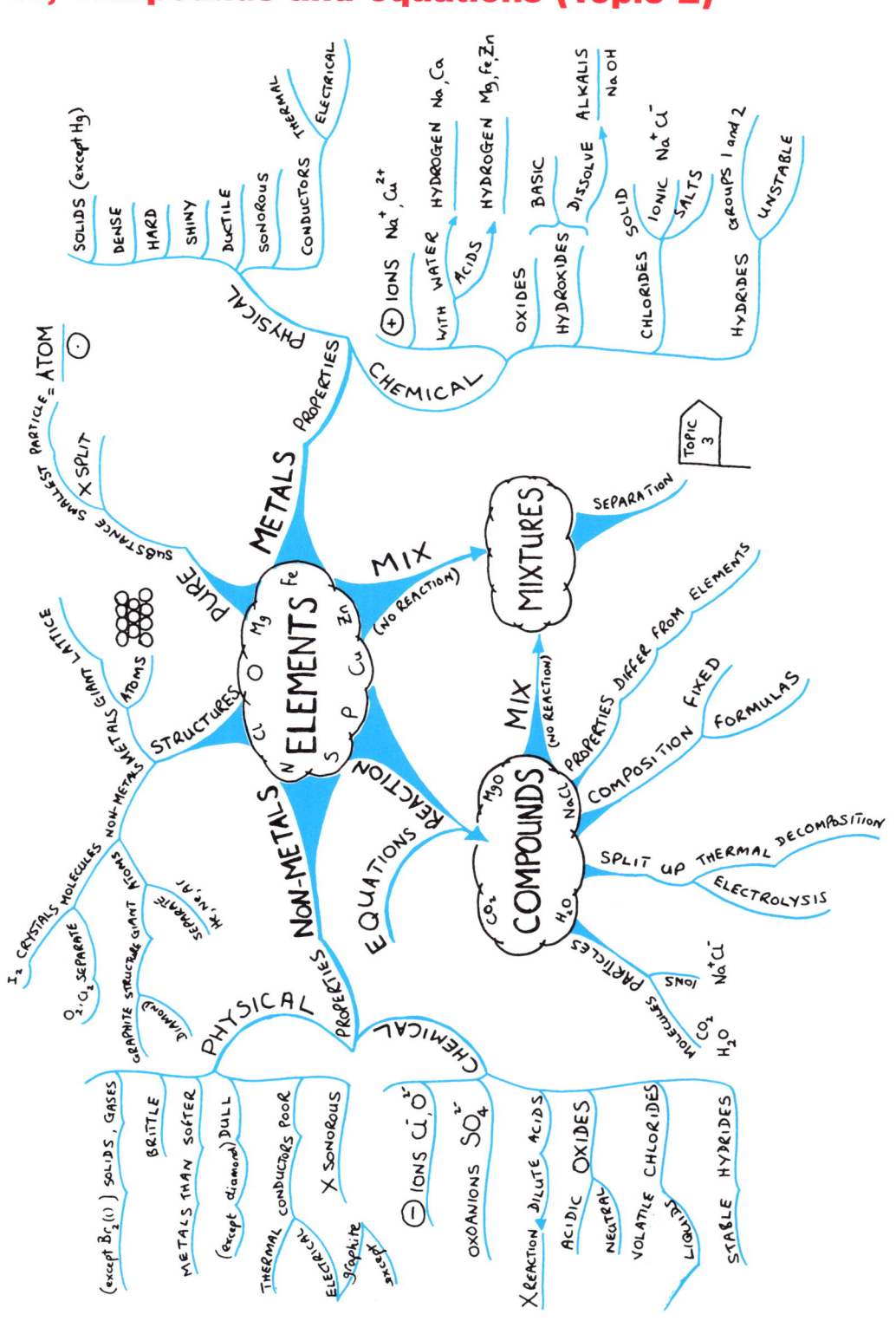

ELEMENTS (Fe, Mg, O, Cl, N, S, P, Cu, Zn)

- **METALS**
  - **PROPERTIES**
    - **PHYSICAL**: SOLIDS (except Hg), DENSE, HARD, SHINY, DUCTILE, SONOROUS, CONDUCTORS (THERMAL, ELECTRICAL)
    - **CHEMICAL**:
      - (+) IONS Na^+, Cu^{2+}
      - WITH WATER → HYDROGEN (Na, Ca)
      - ACIDS → HYDROGEN (Mg, Fe, Zn)
      - OXIDES: BASIC, DISSOLVE → ALKALIS (NaOH)
      - HYDROXIDES: SOLID
      - CHLORIDES: IONIC Na^+Cl^-, SALTS
      - HYDRIDES: GROUPS 1 and 2, UNSTABLE
  - **PURE SUBSTANCE SMALLEST PARTICLE = ATOM** ✗ SPLIT
  - **STRUCTURES**: ATOMS, GIANT LATTICE

- **NON-METALS**
  - **STRUCTURES**: I_2 CRYSTALS, MOLECULES, GIANT STRUCTURE (GRAPHITE, DIAMOND), SEPARATE ATOMS (O_2, Cl_2 SEPARATE), (He, Ne, Ar)
  - **PROPERTIES**
    - **PHYSICAL**: (except $Br_2(l)$) SOLIDS, GASES, BRITTLE, METALS THAN SOFTER, DULL (except diamond), THERMAL CONDUCTORS POOR, ✗ SONOROUS, ELECTRICAL except graphite
    - **CHEMICAL**:
      - (−) IONS Cl^-, O^{2-}
      - OXOANIONS SO_4^{2-}
      - ✗ REACTION DILUTE ACIDS
      - ACIDIC OXIDES, NEUTRAL
      - VOLATILE CHLORIDES, LIQUIDS
      - STABLE HYDRIDES

- **EQUATIONS** (REACTION)

- **MIX** (NO REACTION) → **MIXTURES** → SEPARATION → Topic 3

- **MIX** (NO REACTION) → **COMPOUNDS** (MgO, NaCl, CO_2, H_2O)
  - PROPERTIES DIFFER FROM ELEMENTS
  - COMPOSITION FIXED
  - FORMULAS
  - SPLIT UP: THERMAL DECOMPOSITION, ELECTROLYSIS
  - PARTICLES: IONS (Na^+Cl^-), MOLECULES (CO_2, H_2O)

149

Materials and their properties

Acids, bases and salts (Topic 7)

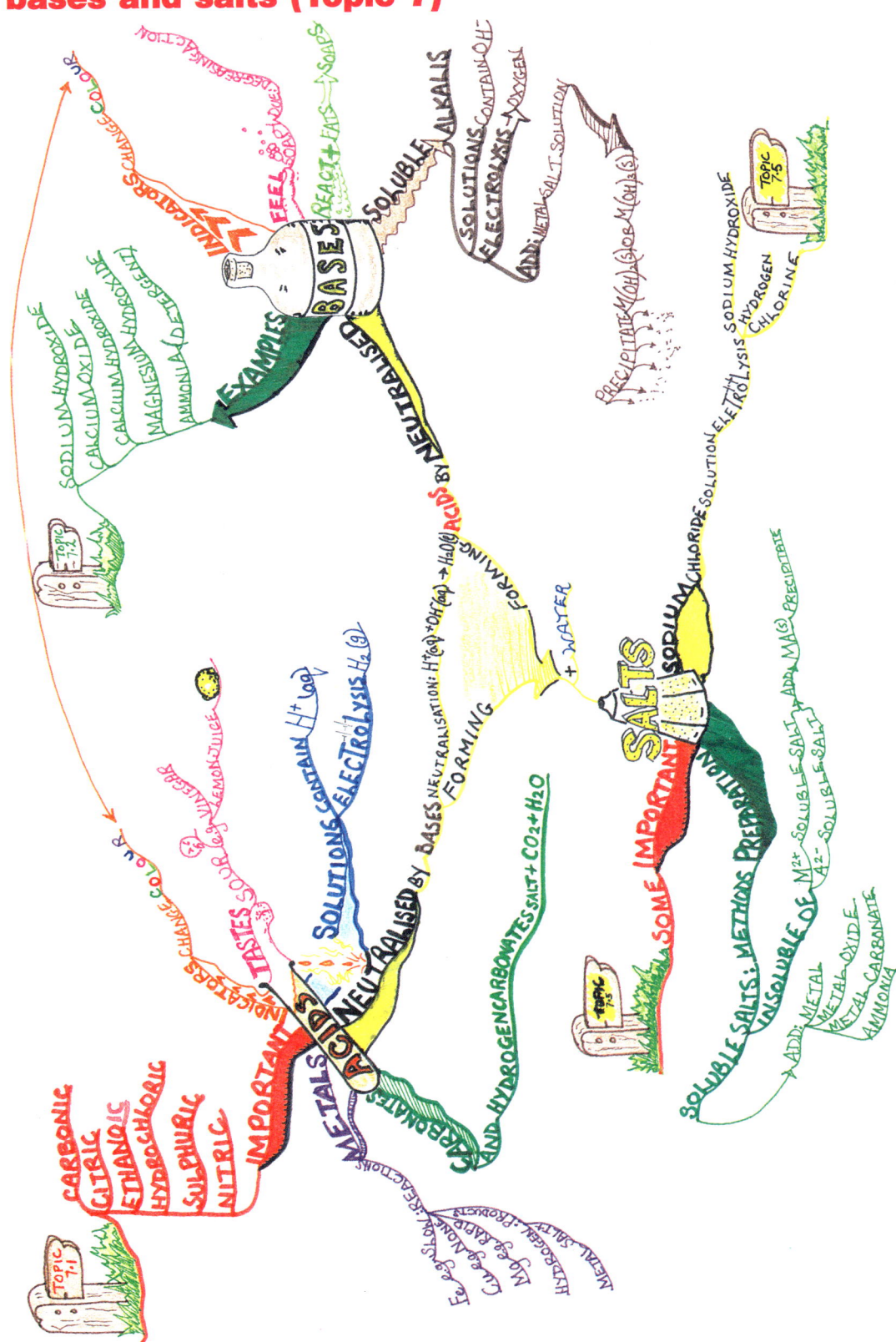

Mind Maps

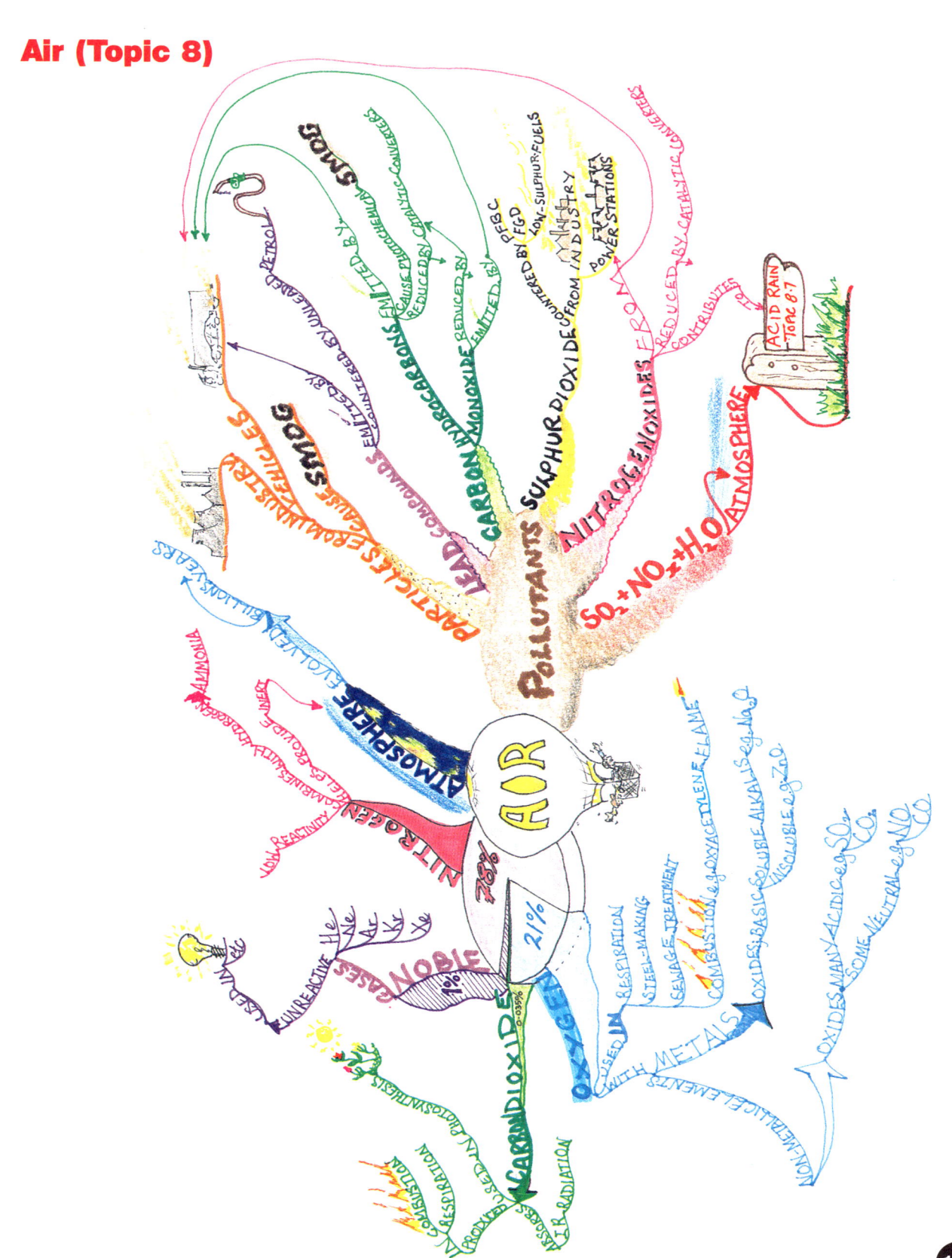

Air (Topic 8)

Materials and their properties

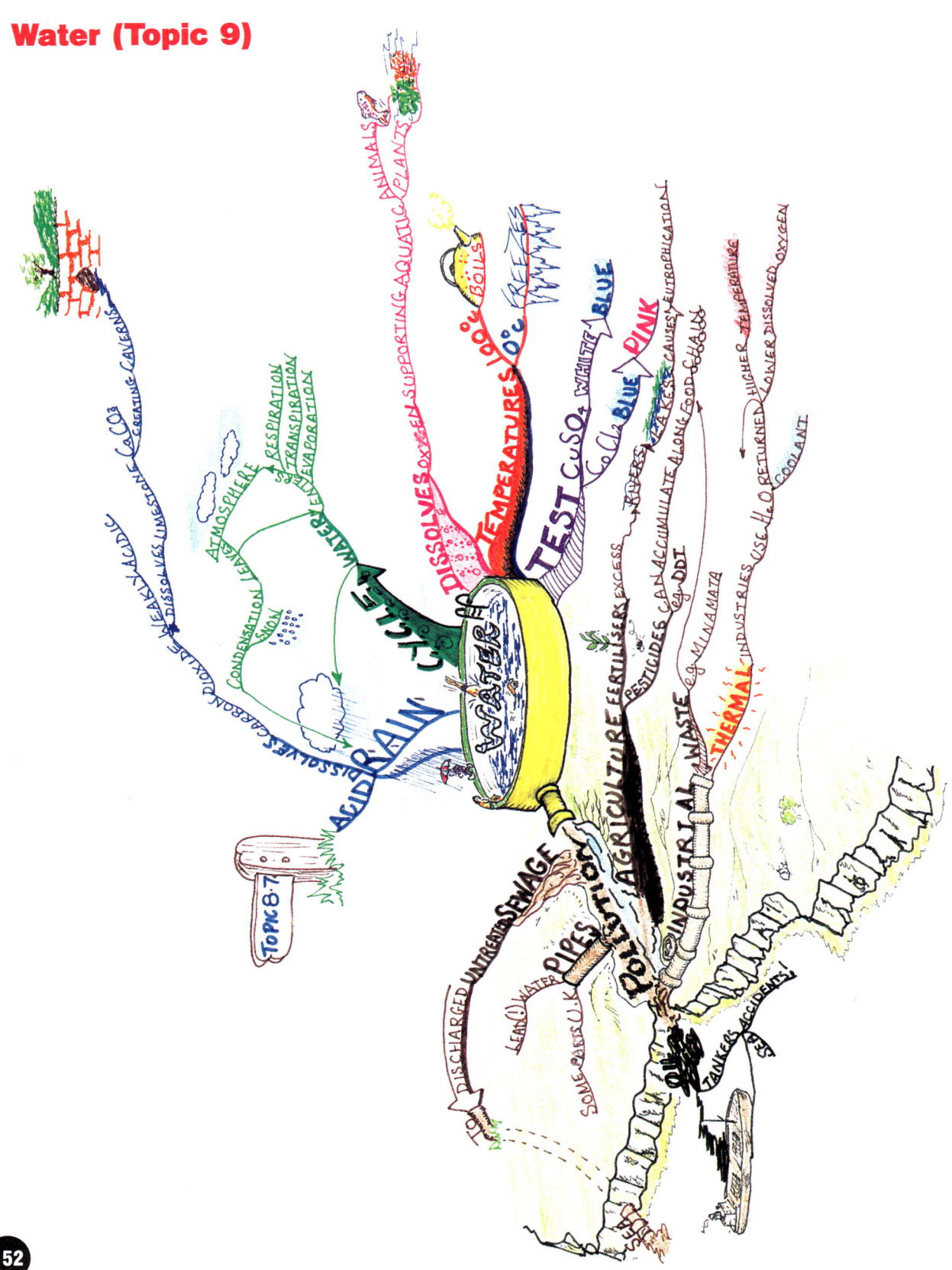

Water (Topic 9)

Metals and alloys (Topic 11)

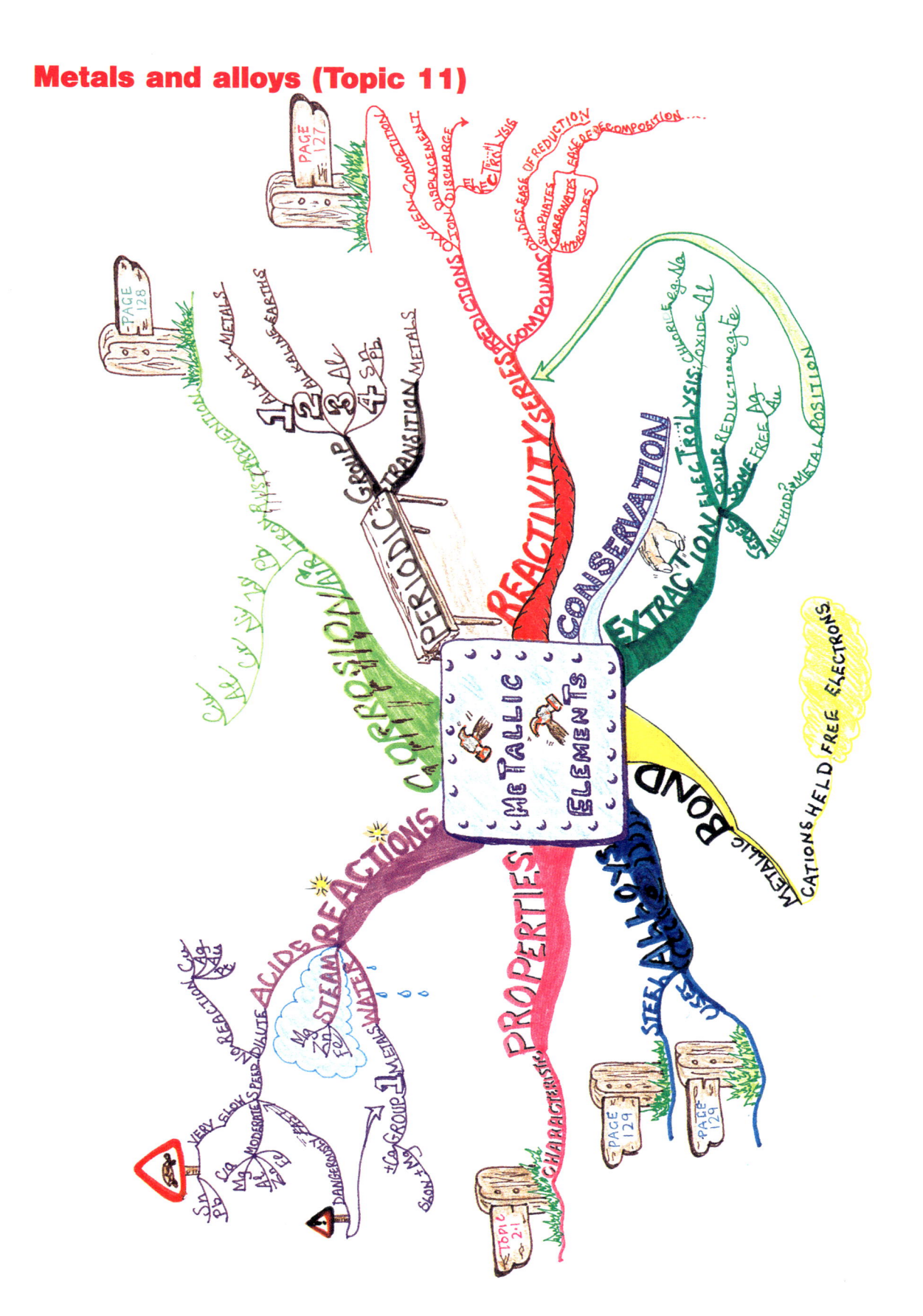

Materials and their properties

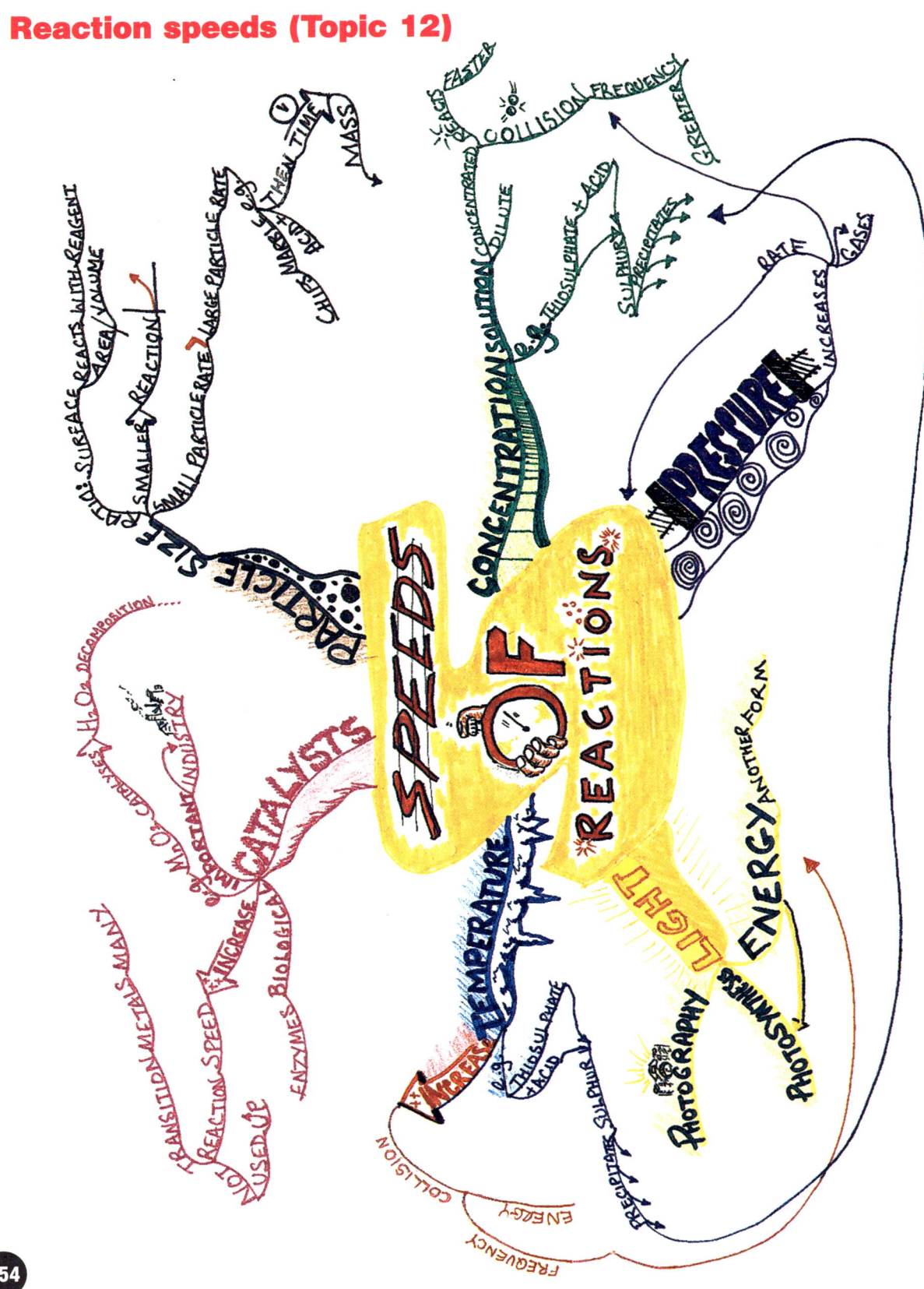

Reaction speeds (Topic 12)

Mind Maps

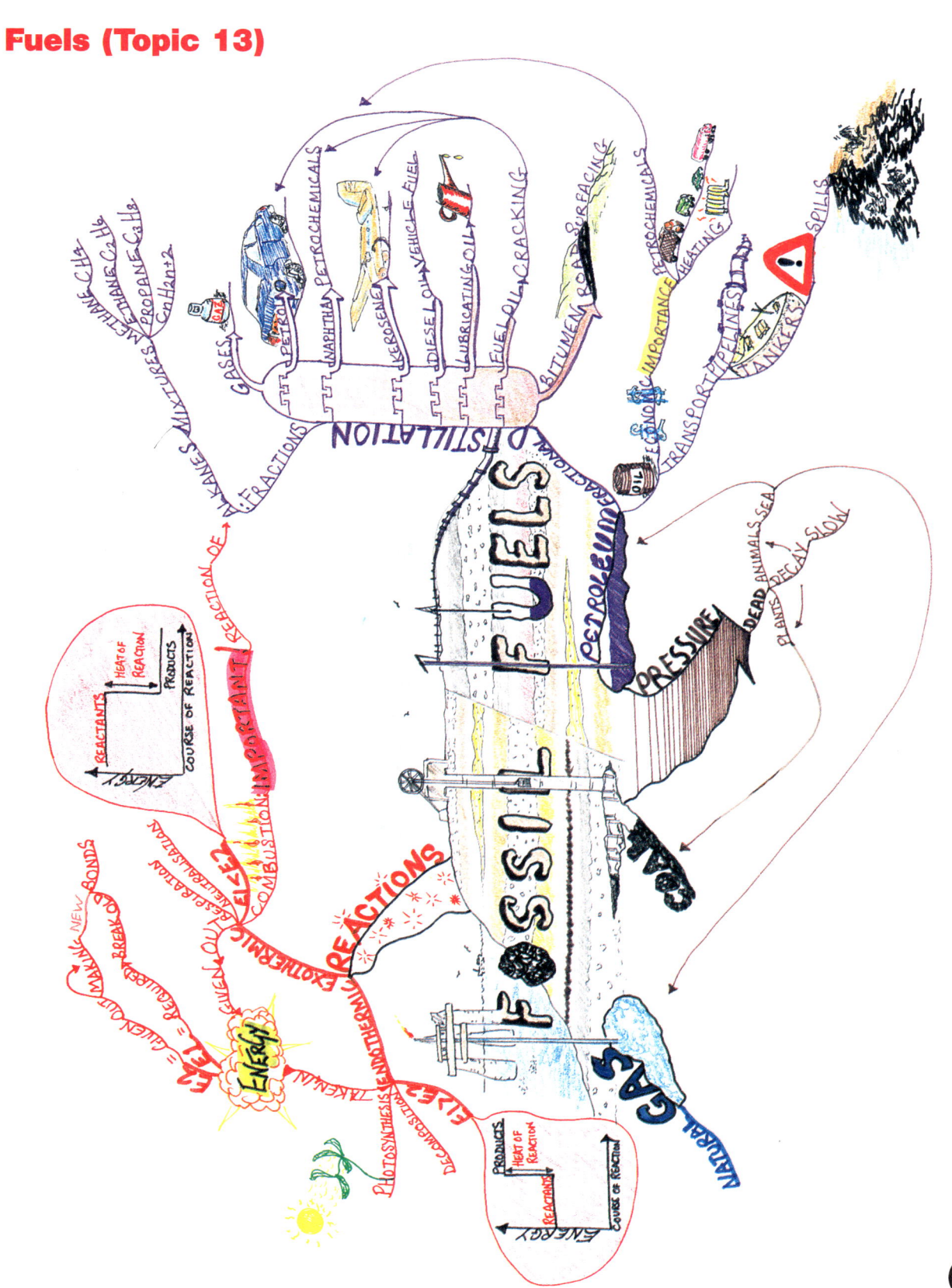

Fuels (Topic 13)

Materials and their properties

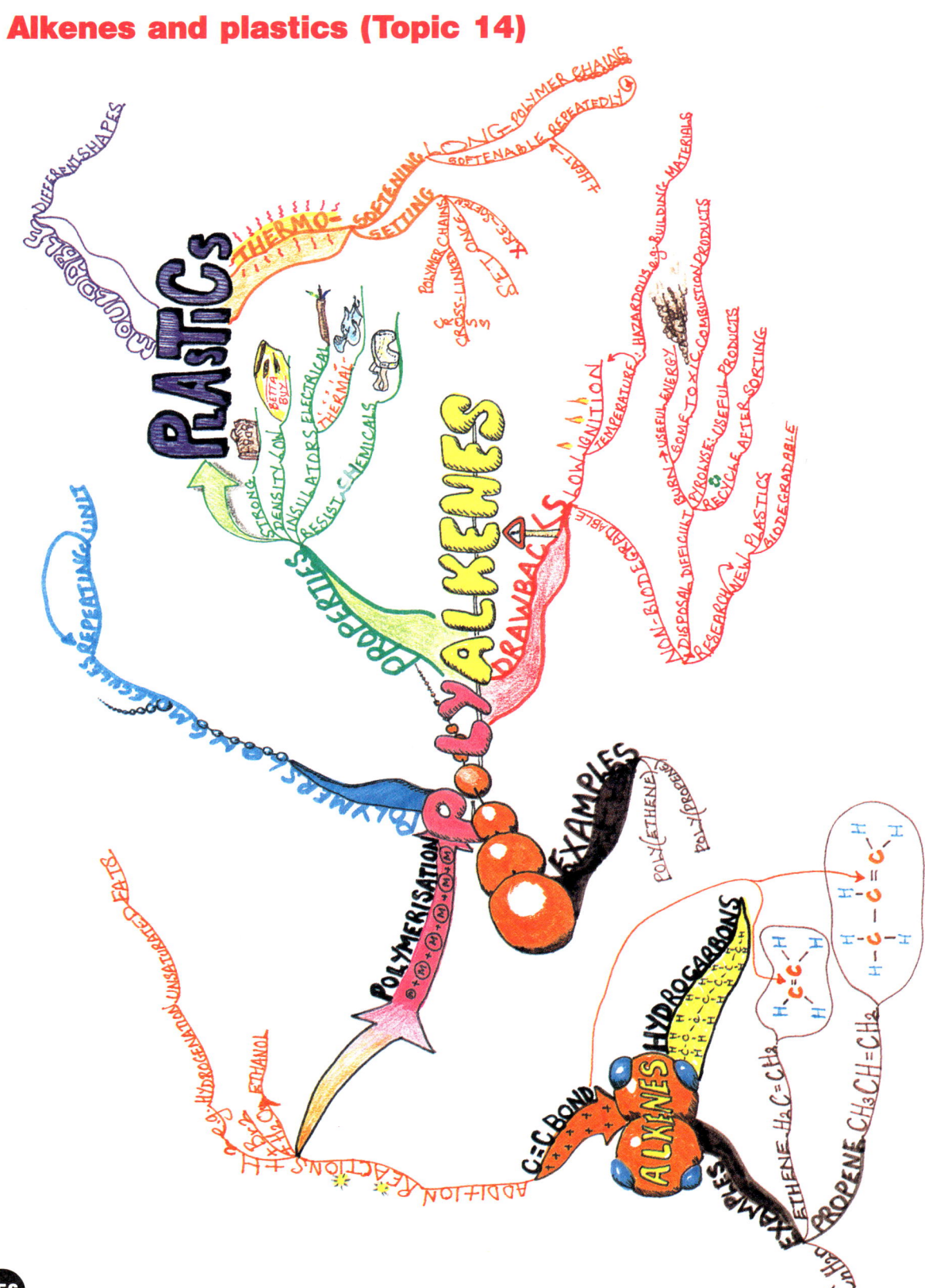

Alkenes and plastics (Topic 14)

Mind Maps: Physical processes

Beyond the Earth (Topic 1)

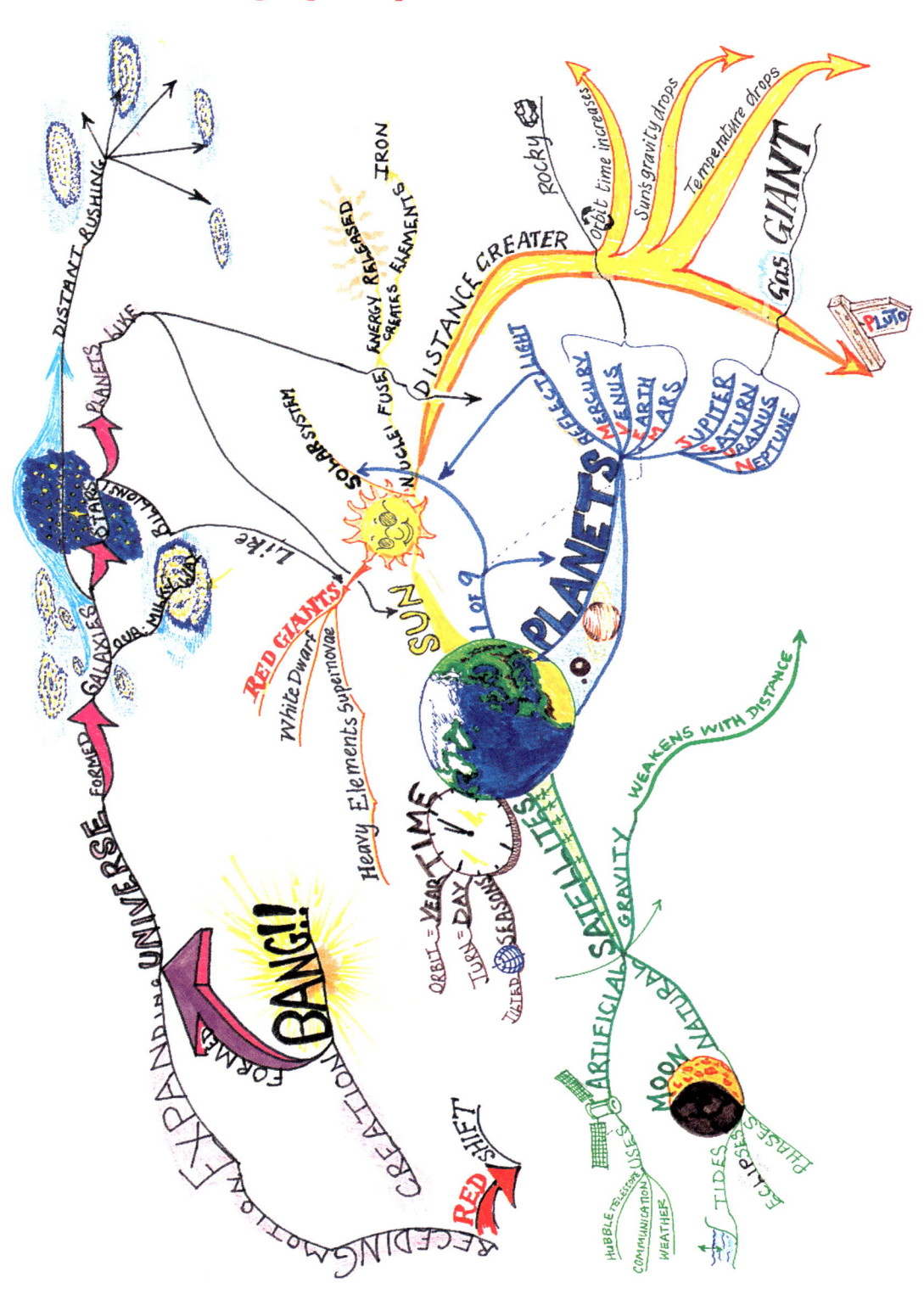

Physical processes

Energy (Topic 2)

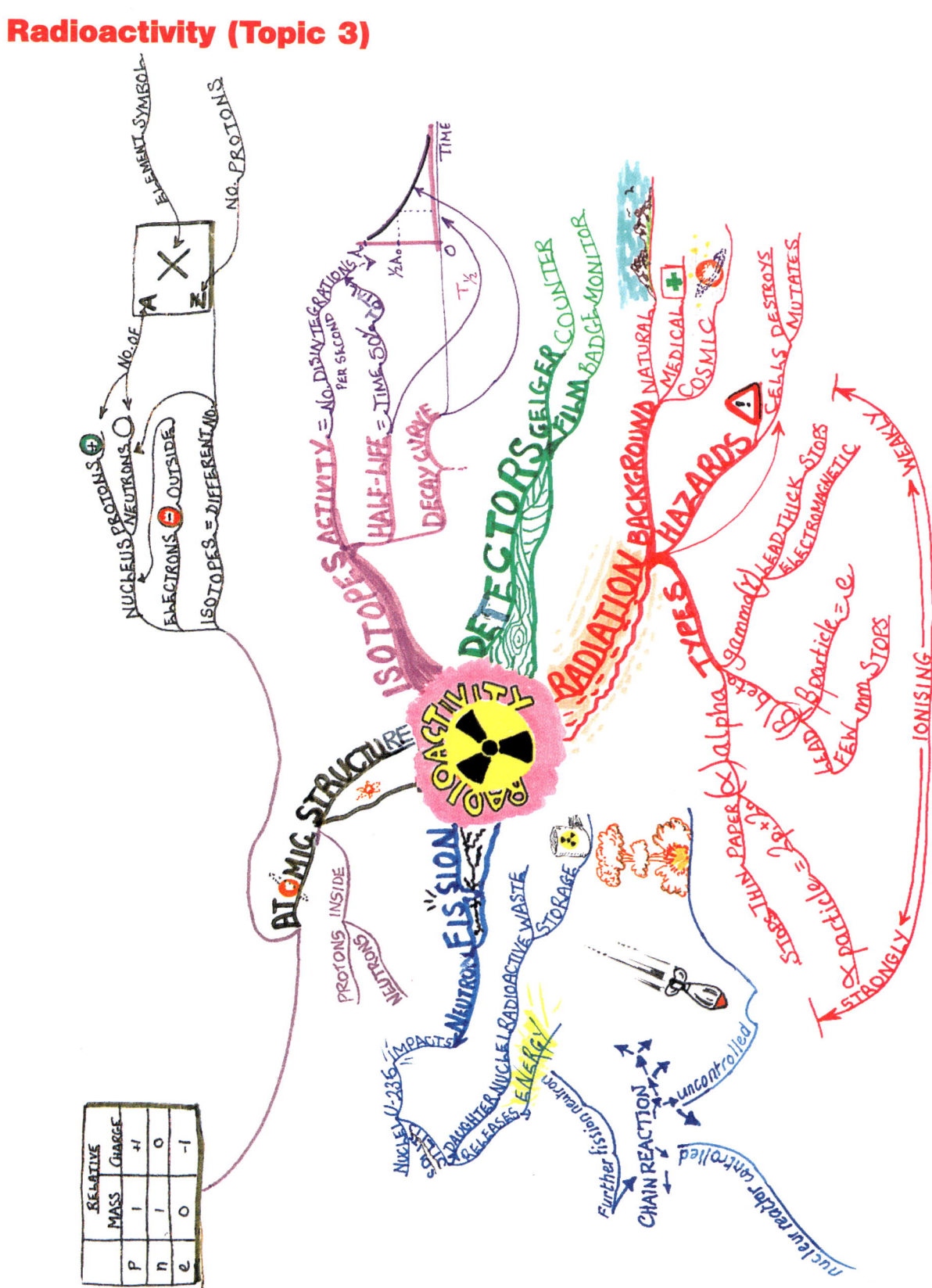

Radioactivity (Topic 3)

Physical processes

Light and electromagnetic waves (Topics 4 and 5)

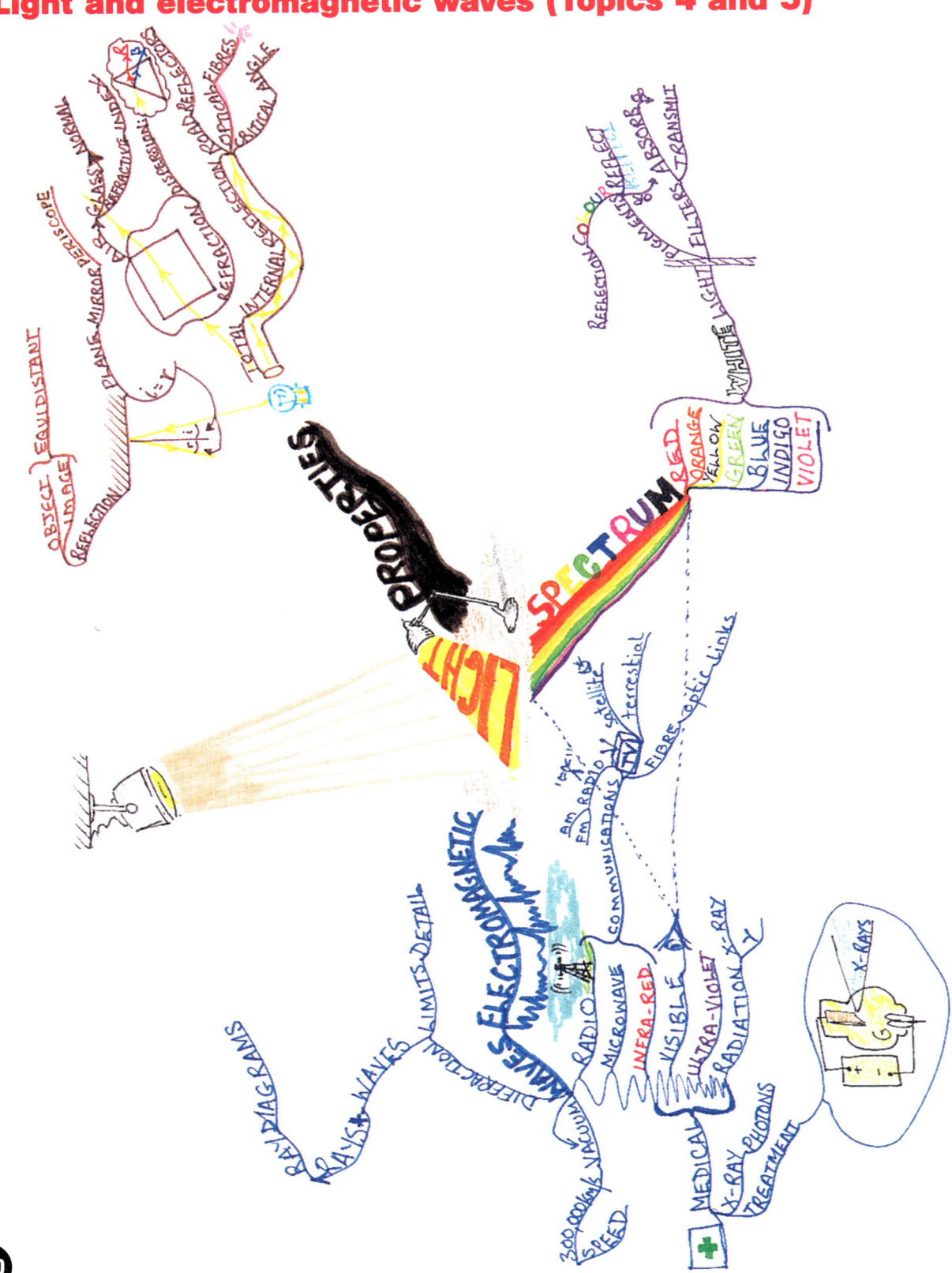

Mind Maps

Force (Topic 6)

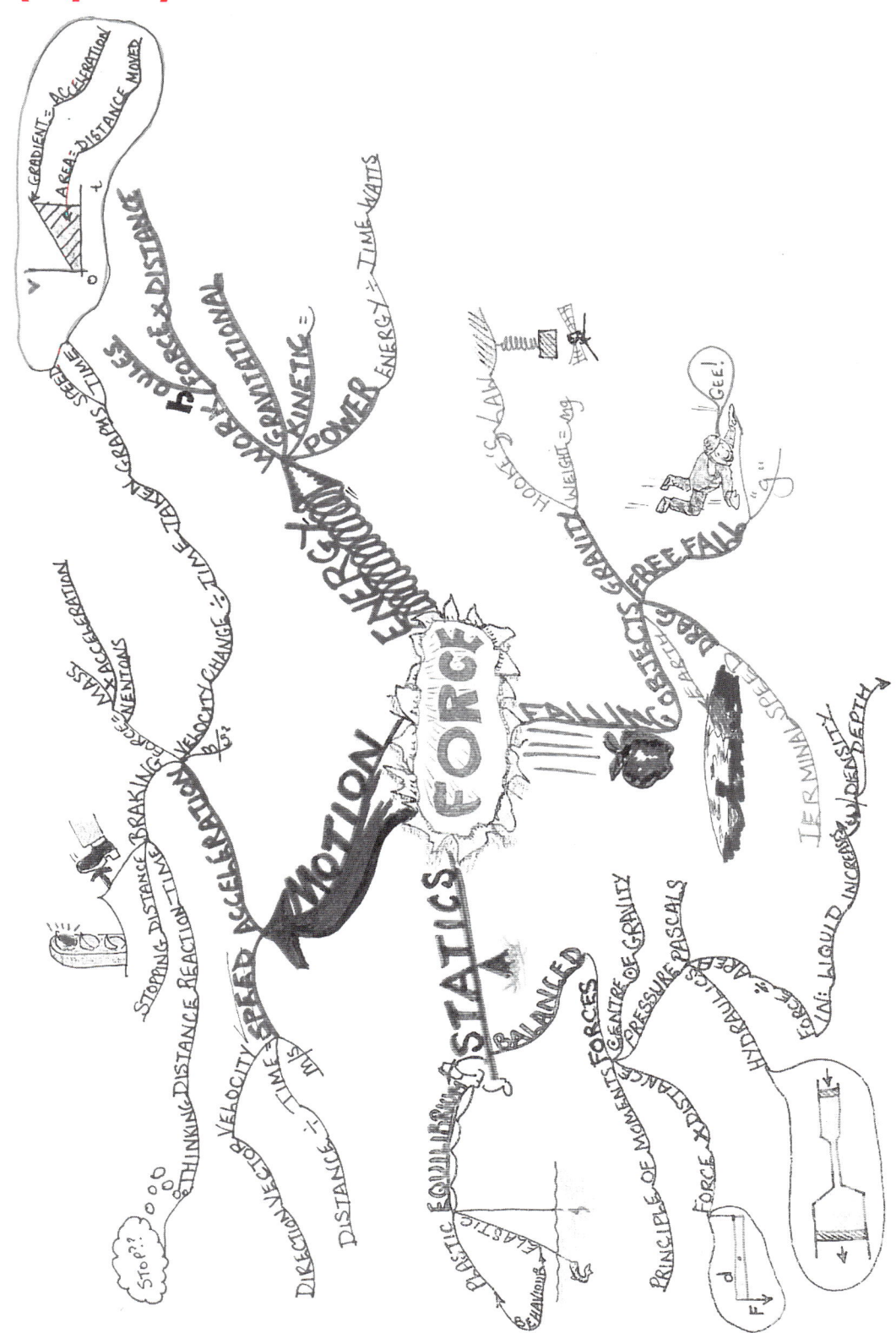

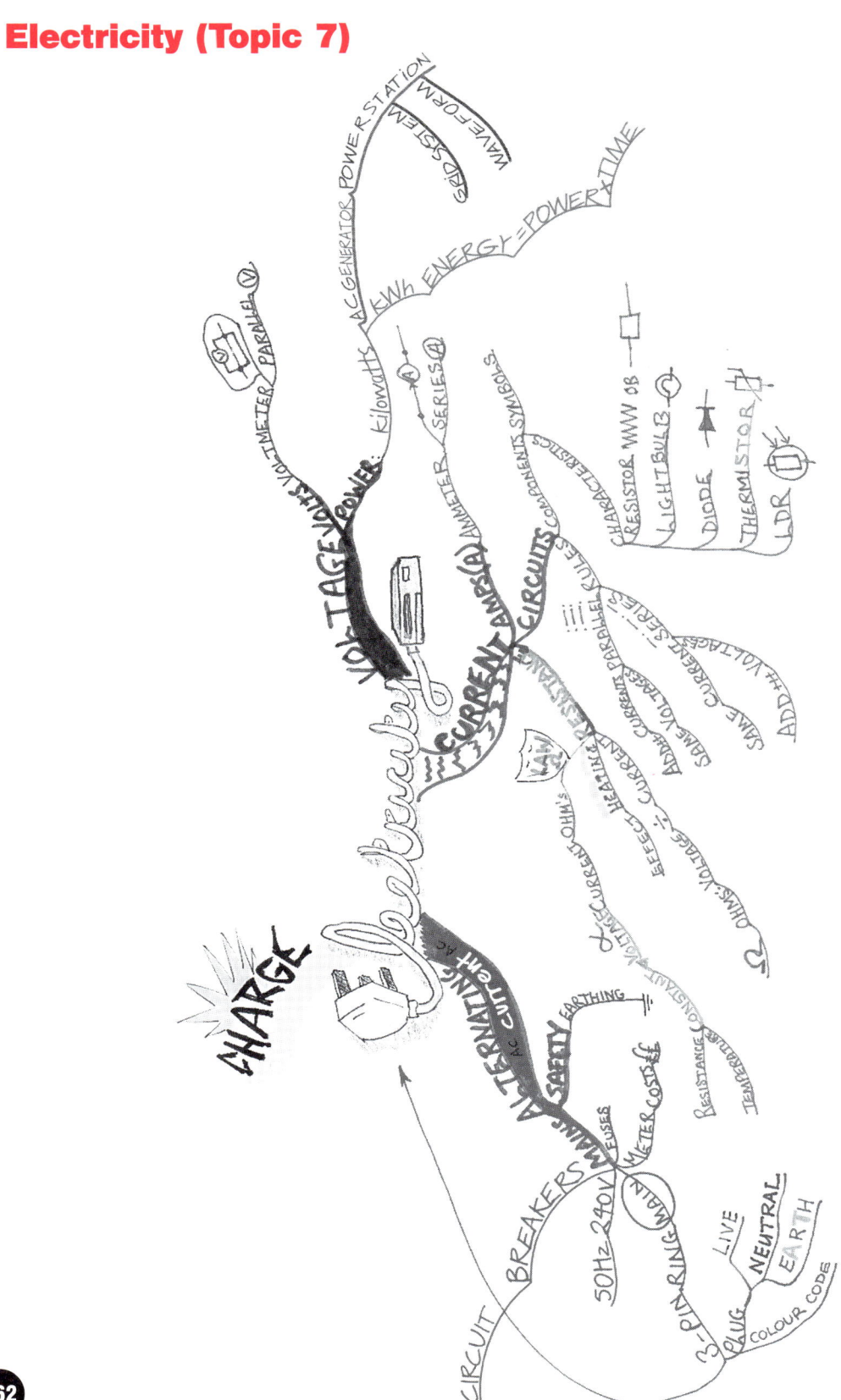

Physical processes

Electricity (Topic 7)

Physical processes

Mind Maps		**157**
1	**Beyond the Earth**	**164**
1.1	About the Earth	165
1.2	Over the Moon	166
1.3	The Solar System	167
1.4	Gravity	168
1.5	Life as a star	169
1.6	The expansion of the Universe	170
2	**Energy resources and energy transfer**	**172**
2.1	Work and energy	172
2.2	Temperature and heat	174
2.3	Heat transfer	175
2.4	Controlling heat transfer	176
2.5	Energy resources	177
3	**Radioactivity**	**179**
3.1	Inside the atom	180
3.2	Radioactive isotopes	181
3.3	Radioactive emissions	182
3.4	Half-life	183
3.5	Radiation effects	184
4	**Waves**	**186**
4.1	Measuring waves	186
4.2	Reflection of light	188
4.3	Refraction of light	189
5	**The electromagnetic spectrum**	**192**
5.1	Using electromagnetic waves	193
5.2	Electromagnetic waves in medicine	194
5.3	Communications	195
6	**Force**	**197**
6.1	Speed and distance	198
6.2	Force and acceleration	199
6.3	Equilibrium	200
6.4	Strength of solids	201
6.5	Pressure	202
7	**Electricity and magnetism**	**204**
7.1	Current, potential difference and resistance	205
7.2	Components in circuits	206
7.3	Mains electricity	207
7.4	Electrical safety	208
7.5	Electromagnetic induction	209
Equations you should know		**212**
Answers		**213**
Index		**220**

Beyond the Earth

preview

At the end of this topic you will be able to:

- explain what causes day and night, the seasons, and the rising and setting of the Sun, Moon and stars
- describe and explain the phases of the Moon and solar and lunar eclipses
- recall the main features of the planets
- use the theory of gravity to explain the motion of the planets, the Moon, satellites and comets
- describe the life cycle of a star
- describe evidence for the expansion of the Universe.

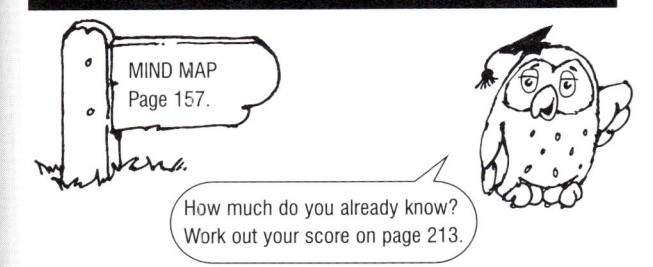

MIND MAP Page 157.

How much do you already know? Work out your score on page 213.

Test yourself

1 List the planets Mars (M), Jupiter (J), Neptune (N), Uranus (U) and Venus (V) in order of *increasing* distance from the Sun. [5]

2 When it is summer in the northern hemisphere, it is winter in the southern hemisphere. Why? [2]

3 What causes a lunar eclipse? [2]

4 Why can you see different constellations in the night sky during the year? [2]

5 a) Of the planets Mercury, Venus, Mars and Jupiter, which one is rocky and further from the Sun than Earth is? [1]
   b) Which of the above four planets does not have a solid surface? [1]

6 A comet X orbits the Sun once every 76 years. It was last seen from Earth in 1985 when it was visible for about a year. By the year 2050, is it likely to be
   a) slowing down or speeding up [1]
   b) moving towards or away from the Sun? [1]

7 What is the name of the process that releases energy in the core of a star? [1]

8 What is a supernova? [2]

9 What is meant by 'red shift'? [2]

10 What did the astronomer Edwin Hubble discover? [2]

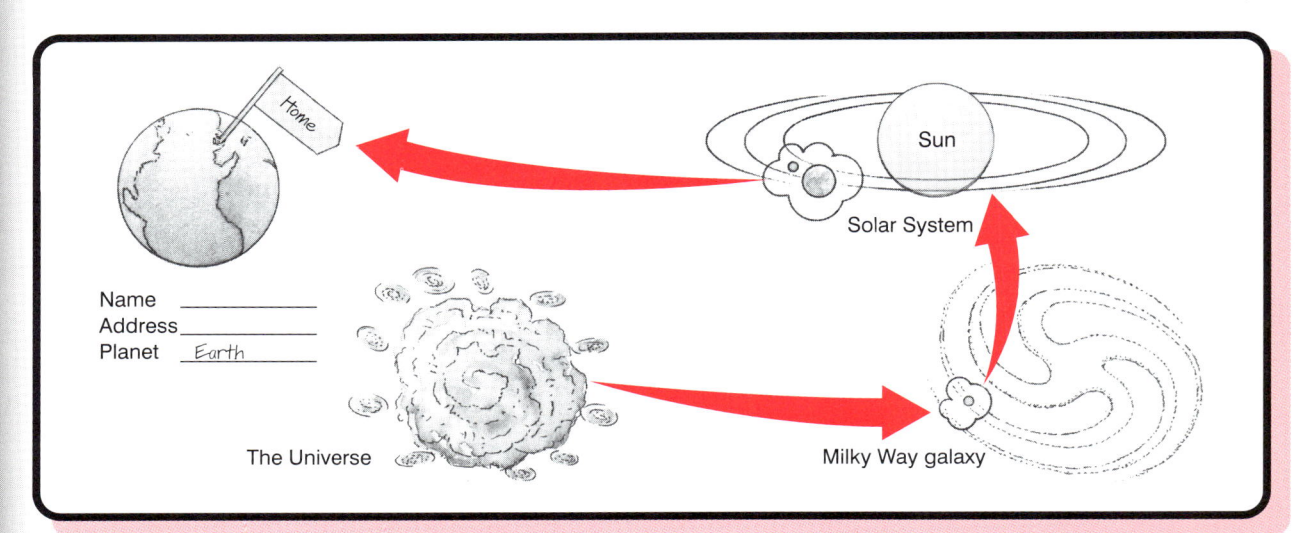

Name _____
Address _____
Planet Earth

Where do you fit in?

Beyond the Earth

1.1 About the Earth

Did you know?

The Earth is one of nine planets in orbit round a star we call the Sun. It takes about 8 minutes for light to reach Earth from the Sun. It takes over four years for light to reach Earth from the next nearest star, Proxima Centauri.

One day in your life

★ The Earth spins steadily on an axis passing through its poles.

★ One full day is the time it takes for the Earth to spin one full turn.

★ At night, our part of the Earth faces away from the Sun.

★ Sunrise happens when our part of the Earth moves into daylight.

★ Sunset happens when our part of the Earth moves out of daylight.

One year in your life

★ The Earth moves round the Sun on an orbit which is almost circular.

★ The Earth takes $365\frac{1}{4}$ days to orbit the Sun once.

★ The Earth's axis is tilted and always points towards the Pole star in the northern sky.

★ In the northern summer, the North Pole is tilted towards the Sun.

★ In the northern winter, the North Pole is tilted away from the Sun.

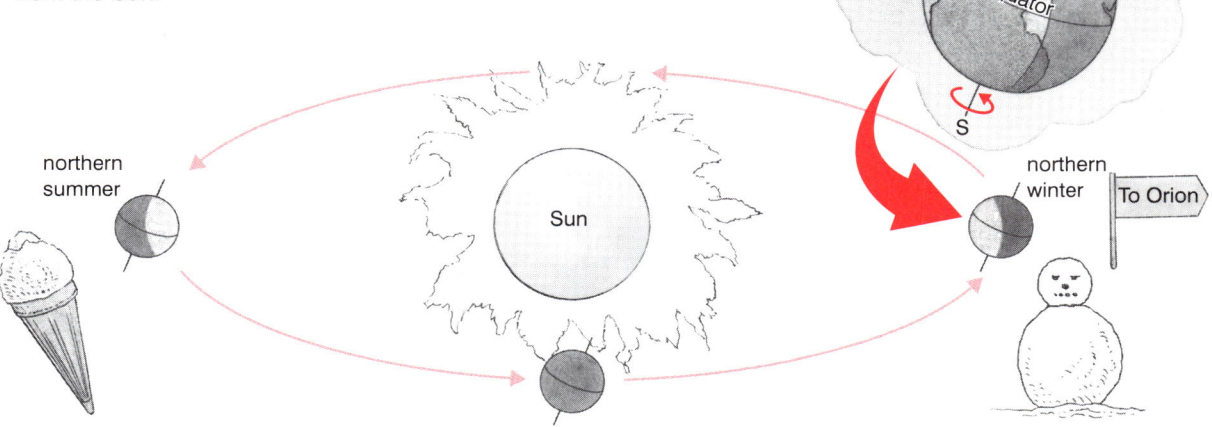

The Earth in orbit

What's on tonight?

The stars are mapped out in patterns called **constellations**. As the Earth moves round the Sun, the constellations we see at night change. Orion the Hunter is a spectacular constellation that we can see in the winter night sky, when the night side of Earth faces towards it.

Daily News

Happy Birthday Mary

Mary Davis is a sprightly 84-year-old who has just celebrated her twenty-first birthday. She was born on the 29th February 1912 and has a birthday every leap year.

Question

What difference would it make if leap years were abolished and we had 365 days in every calendar year?

Answer

The seasons would fall back by one day every four years. After a century, midwinter would be 25 days later than 21 December.

You are here at nightfall in winter. Brr!

Physical processes

1.2 Over the Moon

The Moon in perspective

★ The Moon orbits the Earth once every $27\frac{1}{4}$ days.

★ Its orbit is tilted a few degrees to the Earth's orbit.

★ Its diameter is about $\frac{1}{4} \times$ the diameter of Earth.

★ Its distance from Earth is about 30 Earth diameters.

★ Its gravity is too weak to retain an atmosphere.

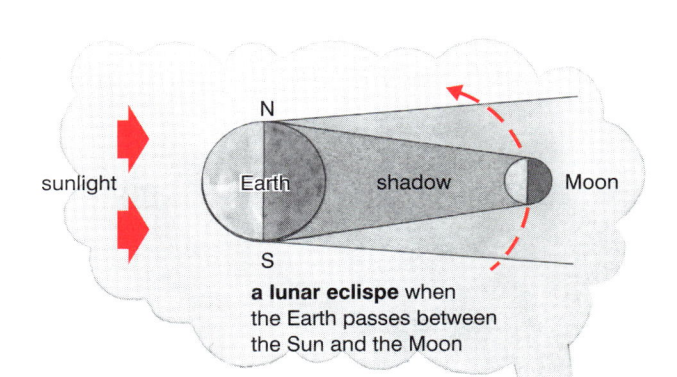

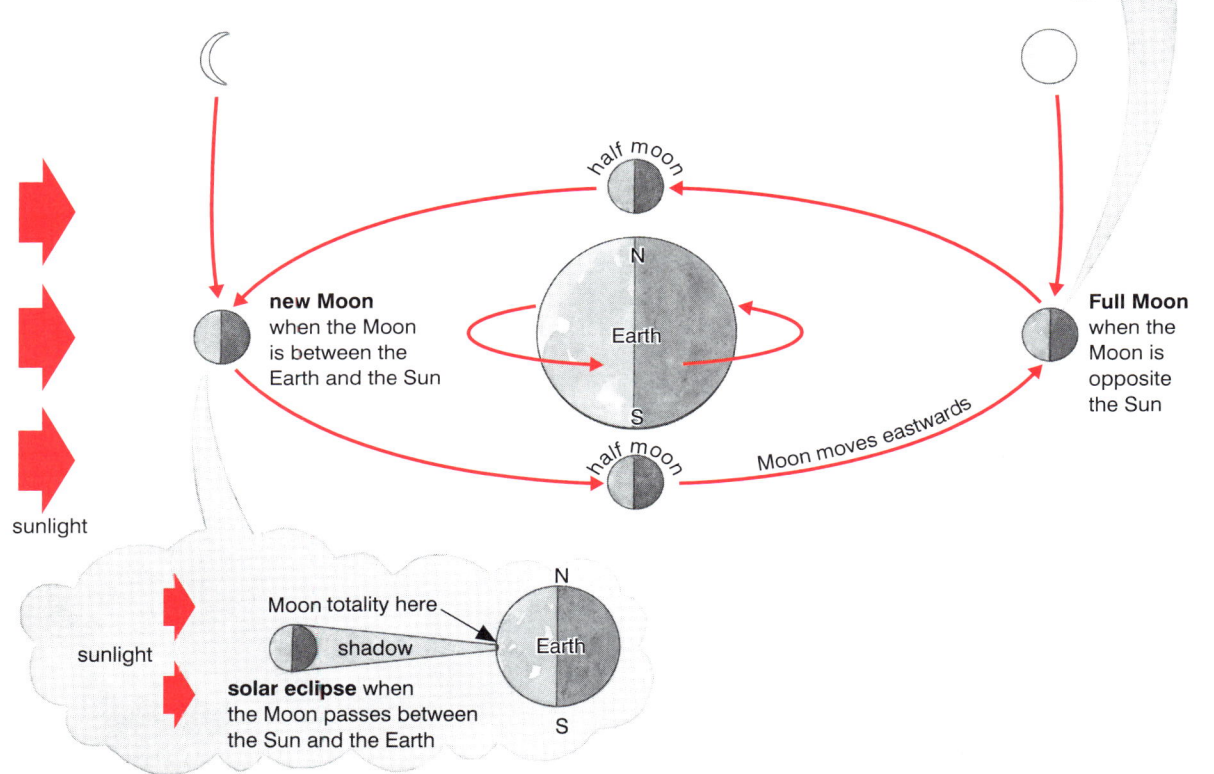

a lunar eclispe when the Earth passes between the Sun and the Moon

new Moon when the Moon is between the Earth and the Sun

Full Moon when the Moon is opposite the Sun

Moon moves eastwards

solar eclipse when the Moon passes between the Sun and the Earth

Phases and eclipses

Question

Why don't eclipses happen every month?

Larger than life

The Sun is 400 times further away from Earth than the Moon is. The Sun's diameter is also 400 times greater than the Moon's. This is why the Sun and the Moon look about the same size.

Answer

The Moon's orbit is at about 7° to the Earth's orbit. An eclipse can only happen if the Moon is exactly on the line between the Earth and the Sun. Usually, the Moon is below or above this line because of the tilt of its orbit.

Beyond the Earth

1.3 The Solar System

Planets in perspective

★ The planets all move round the Sun in the same direction.

★ Their orbits are almost circular, except for Pluto, and in the same plane as the Earth's orbit.

★ The planets reflect sunlight, which is why we can see them.

★ The further a planet is from the Sun, the longer it takes to go round its orbit.

★ When we observe the planets from Earth, they move through the constellations as they go round the Sun.

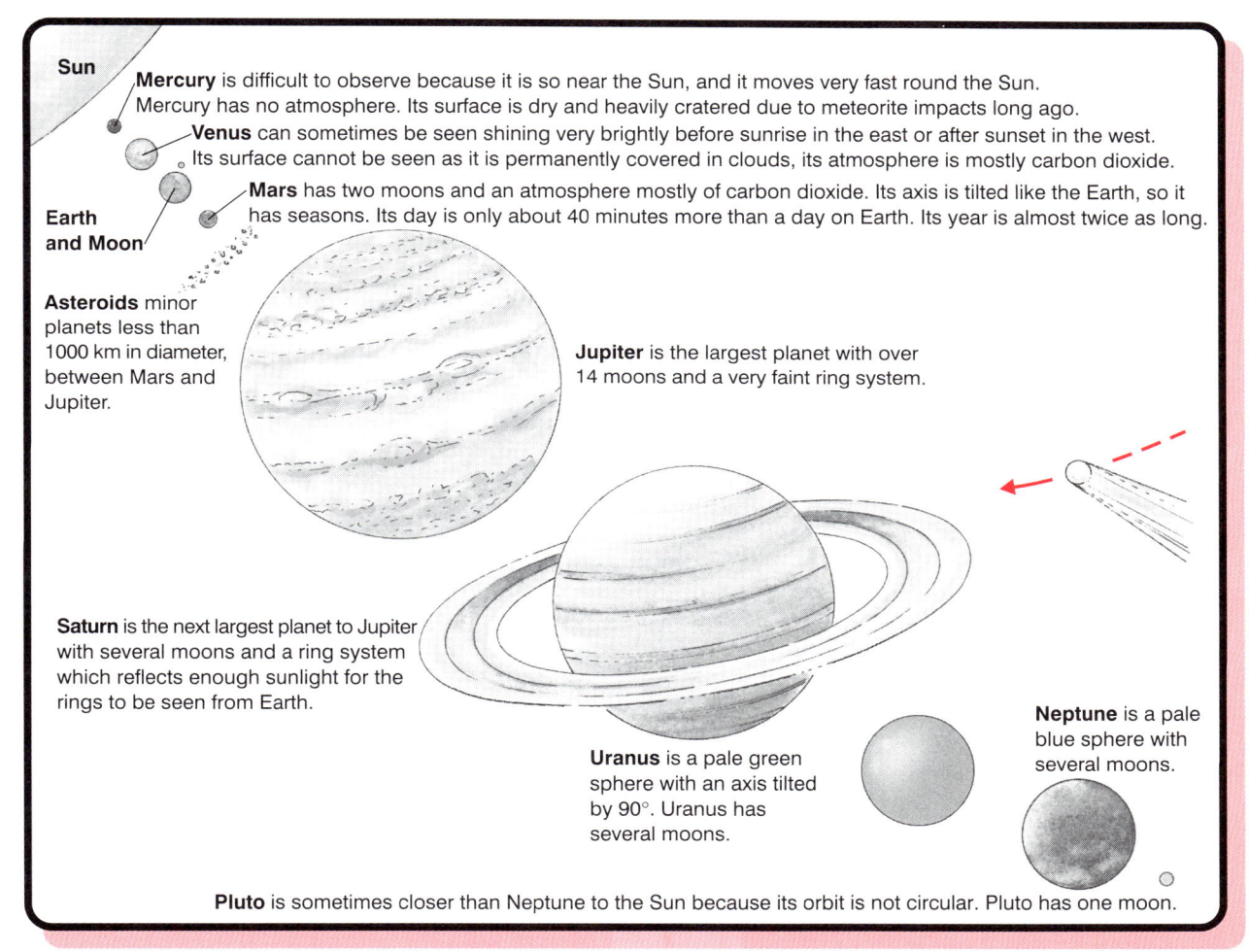

Sun

Mercury is difficult to observe because it is so near the Sun, and it moves very fast round the Sun. Mercury has no atmosphere. Its surface is dry and heavily cratered due to meteorite impacts long ago.

Venus can sometimes be seen shining very brightly before sunrise in the east or after sunset in the west. Its surface cannot be seen as it is permanently covered in clouds, its atmosphere is mostly carbon dioxide.

Earth and Moon

Mars has two moons and an atmosphere mostly of carbon dioxide. Its axis is tilted like the Earth, so it has seasons. Its day is only about 40 minutes more than a day on Earth. Its year is almost twice as long.

Asteroids minor planets less than 1000 km in diameter, between Mars and Jupiter.

Jupiter is the largest planet with over 14 moons and a very faint ring system.

Saturn is the next largest planet to Jupiter with several moons and a ring system which reflects enough sunlight for the rings to be seen from Earth.

Uranus is a pale green sphere with an axis tilted by 90°. Uranus has several moons.

Neptune is a pale blue sphere with several moons.

Pluto is sometimes closer than Neptune to the Sun because its orbit is not circular. Pluto has one moon.

The planets

On another planet

Mercury and **Venus** are called the 'inner planets' because they are closer to the Sun than Earth is. They are rocky, without moons. **Mars** is a rocky planet like the Earth and the inner planets. **Jupiter**, **Saturn**, **Uranus** and **Neptune** are giant spinning balls of fluid. **Pluto** is a small rocky planet.

Handy hint

To remember the order of the planets from the Sun, use the mnemonic '**M**ake **V**ery **E**asy **M**ash, **J**ust **S**tart **U**sing **N**ew **P**otatoes'!

Physical processes

1.4 Gravity

A mysterious force

Any two objects attract each other. This force of attraction is called **gravity**. The greater the masses of the two objects or the closer they are, the stronger the force of gravity between them. The planets, the Moon, satellites and comets all stay in their orbits because of the force of gravity. You stay on the Earth because of the force of gravity between you and the Earth.

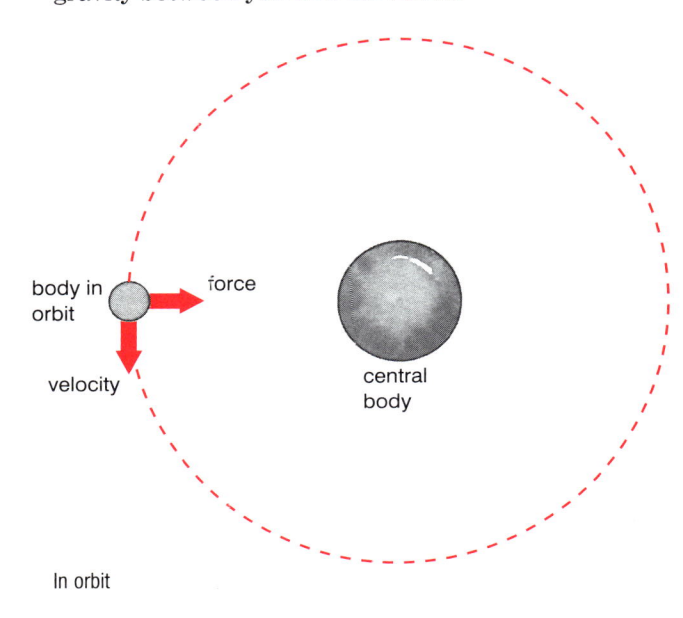

In orbit

Comets

★ Comets move round the Sun in elliptical orbits, usually in a different plane from the Earth's orbit.

★ As a comet approaches the Sun, it moves faster because the Sun's gravity is stronger closer in.

★ It also becomes visible near the Sun because solar heating raises the comet's temperature until it glows.

★ A comet usually develops a tail when it is near the Sun, as particles streaming from the Sun 'blow' glowing matter away from the comet.

★ Comets disappear into darkness as they move away from the Sun, but the Sun's gravity pulls them back towards the Sun again.

Scaling down

If the Sun was represented by a football, the Earth would be a pea 50 metres away from it. Pluto would be a small seed over 2 km away, still held in the Solar System by the force of gravity between it and the Sun.

Satellites

★ **Artificial satellites** are kept in their orbits because of the Earth's gravity. The greater the radius of orbit, the longer its **time period** (the time it takes to go round Earth once).

★ **Communication satellites** orbit the Earth at a certain height above the equator, with a time period of 24 hours. This means that they are always in the same place as seen from the Earth.

★ **Polar satellites** are in low orbits which take them over both poles once every few hours. They have a wide range of uses, including weather forecasting, surveying and spying.

★ **The Moon** is a natural satellite of the Earth. Its radius of orbit is so great that it takes over 27 days to orbit the Earth once.

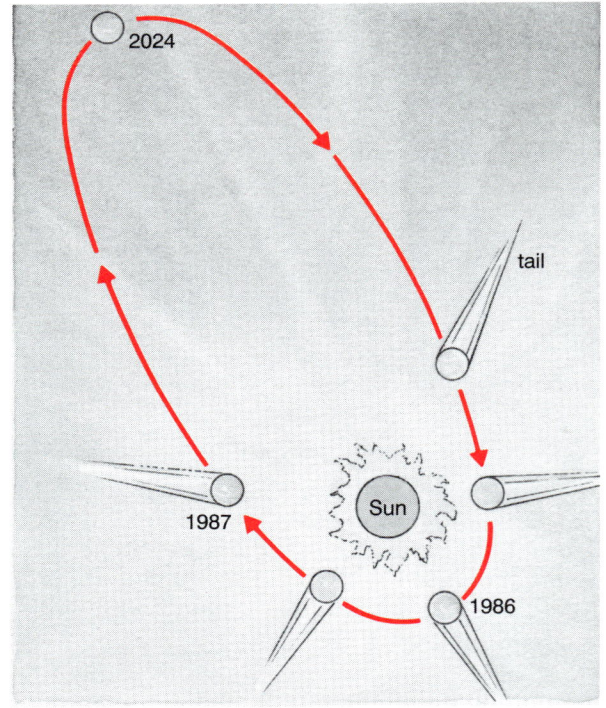

A comet orbit

Beyond the Earth

1.5 Life as a star

The stars we see in the night sky are at different stages of evolution and they vary in size and brightness. Massive bright stars last no more than a few million years. Small dim stars shine for thousands of millions of years. The Sun is thought to be a typical middle-aged star about half-way through its life cycle of about 10 000 million years.

Formation – The star forms from dust and gas in space being pulled together by their own gravity. As the density rises, the star becomes hotter and hotter due to the release of gravitational energy. The planets are thought to have formed from dust clouds left over at this stage when the Sun was formed.

Birth – at a temperature of about 10 million degrees, the nuclei of hydrogen atoms fuse together releasing nuclear energy. This energy keeps the temperature of the star high enough for nuclear fusion to continue. A star is born!

Equilibrium – for most of its life, the star gradually fuses the hydrogen nuclei in its core into heavier nuclei such as helium. The nuclear reactions in the core release vast amounts of electromagnetic and particle radiation. The inward gravitational attraction on the core is balanced by outward pressure due to this radiation.

Expansion – eventually, the hydrogen in the core is used up and the star expands to become a **red giant**. This is thought to happen because the helium nuclei and other light nuclei formed in the star fuse to form heavier nuclei, releasing more radiation which forces the star to swell out.

Collapse – once there are no more light nuclei to fuse together, the star collapses due to its own gravity. It becomes very hot, very dense and very small. It is now a **white dwarf**.

low mass → oblivion as a dark object

high mass

Explosion – if the star is massive enough, it will explode, releasing huge amounts of matter and radiation in a very short time. This supernova event is thought to leave behind an extremely dense object known as a neutron star.

The life cycle of a star

Sandaluk II

Supernovae are rare events. The Crab Nebula in the constellation Taurus is thought to be the remnants of an eleventh century supernova. In 1987, a supernova was observed in the Andromeda galaxy. It was thought to be the death throes of a star called Sandaluk II.

In a supernova explosion, large heavy nuclei are formed from the fusion of lighter nuclei. Dense elements like uranium found in the Earth mean that the Earth and the Sun probably formed from the debris of a supernova explosion.

Question

When a star forms from dust clouds, it becomes so hot that its nuclei fuse together and release more energy. Why does it become so hot when it forms from dust?

Answer

The dust clouds attract each other because of their own gravity, and become more and more dense. Gravitational potential energy is converted into kinetic energy of the dust particles, which become very hot when they collide with each other.

Physical processes

1.6 The expansion of the Universe

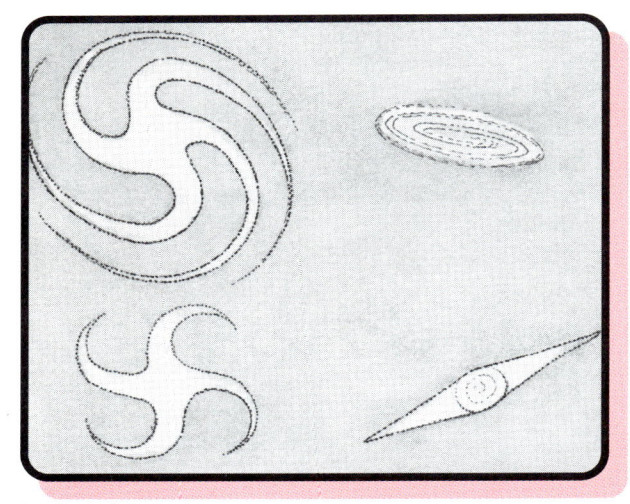

Local galaxies

Galaxies

★ The Sun is just one of billions of stars in the Milky Way galaxy.

★ There are many other galaxies.

★ The nearest galaxy is about 10 million light years away.

★ The furthest is about 12 000 million light years away.

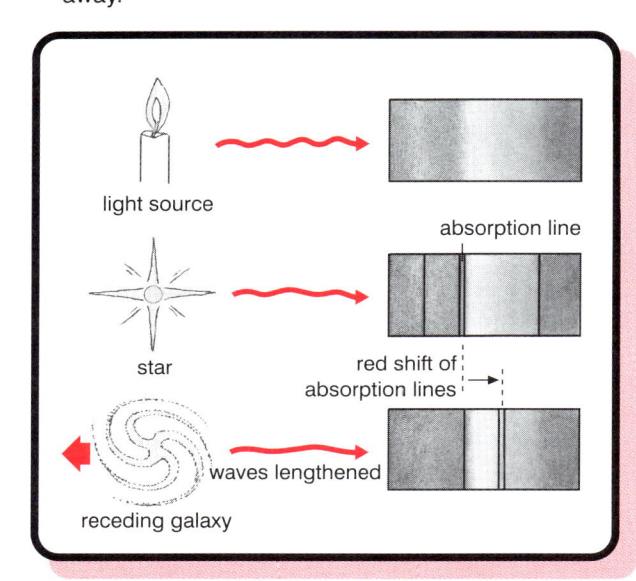

Starlight spectra

The red shift

The spectrum of light from a star is crossed by dark vertical lines. These are caused by the star's outer layers absorbing light of certain wavelengths. **Edwin Hubble** discovered that the absorption lines in the light spectra of distant galaxies are red-shifted towards longer wavelengths in the spectrum. This is because these galaxies are moving away from us very quickly so their light waves are lengthened.

Hubble made precise measurements and discovered that the speed of a galaxy is greater the more distant the galaxy is. This important discovery is known as **Hubble's law**.

The Big Bang

All the distant galaxies are rushing away from us. Scientists think the Universe is expanding. This would explain why distant galaxies are moving away faster and faster the further away they get. The expansion started billions of years ago in a huge explosion called the **Big Bang**. At present, it is not known whether the expansion will continue indefinitely or reverse – ending perhaps in the Big Crunch!

In the beginning

The edge of the Universe

No object can travel faster than light. Light from the Big Bang defines the edge of the Universe, which is expanding at present. Hubble estimated that the edge of the Universe is about 12 000 million light years away!

Question

If the age of the Universe was scaled down to start 24 hours ago, when would life on Earth (one million years ago) have started?

Answer

7 seconds ago

Beyond the Earth

round-up

How much have you improved?
Work out your improvement index on page 213.

1 A student made two sketches of the Moon one week apart.
   a) Explain why the Moon appears different in each sketch. [2]
   b) Make a further sketch to show how you think the Moon appeared after one more week. [1]

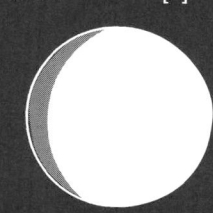

2 During the night, the constellations move across the sky. Explain why this happens. [2]

3 a) Stars produce their own light but planets do not. Explain why we can see the planets. [1]
   b) The diagram shows the planet Venus in two different positions on its orbit relative to the Earth. A sketch was made of Venus in each of these positions, viewed through a large telescope. Decide which sketch is for which position, and explain your reasons. [2]

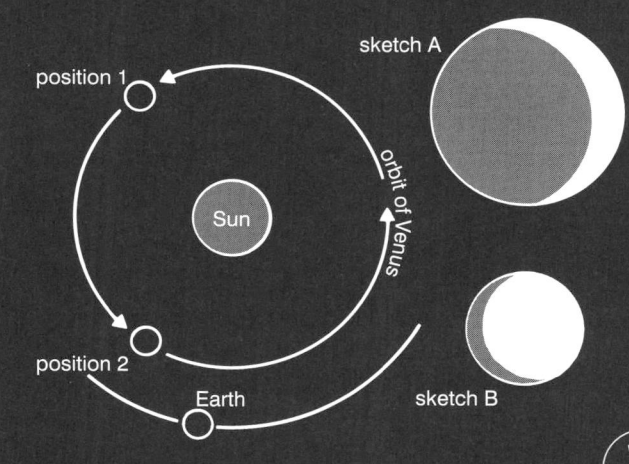

4 a) Sketch a diagram to show how an eclipse of the Sun occurs. [2]
   b) The next total eclipse of the Sun visible from Britain will be in 1999. The last one was many years ago. Why is an eclipse of the Sun such a very rare event? [2]

5 a) Draw a sketch to show the relative positions of the Sun, the Earth and Jupiter when Jupiter is easily visible in the night sky. [1]
   b) State four differences between the Earth and (i) Mars (ii) Jupiter (iii) Saturn. [12]

6 a) Mercury is very difficult to observe. Why? [3]
   b) Pluto is the most distant planet, yet it can be closer than Neptune to the Sun. Why? [2]
   c) Uranus is closer to the Sun than Neptune is. Which takes longer to go round the Sun? [1]
   d) Why do comets disappear then return? [3]

7 a) Betelgeuse is a red giant star. Why is it described as a red giant? [2]
   b) Describe what will happen to the Sun when it uses up all the hydrogen nuclei in its core. [4]
   c) What is a supernova? [2]

8 a) Why is it difficult to launch satellites into orbit? [3]
   b) The Earth's surface gravity is 10 N/kg. The Moon's surface gravity is 1.6 N/kg. Why is the Moon's gravity smaller? [2]

9 The Universe is thought to be expanding. Describe the evidence for this. [4]

10 a) Write a short account of a space mission to a planet. [4]
   b) Light takes 8 minutes to reach the Earth from the Sun, and about 4 years from Proxima Centauri, the nearest star to the Sun. Do you think a space mission to this star is feasible? Explain your answer. [4]

Well done if you've improved. Don't worry if you haven't. Take a break and try again.

Energy resources and energy transfer

preview

At the end of this topic you will be able to:

- describe different forms of energy
- describe the energy changes when work is done or when heat transfer takes place
- explain what is meant by conservation of energy, efficiency and energy waste
- describe the relative merits of different fuels and renewable energy sources.

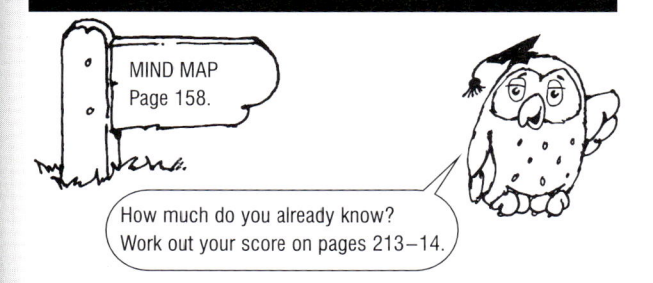

MIND MAP Page 158.

How much do you already know? Work out your score on pages 213–14.

Test yourself

Assume $g = 10$ N/kg where necessary.

1 A cyclist freewheels down a road and eventually comes to rest. Which one of the following sequences **A** to **D** best describes the energy changes in this process?

- **A** Chemical ⟶ potential ⟶ kinetic
- **B** Potential ⟶ kinetic ⟶ thermal
- **C** Potential ⟶ chemical ⟶ kinetic
- **D** Chemical ⟶ kinetic ⟶ thermal [1]

2 Why are metals good conductors of heat? [3]

Home heating bills may be reduced by installing
a) double glazed windows instead of ordinary windows
b) felt insulation in the loft
c) draught excluders round the door frames.

3 Which of the above measures reduces heat loss due to thermal conduction and thermal radiation? [2]

4 Which of the measures reduces heat loss due to thermal convection? [1]

5 State one further method of reducing heat losses from the home. [1]

6 State three different fuels, including one type which is not a fossil fuel. [3]

7 State three renewable energy sources which depend on the Sun. [3]

8 What is the origin of geothermal energy? [2]

9 What is the origin of tidal energy? [2]

10 A falling weight is used to turn an electricity generator which is used to light a bulb, as shown in the diagram. Complete the energy flow diagram. [5]

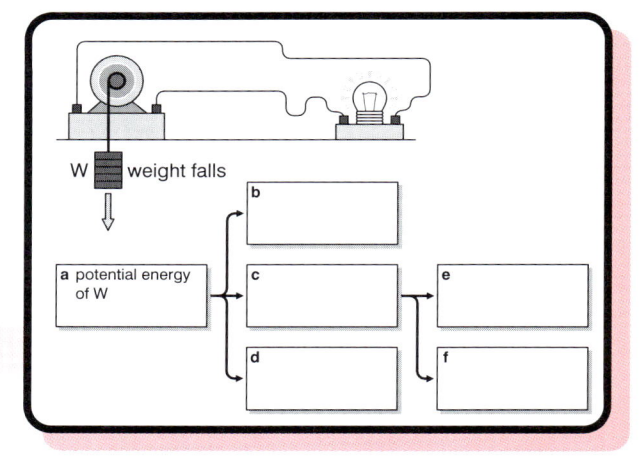

2.1 Work and energy

Time for work

Work is done when a force makes an object move. The greater the force or the further the movement, the greater the amount of work done. For example, the work done to lift a box to a height of 2 m is twice the work done to lift the same box to a height of 1 m.

Energy is the capacity to do work. A battery-operated electric motor used to raise a weight

Energy resources and energy transfer

does work on the weight. The battery therefore contains energy because it has the capacity to make the motor do work.

Energy can be transferred from one object to other objects. A raised weight has the capacity to do work and therefore contains energy. For example, it could be used to keep a clock running.

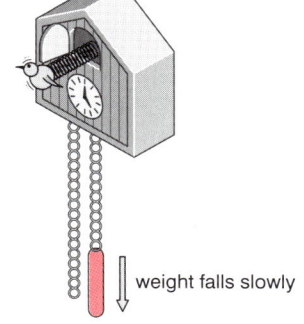

weight falls slowly

Transferring energy

Heat is energy transferred due to a difference of temperature. Heat and work are two methods by which energy can be transferred to or from a body. Work is energy transferred due to force and heat is energy transferred due to temperature difference. Heat as a method of transferring energy is discussed in more detail on page 175.

Work and energy are measured in joules (J), where one joule is defined as the work done when a force of one newton acts over a distance of one metre in the direction of the force.

Energy can be changed from any one form into other forms. In other words, it can be transformed from one form into other forms.

Power is the rate of transfer of energy. The unit of power is the watt (W), equal to the rate of transfer of energy of one joule per second.

Forms of energy

Energy exists in different forms, including

- **kinetic energy** which is the energy of a moving body due to its motion
- **potential energy** which is the energy of a body due to its position
- **chemical energy** which is energy released by chemical reactions
- **light energy** which is energy carried by light
- **elastic energy** which is energy stored in an object by changing its shape
- **electrical energy** which is energy due to electric charge
- **nuclear energy** which is energy released in nuclear reactions
- **sound energy** which is energy carried by sound waves
- **thermal energy** which is the energy of an object due to its temperature.

Make an anagram of the first letter of each line to help remember all these forms of energy. No doubt you can do better than 'KP Cleenst' or 'NT Speckle'!

Question

a) A student applies a force of 600 N to a wardrobe and pushes it a distance of 2.0 m across a floor. Calculate the work done by the student.

b) If the wardrobe had been emptied, it could have been pushed across the floor using a force of 200 N. How far could it have been moved for the same amount of work?

A Very Important Principle

The principle of conservation of energy states that in any change, the total energy before the change is equal to the total energy after the change. In other words, the total amount of energy is conserved, even though it may change from its initial form into other forms as a result of the change.

But

The trouble with energy is that it tends to spread out when it changes from one form into other forms. For example, in a bicycle freewheeling down a slope, friction at the wheel bearings causes the bearings to become warm. Some of the initial potential energy is therefore converted into thermal energy. Such thermal energy is lost to the surroundings and can never be recovered and used to do work. The thermal energy is therefore wasted.

Even where energy is concentrated, such as when a car battery is charged, energy is wasted in the process. For example, the electric current passing through a car battery when it is being charged would warm the circuit wires a little.

Answers a) 1200 J b) 6.0 m

Physical processes

2.2 Temperature and heat

Temperature scales

Temperature is a measure of 'hotness'. If a solid substance is heated and heated, its temperature rises until it reaches the melting point of the substance. At this point the solid changes its physical state into a liquid without a change of temperature. Continued heating of the liquid raises its temperature to the boiling point.

A **scale of temperature** is defined by using fixed points which are easily reproduced 'degrees of hotness', such as the temperature of melting ice (the ice point), or of water boiling at atmospheric pressure (the steam point).

★ The **Celsius** scale of temperature, in °C, is defined in terms of the ice point (0°C) and the steam point (100°C).

★ The **absolute** scale of temperature, in kelvins (K), is defined in terms of the lowest possible temperature (0 K) as one fixed point, and the temperature of ice and water in equilibrium with water vapour (273 K) as the other fixed point. This scale is used for scientific work and is defined as

absolute temperature = Celsius temperature + 273
(in kelvins)   (in °C)

Thermal energy

Thermal energy is the energy gained by a substance when its temperature rises or it melts or vaporises.

★ **When a substance is heated and its temperature rises**, its atoms gain kinetic energy. In a solid, the atoms vibrate more; in a liquid or a gas, the atoms move about faster.

★ **When a substance is heated and its physical state changes**, the potential energy of its atoms changes. When a solid melts, energy is required to let the atoms break free from each other. In a liquid, the atoms move about at random, with weak forces of attraction acting between them. When a liquid vaporises, the atoms or molecules break away from each other completely and only come into contact with each other when they collide.

★ **The thermal energy of a substance can also be changed by doing work**. For example, the work done by the frictional force between two moving parts in a machine causes the moving parts to gain thermal energy (warm up).

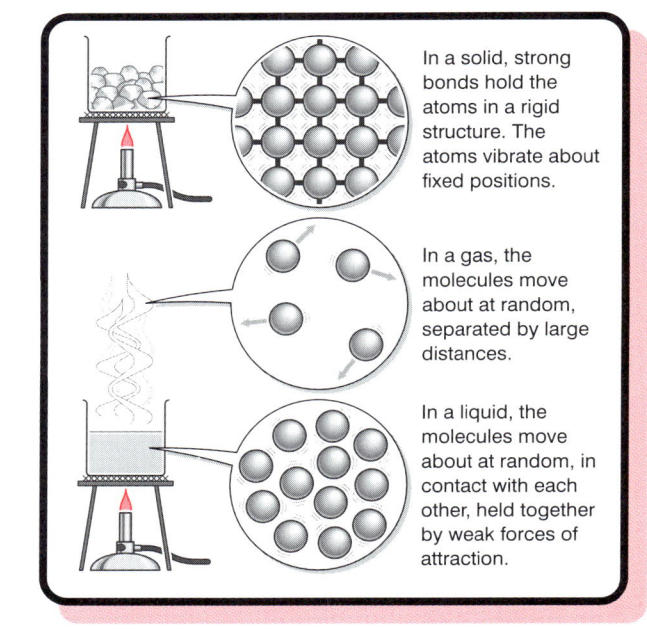

In a solid, strong bonds hold the atoms in a rigid structure. The atoms vibrate about fixed positions.

In a gas, the molecules move about at random, separated by large distances.

In a liquid, the molecules move about at random, in contact with each other, held together by weak forces of attraction.

States of matter

Question

The graph shows how the temperature of a hot substance, initially in the liquid state, changed as it cooled.

a) Use the graph to estimate the melting point of the substance.
b) Describe how the arrangement of the atoms of the substance changed during the cooling process.

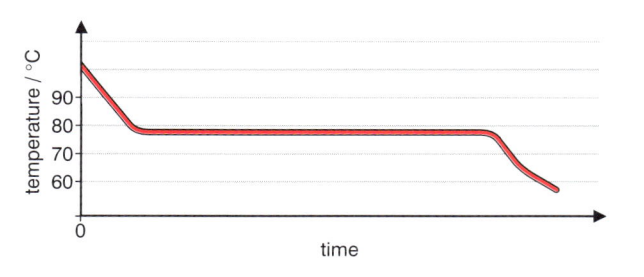

Answers

a) 78°C b) Above 78°C, the atoms move about at random in contact with each other; at 78°C, they take up fixed positions into which they are locked below this temperature.

2.3 Heat transfer

Heat transfer occurs by means of thermal **conduction**, **convection** and **radiation**. Cooling also takes place during **evaporation** from a hot liquid, and matter as well as heat is transferred in this process, which is not the case with conduction, convection or radiation.

Thermal conduction – five facts

1. Thermal conduction is heat transfer through a substance without the substance moving.
2. Solids, liquids and gases all conduct heat.
3. Good thermal conductors are also good electrical conductors. They contain free electrons which can transport both energy and charge through the substance.
4. Metals and alloys are the best conductors of heat.
5. Insulating materials such as wood, fibreglass and air are very poor conductors of heat. The presence of air pockets in an insulating material improves its insulating properties.

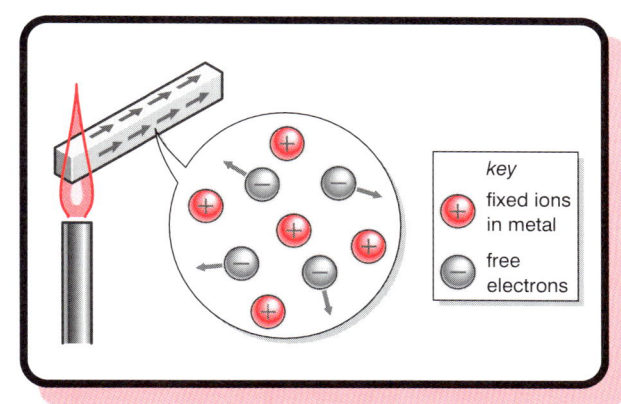

Thermal conduction in a metal

Thermal convection – five facts

1. Thermal convection is heat transfer in a liquid or a gas due to internal circulation of particles.
2. Thermal convection occurs only in fluids (liquids or gases).
3. Natural convection occurs because hot fluids, being less dense than cold fluids, rise, whereas cold fluids sink. When a fluid is heated, circulation is caused by hot fluid rising and cold fluid sinking.
4. Forced convection happens when a cold fluid is pumped over a hot surface and takes away energy from the surface.
5. Cooling fins on an engine increase the surface area of the engine and therefore enable more thermal convection to occur.

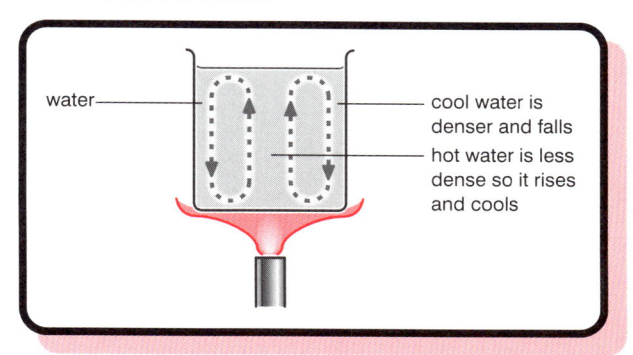

Thermal convection in water

Thermal radiation – five facts

1. Thermal radiation is electromagnetic radiation emitted by any surface at a temperature greater than absolute zero.
2. The hotter a surface is, the more thermal radiation it emits.
3. Thermal radiation can pass through a vacuum and does not need a substance to carry it.
4. A black surface is a better emitter and absorber of thermal radiation than a white surface.
5. A matt (rough) surface is a better emitter and absorber of thermal radiation than a shiny surface.

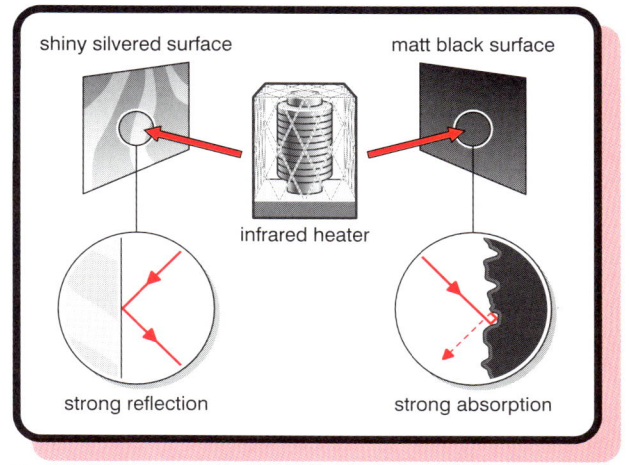

Thermal radiation

Physical processes

2.4 Controlling heat transfer

Designers need to take account of the thermal properties of materials when considering what materials to use in any given device or situation.

★ A car radiator transfers heat from the engine to the surroundings. Forced convection occurs as water pumped round the engine block carries away heat to the radiator. Heat is conducted through the radiator walls so the outside of the radiator becomes hot. Air circulates round the outside of the radiator, carrying away heat, and the radiator surface is blackened so it emits thermal radiation.

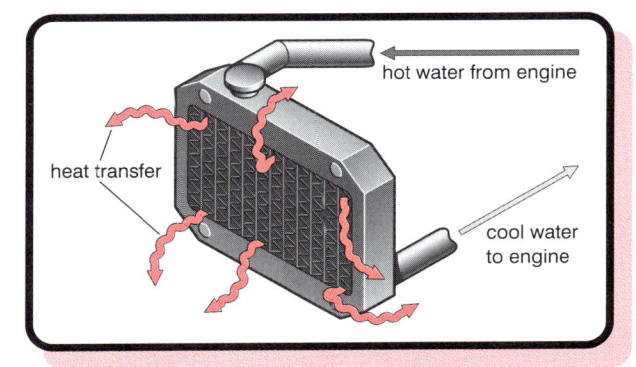

A car radiator

★ A domestic hot water tank is fitted with an insulating jacket to reduce heat losses. The outer surface of the jacket is shiny to reduce heat losses due to thermal radiation.

Keeping warm in winter

Home heating bills can be greatly reduced by fitting loft insulation and double glazing. The picture of the house shows these and other measures that can be taken to reduce fuel bills.

Question

1 Tick boxes in the table to show which heat transfer processes have been reduced by each measure.

Maintaining body temperature

If you are outdoors in winter, you need warm dry clothing made of fibres which trap layers of air. Since air is a very poor conductor of heat, it reduces heat transfer from the body to the surroundings. A white outer surface reduces thermal radiation. A smooth shiny surface would be even better but might be expensive! In addition, the outer surface needs to be waterproof and the inner layers need to prevent water vapour caused by sweat penetrating the fibres.

Question

2 List the materials you would use to make a winter coat, giving a reason for each material chosen.

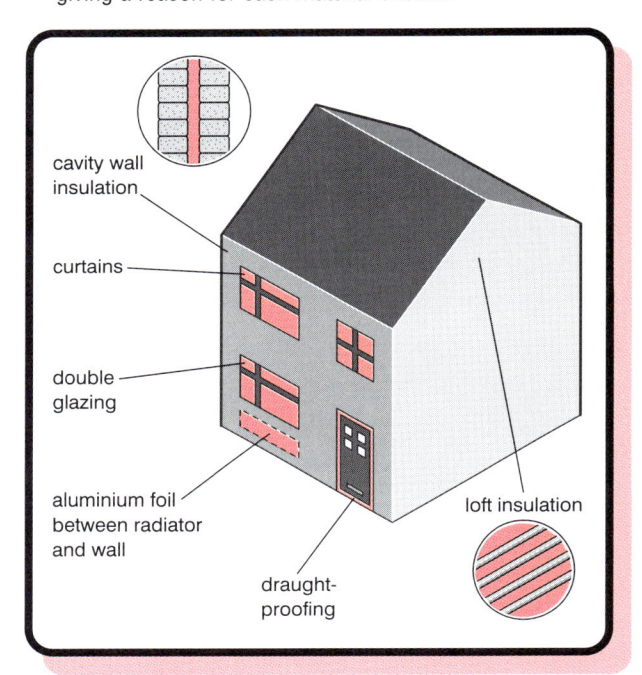

Reducing home heating bills

Answer

1 conduction ✓✓✓XXX convection X✓✓XXX radiation ✓✓XX✓X

	loft insulation	double glazing	cavity wall insulation	radiator foil	heavy curtains	draught excluder
conduction						
convection						
radiation						

2.5 Energy resources

Demand and supply

The total energy demand for the United Kingdom in one year is about 10 million million million joules. This works out at about 5000 joules per second for every person in the country. The pie charts show how the total energy is obtained and how it is used.

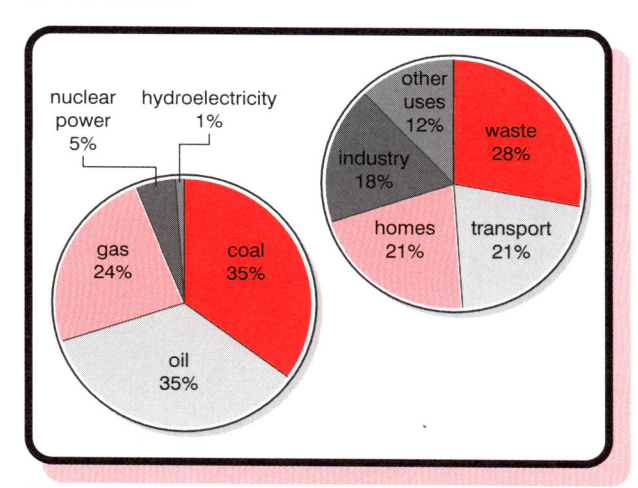

UK energy supplies — UK energy demands

Fuels are substances which release energy as a result of changing into another substance. Fuels cannot be reused.

- fossil fuels – coal, oil, gas, wood
- nuclear fuels – uranium, plutonium

Renewable energy resources are sources of useful energy which do not change the substances involved, allowing them to be reused. The energy usually comes from the Sun.

- solar-driven resources – solar panels for water heating, solar cells
- weather-driven resources (indirectly powered by the Sun's heating effect on the atmosphere) – hydroelectricity, aerogenerators (wind), wave powered generators
- tidal generators (powered by the gravitational potential energy between the Earth and the Moon)
- geothermal power (powered by thermal energy in the Earth's interior)

Energy efficiency

Reasons why energy should not be wasted:

1. Fuel supplies are finite and cannot be renewed.
2. Fossil fuels release carbon dioxide gas which is thought to be causing global warming, resulting in melting icecaps and rising sea levels. Sulphur dioxide from power stations is a cause of acid rain.
3. Nuclear fuel creates radioactive waste which must be stored safely for hundreds of years to prevent it harming us.
4. Small-scale renewable resources may damage the environment, for example turbine noise from aerogenerators and effects on plant and animal life when tidal power stations are made.
5. It costs money to make energy useful and to distribute it.

Using energy resources efficiently

★ Use machines and vehicles more efficiently.

★ Replace inefficient machines and vehicles with more efficient ones.

★ Improve thermal insulation in buildings.

★ Fit automatic lighting and temperature sensors to reduce unnecessary lighting and heating.

★ Supply waste heat from power stations for district heating (combined heat and power stations).

★ Use more pumped storage schemes (see below).

★ Make energy-efficient lifestyle choices, for example teleworking, car sharing, better public transport.

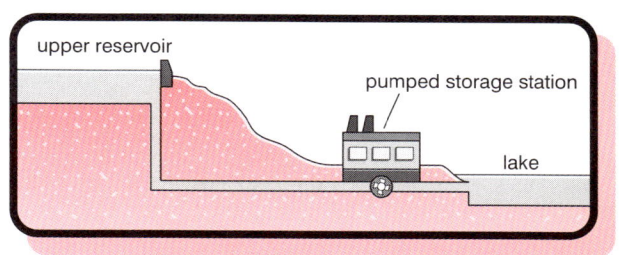

A pumped storage station. Electricity is used to pump water uphill when the demand for electricity is low. Electricity is generated by allowing water to flow downhill when demand is high.

2 Physical processes

Machines at work

The useful work done by a machine is always less than the energy supplied to it because of friction between its moving parts. This causes heating and therefore wastes energy.

$$\text{efficiency} = \frac{\text{useful work done by the machine}}{\text{energy supplied to the machine}}$$

$$= \frac{\text{output power}}{\text{input power}}$$

Notes

1. *Efficiency is sometimes expressed as a percentage (the fraction above multiplied by 100).*
2. *The efficiency of any machine is always less than 100% because of friction.*

Machines at work

round-up

How much have you improved? Work out your improvement index on page 214.

1. Describe the energy changes that take place when
   a) the alarm sounds on a battery-operated clock [1]
   b) a parachutist jumps from a plane and descends safely to the ground. [2]

2. A 12 V 25 W electric heater designed for use in a car is capable of heating a flask of tea from 20 °C to 50 °C in 15 minutes.
   a) Calculate the energy supplied by a 25 W electric heater in 15 minutes. [1]
   b) A student decides to test the heater by filling the flask with 0.20 kg of water. She has discovered in a separate test that 4200 J of energy are needed to raise the temperature of 1.0 kg of water by 1 °C. She finds that the heater takes 650 s to heat the water from 20 °C to 40 °C.
      (i) Calculate the energy needed to heat 0.20 kg of water from 20 °C to 40 °C. [1]
      (ii) Calculate the power of the heater. [1]

3. a) Explain whether hot tea in a china teapot would cool faster than hot tea in a shiny metal teapot. [2]
   b) Explain why hot tea cools faster in a wide-brimmed cup than in a narrow cup. [3]
   c) Explain why heat loss through a single-glazed window can be reduced by fitting double glazing. [2]

4. In a geothermal power station, water at 10 °C is pumped through pipes which pass through hot underground rocks at 90 °C. Given that 4200 J of energy are needed to raise the temperature of 1.0 kg of water by 1 °C,
   a) calculate
      (i) the energy needed to heat 1.0 kg of water from 10 °C to 90 °C
      (ii) the mass of water that must be pumped through the pipes each second to extract thermal energy at a rate of 100 million joules per second [3]
   b) discuss whether or not geothermal power is a renewable resource. [3]

Well done if you've improved. Don't worry if you haven't. Take a break and try again.

Radioactivity

preview

At the end of this topic you will be able to:

- explain the structure of the atomic nucleus and the term isotope
- explain radioactivity in simple terms
- describe the characteristics of the three main types of emission from radioactive substances
- explain what is meant by background radioactivity
- explain the term half-life and interpret half-life graphs and related data
- understand that emissions from radioactive substances have harmful effects.

MIND MAP Page 159.

How much do you already know? Work out your score on page 214.

Test yourself

1 State whether each of the following particles carries positive charge, negative charge or is uncharged.
 a) the electron **b)** the proton **c)** the neutron
 d) the alpha particle **e)** the beta minus particle [5]

2 State how many protons and how many neutrons are present in each nucleus of the following isotopes.
 a) ^4_2He **b)** $^{235}_{92}\text{U}$ [4]

3 What type of charge does the nucleus of the atom carry? [1]

4 State the three types of emissions from naturally occurring radioactive substances, and state which type of radioactive emission is most easily absorbed. [4]

5 What is background radioactivity? [1]

6 Name a scientific instrument used to measure radioactivity. [1]

7 The *half-life* of the *isotope* of carbon $^{14}_6\text{C}$ is 5500 years. Explain what is meant by the terms in italics. [2]

8 What is meant by nuclear fission? [2]

9 Why is it important to store radioactive waste from a nuclear reactor for thousands of years? [2]

10 A radioactive source is placed near the end of a Geiger tube. The particles emitted by the source are stopped when a 50p coin is placed between the source and the tube. What types of radiation could be emitted by the source? [2]

Symbol for radioactive sources

A scientific puzzle

Radioactivity was discovered in 1896 by **Henri Becquerel**. When he developed an unused photographic plate, he found an image of a key on it. He realised this was caused by radiation from a packet containing uranium salts, which had been on top of a key with the photographic plate underneath. The puzzle of explaining the radiation was passed by Becquerel to a young research worker, **Marie Curie**. She painstakingly analysed the uranium salts and discovered the radiations were emitted from the uranium atoms, which formed other types of atoms in the process. She and her husband Pierre discovered and named two new radioactive elements, polonium and radium. It was shown that the emissions contained two types of radiation, alpha radiation which is positively charged and easily absorbed, and beta radiation which is negatively charged and much less easily absorbed. Later gamma radiation was discovered which is uncharged and much more penetrating.

Physical processes

3.1 Inside the atom

The structure of the atom

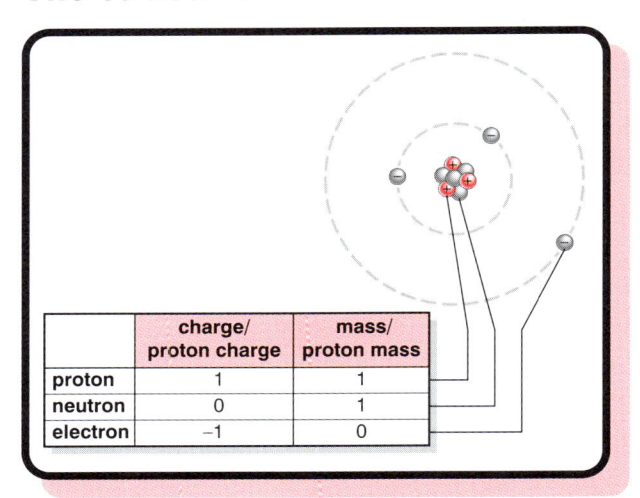

	charge/proton charge	mass/proton mass
proton	1	1
neutron	0	1
electron	−1	0

A lithium atom

Ernest Rutherford used alpha radiation to probe the atom. He knew that alpha radiation consisted of positively charged particles. He found that when a beam of alpha particles was directed at a thin metal foil, some of the particles bounced back off the foil. He deduced that

- the atom contains a tiny positively charged nucleus, where most of its mass is located
- the rest of the atom consists of empty space through which negatively charged electrons move as they orbit the nucleus.

Further investigations showed that the nucleus contains two types of particles, **protons** and **neutrons**.

Atoms and molecules

1 An **element** is a substance which cannot be split into simpler substances. A **compound** is a substance containing two or more elements combined in fixed proportions.

2 An **atom** is the smallest particle of an element which is characteristic of that element.

3 A **molecule** is formed when two or more atoms join together.

4 The lightest atom is hydrogen. The heaviest naturally occurring atom is uranium.

5 The **periodic table of the elements** places the elements in order of increasing **atomic number** (symbol Z). The atomic number of an element is the number of protons in its nucleus.

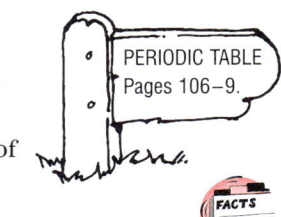

PERIODIC TABLE Pages 106–9.

Isotopes

★ The number of protons in the atomic nucleus of an element (the **atomic number Z** of the element) is constant for that element.

★ The number of neutrons in the atomic nuclei of a given element can vary from one atom to another.

★ The term **isotope** describes a particular type of atom of a given element. For example, chlorine has two isotopes, one with 17 protons and 18 neutrons, and the other with 17 protons and 20 neutrons.

★ Since protons and neutrons each have a mass of one atomic mass unit, the total number of protons and neutrons in a nucleus gives the mass of the nucleus in atomic mass units. This is called the **mass number A** of the nucleus. Because electrons have very little mass in comparison, the mass of an atom in atomic mass units is equal to A.

★ An isotope is defined by the symbol

$$^A_Z X$$

where X is the chemical symbol of the element, Z is the number of protons in the nucleus (the atomic number) and A is the number of protons and neutrons in the nucleus (the mass number).

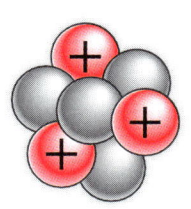

Why doesn't the nucleus fly apart due to repulsion of the positive protons? The nucleus is held together by the **strong nuclear force**.

Question

Work out the number of protons and neutrons in each of the following isotopes. **a)** $^{235}_{92}U$ **b)** $^{14}_{6}C$ **c)** $^{22}_{10}Ne$

Answers a) 92p + 143n b) 6p + 8n c) 10p + 12n

Radioactivity

3.2 Radioactive isotopes

Stable and unstable nuclei

A nucleus is **stable** if the strong nuclear force between its neutrons and protons is much greater than the electrostatic force of repulsion between the protons. Some nuclei are **unstable** because the electrostatic forces of repulsion are larger than the strong attractive forces.

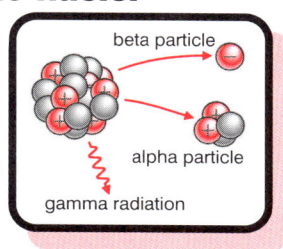

An unstable nucleus

★ A large nucleus with **too many protons and neutrons** is unstable. It becomes stable by emitting an **alpha particle**. This is a particle consisting of two protons and two neutrons.

★ A smaller nucleus with **too many neutrons** is unstable. It becomes stable by emitting a **beta particle**. This is an electron created in the nucleus and instantly emitted.

★ A nucleus may still possess **excess energy** after an alpha or beta particle has been emitted. It may then release the excess energy as **gamma radiation**. This is electromagnetic radiation of very short wavelength.

★ The daughter nucleus might itself be radioactive, and may emit a further alpha or beta particle.

★ An unstable nucleus is said to **disintegrate** when it emits an alpha particle or beta particle. When it emits gamma radiation, it is said to **de-excite**.

★ The **activity** of a radioactive source is the number of nuclei per second that disintegrate.

The Geiger counter

This consists of a Geiger tube connected to an electronic counter. Each particle from a radioactive source that enters the tube is registered on the electronic counter as one count. If the Geiger tube is pointed at a radioactive source, the activity of the source can be monitored by counting the number of particles entering the tube in a measured time interval and calculating the **count rate** (the number of counts per second), which is proportional to the activity.

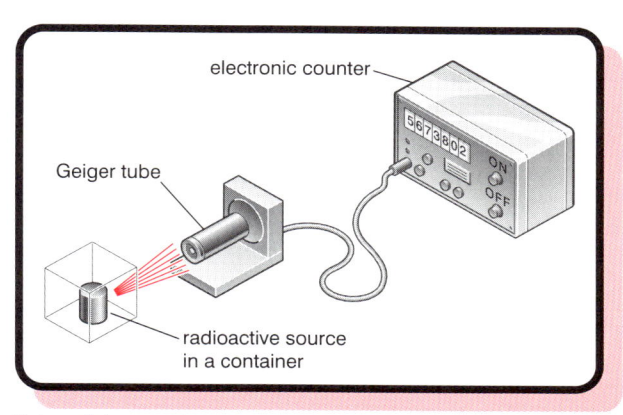

Using a Geiger counter

Background radioactivity

A Geiger counter will detect a low level of radioactivity even with no source present. This is called **background radioactivity** and is due to cosmic radiation and naturally occurring radioactive isotopes in rocks such as granite.

Question

A Geiger counter records 1980 counts in 300 seconds when it is held at a fixed distance from a radioactive source. Without the source present, it records 120 counts in 300 seconds.

a) Why does the Geiger tube count when no source is present?
b) Calculate the count rate due to the source.
c) Give two reasons why the count rate is less than the activity of the source.

$E = mc^2$

This famous equation was first derived by **Albert Einstein**. He showed that if energy E is given to (or taken away from) an object, the mass of the object increases (or decreases) by a mass m in accordance with the equation $E = mc^2$, where c is the speed of light. The energy given out when a nucleus disintegrates can be calculated from the difference in mass of the parent nucleus and its products.

Answer

a) background radioactivity
b) 6.2 counts per second
c) The radiation spreads out from the source in all directions so most of it misses the tube; absorption by the air between the tube and the source.

3.3 Radioactive emissions

Ionisation

Ions are atoms that have become charged, either by removing electrons or by adding them. When the particles produced from radioactive substances pass through a gas, they cause the gas molecules to ionise. In a **cloud chamber**, tiny droplets form along the path of an alpha particle due to the trail of ions created by the particle. The path of each alpha particle is visible in the cloud chamber.

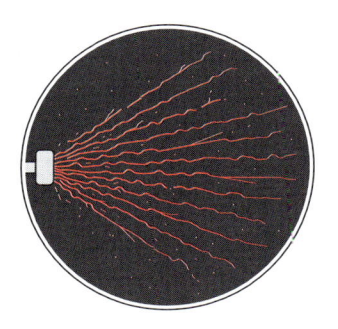

Alpha-particle tracks in a cloud chamber

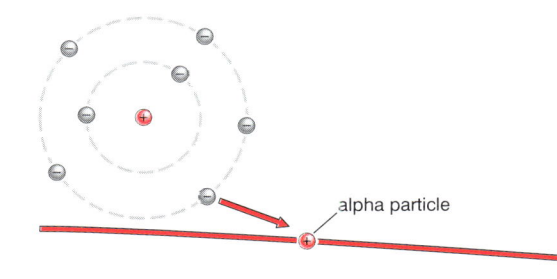

Ionisation

The properties of alpha, beta and gamma radiation

	alpha	beta	gamma
charge	+2	−1e	0
absorption	thin paper	few mm of aluminium	several cm of lead
range in air	fixed, up to 10 cm	variable, up to 1 m	spreads without limit
ionising effect	strong	weak	very weak

Equations for radioactive change

Alpha emission

An alpha particle (symbol $^4_2\alpha$) consists of two protons and two neutrons. An unstable nucleus that emits an alpha particle therefore loses two units of charge and four units of mass. (Remember each proton has a mass of 1 atomic mass unit and a charge of +1 and a neutron has the same mass as a proton and is not charged.)

An unstable nucleus $^A_Z X$ has Z protons and $(A-Z)$ neutrons in its nucleus. If it emits an alpha particle, it becomes a nucleus with two fewer protons and two fewer neutrons.

$$^A_Z X \longrightarrow {^{A-4}_{Z-2}} Y + {^4_2}\alpha$$

Beta minus emission

A beta particle (symbol β) is an electron created in an unstable nucleus, then instantly emitted. A neutron in the nucleus suddenly becomes a proton, creating the beta particle at the same time. The total number of neutrons and protons in the nucleus is therefore unchanged, but there is one more proton.

$$^A_Z X \longrightarrow {^A_{Z+1}} Y + {^{\ 0}_{-1}}\beta$$

The mass number of the beta particle is 0 because it is an electron. Its charge is opposite to that of a proton, so its proton number is written as −1.

Note
In both equations, the numbers balance along the top and along the bottom.

Question

a) Write down the equation representing
   (i) alpha emission from the unstable nucleus $^{238}_{92}$U to form a nucleus of thorium (Th)
   (ii) beta emission from the unstable nucleus $^{27}_{12}$Mg to form a nucleus of aluminium (Al).

b) State how many protons and how many neutrons are present in each nucleus in your equations.

Answers

a) (i) $^{238}_{92}U \longrightarrow {^{234}_{90}}Th + {^4_2}\alpha$
   (ii) $^{27}_{12}Mg \longrightarrow {^{27}_{13}}Al + {^{\ 0}_{-1}}\beta$

b) U-238 = 92p + 146n; Th-234 = 90p + 144n; Mg-27 = 12p + 15n; Al-27 = 13p + 14n

Radioactivity

3.4 Half-life

The **half-life** of a radioactive isotope is the time taken for half its atoms to disintegrate. This time is a characteristic of the isotope. Long-lived radioactive isotopes have nuclei that are less unstable than short-lived isotopes. For example, uranium-238 has a half-life of more than 4500 million years.

The **number of atoms** of a radioactive isotope decreases with time. Radioactive disintegration is a **random** process, and the number of atoms that disintegrate per second is proportional to the number of radioactive atoms present at that time. For example, suppose 10% of the atoms of a certain radioactive isotope X disintegrate every 10 seconds. The table below shows how the number of atoms of X changes, starting with 10 000.

A graph showing how the number of atoms of X decreases with time is shown below. This type of curve is called a **decay curve**.

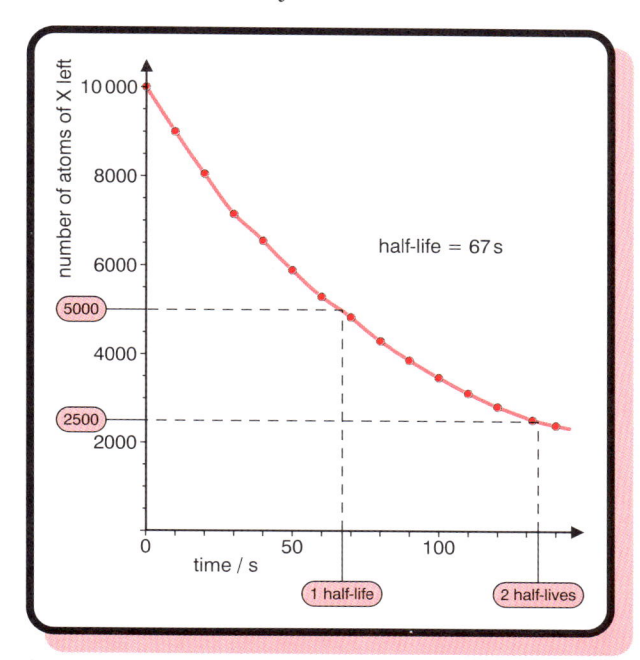

A decay curve

> **Question**
>
> a) Use the graph to estimate the half-life of X.
> b) Use a calculator to estimate the time taken for the number of atoms to fall to 25% of 10 000. This should be equal to 2 half-lives.

The **activity** of a radioactive isotope decreases with time. This is because the activity is proportional to the number of atoms of the isotope left. The shape of the activity–time curve is the same as the decay curve, provided the 'daughter' isotope is stable.

Radioactive dating

Rocks formed millions of years ago can be dated using radioactivity. Ancient materials can also be dated using radioactivity.

★ Some igneous rocks contain the uranium isotope U-238, formed by volcanic activity long ago. These can be dated by measuring the proportion of an isotope of lead, Pb-206, relative to U-238. The uranium isotope has a half-life of 4500 million years, emitting alpha particles and forming the stable isotope Pb-206 via a series of relatively short-lived radioactive isotopes. A decay curve like the one here may be used to work out the age of a rock from the proportion of U-238 remaining.

★ Rocks containing trapped argon gas can be dated by measuring the proportion of the gas to the radioactive potassium isotope, K-40, which produces the gas as a result of radioactive change. K-40 is an unstable isotope with a half-life of 1250 million years, producing the argon isotope Ar-40. This gas is trapped when the molten rock solidifies. Hence the age of the rock can be determined by measuring the relative proportions of the two isotopes and then using a decay curve.

> **Answer**
>
> a) 66 s

Time/s	0	10	20	30	40	50	60	70
Number of atoms left	10 000	9000	8100	7290	6561	5905	5314	4783
Decrease in number of atoms of X	1000	900	810	729	656	591	531	478

Physical processes

3.5 Radiation effects

Why radioactivity is harmful

Radiation from radioactive substances produces ions. Ionising radiation damages living cells in two ways:

1. by penetrating the cell membranes which causes the cell to die
2. by breaking the strands of DNA molecules in the cell nucleus, which may cause cell mutation.

★ **Alpha radiation** is easily absorbed, highly ionising and therefore very harmful.

★ **Beta radiation** is less easily absorbed and less ionising. However, it can penetrate deep into the body from outside so it too is very harmful.

★ **Gamma radiation** easily penetrates soft tissue and is absorbed by bones, where its ionising effect can produce immense damage.

★ Harmful microorganisms and cancer cells can be killed by controlled high doses of ionising radiation. For example, gamma radiation from the radioactive isotope cobalt-60 is used to treat cancer.

There is no lower limit below which ionising radiation is harmless. Therefore, extreme care is essential when radioactive substances are used and legal regulations for using radioactive substances must be observed. In a school laboratory, students under the age of 16 are not allowed to carry out experiments with radioactive materials.

Question

a) Why is a storage box for radioactive substances made of lead?
b) Why is it essential for handling tongs to have long handles?

Fission

In a nuclear reactor, U-235 nuclei in the fuel rods split into two and release energy. This process is called **fission**. Neutrons are also released, and they produce further fission.

Radioactive waste

Radioactive waste from a nuclear reactor is classified as

- **low level waste** such as clothing worn by personnel – the clothing fibres may contain radioactive dust particles
- **intermediate level waste** such as metal cladding from spent fuel rods – the cladding becomes radioactive inside the reactor
- **high level waste** such as fission products, unused uranium and plutonium.

Treatment and storage of radioactive waste

★ Low level radioactive waste from Britain's nuclear reactors is stored in sealed containers in a shallow trench at Sellafield.

★ Intermediate level waste is stored in sealed drums at several sites in Britain. An underground storage site at Sellafield is being developed to store all Britain's intermediate level and low level waste.

★ High level waste includes spent fuel rods, which are highly radioactive because the nuclei produced by fission of uranium-235 are unstable. The spent fuel rods therefore generate heat due to radioactive decay. The rods are placed initially in cooling ponds until they are cool enough to be transported safely to Sellafield. There they are reprocessed to recover unused uranium and plutonium. The rest of the high level waste is stored in sealed containers at Sellafield.

Answers
a) Lead is the best absorber of radioactivity.
b) The tongs keep the source as far away from the user as possible.

TAKE A BREAK

round-up

How much have you improved?
Work out your improvement index on pages 214–15.

1. Natural uranium consists of about 99% $^{238}_{92}$U and about 1% $^{235}_{92}$U.
   a) How many protons and how many neutrons are present in each type of atom? [4]
   b) What is the name for different types of atoms of the same element? [1]
   c) $^{238}_{92}$U has a *half-life* of about 4500 million years. Explain what is meant by *half-life*. [1]

2. One type of smoke detector uses an alpha particle source, as shown.

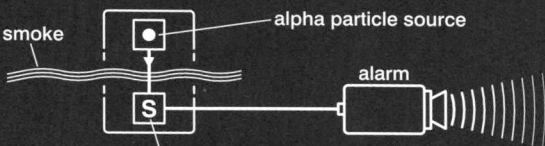

   alpha particle sensor is on whenever smoke prevents the particles reaching it

   a) Why is an alpha source used rather than a beta or a gamma source? [2]
   b) Why is it important for the alpha source to have a half-life of more than 5 years? [1]

3. a) $^{220}_{82}$Rn emits alpha particles to form an isotope of the element polonium (Po). Write down the equation for this process. [2]
   b) Radon-220 has a half-life of 52 s. A pure sample of this isotope had an initial activity of 400 disintegrations per second. What was its activity after (i) 104 s (ii) 208 s? [2]

4. The thickness of hot rolled steel plate produced in a factory was monitored using a gamma source and detector, as shown below.

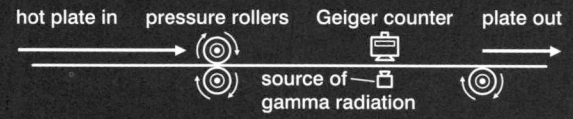

   a) Why was gamma radiation used instead of alpha or beta radiation? [3]
   b) The counter reading increased every second as shown in the table below.

Time / s	0	1	2	3	4	5	6	7	8	9	10
Counter reading	0	204	395	602	792	1004	1180	1340	1505	1660	1825

   (i) What was the average count rate over the first 5 seconds? [1]
   (ii) What was the average count rate over the last 2 seconds? [1]
   (iii) What happened to the thickness of the plate? [1]

5. a) Background radioactivity accounts for 87% of the exposure to ionising radiations of the average person in Britain. Explain what is meant by
      (i) background radioactivity [1]
      (ii) ionising radiation. [1]
   b) State two further sources of ionising radiation. [2]
   c) Explain how you would use a Geiger counter and a stopwatch to measure background radioactivity. [2]

6. In a test to identify the type of radioactivity produced by a radioactive source, the following results were obtained with different sheets of materials placed between the source and the Geiger tube.

material	count rate / counts per second
none	450
tin foil	235
1 mm aluminium	230
10 mm aluminium	228
10 mm lead	160

Use these results to decide what types of radiation are emitted by the source. Explain your answer. [4]

7. a) Why is it essential to use long-handled tongs to move a radioactive source? [1]
   b) Cobalt-60 is a radioactive isotope that emits gamma radiation. It is used in hospitals to treat cancer. What is gamma radiation and why is it necessary to use gamma radiation for this purpose? [2]

8. a) Explain why spent fuel from a nuclear reactor is highly dangerous. [2]
   b) Describe what happens to the fuel rods from a nuclear reactor after they have been removed. [3]

Waves

preview

At the end of this topic you will be able to:

- describe different types of waves
- explain what is meant by the amplitude, wavelength and frequency of a wave
- describe reflection and refraction as wave properties
- state the law of reflection of light and explain what is meant by refraction of light
- explain how total internal reflection can occur
- describe examples of reflection and refraction of sound.

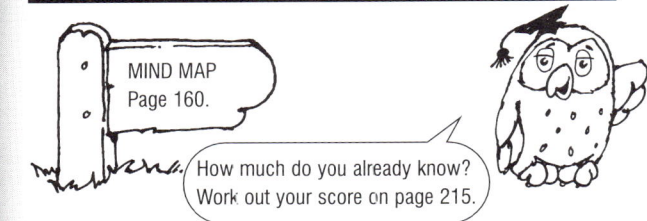

MIND MAP Page 160.

How much do you already know? Work out your score on page 215.

Test yourself

1 State four different types of waves. [4]

2 State one type of wave that can travel through a vacuum, and one type that cannot. [2]

3 The diagram shows a snapshot of a wave travelling from left to right, at a speed of 20 mm/s.

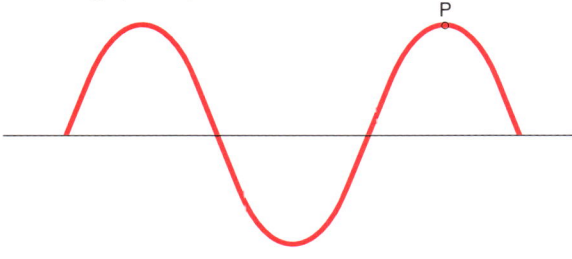

Use a millimetre rule to measure its wavelength and its amplitude. [2]

4 In the diagram in **3**, what is the displacement of point P
  a) exactly 1.0 s after the snapshot shown
  b) exactly 4.0 s after the snapshot shown? [2]

5 a) State the law of reflection of light at a plane mirror. [1]
  b) A woman stands in front of a vertical mirror at a distance of 1.0 m from the mirror. The woman is able to see an image of her face in the mirror, but is unable to see her image below knee level. 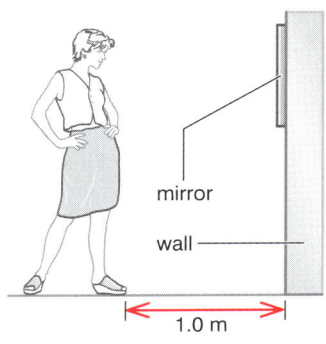
   (i) How far is the woman from her own image? [1]
   (ii) Would she be able to see her image below knee level if she moved nearer the mirror? Explain your answer. [3]

6 a) Why are waves on the sea shore not reflected when they run up the shore? [2]
  b) A child stands in shallow water at the beach and counts 50 waves passing him in 5 minutes. Calculate: (i) the time between successive waves
   (ii) the frequency of these waves. [2]

7 a) When a light ray passes from air into glass at a non-zero angle to the normal, does it bend towards or away from the normal? [1]
  b) When light passes from air to glass, state whether there is an increase, a decrease or no change in
   (i) the speed (ii) the wavelength (iii) the frequency
   of the light waves. [3]

8 What causes echoes? [2]

9 A beam of white light is split into a spectrum by passing it through a glass prism.
  a) State the colours of the spectrum. [2]
  b) Which colour of the spectrum is refracted least? [1]

4.1 Measuring waves

Look at the snapshot of a transverse wave in the diagram on the left. The wave is travelling from left to right, but you can't tell this from the snapshot. Each point on the wave vibrates at 90° to the wave direction.

Waves

- ★ **One complete cycle** of vibration of any point returns the point to the same position and direction it had at the start of the cycle. In this time, a wave crest at the point is replaced by the next wave crest.

- ★ **The amplitude of a wave** is the height of the wave crest above the centre.

- ★ **The wavelength of a wave** (symbol λ, pronounced 'lambda') is the distance from one crest to the next crest.

- ★ **The frequency of a wave** (symbol f) is the number of crests passing a given position each second. This is the same as the number of complete cycles of vibration per second of any point. The unit of frequency is the hertz (symbol Hz), equal to 1 cycle per second.

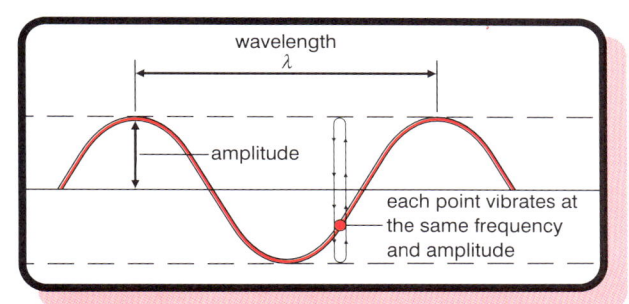

Question

1 What are the wavelength and the amplitude of the wave shown above?

Refraction

When a plane wave passes across a straight boundary,

1. its wavelength changes if the wave speed changes at the boundary. The frequency does not change.

2. its direction of motion changes if its direction is not perpendicular to the boundary.

- ★ A light ray is refracted towards the normal when it passes from air into glass. This happens because light waves travel slower in glass than in air.

- ★ Sound waves are refracted away from the normal when they travel from air into water. This happens because sound waves travel faster in glass than in air.

Reflection

The diagram shows a straight wave reflecting off a straight reflector. The waves reflect off the reflector at the same angle to its surface as they hit it.

- ★ A light ray reflects off a plane mirror at the same angle to the surface as the angle at which it strikes the mirror. This happens because light consists of waves.

- ★ Echoes are sound waves from a well defined source that reflect from a hard surface.

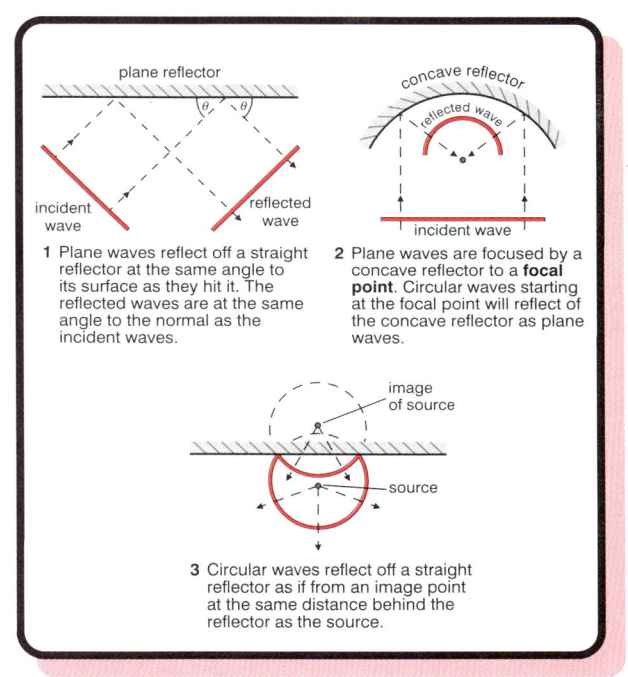

1 Plane waves reflect off a straight reflector at the same angle to its surface as they hit it. The reflected waves are at the same angle to the normal as the incident waves.

2 Plane waves are focused by a concave reflector to a **focal point**. Circular waves starting at the focal point will reflect of the concave reflector as plane waves.

3 Circular waves reflect off a straight reflector as if from an image point at the same distance behind the reflector as the source.

Reflections on reflection

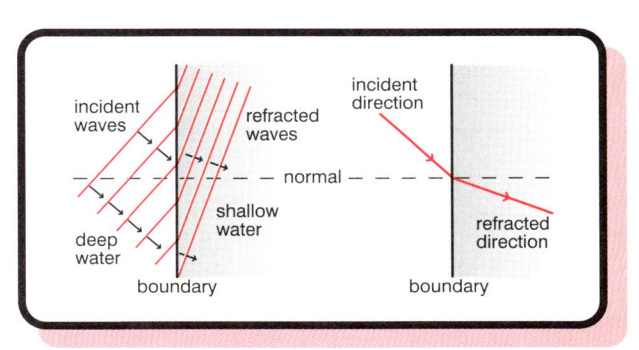

Refraction

Answer: Amplitude = 10 mm, wavelength = 40 mm

Physical processes

4.2 Reflection of light

Ray diagrams

A light ray shows the direction in which light travels. Ray diagrams are used to describe how light is affected by mirrors, prisms and lenses.

Mirror images

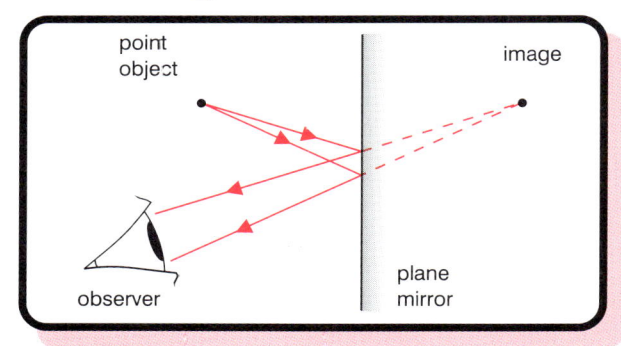

Image formation

The diagram shows how a plane mirror forms an image. Note that the image of an object viewed by reflection using a plane mirror is

- the same distance behind the mirror as the object is in front
- upright and the same size as the object
- virtual, which means it is formed where the reflected rays *appear* to come from
- laterally inverted, which means the image of a left-handed person is right-handed and vice versa. Try it if you don't believe it!

The **law of reflection** states that the angle between the reflected ray and the normal is equal to the angle between the incident ray and the normal.

The diagram shows how this can be tested using a ray box and a plane mirror. Note that the normal is the line which is perpendicular to the mirror at the point where the light ray meets the mirror.

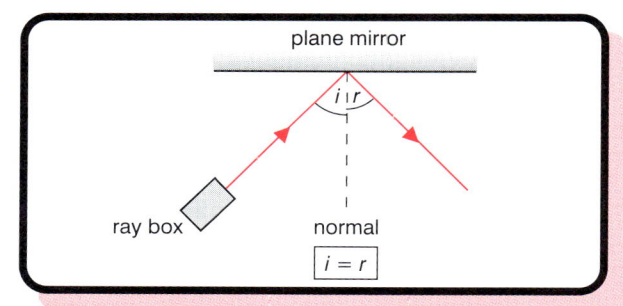

Uses of a plane mirror

1. A **wall mirror** needs to be at least half the height of the tallest person who uses it. It also needs to be mounted with its top edge level with the top of the head.

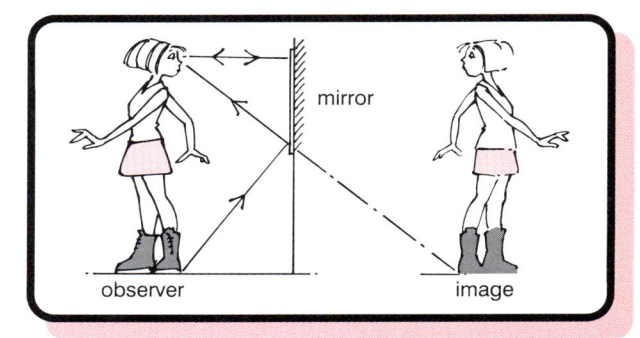

Using a wall mirror

2. A **periscope** is useful for seeing over a crowd. It is also used in submarines to see above the surface when the submarine is under water.

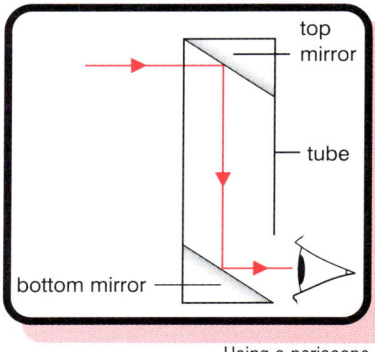

Using a periscope

3. **Parallax errors** caused by incorrectly reading the position of a pointer on a scale can be eliminated using a plane mirror. The image of the pointer must be directly under the pointer when reading the scale.

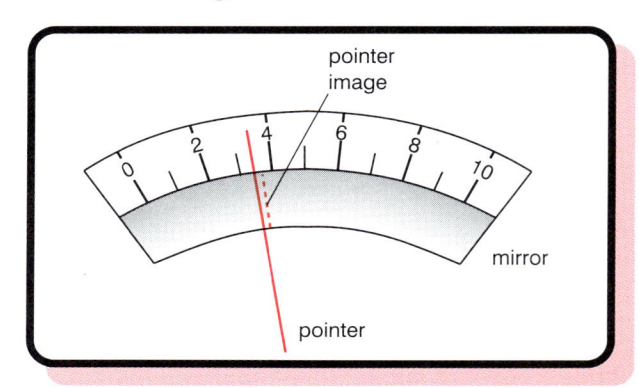

The law of reflection

Parallax errors

4.3 Refraction of light

Investigating refraction

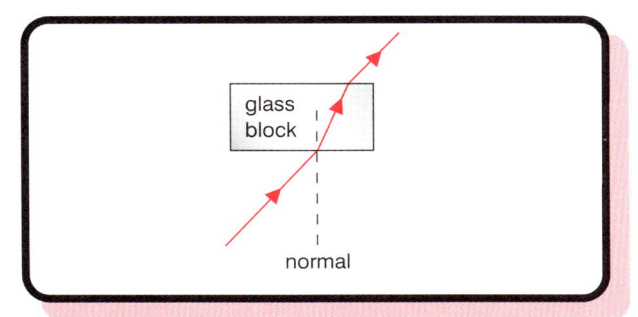

Refraction in a glass block

★ If a light ray is directed at a glass block as shown, the light ray changes its direction when it enters the glass. It is closer to the normal in glass than in air. This is an example of the **refraction** of light. It occurs because light waves travel more slowly in glass than in air.

★ When a light ray passes from glass into air at a non-zero angle to the normal, it bends away from the normal. This happens because the light waves speed up when they pass from glass into air.

★ Refraction happens when light passes from one transparent medium into another. The light ray is always closer to the normal in the 'slower' medium.

In deep water

A swimming pool appears shallower than it really is because light from the bottom of the pool is refracted away from the normal when it passes into air at the surface. Someone looking into the water from above sees an image of the bottom of the pool nearer the surface.

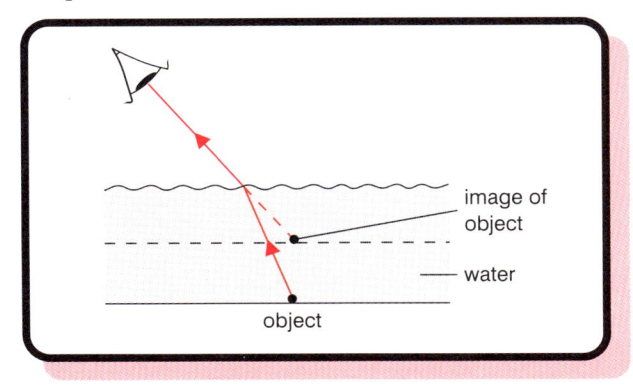

Fact file

The speed of light through air is 300 000 km/s. Light travels more slowly in a transparent medium than in air. For example, its speed in glass is 200 000 km/s. The ratio of its speed in air to its speed in glass is therefore 1.5. This ratio is called the **refractive index** of the medium.

The visible spectrum

This is produced by passing a beam of white light through a prism. Because the speed of light in glass decreases from red to blue, blue light is bent more than red light.

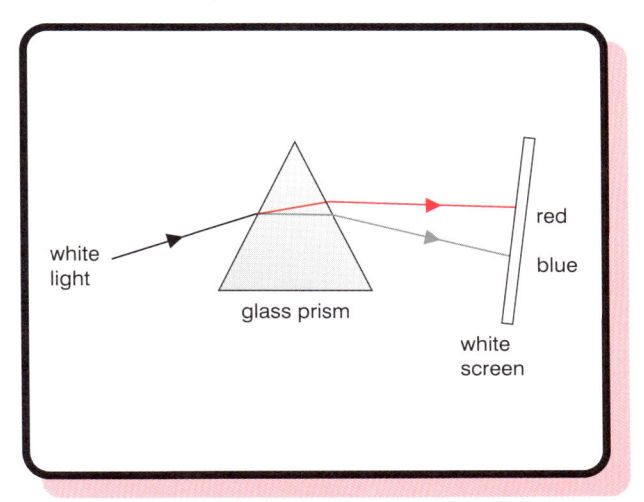

Handy hints

★ Remember that **Blue Bends Better than red!**

★ Also remember the colours of the spectrum (**R**ed **O**range **Y**ellow **G**reen **B**lue **I**ndigo **V**iolet) from a mnemonic, such as Richard Of York Gave Battle In Vain, or remember Roy G Biv.

★ The frequency of light does not change on passing from one transparent medium to another. However, the speed and the wavelength do change.

Physical processes

Total internal reflection

This occurs when light in a transparent medium strikes the boundary at an angle of incidence greater than a **critical angle**. The light ray reflects internally just as if the boundary is a mirror.

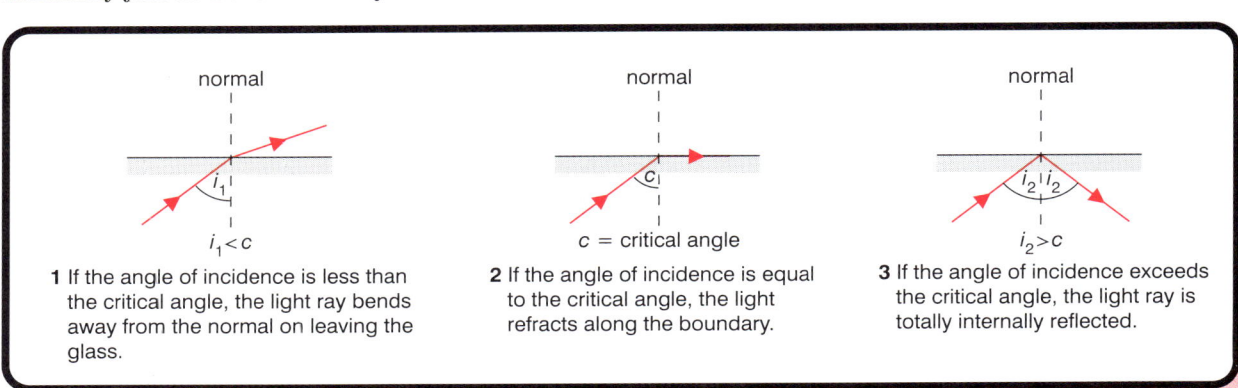

1 If the angle of incidence is less than the critical angle, the light ray bends away from the normal on leaving the glass. ($i_1 < c$)

2 If the angle of incidence is equal to the critical angle, the light refracts along the boundary. (c = critical angle)

3 If the angle of incidence exceeds the critical angle, the light ray is totally internally reflected. ($i_2 > c$)

Total internal reflection

Optical fibres

An optical fibre is a thin fibre of transparent flexible material. A light ray that enters the fibre at one end emerges at the other end, even if the fibre is curved round. This happens because the light ray is totally internally reflected at the fibre surface wherever it hits the boundary. Each light ray in the fibre travels along a straight line through the fibre between successive reflections. Provided the bends in the fibre are not too tight, light rays in the fibre do not emerge from its sides. Optical fibres are used in medicine (to see inside the body) and in communications (to guide light signals).

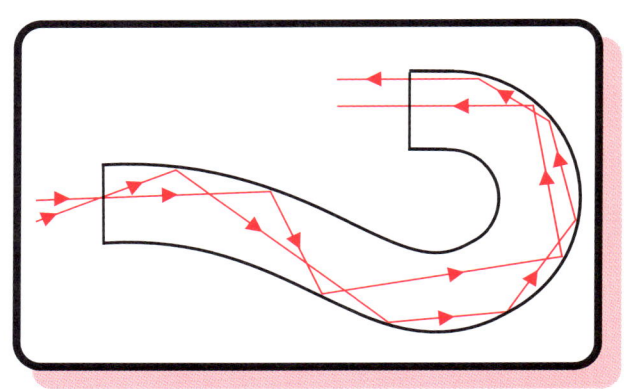

An optical fibre

Reflectors for road safety

The back surface of a cycle reflector consists of lots of triangles. Light rays falling directly on the reflector are totally internally reflected twice at this surface, so they are reflected back.

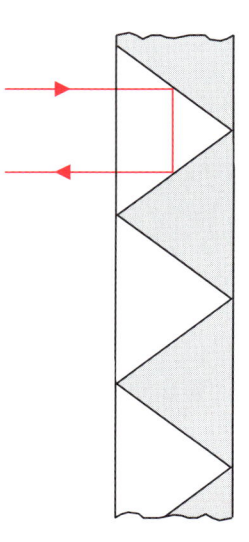

A reflector

round-up

How much have you improved? Work out your improvement index on page 215.

1 a) Complete the sketch, showing the wave after reflection. [4]

b) Two plane mirrors are placed perpendicular to each other and a light ray is directed at an angle of 30° to one of the mirrors. Mark the direction of the light ray after reflection at each mirror. [2]

2 a) When light passes from air into glass, it slows down. What happens to its wavelength and its frequency? [2]

b) The diagram shows plane waves about to cross a boundary between shallow and deep water. Complete the diagram by showing the waves in the deep water as well as the shallow water. [2]

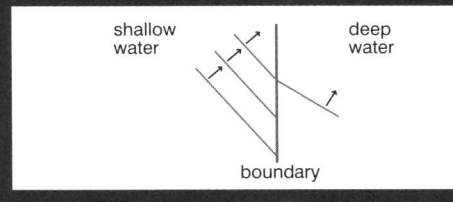

3 A student stands in a paved area at a distance of 100 m from a large vertical brick wall. She calls to a friend nearer the wall and notices that her voice echoes.

a) Explain why she hears an echo of her own voice. [2]

b) When her friend calls back, there is no echo. Why? [2]

4 a) Complete the ray diagram to show where the image of point object O_1 is formed. [2]

b) Without drawing further rays on your diagram, mark the position where the image of point object O_2 is formed. [1]

c) Hence explain why the image of the arrow is the same length as the arrow itself. [2]

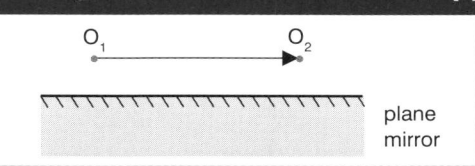

5 a) A student stands 1.0 m in front of a wall-mounted plane mirror. What is the distance from the student to her image? [1]

b) The student is 1.80 m tall. With the aid of a diagram, explain why the mirror needs to be at least 0.9 m in length if she is to be able to see a full-length image. [4]

c) State two further uses of a plane mirror. [2]

6 a) With the aid of a diagram, explain why a swimming pool appears shallower than it really is when observed from above. [4]

b) Sketch an arrangement to show how a prism can be used to split a narrow beam of white light into a spectrum. [2]

7 a) Explain with the aid of a diagram what is meant by total internal reflection of light. [2]

b) The diagram shows a light ray entering an optical fibre. Complete the diagram showing the path of the light ray after it enters the optical fibre. [2]

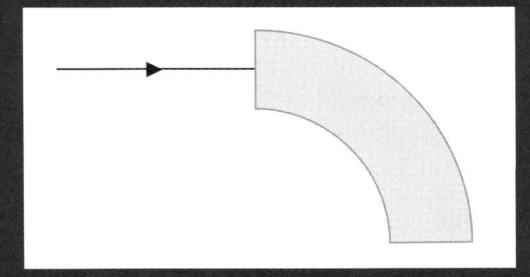

Well done if you've improved. Don't worry if you haven't. Take a break and try again.

The electromagnetic spectrum 5

preview

At the end of this topic you will be able to:

- state the six main bands of the electromagnetic spectrum in order of increasing wavelength
- outline the similarities and the main differences between the different bands
- describe some uses of electromagnetic waves in the home, in medicine and in communications
- relate uses of electromagnetic waves to their properties.

MIND MAP Page 160.

How much do you already know? Work out your score on page 216.

Test yourself

1. Name the six main bands of the electromagnetic spectrum in order of increasing frequency. [6]

2. State one use for each of the main bands of the electromagnetic spectrum. [6]

3. Which two bands of the electromagnetic spectrum are not absorbed by the atmosphere? [2]

4. a) Which type(s) of electromagnetic radiation can cause ionisation? [2]
   b) Which type of electromagnetic radiation are you emitting at this very moment? [1]
   c) Which type of electromagnetic radiation causes sunburn? [1]

5. Name one type of electromagnetic radiation that can pass through a metal plate and one type that cannot. [2]

6. Which type of electromagnetic radiation is emitted when
   a) high-speed electrons are suddenly stopped [1]
   b) a sunbed is used? [1]

7. a) A satellite broadcasts at a frequency of 10 GHz. What type of electromagnetic radiation is at this frequency? [1]
   b) Why is a satellite dish (i) concave (ii) made from metal? [2]

8. How does an invisible marker pen work? [3]

9. a) What type of electromagnetic radiation is detected by (i) a blackened thermometer (ii) a Geiger counter? [2]
   b) Which type(s) of electromagnetic radiation cannot be detected using photographic film? [1]

10. a) A fibre optic link uses electromagnetic radiation of wavelength 1000 nm. What part of the electromagnetic spectrum is this? [1]
    b) Which two types of electromagnetic radiation are emitted by a filament lamp? [1]

All electromagnetic waves

1. do not need to be carried by a medium
2. travel at the same speed of 300 000 km/s in a vacuum
3. can be diffracted, refracted and reflected (although X-rays and gamma rays need special techniques)
4. make charged particles vibrate
5. are transverse waves and can be polarised.

The electromagnetic spectrum

5.1 Using electromagnetic waves

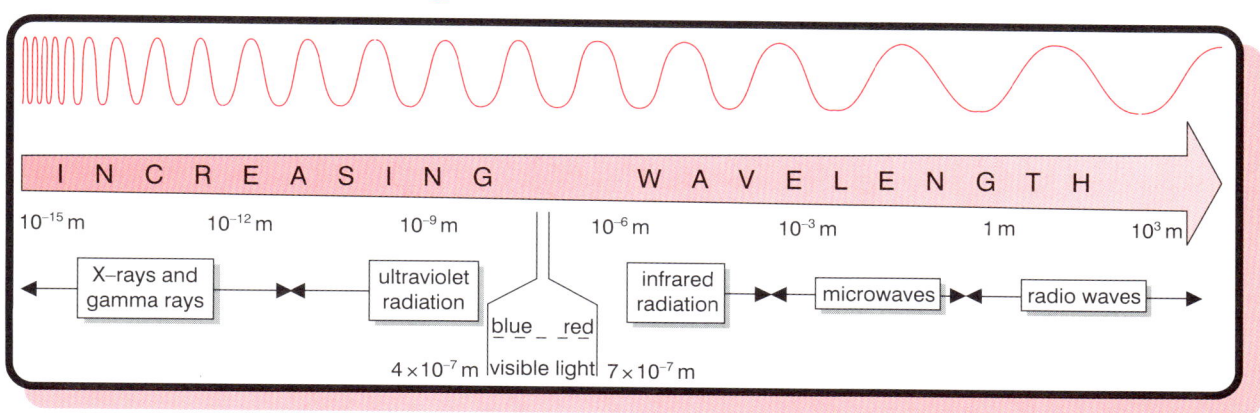

INCREASING WAVELENGTH

10^{-15} m, 10^{-12} m, 10^{-9} m, 10^{-6} m, 10^{-3} m, 1 m, 10^{3} m

X-rays and gamma rays — ultraviolet radiation — visible light (blue 4×10^{-7} m – red 7×10^{-7} m) — infrared radiation — microwaves — radio waves

	production	detection	absorption or reflection	uses
radio waves	transmitter aerial, Sun	receiver aerial	reflected by metal	communications
microwaves	microwave transmitter	microwave detector	reflected by metal	communications, heating
infrared light	any object	blackened thermometer	reflected by shiny silvered surfaces, absorbed best by matt black surfaces	communications, heating
visible light	glowing objects	eye, photographic film	reflected by metal, absorbed by pigments	sight, communications
ultraviolet light	UV lamps, Sun	photocell, photographic film	absorbed by skin	security coding, sunbeds
X-rays and gamma rays	X-ray tube, radioactive isotopes	Geiger tube, photographic film	penetrates matter	medical

Electromagnetic waves at home

Microwave cookers: microwaves penetrate food and agitate water molecules within the food. This happens if the frequency is 2.5 GHz, so microwave cookers operate at this frequency. The oven case is metal, which reflects microwaves, so the oven does not heat up. All the electrical power supplied is used to heat the food.

Microwaves are also used for industrial heating, for example to dry wet fabrics after dyeing.

Infrared sensors: these are used for security purposes. **Passive** sensors detect infrared radiation emitted by intruders. **Active** sensors emit infrared rays and detect reflections from intruders. Infrared sensors fitted to TV cameras allow surveillance in the dark.

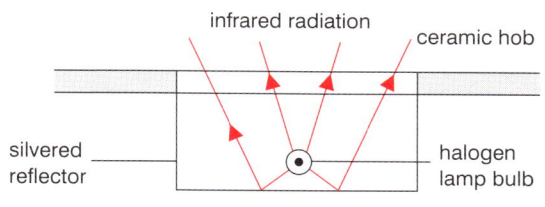

A halogen hob

Halogen hobs: cookers fitted with transparent ceramic cooker rings use halogen lamp bulbs that emit mostly infrared radiation. Little energy is used to heat the ceramic plate, and when the cooker ring is switched off it cools much more rapidly than an ordinary cooker ring.

UV-sensitive inks: these inks can only be seen using ultraviolet light. They are used for security marking.

5 Physical processes

5.2 Electromagnetic waves in medicine

A health warning

X-rays and gamma rays penetrate living tissues and so can be used in medicine to diagnose disorders and for treatment. These electromagnetic radiations are ionising, so excessive amounts will damage living cells. Great care is taken to ensure radiation doses given to patients are as low as possible and to ensure personnel are not exposed.

X-rays

These are produced in an **X-ray tube**. The X-ray beam consists of a continuous spread of wavelengths. The longer wavelengths are easily absorbed by tissues, unlike the shorter wavelengths which easily pass through tissues. A metal plate is placed in the path of the beam before the patient to remove longer wavelengths. This reduces absorption of X-rays by the patient.

X-ray photographs of internal organs are made with the aid of a suitable contrast medium. For example, a patient about to undergo a stomach X-ray may be given a barium meal in advance. Barium absorbs X-rays so the X-ray photograph shows a light image of the stomach on a darker background.

Personnel in a hospital X-ray department wear **film badges** to monitor their exposure to ionising radiations. If a film badge is over-exposed when it is developed, the wearer has been over-exposed too!

Gamma radiation

This is produced by radioactive isotopes. Gamma radiation is used at high doses to destroy unwanted tissue inside the body, and at low doses to 'image' internal organs.

1. **Treatment** – gamma radiation from the radioactive isotope cobalt-60 is used to destroy cancerous tissue.

2. **Diagnosis** – the **gamma camera** is used with a suitable radioactive tracer to form an image of an internal organ. The tracer must emit gamma radiation and its half-life must be a suitable length. The tracer is given to the patient in advance, either by mouth or by injection.

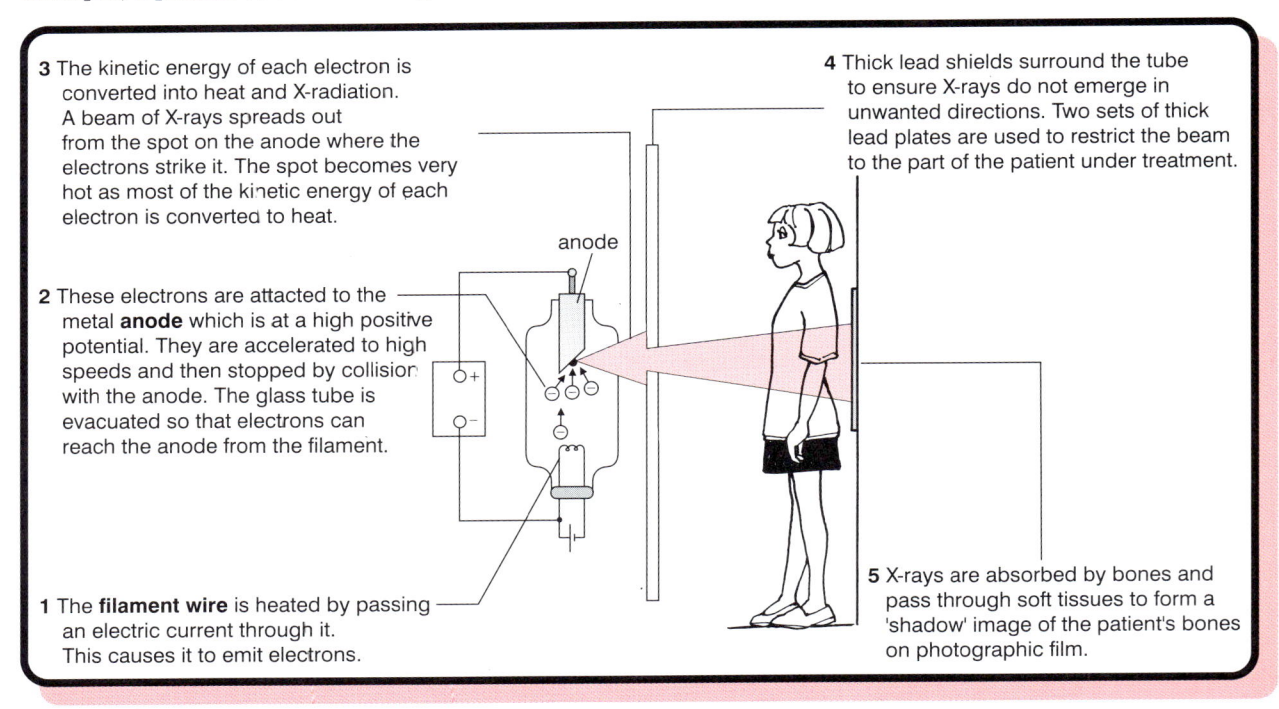

---

3. The kinetic energy of each electron is converted into heat and X-radiation. A beam of X-rays spreads out from the spot on the anode where the electrons strike it. The spot becomes very hot as most of the kinetic energy of each electron is converted to heat.

2. These electrons are attacted to the metal **anode** which is at a high positive potential. They are accelerated to high speeds and then stopped by collision with the anode. The glass tube is evacuated so that electrons can reach the anode from the filament.

1. The **filament wire** is heated by passing an electric current through it. This causes it to emit electrons.

4. Thick lead shields surround the tube to ensure X-rays do not emerge in unwanted directions. Two sets of thick lead plates are used to restrict the beam to the part of the patient under treatment.

5. X-rays are absorbed by bones and pass through soft tissues to form a 'shadow' image of the patient's bones on photographic film.

An X-ray tube in use

5.3 Communications

Radio waves, microwaves, infrared light and visible light are all used to carry information. The higher the frequency of the **carrier waves**, the more information can be carried. The information is carried by **modulating** the carrier wave:

1. in **analogue form**, by modulating the amplitude (AM) or the frequency (FM) of the carrier wave
2. in **digital form** as a stream of pulses.

The spread of frequencies in the signal determines the **bandwidth** of the carrier wave. Each carrier wave is allocated a frequency channel wide enough to transmit the bandwidth of the signal. For example, a channel width of 4000 Hz in telephone channels covers most of the audio range. A TV channel needs to be 8 MHz wide to carry all the information for TV pictures.

Electrical **noise** is created in amplifiers used to boost weak signals, causing loss of information. Digital pulses can be 'cleaned up' to eliminate noise.

Optical fibre communications

Optical fibres can carry pulses of infrared light hundreds of kilometres without interruption. The frequency of light is about 1 million times higher than the frequency of microwave radiation, so an optical fibre can carry much more information than a microwave beam or an electrical cable.

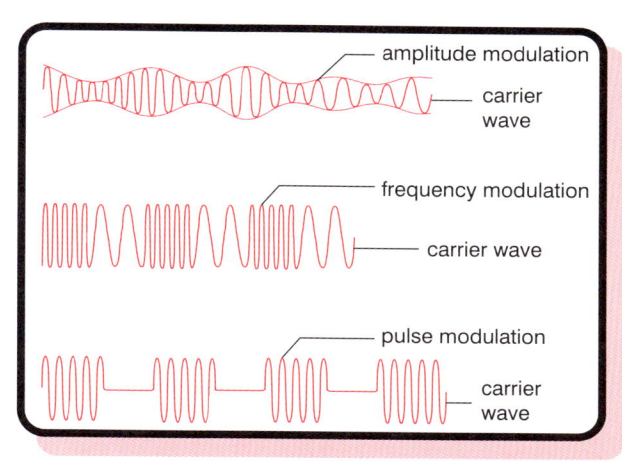

Amplitude modulation, frequency modulation and pulse modulation

Frequency bands

	frequency range	uses
long wave (LW)	up to 300 kHz	international AM radio
medium wave (MW)	300 kHz–3 MHz	AM radio
high frequency (HF)	3–30 MHz	AM radio
very high frequency (VHF)	30–300 MHz	FM radio
ultra high frequency (UHF)	300–3000 MHz	TV broadcasting, mobile phones
microwave	above 3000 MHz	satellite TV, global phone links
light	500 THz approx	fibre optic communication links

Note: 1 MHz = 1 000 000 Hz. 1 THz = 1 million MHz.

Mobile phone links are only possible if the receiver is near a transmitter. A mobile phone signal is allocated a channel of bandwidth 25 kHz in the UHF band at a frequency of about 900 MHz. The transmitter is linked to the international phone network which uses undersea cable links, local microwave links and satellite links.

Radio broadcasts at frequencies below 30 MHz travel long distances due to reflection from a layer of ionised gases in the upper atmosphere. Long wave broadcasts spread round the Earth because long wavelength radio waves follow the Earth's curvature.

Satellite TV signals are carried by microwaves from a geostationary satellite. This orbits the Earth once every 24 hours round the equator, so stays in the same place above the Earth. A reflecting dish pointed towards the satellite focuses the microwaves on an aerial, which detects the signal and passes it onto a decoder.

Terrestrial TV signals are carried by radio waves in the UHF band range. Receiving aerials need to be in the line of sight of the transmitter. TV pictures from the other side of the world reach us via satellite links and ground stations.

Physical processes

round-up

How much have you improved? Work out your improvement index on page 216.

1 a) List the six main bands of the electromagnetic spectrum in order of increasing wavelength. [6]
  b) (i) State two common properties of all electromagnetic waves. [2]
   (ii) List the types of electromagnetic waves that blacken photographic film. [3]
   (iii) List the types of electromagnetic waves that are used in communications. [4]

2 a) Microwave cookers operate at 2500 MHz and microwave satellites operate at about 10 000 MHz. Use the formula   wavelength × frequency = speed   to calculate the wavelength in air in each case. The speed of light in air is 300 000 km/s. [2]
  b) Food can be heated using a microwave oven or an ordinary oven. What are the advantages of using a microwave oven? [1]

3 a) Why is it possible to detect radio broadcasts from distant countries? [2]
  b) (i) What is meant by the carrier frequency of a radio or TV broadcast? [1]
   (ii) Why is necessary for TV transmitter stations in adjacent regions to broadcast at different carrier frequencies? [1]
  c) Why is it necessary to use a concave metal dish to detect electromagnetic waves from a satellite but not from a TV transmitter mast? [2]

4 a) A soap powder manufacturer decides to mix a substance into the powder which absorbs ultraviolet light and emits visible light as a result. Why would this make clothes washed in this powder seem very white in bright sunlight? [2]
  b) (i) Why is ultraviolet light harmful? [2]
   (ii) Why is it important to use protective skin cream if you are outdoors for a long time in summer? [2]

5 a) Why can an infrared TV camera see people and animals in darkness? [1]
  b) (i) What main type of electromagnetic radiation is emitted by a halogen lamp in a ceramic cooker hob? [1]
   (ii) Why does a ceramic hob heat food up more quickly than a conventional cooker ring does? [2]

6 a) In an X-ray tube, why is it essential to
   (i) make the anode positive relative to the filament
   (ii) focus the electron beam onto a small spot of the anode? [3]
  b) (i) A photograph of a broken limb can be obtained using X-rays. What properties of X-rays are made use of in this process? [2]
   (ii) Before a stomach X-ray is taken, the patient is given a barium meal. Why? [2]

7 a) The diagram shows the waveform of two carrier waves with different frequencies. Identify the high frequency carrier wave and explain why it can carry more pulses than the low frequency carrier wave. [3]

  b) Mobile phones operate at a frequency of about 900 MHz, each channel occupying a bandwidth of 25 kHz.
   (i) How many mobile phone channels can be carried in the frequency band from 900 to 925 MHz? [1]
   (ii) Terrestrial TV programmes are carried at lower frequencies and satellite TV is carried at higher frequencies. Why are no TV channels allocated to the frequency band from 900 to 925 MHz? [1]

8 A communications satellite must be in a geostationary orbit.
  a) What is meant by a geostationary orbit? [2]
  b) Why is it necessary for a communications satellite to be in such an orbit? [1]

Well done if you've improved. Don't worry if you haven't. Take a break and try again.

Force

preview

At the end of this topic you will be able to:

- define speed and state its unit
- sketch and interpret graphs of distance against time and speed against time
- explain changes in the motion of an object in terms of unbalanced forces acting on it
- describe the motion of a falling object with and without drag forces
- identify the forces acting on a body in equilibrium
- state and use Hooke's law and describe elastic and plastic behaviour
- carry out simple pressure and density calculations
- describe pressure applications, including hydrostatic pressure and hydraulics.

MIND MAP Page 161.

How much do you already know? Work out your score on pages 216–17.

Test yourself

1. A walker travelled a distance of 10 km in 2 hours. Calculate the walker's average speed in **a)** km/h **b)** m/s. [2]

2. **a)** What feature of a graph of speed against time gives the distance travelled? [1]
   b) What does the gradient of a distance against time graph represent? [1]

3. What forces are acting on your body at the moment? [2]

4. State whether each of the following is in stable, unstable or neutral equilibrium
   a) a ball at rest on the floor
   b) a child sitting on a fence
   c) a coat hanger hanging from a rail. [3]

5. An object released in water falls at constant speed. Why? [4]

6. Why does the shape of a vehicle affect its petrol consumption? [3]

7. **a) (i)** Explain why a sharp knife cuts more easily than a blunt knife. [1]
   (ii) Explain why a suction cap pushed onto a smooth vertical tile doesn't fall off. [2]
   b) A spade has a rectangular blade which measures 25 cm × 20 cm. It is used to flatten a mound of earth. Each impact of the blade's flat surface on the mound creates a force of 300 N. Calculate the pressure due to this force. [2]

8. **a)** What is meant by elastic behaviour? [1]
   b) What is meant by plastic behaviour? [1]

9. A steel spring stretches by 4 cm when it is stretched by a force of 1 N applied at either end.
   a) What is the extension of the spring when it is stretched by a force of 5 N? [1]
   b) How much force is needed to extend the spring by 10 cm? [1]

10. State one situation in which friction is
    a) useful **b)** a nuisance. [2]

Galileo and the Leaning Tower of Pisa

Galileo demonstrated to his friends that falling objects descend at the same rate, regardless of their mass. He is reported to have released two different objects at the same time from the top of the Leaning Tower of Pisa to show that they hit the ground simultaneously.

197

6 Physical processes

6.1 Speed and distance

Fact file
★ **Speed** is defined as distance travelled per unit time.

★ The **unit** of speed is the metre per second (m/s).

★ Average speed (in m/s) = $\dfrac{\text{distance travelled (in m)}}{\text{time taken (in s)}}$

★ **Velocity** is speed in a given direction.

Distance–time graphs for a moving object

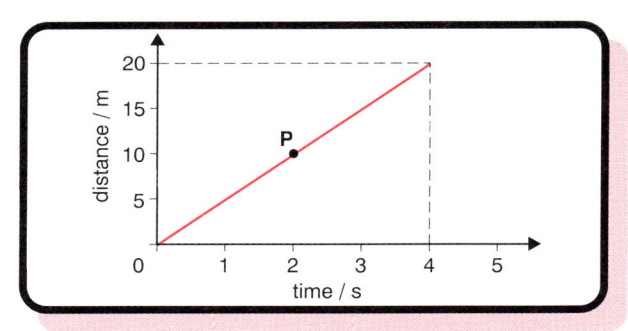

Constant speed

At **constant speed**, the distance travelled increases steadily with time as shown on the graph above.

1. The graph is a straight line with a constant gradient.
2. The steeper the line, the greater the speed.
3. The gradient of the graph is equal to the speed of the object.

The equation for constant speed

1. Rearranging the equation speed = $\dfrac{\text{distance}}{\text{time}}$

   gives **distance = speed × time**.

   This can be used to work out the distance an object moves in a given time if its speed is constant.

2. Rearranging distance = speed × time

   gives the equation **time** = $\dfrac{\textbf{distance}}{\textbf{speed}}$.

   This can be used to work out the time taken to travel a given distance for an object moving at constant speed.

When speed is not constant

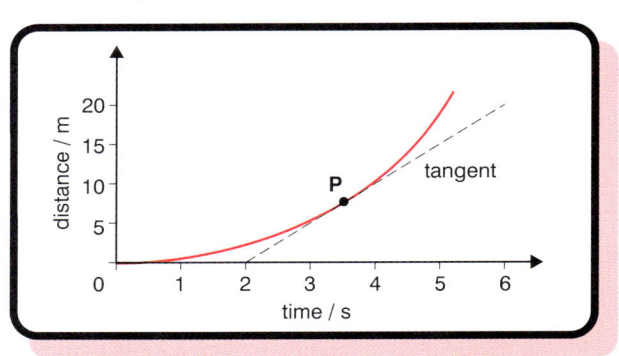

Distance–time graph for an object that accelerates from rest

At **changing speed**, the gradient of the line changes, as in the distance–time graph for an object that accelerates from rest.

1. The gradient changes with time.
2. The speed at any point is equal to the gradient of the tangent to the curve.
3. The speed is zero where the gradient is zero. This is at the origin O on the graph.

Question

a) Determine the speed at point P on each of the two graphs on this page.

b) On the second graph, how can you tell if the object is moving faster or slower after point P?

Did you know?
Scientists reckon that nothing can travel faster than light in free space. Its speed is 300 000 km/s. Light takes about 8 minutes to travel to Earth from the Sun and about 4 years from the star nearest the Sun. Show that this distance is about 36 million million kilometres.

Speed and velocity

Velocity is defined as speed in a given direction. A car moving at 20 m/s due north has the same speed as a car moving at 20 m/s due south, but not the same velocity.

Answer

a) 5 m/s b) The gradient becomes steeper so the speed is increasing.

6.2 Force and acceleration

★ **For an object moving along a straight line**, its acceleration is its change of speed per second.

★ **For an object falling freely**, its acceleration is constant, referred to as the acceleration due to gravity g. Near the Earth's surface, $g = 10\,\text{m/s}^2$. A falling object gains speed at a rate of 10 m/s each second.

Balanced forces

★ A **force** is anything that can change the velocity of an object.

★ If there is no force acting on an object, the object moves at constant velocity (constant speed without changing direction) or remains stationary.

★ If an object is acted on by two or more forces which balance each other out, the object either remains at rest or continues to move at constant velocity.

★ A force acting on an object is usually represented by an arrow in the direction of the force pulling on the object at the point where the force acts. This is called a **force diagram**.

Unbalanced forces

The speed or direction of motion of an object changes if the object is acted on by a force or by several forces which do not balance out. The combined effect of different forces acting on an object is called the **resultant force** on the object.

If an object is at rest or moving at constant velocity, the resultant force on it must be zero. This is known as **Newton's first law of motion**.

If an object's velocity is changing, the resultant force on it is not zero. Experiments show that the acceleration of an object is proportional to the resultant force on the object. This is known as **Newton's second law of motion** and it can be written as an equation.

$$\begin{array}{ccc} \text{force} & = \text{mass} & \times \text{ acceleration} \\ (\text{in newtons, N}) & (\text{in kg}) & (\text{in m/s}^2) \end{array}$$

Weight

The **weight** of an object is the force of gravity on it. An object falling freely is acted on by gravity only. Since the acceleration due to gravity g is constant, then the force of gravity on an object (its weight) must be equal to its mass × g.

$$\begin{array}{ccc} \text{weight} & = \text{mass} \times & g \\ (\text{in N}) & (\text{in kg}) & (\text{in m/s}^2) \end{array}$$

Note that the unit of g may be written as N/kg or m/s^2 since $1\,\text{N} = 1\,\text{kg}\,\text{m/s}^2$.

Terminal speed

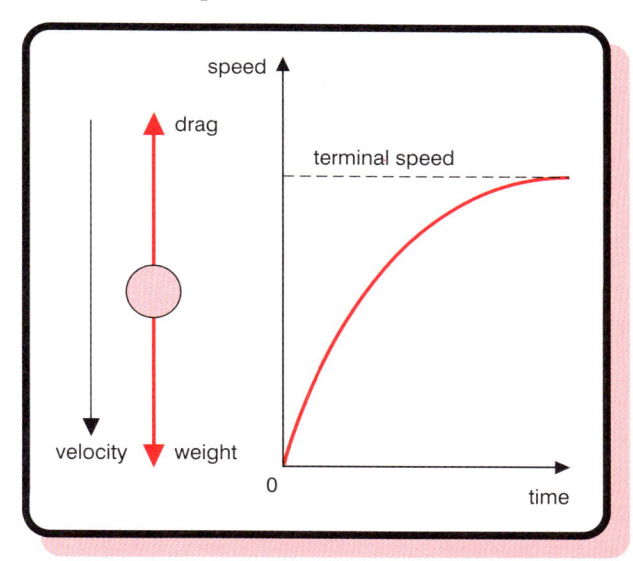

Terminal speed

When an object moves through a liquid or a gas, it experiences friction due to the liquid or gas, which opposes its motion. This resistance to its motion is called **drag**. The drag force increases with speed, and depends on the shape of the object and the substance the object is moving through.

★ An object released in air accelerates gradually until its speed is such that the drag force is equal and opposite to its weight. This speed is called the **terminal speed**.

★ A vehicle reaches its top speed when the drag force is equal and opposite to the engine force. The top speed can be increased by reshaping a vehicle to reduce the drag force on it.

Physical processes

6.3 Equilibrium

Fact file

★ Different types of force include **weight** (the force of gravity), **tension** (forces that stretch), **compression** (forces that squeeze), **twisting forces**, **electrical forces** and **magnetic forces**.

★ The unit of force is the **newton** (N). Note that 10 N is the weight of a mass of 1 kg at the Earth's surface.

★ The **centre of gravity** of an object is the point where its weight may be considered to act.

Stability

If an object at equilibrium is displaced slightly then released, it is said to be

1 **in stable equilibrium** if it returns to equilibrium

2 **in neutral equilibrium** if it stays at its new position

3 **in unstable equilibrium** if it moves away from the point where it was in equilibrium.

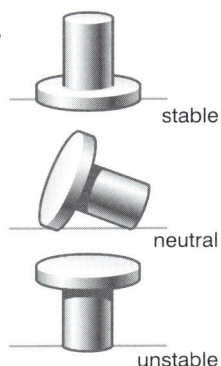

At rest

An object in equilibrium is **at rest** because **the forces acting on it balance each other out**. Some examples of objects in equilibrium are shown in the following diagram.

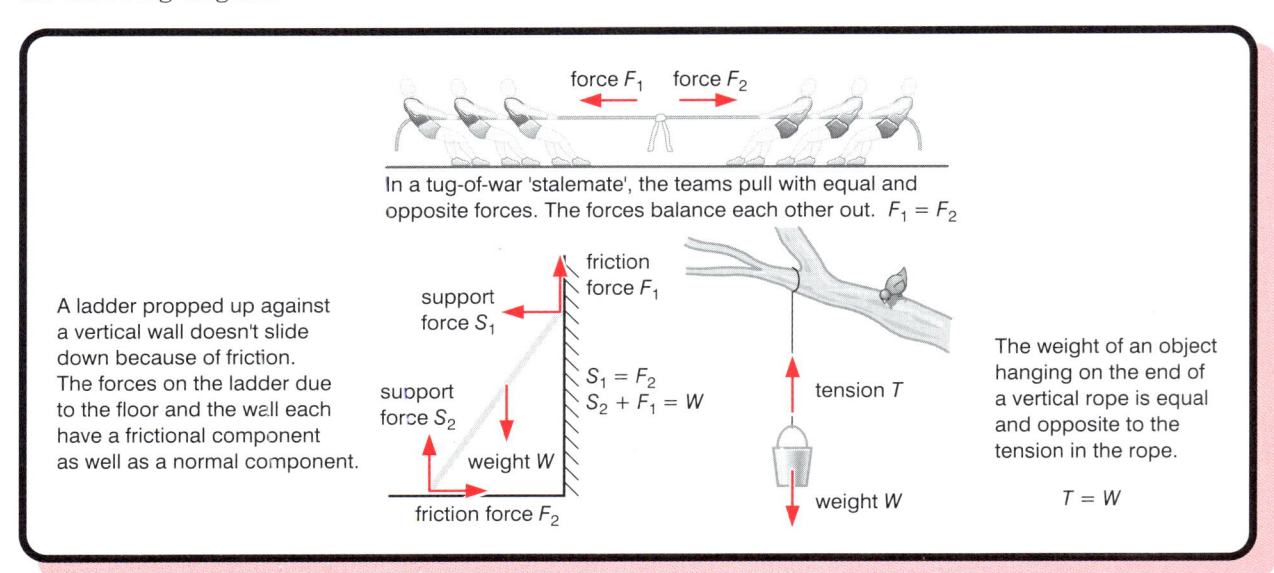

Action and reaction

Whenever two objects interact, they exert equal and opposite forces on each other. For example, if you lean on a wall with a certain force, you experience an equal and opposite force from the wall. The same rule applies when two objects collide; they push on each other with an equal and opposite force.

Question

A plank of weight 200 N rests horizontally on two bricks, one at either end as shown.
a) What force does the plank exert on each brick?
b) What force is necessary to lift the plank at one end?

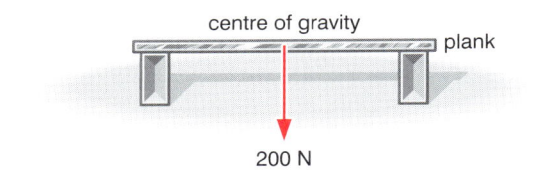

Answer a) 100 N b) 100 N

In a tug-of-war 'stalemate', the teams pull with equal and opposite forces. The forces balance each other out. $F_1 = F_2$

A ladder propped up against a vertical wall doesn't slide down because of friction. The forces on the ladder due to the floor and the wall each have a frictional component as well as a normal component.

$S_1 = F_2$
$S_2 + F_1 = W$

The weight of an object hanging on the end of a vertical rope is equal and opposite to the tension in the rope.

$T = W$

Equal and opposite forces

6.4 Strength of solids

Solids under test

The particles in a solid are locked together by strong chemical bonds. This is why a solid has its own shape and cannot flow. The diagram on the right shows a solid acted upon by external forces. These forces can alter the shape of the solid, depending on whether or not the forces between the particles are strong enough to withstand the external forces.

Under tension: the solid is stretched by the external forces. The solid is said to be in a state of tension when it is stretched. The tension in the solid is equal and opposite to the external force.

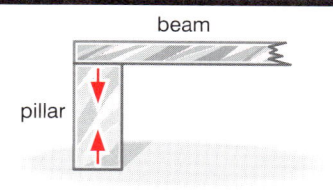

In compression: the solid is compressed by the external forces. Most solids are very difficult to compress and huge forces are needed, such as using a vice.

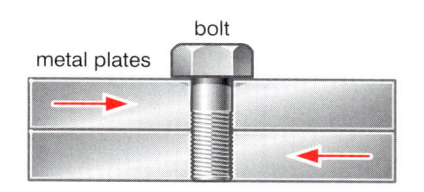

Shear: the external forces are trying to shear the bolt because they are not acting along the same line.

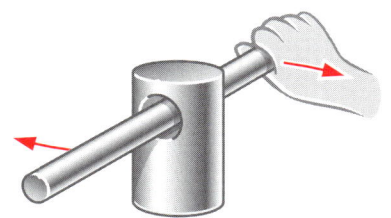

Twist: the external forces are twisting the solid.

Solids under test

Solids and strength

★ **Stiffness** is the ability to withstand being stretched or bent.

★ **Toughness** is the ability to withstand fracture.

★ **Strength** is a measure of how much force is needed to break an object.

★ **Brittleness** is a measure of how easily an object snaps.

Hooke's law

This law states that **the extension of a spiral spring is proportional to the force used to stretch it**. The diagram shows how Hooke's law may be tested, and a graph of some typical results for a steel spring. Note that the extension is the change of length from its unstretched length.

Hooke's law may be written in the form $T = ke$ where T is the tension in the spring, e is the extension of the spring and k is a constant. This is the equation for the line in the graph. The line is straight and it passes through the origin because the tension is proportional to the extension. Its gradient is equal to the spring constant k. Note that the equation $T = ke$ may be rearranged to give

$$e = \frac{T}{k} \text{ or } k = \frac{T}{e}$$

Elastic and plastic behaviour

★ **Elastic behaviour** is the ability of a solid to regain its shape when the external forces are removed. The atoms return to their original positions when the external forces are removed.

★ **The elastic limit** of a solid is the limit of its ability to regain its shape. Beyond its elastic limit, it deforms permanently.

★ **Plastic behaviour** occurs when the shape of a solid is permanently changed by external forces. The atoms are pulled out of position permanently.

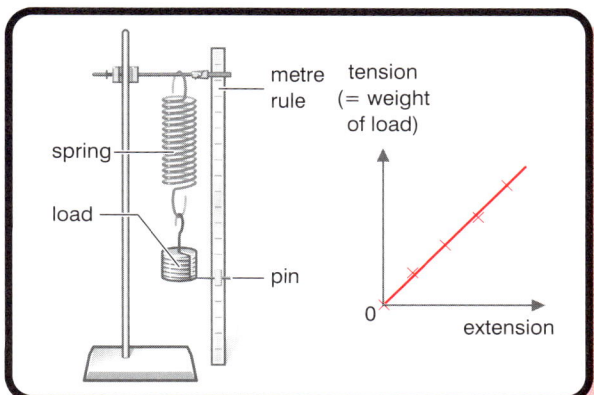

Hooke's law

Physical processes

The graphs below show how the extension of different objects under tension increases with the external force.

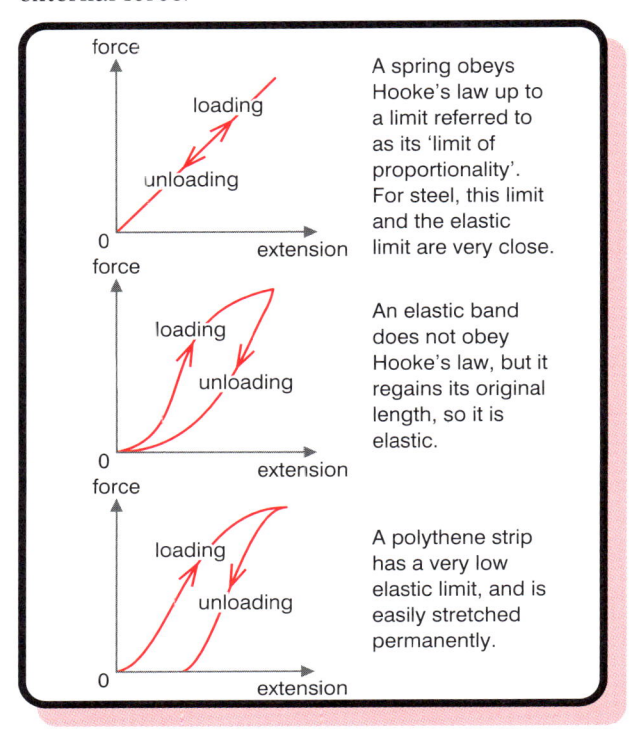

A spring obeys Hooke's law up to a limit referred to as its 'limit of proportionality'. For steel, this limit and the elastic limit are very close.

An elastic band does not obey Hooke's law, but it regains its original length, so it is elastic.

A polythene strip has a very low elastic limit, and is easily stretched permanently.

Stretching materials

6.5 Pressure

Fact file

★ **Pressure** is defined as force per unit area acting normally on a surface.

★ The unit of pressure is the **pascal** (Pa), equal to 1 N/m².

★ Density = $\frac{mass}{volume}$

★ The unit of density is the **kilogram per cubic metre** (kg/m³).

Pressure points

The larger the area of surface over which a force acts, the smaller the pressure. The smaller the area, the greater the pressure.
(Note: $1\,m^2 = 10\,000\,cm^2$.)

Question

1 Calculate the pressure in N/m² exerted by a 60 kg person standing on the floor if the area of contact between the person's feet and the floor is 0.01 m². Assume $g = 10$ N/kg.

Hydraulic brakes

A vehicle brake system exerts a large braking force on the wheels as a result of a much smaller force being applied to the foot pedal.

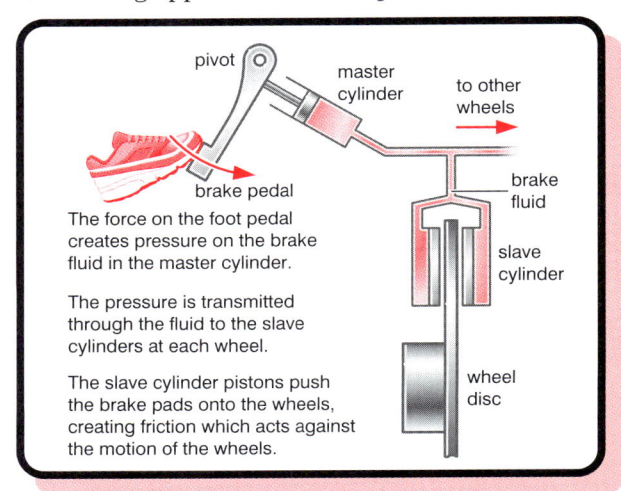

The force on the foot pedal creates pressure on the brake fluid in the master cylinder.

The pressure is transmitted through the fluid to the slave cylinders at each wheel.

The slave cylinder pistons push the brake pads onto the wheels, creating friction which acts against the motion of the wheels.

Disc brakes

Using the pressure equation

1 The pressure exerted on the fluid is given by the equation $p = \frac{F_1}{A_1}$ where F_1 is the force on the master cylinder and A_1 is the area of the master cylinder.

2 This pressure is transmitted to the slave cylinders without loss. This assumes no air in the brake system.

3 The force exerted by each slave cylinder $F_2 = pA_2$, where A_2 is the area of each slave cylinder.

4 Hence $F_2 = \frac{F_1 A_2}{A_1}$. Since A_2 is much larger than A_1, then it follows that F_2 is much larger than F_1.

Question

2 A brake system has a master cylinder of area 5 cm² and each slave cylinder has an area of 100 cm². A force of 20 N is applied to the master cylinder.
   a) Calculate (i) the pressure in the system, in pascals (ii) the force exerted by each slave piston.
   b) Why is it important not to allow any air into the brake system?

Answers

1 60 kPa
2 a) (i) 40 000 Pa (ii) 400 N
  b) Unlike a liquid, air can be compressed. Therefore the pressure would not be transmitted to the slave cylinders.

round-up

How much have you improved? Work out your improvement index on page 217.

The acceleration of a freely falling object $g = 10 \text{ m/s}^2$.

1 a) A walker leaves a car park and walks at a steady speed of 1.2 m/s for 1 hour. How far did the walker travel in this time in
  (i) metres **(ii)** kilometres? [2]
b) A runner leaves the same car park 40 minutes after the walker and catches up with the walker at a distance of 4 km from the car park. What was the runner's speed? [1]

2 The graph shows the progress of two cyclists in a 10 km road race.

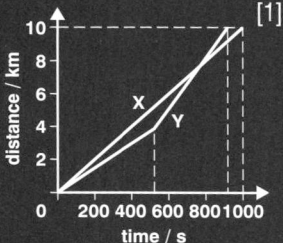

a) One cyclist X maintained a constant speed throughout. What can you deduce from the graph about the speed of the other cyclist Y? [4]
b) (i) From the graph, calculate the speed of X. [1]
  (ii) From the graph, calculate the speed of Y when Y overtook X. [1]

3 a) Explain the difference between speed and velocity. [2]
b) A police car joins a motorway and travels north at a constant speed of 30 m/s for 5 minutes. It then leaves the motorway at a motorway junction, rejoins it immediately and travels south in the opposite direction for 20 minutes at a steady speed of 20 m/s to the scene of an accident.
  (i) How far did the police car travel in each direction? [2]
  (ii) How far from the point where the police car first joined the motorway was the scene of the accident? [1]

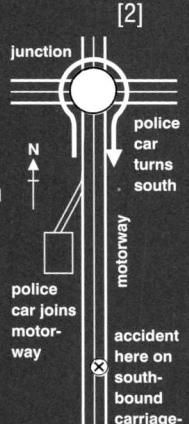

4 a) Why do the rear wheels of a tractor need to be much larger than the wheels of a van of equal weight? [2]
b) With the aid of a diagram, explain why the shape of a bowling alley pin makes it easy to knock over. [2]

5 a) Calculate the pressure exerted by a person of weight 600 N when she is
  (i) standing on both feet, with an area of contact between each foot and the floor of 0.0015 m² [1]
  (ii) sitting on a chair, with a total area of contact on the chair of 0.10 m². [1]
b) Calculate the total area of contact between the tyres of a bicycle and the ground if the air pressure in each tyre is 150 kPa and the total weight of the bicycle and cyclist is 600 N. [1]

6 A student proposes to replace a steel spring in a spring balance with an elastic band. She tests the stiffness of the elastic band and the spring in separate experiments. The graphs show her results.

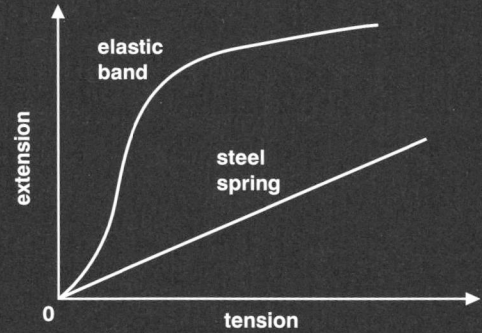

a) Use these results to compare the stiffness of the elastic band and the steel spring. [2]
b) Would the elastic band be satisfactory in place of the steel spring? Give a reason for your answer. [2]

7 A steel spring of length 300 mm was used to measure the weight of an object. With the spring hanging vertically from a fixed point, its length was measured when it supported different known weights. Then its length was measured when it supported the unknown weight W. The measurements are given below.

weight / N	0	1	2	3	4
spring length / mm	300	340	382	419	461

Spring length for the unknown weight = 376 mm
a) Plot a graph of weight (vertical axis) against the extension of the spring. [4]
b) Use your graph to determine the unknown weight W. [1]

Electricity and magnetism

7

preview

At the end of this topic you will be able to:

- explain what is meant by potential difference
- describe series and parallel circuits in terms of current and voltage
- describe how to use an ammeter to measure current and a voltmeter to measure voltage
- recognise the circuit symbols for common electrical components and know their characteristics
- define resistance and carry out calculations involving current, voltage and resistance
- describe how mains electricity is supplied and costed
- identify dangers of mains electricity and explain safety features and devices to minimise dangers
- explain the principle and operation of an alternating current generator.

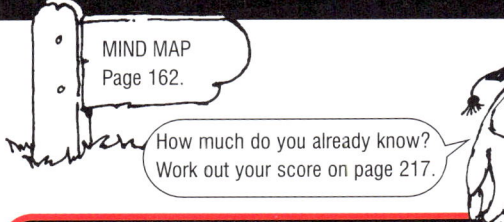

MIND MAP Page 162.

How much do you already know? Work out your score on page 217.

Test yourself

1 A 1.5 V cell was connected in series with an ammeter, a switch and a 1.5 V, 0.5 W torch bulb X. A second identical torch bulb Y was connected in parallel with X. The switch was then closed to light both torch bulbs.
   a) Draw the circuit diagram. [2]
   b) Calculate the energy supplied by the cell in
      (i) one second (ii) one minute. [2]

2 In the circuit shown, ammeter A_1 reads 0.5 A and ammeter A_2 reads 0.3 A.

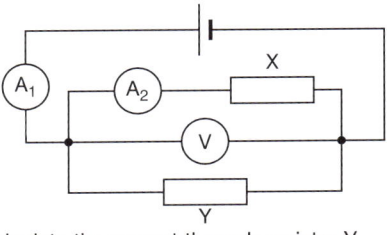

   a) Calculate the current through resistor Y. [1]
   b) The voltmeter in parallel with resistor Y reads 1.0 V when ammeter A_1 reads 0.5 A. Calculate the resistance of resistor Y. [2]

3 A current of 2.5 A is passed through a 6.0 Ω resistor. Calculate a) the p.d. across the resistor
   b) the current through this resistor if a 3.0 V battery is connected across it. [2]

4 a) Draw a circuit diagram to show a diode connected in series with a 1.5 V cell and a torch bulb lit up. [2]
   b) If the 1.5 V cell is connected in the circuit in the reverse direction, the torch bulb will not light. Why? [2]

5 Give the symbol and state the main characteristic of each of the following components:
   a) a light-dependent resistor
   b) a thermistor. [4]

6 An electric heater is rated at 240 V, 1000 W. Calculate
   a) the electrical energy delivered to the heater in 300 s
   b) the number of units of electricity used by the heater in 4 hours. [3]

7 a) State the purpose of a fuse in an electric circuit.
   b) Explain how a fuse achieves its purpose. [3]

8 A microwave oven rated at 800 W is used for 15 minutes to heat some food. Calculate
   a) the number of units of electricity used
   b) the cost of the electricity used, if each unit of electricity is priced at 6.0p. [3]

9 a) Sketch the waveform of the output voltage from an alternating current generator. [2]
   b) What is the angle between the coil and the lines of the magnetic field in an alternating current generator when the induced voltage is
      (i) at its maximum value (ii) zero? [2]

10 a) State two ways in which the voltage from an alternating current generator would change if its rate of rotation was reduced. [2]
   b) State two factors in the design of an alternating current generator that affect the size of the induced voltage. [2]

7.1 Current, potential difference and resistance

Fact file

★ An **electric current** is a **flow of charge**. The unit of electric current is the **ampere** (A).

★ A source of **potential difference** is necessary to force charge around a circuit. **Voltage** is an alternative word for potential difference.

★ The unit of potential difference is the **volt** (V), equal to one joule per coulomb.

★ The **resistance** of an electrical component in a circuit
$$= \frac{\text{the voltage across the component}}{\text{the current through the component}}$$

★ The unit of resistance is the **ohm** (Ω), defined as one volt per ampere.

Four rules about current

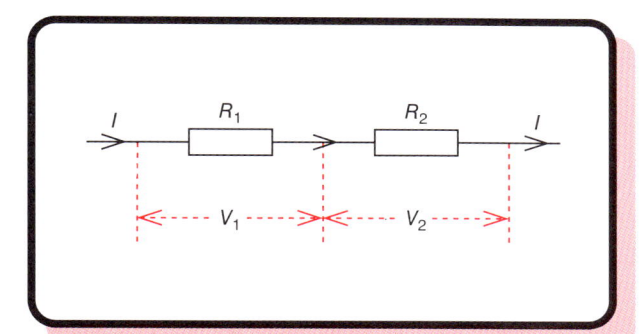

Series resistors

1. The current entering a component is the same as the current leaving it. A component does not use up current; it uses the electrical energy supplied to it by the charge that passes through it.

2. At a junction, the total current leaving the junction is equal to the total current entering the junction.

3. Components in series pass the same current.

4. An ammeter is a meter designed to measure current. It is always connected in series with a component. An ideal ammeter has zero resistance.

Four rules about voltage

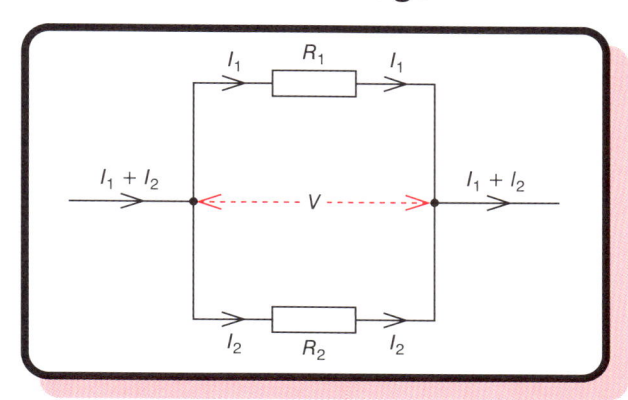

Parallel resistors

1. The voltage across a component is a measure of the energy delivered to the component by the charge that passes through it.

2. Components in parallel have the same voltage across them.

3. For two or more components in series, the total voltage is equal to the sum of the individual voltages.

4. A voltmeter is a meter designed to measure voltage (potential difference). It is always connected in parallel with a component. An ideal voltmeter has infinite resistance.

Three rules about resistance

1. **To calculate resistance**, use the equation
$$\text{resistance} = \frac{\text{voltage}}{\text{current}}.$$

2. **Ohm's law** states that for a wire under constant physical conditions, the current is proportional to the voltage. This is equivalent to stating that its resistance is constant.

3. A **resistor** is a component designed to have a particular value of resistance. This resistance is caused by opposition to the motion of electrons round the circuit.

Note
The following prefixes are used for large or small values of current, voltage or resistance:

mega (M)	kilo (k)	milli (m)	micro (μ)
1 000 000	1000	0.001	0.000 001
10^6	10^3	10^{-3}	10^{-6}

Physical processes

7.2 Components in circuits

What does current depend on?

1. the voltage of the cell, battery or power supply unit
2. the resistance of the components in the circuit.

Resistors can be used to control the current in a circuit.

Measuring resistance

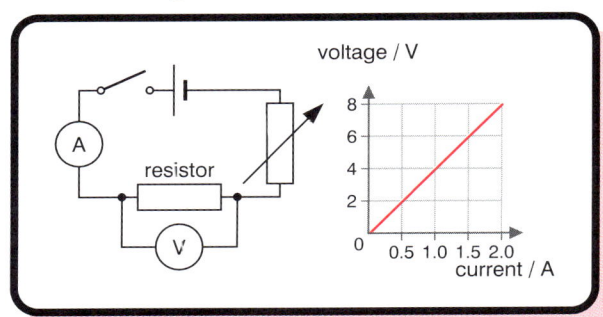

Measuring resistance   Voltage against current

The circuit above may be used to investigate the variation of current with voltage for any device. The graphs show the results of such investigations for different components, plotted with current on the y-axis and voltage on the x-axis.

1. For a wire-wound resistor at constant temperature, the graph is a straight line – the resistance is constant.

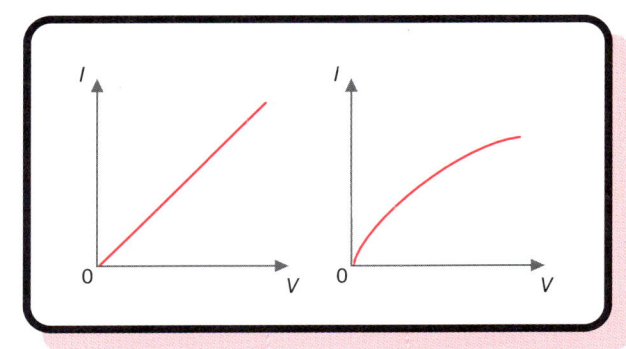

Fixed resistor   Filament bulb

2. For a filament bulb such as a torch bulb, the graph is a curve – the resistance increases as the filament becomes hotter.

3. For a diode in its forward direction, the graph shows that the resistance decreases as the current increases. In the reverse direction, the graph shows that the diode has an extremely high resistance.

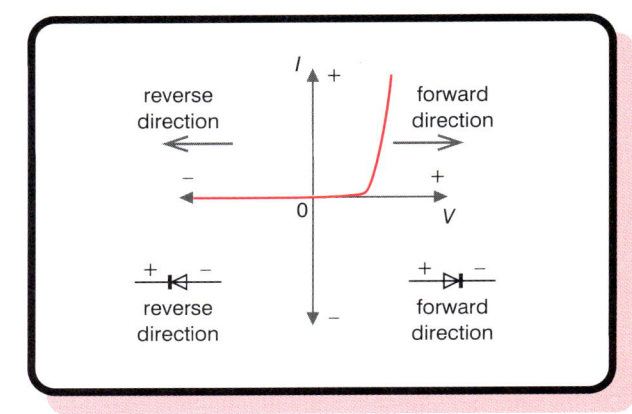

Diode

4. For a light-dependent resistor (LDR), its resistance depends on the intensity of light falling on it. Increasing the intensity makes the resistance lower; conversely, decreasing the intensity makes the resistance higher. More electrons are freed from the atoms if the light intensity is increased, causing the resistance to fall.

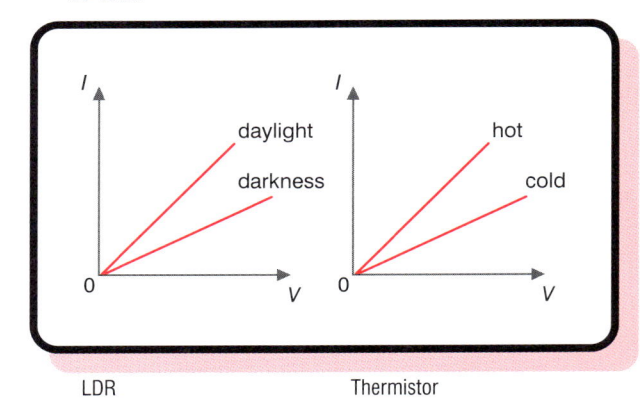

LDR   Thermistor

5. For a thermistor, the resistance decreases with increasing temperature and vice versa. More electrons are freed from the atoms if the temperature is increased, causing the resistance to fall.

7.3 Mains electricity

Alternating current

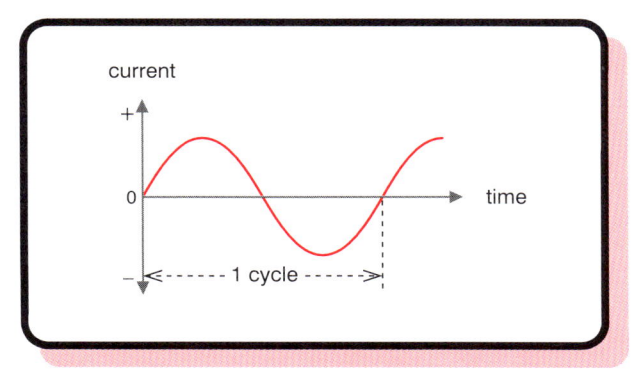

Alternating current

1. The electric current through a mains appliance alternates in direction. The current reverses direction then reverses back each cycle.

2. The **frequency** of an alternating current is the number of cycles per second. In the UK, the mains frequency is 50 Hz.

Mains circuits

The three-pin plug

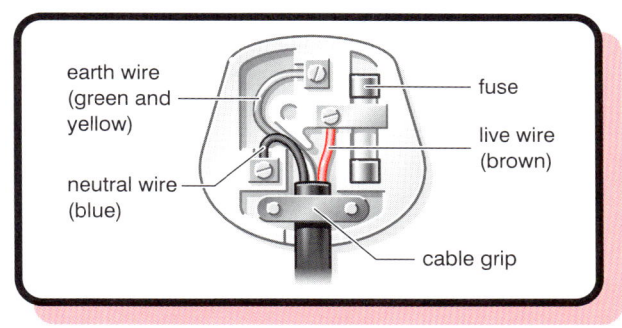

A mains plug

Electricity costs

★ Energy transferred = power × time
   (in joules)   (in watts) (in seconds)

★ One kilowatt hour (kW h) is the electrical energy supplied to a one kilowatt appliance in exactly one hour.

★ The kilowatt hour is the unit of electricity for costing purposes.

★ A domestic electricity meter records the total number of units used.

Each circuit from the fuse board is protected with its own fuse. If the fuse 'blows', the live wire is therefore cut off from appliances supplied by that circuit.

The mains cable from the substation to a building is connected via the electricity meter to the circuits in the building at the distribution fuse board. The live wire from the substation is connected via a main fuse to the electricity meter.

The two wires used to supply an electric current to an appliance are referred to as the **live** and the **neutral** wires. The neutral wire is earthed at the nearest mains substation.

Mains wires need to have as low a resistance as possible, otherwise heat is produced in them by the current. This is why mains wires are made from copper. All mains wires and fittings are insulated.

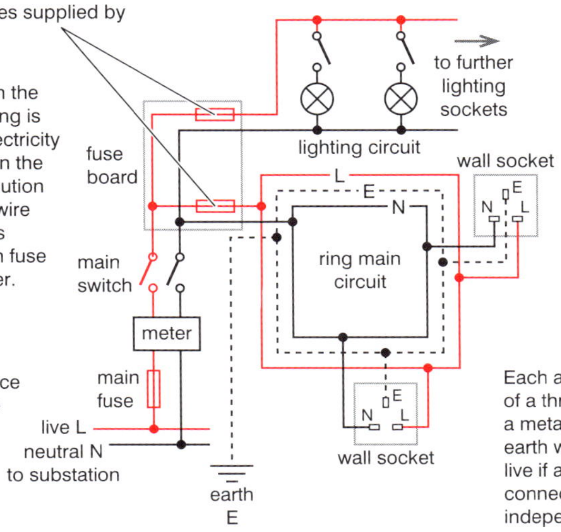

The fuse in a lighting circuit is in the fuse box. Each light bulb is turned on or off by its own switch. When the switch is in the off position, the appliance is not connected to the live wire of the mains supply.

A **ring main** is used to supply electricity to appliances via wall sockets. A ring main circuit consists of a live wire, a neutral wire and the **earth wire** which is earthed at the fuse board. The wires of a ring main are thicker than the wires of a lighting circuit because appliances connected to a ring main require more current than light bulbs do.

Each appliance is connected to the ring main by means of a three-pin plug which carries a fuse. An appliance with a metal chassis is earthed via the three-pin plug and the earth wire. This prevents the metal chassis from becoming live if a fault develops in the appliance. Appliances connected to the ring main can be switched on or off independently since they are in parallel with each other.

Mains circuits

Physical processes

7.4 Electrical safety

Faults and fuses

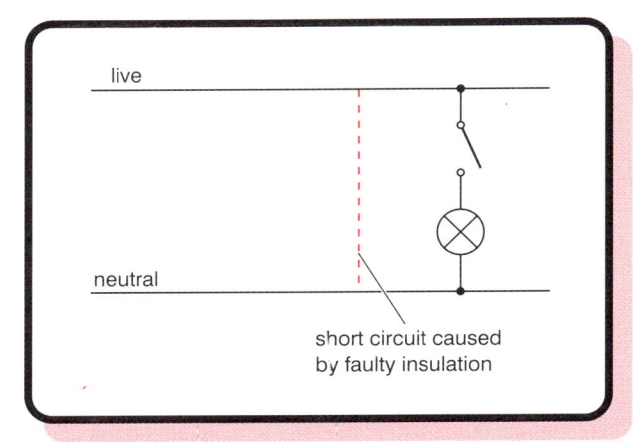

A short circuit

A **short circuit** occurs where a fault creates a low resistance path between two points at different voltages. The current through the short circuit is much greater than the current along the correct path between the two points, enough to create a fire through overheating.

Fuses are intended to prevent excessive currents flowing. A fuse is a thin piece of resistance wire which overheats and melts if too much current passes through it. The fuse wire breaks when it melts, thus cutting the current off and protecting the appliance or the wires leading to it from overheating due to excessive current.

Faults in mains circuits can arise due to
- **poor maintenance** e.g. frayed cables or damaged plugs or fittings such as sockets and switches
- **carelessness** e.g. cables that are too long, coiling a cable (which prevents heat from escaping from it)
- **overloading a circuit** e.g. too many appliances connected to the same circuit or connecting a powerful appliance to a low current circuit.

Earthing

Any appliance with a metal case must be earthed through the ring main to protect the user. If such an appliance is not earthed and a fault develops in which a live wire touches the case, anyone who subsequently touches the case will be electrocuted. The victim effectively provides a short circuit path to earth from the live case.

Circuit breakers

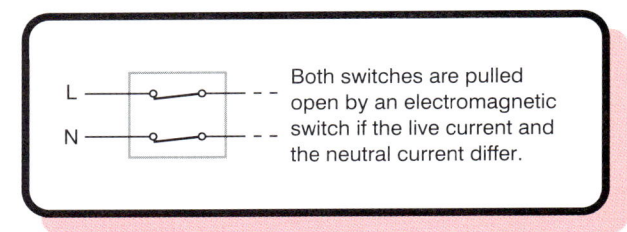

A residual current circuit breaker

A lethal electric shock is possible with currents as small as 50 mA passing through the body. The **residual current circuit breaker** is designed to cut an appliance off from the mains if the current in the live wire differs from the current in the neutral wire by more than 30 mA. This difference would arise if current leaks to earth from a poorly insulated live wire.

A **simple circuit breaker** is a switch operated by an electromagnet in series with the switch. When the switch is closed, if the current reaches a certain value, the electromagnet pulls the switch open and cuts the current off. The circuit breaker switch then needs to be reset once the fault causing the current rise has been remedied. A circuit breaker does not need to be replaced like a fuse each time it cuts the current off.

Double insulation

This is a safety feature of mains appliances like hand-held hair dryers and electric shavers which have insulated cases.

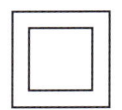

Double insulation symbol

Question

State the purpose of **a)** a fuse **b)** a residual current circuit breaker.

Answers
a) To protect the appliance or the wiring from overheating due to excessive current.
b) To protect the user from shocks.

7.5 Electromagnetic induction

Fact file

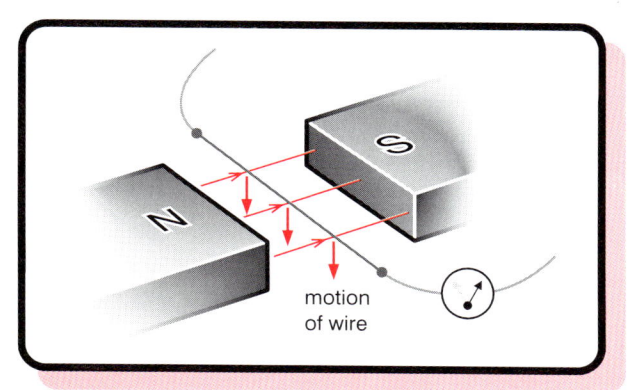

Electromagnetic induction

★ When a wire cuts across the lines of force of a magnetic field, a voltage is induced in the wire.

★ If the wire is part of a complete circuit in which there is no other voltage source, the induced voltage drives a current round the circuit.

★ The faster the wire moves across the field lines, the greater the induced voltage.

★ The stronger the magnetic field, the greater the induced voltage.

Laws of electromagnetic induction

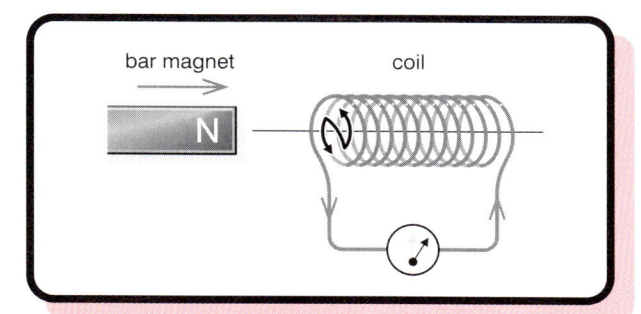

Lenz's law

Lenz's law: the induced current in a circuit is always in such a direction as to oppose the change which causes it. This can be tested by inserting a bar magnet into a coil connected to a centre-reading milliammeter. The direction of the induced current is given by the deflection of the pointer of the meter. Inserting the magnet generates a current which creates a magnetic pole to oppose the incoming pole.

Faraday's law of electromagnetic induction: the induced voltage is proportional to the speed at which the wire cuts the magnetic field lines. The induced current is small if the magnet is inserted slowly. If the magnet is inserted rapidly, the induced current is much larger.

The alternating current generator

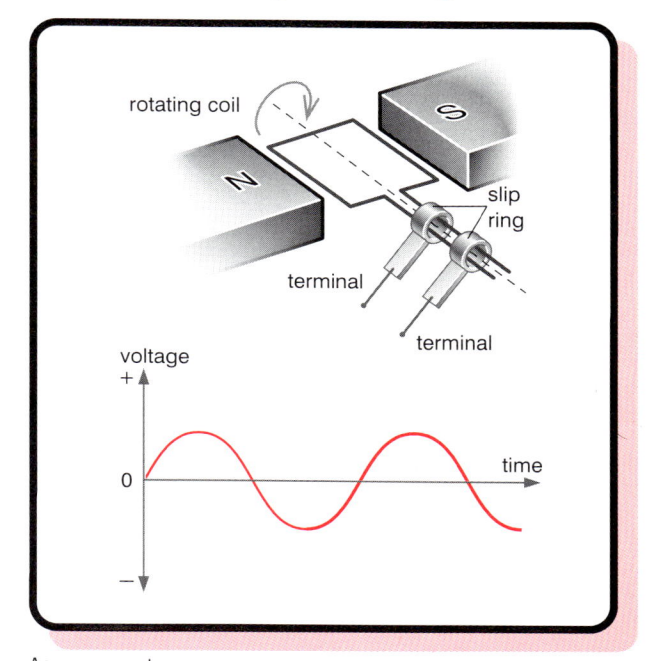

An a.c. generator

The a.c. generator consists of a rectangular coil of insulated wire which is made to rotate at steady speed in a uniform magnetic field. Work done to turn the coil is converted into electrical energy. The alternating voltage induced across the terminals of the coil can be displayed on an oscilloscope.

★ The frequency of the alternating voltage is equal to the frequency of rotation of the coil.

★ The peak voltage is proportional to the speed of rotation of the coil.

★ The peak voltage occurs when the sides of the coil cut across the field lines at 90°. The voltage is zero when the coil sides move parallel to the field lines.

Physical processes

★ A direct voltage can be generated if the two slip rings are replaced by a split-ring commutator, as shown. This makes the connections to the coil change each half-cycle so the voltage polarity does not change. However, the voltage is not steady.

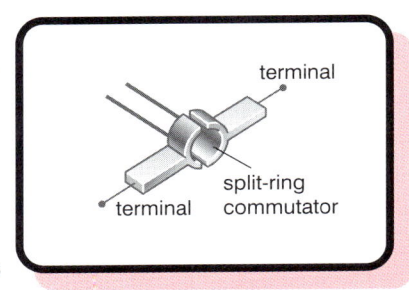

Producing direct current

The dynamo

In a dynamo, the magnet rotates and the coil remains stationary. The magnet and coil move relative to each other such that the coil windings cut across the magnetic field lines. Hence a voltage is induced.

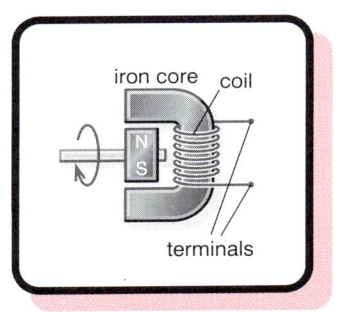

A dynamo

Question

A bicycle is fitted with a dynamo lamp. Explain why the cyclist must pedal harder after switching the lamp on.

High voltage transmission of electrical power

The grid system operates at high voltage because the higher the voltage, the less the current needed for the same power. Less power is therefore wasted due to resistance heating in the cables used to carry the current. Such cables are either carried on pylons or buried underground.

Answer

Electrical energy for the lamp is provided from work done by the cyclist. Hence the cyclist must do more work by exerting more force to keep the speed the same.

round-up

How much have you improved?
Work out your improvement index on page 218.

1 In this circuit, the ammeter reading was 0.25 A and the voltmeter reading was 3.0 V.

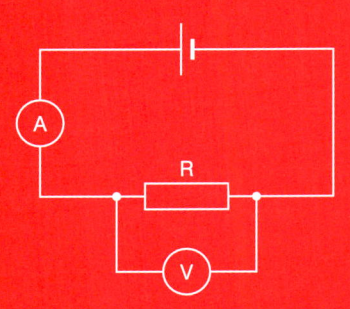

a) Calculate the resistance of resistor R. [1]
b) If a second resistor identical to R was connected in parallel with R how would the ammeter and voltmeter readings alter? [2]

2 The circuit diagram shows two 5 Ω resistors P and Q in series with each other, an ammeter and a 3.0 V cell.

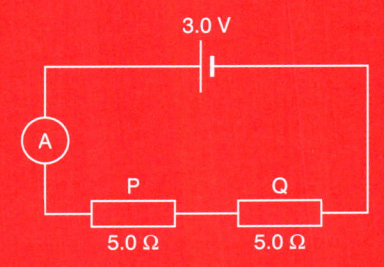

a) (i) What is the voltage across each resistor? [1]
   (ii) What is the current through each resistor? [1]
b) A third 5 Ω resistor R is then connected in parallel with resistor P. How does this affect the current passing through each of the other two resistors? [2]

210

round-up

3 With the aid of a circuit diagram, describe how you could check the resistance per metre of a reel of resistance wire rated at 5.0 Ω/m. [5]

4 A light-dependent resistor has a resistance in darkness of 100 000 Ω. In daylight, its resistance falls to 1000 Ω. It is connected in series with a 1000 Ω resistor R to form a potential divider, as shown.

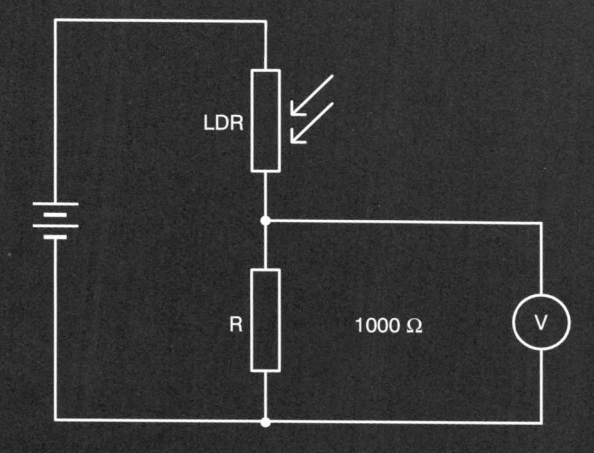

a) In daylight, the voltmeter across R reads 2.0 V. Calculate the current through R and the voltage across the potential divider. [2]

b) The light-dependent resistor is then covered, causing the voltmeter reading to fall. Explain why this happens. [3]

5 The following mains appliances were used in a household over a period of 24 hours:
 (i) two 100 W light bulbs, each for 6 hours
 (ii) a 5000 W electric oven for 2 hours
 (iii) a 3000 W electric kettle used four times for five minutes each time.

a) Calculate the number of units of electricity used in each case. [3]

b) Calculate the total cost of the electricity used if the unit price of electricity was 5p. [1]

c) How long would it take a 5000 W electric oven to use the same number of electricity units as a 100 W electric light bulb would use in 24 hours? [2]

6 a) Why is it dangerous to touch a mains appliance when you have wet hands? [3]

b) A mains electric mower should never be connected to the mains unless a residual current circuit breaker is used. Why? [3]

c) Why is it dangerous to use a mains electric mower with its mains cable coiled up? [2]

d) A microwave oven rated at 650 W, 240 V requires a 3 A fuse. If the wrong fuse is chosen, what problems might occur? [2]

7 a) With the aid of a labelled diagram, explain the operation of an alternating current generator. [6]

b) (i) Sketch the waveform produced by an alternating current generator. [2]

(ii) Show on the waveform you have drawn a point where the coil is parallel to the magnetic field. [1]

c) How does the voltage waveform of an alternating current generator change if the generator turns faster? [2]

8 a) Domestic consumers in the UK are supplied with mains electricity at 240 V. In the USA, the mains voltage is lower, but more current is needed to deliver the same power. Which system is safer and why? [2]

b) The cables used to distribute electricity through the grid system are often carried by pylons. Give one advantage and one disadvantage of using pylons rather than underground cables for this purpose. [2]

Well done if you've improved. Don't worry if you haven't. Take a break and try again.

Equations you should know

Read, learn and inwardly digest the formulas and units below. To test yourself, cover each line with a blank card after the first word and see if you can write the rest of the equation on the card.

voltage = current × resistance

energy transferred = power × time
$\quad\quad$ (J) $\quad\quad\quad\quad$ (W) $\quad$ (s)

energy transferred = power × time
$\quad\quad$ (kW h) $\quad\quad\quad$ (kW) $\quad$ (h)

pressure = $\dfrac{\text{force}}{\text{area}}$

speed = $\dfrac{\text{distance}}{\text{time}}$

work done = force × distance moved in direction of force

energy transferred = work done

efficiency = $\dfrac{\text{useful energy transferred by device}}{\text{total energy supplied to device}}$

power = $\dfrac{\text{work done}}{\text{time taken}}$

weight = mass × gravitational field strength (g)

physical quantity	unit	unit symbol
area	square metres	m^2
current	ampere	A
distance	metres	m
energy	joules	J
force	newtons	N
frequency	hertz	Hz
gravitational field strength	newtons per kilogram	N/kg
mass	kilogram	kg
power	watt	W
pressure	pascal	Pa
resistance	ohm	Ω
speed	metre/second	m/s
time	second	s
voltage	volt	V
volume	cubic metre	m^3
wavelength	metre	m
weight	newton	N

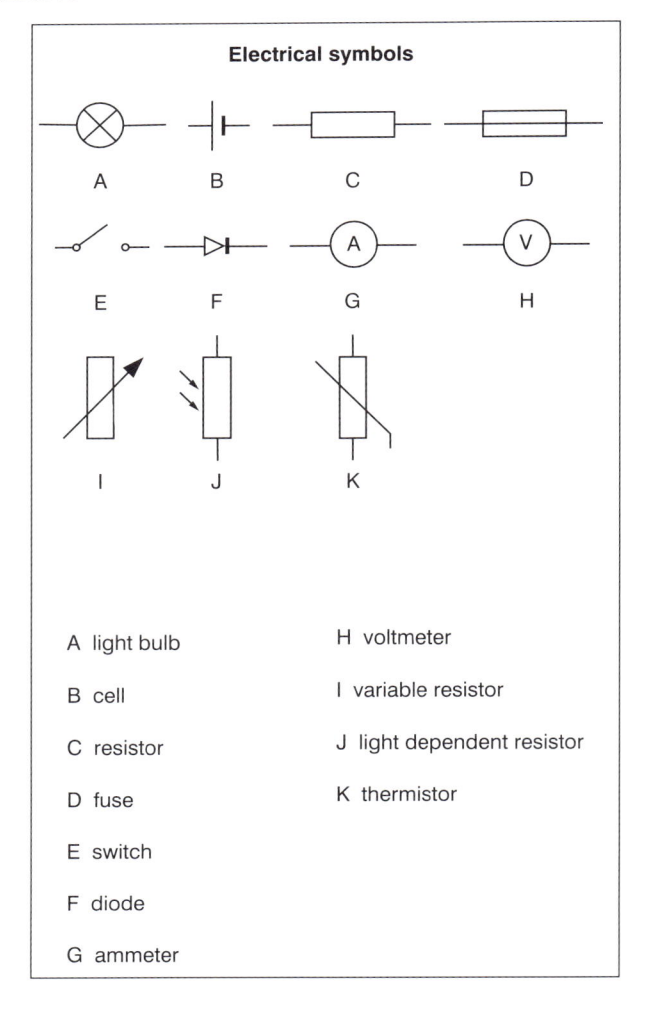

Electrical symbols

A light bulb
B cell
C resistor
D fuse
E switch
F diode
G ammeter
H voltmeter
I variable resistor
J light dependent resistor
K thermistor

Answers

1 Test yourself (page 164)

Beyond the Earth

1. VMJUN (✓ for each correct answer)

2. In northern summer, the Earth's North Pole is tilted towards the Sun and the South Pole is tilted away from the Sun (✓). This is when the northern hemisphere receives more sunlight each day than the southern hemisphere (✓).

3. The Moon moves through the Earth's shadow (✓). Sunlight cannot reach the Moon so it cannot be seen (✓).

4. The stars we see each night are in the opposite direction to the Sun (✓). As the Earth moves round the Sun, the stars we see at night change during the year (✓).

5. a) Mars (✓) b) Jupiter (✓)

6. a) Speeding up (✓). b) Moving towards the Sun (✓).

7. Nuclear fusion (✓).

8. A massive star exploding at the end of its life (✓) releasing an enormous amount of energy in a short time (✓).

9. The light spectrum from the star is shifted towards the red end of the spectrum (✓) due to the star receding (✓).

10. Distant galaxies are moving away from us (✓) at speeds in proportion to their distances away (✓).

Your score: ☐ out of 22

1 Round-up (page 171)

Beyond the Earth

1. a) The first sketch was drawn a few days after the new moon (✓). One week later, the Moon is almost opposite the Sun and will reach full moon a few days later (✓).

   b)

   (✓)

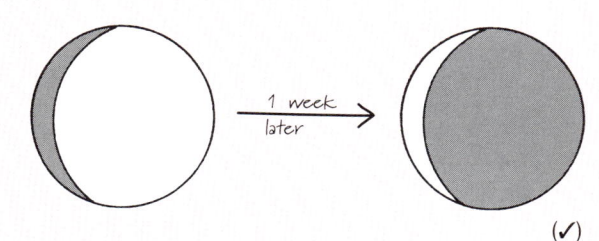

2. The Earth spins eastwards (✓), so the constellations appear to move across the sky westwards (✓).

3. a) Planets reflect sunlight (✓).
   b) Sketch A is when Venus is in position 2, nearer Earth (✓). Its disc appears larger and crescent shaped (✓).

4. a) See page 166 (✓✓).
   b) Totality covers only a small area of the Earth's surface (✓). As the Earth spins, only a small fraction of its surface passes through the area of totality (✓).

5. a) Jupiter shown in the opposite direction to the Sun (Sun Earth Jupiter) (✓).
   b) (i) Mars is smaller, further from the Sun, is colder than Earth, and has no oxygen in its atmosphere (✓✓✓✓).
      (ii) Jupiter is larger, not solid, further from the Sun than Earth, and spins faster (✓✓✓✓).
      (iii) Saturn is larger, not solid, further from the Sun than Earth, and has a ring system (✓✓✓✓).

6. a) It is close to the Sun (✓) and can therefore only be seen just before sunrise (✓) or just after sunset (✓).
   b) Neptune's orbit is circular (✓) whereas Pluto's orbit is elliptical and partly inside Neptune's orbit (✓).
   c) Neptune (✓)
   d) They become cold and dark when they move away from the Sun (✓), so cannot be seen (✓) until the Sun's gravity pulls them round back near the Sun (✓).

7. a) It is red (✓) and much larger than the Sun (✓).
   b) The Sun will become a red giant (✓) and then collapse to become a white dwarf (✓) before radiating all its energy (✓) and becoming invisible (✓).
   c) A massive star which explodes after the white dwarf stage (✓) because its internal pressure is too great (✓).

8. a) They must acquire sufficient speed to overcome gravity (✓) to gain orbital height (✓) then go into orbit (✓).
   b) Its radius (✓) and density are smaller (✓).

9. See page 170 (✓✓✓✓).

10. a) See your textbook or an encyclopedia. Mind map a few brief notes before you write your account. Give a sketch if appropriate (✓✓✓✓).
    b) Voyager 2 took several years to reach Jupiter, a distance which light takes about 30 minutes. The journey to Proxima Centauri would take tens of thousands of years using present rocket technology (✓✓✓✓).

Your score: ☐ out of 59

Your improvement index: $\dfrac{\Box/59}{\Box/22} \times 100\% = \Box\%$

2 Test yourself (page 172)

Energy resources and energy transfer

1. B (✓)

2. Metals contain electrons which move about freely inside the metal (✓). When the metal is heated, the electrons at the point of heating gain kinetic energy (✓) which they transfer to other parts of the metal (✓).

3. a and b (✓✓).

4. c only (✓).

213

Physical processes

5 Cavity wall insulation *or* window blinds *or* thicker carpets (✓).
6 Fossil fuels: oil, coal, gas; non-fossil fuels: uranium, methanol (✓✓✓).
7 Three from: wind power, wave power, solar heating, hydroelectricity (✓✓✓).
8 Radioactive decay inside the Earth (✓) releases energy as heat (✓).
9 The gravitational pull of the Moon (✓) on the Earth's oceans (✓).
10 b) Heat due to friction (✓).   c) Electrical energy (✓).
   d) Sound (✓).   e) Light (✓).   f) Heat due to electrical resistance (✓).

Your score: ☐ out of 23

2 Round-up (page 178)

Energy resources and energy transfer

1 a) Chemical energy in the battery → electrical energy → sound energy (✓).
  b) Gravitational potential energy → kinetic energy (✓) + work done against air resistance (✓).
2 a) 22.5 kJ (✓)   b) (i) 16.8 kJ (✓)   (ii) 26 W (✓)
3 a) China is a better thermal insulator but shiny metal radiates less (✓). The china teapot is likely to be better unless it has very thin walls (✓).
  b) There is a larger open surface in the wide-brimmed cup so there is more evaporation (✓) and thermal radiation (✓) from the wide-brimmed cup. Hence the tea in it loses thermal energy faster and it cools more quickly (✓).
  c) A double-glazed unit traps a layer of still air between its two panes (✓). This is a good thermal insulator (✓).
4 a) (i) 336 kJ (✓) (ii) 298 kg/s (✓✓)
  b) Yes (✓); the water can be re-used and the rocks are not changed into other substances (✓). However, the supply of thermal energy is finite (✓).

Your score: ☐ out of 19

Your improvement index: $\dfrac{\boxed{}/19}{\boxed{}/23} \times 100\% = \boxed{}\%$

3 Test yourself (page 179)

Radioactivity

1 a) Negative (✓)   b) Positive (✓)   c) Uncharged (✓)
  d) Positive (✓)   e) Negative (✓)
2 a) 2p + 2n (✓✓)   b) 92p + 143n (✓✓)
3 Positive (✓)

4 Alpha, beta and gamma radiation (✓✓✓), alpha radiation is most easily absorbed (✓).
5 Radioactivity from the surroundings or caused by cosmic radiation (✓).
6 The Geiger counter (✓).
7 Half-life – the time taken for half the atoms of a given radioactive isotope to disintegrate (✓).
  Isotope – atoms of an element with the same number of neutrons and protons (✓).
8 A nucleus of an atom splits (✓) into two approximately equal halves (✓).
9 The waste from the spent fuel rods contains radioactive isotopes with very long half-lives (✓). Radiation released by radioactive isotopes is harmful (✓).
10 Alpha or beta radiation (✓✓).

Your score: ☐ out of 24

3 Round-up (page 185)

Radioactivity

1 a) U-238 = 92p + 146n (✓✓); U-235 = 92p + 143n (✓✓)
  b) Isotopes (✓)
  c) The time taken for half the initial number of atoms of a given isotope to decay (✓).
2 a) Smoke absorbs alpha radiation (✓) but not beta or gamma radiation (✓).
  b) If the half-life was much shorter than 5 years, the decrease in activity of the source within a year would set the alarm off (✓).
3 a) $^{220}_{82}Rn \rightarrow ^{216}_{80}Po + ^{4}_{2}\alpha$ (✓✓)
  b) (i) 100/s (✓)   (ii) 25/s (✓)
4 a) Steel plate stops alpha and beta radiation (✓✓) but not gamma radiation (✓).
  b) (i) 200/s (✓)   (ii) 160/s (✓)
  (iii) It became thicker (✓).
5 a) (i) See page 181 (✓).   (ii) It produces ions (✓).
  b) X-rays, radioactive waste (✓✓).
  c) Start the Geiger counter and the stopwatch together. Stop the Geiger counter after exactly 600 seconds (✓). Measure the number of counts recorded by the counter. Divide this number by 600 to give the count rate (✓).
6 Alpha and gamma radiation (✓✓), the tin foil stops alpha radiation (✓) whereas even thick lead is unable to stop the gamma radiation completely (✓).
7 a) The radiation becomes weaker with distance (✓).
  b) Electromagnetic radiation of very short wavelength (✓), it penetrates the body (✓).
8 a) It contains long-lived radioactive isotopes (✓) which emit harmful radiation (✓).
  b) The rods are allowed to cool first (✓). Unused uranium is then removed from them chemically (✓). The chemical waste is stored in sealed containers (✓).

Your score: ☐ out of 37

Your improvement index: $\dfrac{\Box/37}{\Box/24} \times 100\% = \Box\%$

4 Test yourself (page 186)

Waves

1. Any four from: sound waves, water waves, waves on a string, electromagnetic waves (radio, microwaves, infrared, visible, ultraviolet, X-rays, gamma rays) (✓✓✓✓).

2. Any electromagnetic wave can pass through a vacuum (✓); any other type of wave needs a medium (✓).

3. Wavelength = 40 mm (✓); amplitude = 15 mm (✓).

4. a) −15 mm (✓) b) +15 mm (✓)

5. a) The angle between the incident ray and the normal = the angle between the reflected ray and the normal (✓).
   b) (i) 2.0 m (✓) (ii) No (✓), because the lowest part of the image visible depends only on the position of the lower edge of the mirror (✓), not on the distance of the person from the mirror (✓).

6. a) There is no hard surface they can reflect off (✓). The amplitude becomes less and less as they run up the shore (✓).
   b) (i) 6 seconds (✓) (ii) 0.17 ($=\frac{1}{6}$) Hz (✓)

7. a) Towards (✓)
   b) (i) Decreases (✓) (ii) Decreases (✓) (iii) No change (✓)

8. Echoes are sound waves that reflect (✓) off a hard smooth surface (✓).

9. a) Red, orange, yellow, green, blue, violet (✓ for 4 colours, ✓ for fifth colour).
   b) Red (✓)

Your score: ☐ out of 28

4 Round-up (page 191)

Waves

1. a) (✓✓) (✓✓) 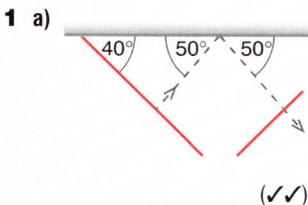 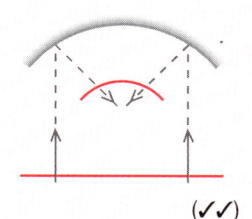
   b) (✓✓)

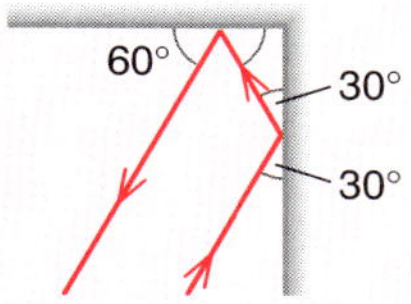

2. a) Its wavelength becomes smaller (✓). Its frequency stays the same (✓).
   b) (✓✓)

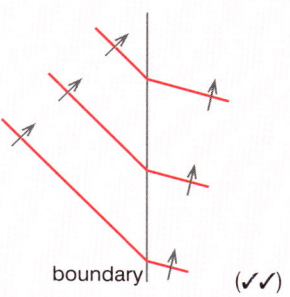

3. a) The sound created by the student travels towards the wall (✓) and reflects off to cause the echo (✓).
   b) The sound from her friend is directed away from the wall (✓), so there is no sound reflected from the wall (✓).

4. a) (✓✓)   b) (✓)
   c) Image I_1 is directly opposite O_1 and image I_2 is directly opposite O_2 (✓). Hence distance I_1I_2 is the same as distance O_1O_2 (✓).

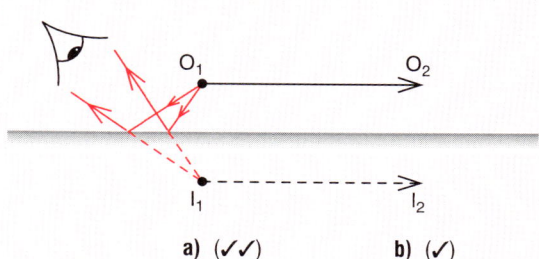

5. a) 2.0 m (✓)
   b) The top of the mirror needs to be just above eye level (✓) to be able to see the head (✓). The bottom of the mirror needs to be opposite the midpoint between the floor and eye level (✓) to be able to see the feet (✓).
   c) Two of: in a periscope; to make a corner cube reflector; to read a scale (✓✓).

6. a) See page 189 for diagram (✓✓) and explanation of diagram (✓✓).
   b) See page 189 for diagram (✓✓).

7. a) See page 190 (✓✓).
   b) (✓✓)

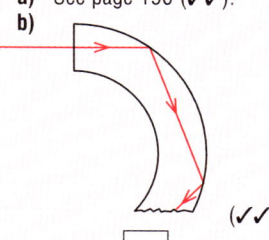

Your score: ☐ out of 36

Your improvement index: $\dfrac{\Box/36}{\Box/28} \times 100\% = \Box\%$

215

Physical processes

5 Test yourself (page 192)

The electromagnetic spectrum

1. Radio (✓), microwaves (✓), infrared (✓), visible (✓), ultraviolet (✓), X-rays and gamma rays (✓).
2. See page 193 (✓✓✓✓✓✓).
3. Visible light (✓) and radio (✓).
4. a) X-rays and gamma radiation (✓✓).
   b) Infrared radiation (✓)
   c) Ultraviolet light (✓)
5. X-rays or gamma radiation can (✓); radio waves cannot (✓).
6. a) X-rays (✓)
   b) Ultraviolet light (✓)
7. a) Microwave radiation (✓)
   b) (i) To focus microwave radiation from the satellite onto the dish aerial (✓).
      (ii) Metal reflects microwaves (✓).
8. The pigment in the ink does not absorb visible light (✓). It absorbs ultraviolet light and emits visible light (✓). Under a UV lamp, the ink is therefore visible (✓).
9. a) (i) Infrared radiation (✓)
      (ii) X-rays and gamma radiation (✓).
   b) Radio waves and microwaves (✓).
10. a) Infrared radiation (✓)
    b) Visible light and infrared radiation (✓).

Your score: ☐ out of 33

5 Round-up (page 196)

The electromagnetic spectrum

1. a) X-rays and gamma rays (✓), ultraviolet (✓), visible (✓), infrared (✓), microwave (✓), radio (✓).
   b) (i) Any two of: travel at the same speed in a vacuum; transverse waves; do not need a substance/pass through a vacuum; can be reflected or refracted or diffracted; make charged particles vibrate (✓✓).
      (ii) Visible (✓), ultraviolet (✓), X-rays and gamma rays (✓).
      (iii) Radio (✓), microwaves (✓), infrared (✓), visible (✓).
2. a) Cooker 0.12 m (✓), satellite 0.03 m (✓).
   b) Faster, uses less energy, cooks the food throughout (✓).
3. a) Long wave radio waves follow the Earth's curvature (✓), medium wave radio waves reflect from the ionosphere (✓).
   b) (i) The frequency of the electromagnetic waves that carry the audio or TV signals (✓).
      (ii) If they broadcast at the same frequency, the broadcasts would interfere with each other where they overlap (✓).
   c) The satellite signals are much weaker (✓); a dish is used to focus them onto an aerial (✓).
4. a) Ultraviolet light in bright sunlight would be absorbed by the powder molecules in the clothing (✓). The molecules would emit visible light, making the clothes seem brighter (✓).
   b) (i) It damages the retinal cells of the eye (✓); it causes sunburn (✓).
      (ii) To absorb ultraviolet light from sunlight (✓), to prevent sunburn (✓).
5. a) Their bodies emit infrared light which can be detected by an infrared camera (✓).
   b) (i) Infrared light (✓)
      (ii) A conventional heating element consists of resistance wire surrounded by an electrical insulator in a metal tubing (✓); conduction of heat from the resistance wire to the metal tubing is very slow and so the hob takes much longer to heat up than a ceramic hob (✓).
6. a) (i) To attract electrons from the heated filament (✓).
      (ii) The X-rays need to originate from a small spot on the anode (✓) otherwise the image they produce will be blurred (✓).
   b) (i) X-rays pass through soft tissues and are absorbed by bone (✓). X-rays blacken photographic film (✓).
      (ii) The stomach consists of soft tissues only (✓). The barium meal in the stomach enables the lining of the stomach to be seen because barium absorbs X-rays (✓).
7. a) There are more cycles per second of the waveform at the higher frequency (✓). Each pulse needs the same number of cycles per second (✓), so more pulses per second are possible at higher frequencies (✓).
   b) (i) 1000 (✓)
      (ii) They would interfere with mobile phone communications (✓).
8. a) An orbit directly above the equator (✓) with an orbital time of exactly 24 hours (✓).
   b) The satellite is always in the same position over the equator (✓).

Your score: ☐ out of 49

Your improvement index: $\dfrac{\boxed{}/49}{\boxed{}/33} \times 100\% = \boxed{}\%$

6 Test yourself (page 197)

Force

1. a) 5 km/h (✓)   b) 1.4 m/s (✓)
2. a) The area under the line (✓).   b) Speed (✓)
3. Your weight (✓), the support force from your chair (✓).
4. a) Neutral (✓) b) Unstable (✓) c) Stable (✓)
5. The drag force on the object increases with speed (✓) until it is equal to the weight of the object (✓). At terminal speed, the two forces balance each other out (✓) and so the object moves at constant speed (✓).
6. The force due to air resistance depends on the shape and the speed of the vehicle (✓). Work done against this force uses energy from petrol (✓). Changing the shape alters the force due to air resistance and therefore alters the fuel consumption (✓).

7 a) (i) The force is applied to a much smaller contact area if the knife is sharp (✓).
   (ii) Atmospheric pressure acting on the outer surface is greater than the pressure of the air trapped between the cap and the tile (✓). The pressure difference creates sufficient force to hold the cap on the tile (✓).
b) 6 kPa (✓✓)

8 a) The original shape is regained after the removal of applied forces (✓).
b) The original shape is not regained after the removal of applied forces (✓).

9 a) 20 cm (✓) **b)** 2.5 N (✓)

10 a) For example, tyre grip for braking, shoe grip for walking, grip for drive belts (✓).
b) For example, energy wasted due to friction in bearings (✓).

Your score: ☐ out of 27

6 Round-up (page 203)

Force

1 a) (i) 4320 m (✓) **(ii)** 4.32 km (✓) **b)** 4.3 m/s (✓)

2 a) It was steady (✓) and less than the speed of X for most of the journey (✓). Then the speed of Y was greater than that of X (✓) and Y overtook X (✓).
b) (i) 10 m/s (✓) **(ii)** 15 m/s (✓)

3 a) Speed is distance travelled per second (✓); velocity is speed in a given direction (✓).
b) (i) 9 km north (✓) then 24 km south (✓).
   (ii) 15 km south (✓).

4 a) The tyres are wider to create less pressure on the soft ground (✓). Also, the tractor can tilt further with big wheels before it topples over (✓).
b) Your diagram should show a small base and a high centre of gravity (✓). The pin needs to tilt only a little before it falls over because of its high centre of gravity in relation to its small base (✓).

5 a) (i) 200 kPa (✓) **(ii)** 6 kPa (✓) **b)** 0.004 m² (✓)

6 a) The stiffness of the steel spring is constant (✓); the stiffness of the elastic band changes as it is stretched (✓).
b) No (✓), it does not give equal changes in length for equal increases in force (✓).

7 a) Your graph should show axes labelled correctly and units shown (✓), points plotted correctly (✓), points covering at least half of each scale (✓), a straight line drawn through the points (✓).
b) 1.9 N (✓)

Your score: ☐ out of 30

Your improvement index: ☐/30 ÷ ☐/27 × 100% = ☐ %

7 Test yourself (page 204)

Electricity and magnetism

1 a) (✓✓)

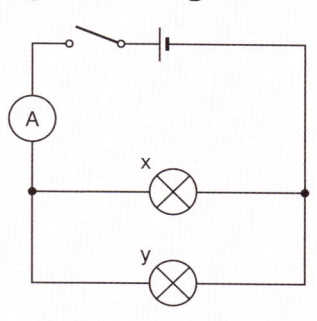

b) (i) 1 J (✓) **(ii)** 60 J (✓)

2 a) 0.2 A (✓) **b)** $\frac{1.0\,V}{0.2\,A}$ (✓) = 5.0 Ω (✓)

3 a) 15.0 V (✓) **b)** 0.5 A (✓)

4 a) (✓✓)

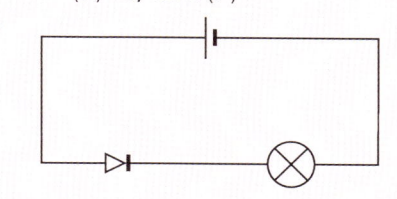

b) The diode is now reverse biased (✓) so it will not conduct (✓).

5

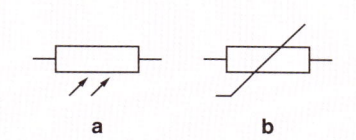

a   b

(✓✓)

a) An LDR's resistance depends on the incident light intensity (✓).
b) A thermistor's resistance depends on temperature (✓).

6 a) 300 kJ (✓) **b)** 1.0 kW × 4 h (✓) = 4 units (✓)

7 a) A fuse is intended to protect an appliance or the connecting wires from excessive current (✓).
b) If the current rises above a certain value, the fuse wire overheats and melts (✓) causing a gap in the circuit (✓).

8 a) 0.8 kW × 0.25 h (✓) = 0.2 (✓)
b) 1.2p (✓)

9 a) See page 209 for diagram (✓✓)
b) (i) 0 (✓) **(ii)** 90° (✓).

10 a) The peak voltage would decrease (✓) and the time for one cycle would increase (✓).
b) Any two from: the strength of the magnet; the number of turns on the coil; the area of the coil (✓✓).

Your score: ☐ out of 34

Physical processes

7 Round-up (pages 210–11)

Electricity and magnetism

1. a) 12 Ω (✓)
   b) The ammeter reading would double (✓); the voltmeter reading would be unchanged (✓).

2. a) (i) 1.5 V (✓) (ii) 0.3 A (✓)
   b) The current in P becomes less (✓); the current in Q becomes greater (✓).

3. Circuit diagram as on page 206 with the resistor label replaced by 'wire under test' (✓). Connect an exact length of 1.0 m into the circuit (✓) and measure the current and p.d. using the ammeter and the voltmeter (✓✓). Calculate the resistance from p.d./current (✓).

4. a) 2.0 mA (✓), 4 V (✓)
   b) The resistance of the LDR increases (✓), which reduces the current through the LDR and resistor R (✓). Hence the voltage across R decreases (✓).

5. a) (i) 1.2 (✓) (ii) 10 (✓) (iii) 1.0 (✓)
   b) 61p (✓)
   c) 29 minutes (✓✓)

6. a) Tap water conducts electricity (✓). Water might run into the appliance and provide a conducting path to earth via the user (✓). Also, the contact resistance between the appliance and the user is reduced by water (✓).
   b) If the case became live (✓), current leakage to earth via the user might not be enough to blow the fuse (✓). An RCCB would cut the mains supply off if the leakage current exceeds 30 mA (✓).
   c) The cable would become warm due to its resistance (✓). If it overheated, the insulation might melt (✓).
   d) If the fuse rating is too low, the fuse will 'blow' when the appliance is switched on (✓). If the fuse rating is too high, the fuse will not 'blow' when the current becomes excessive. This would create a risk of fire due to resistance heating (✓).

7. a) See page 209 for diagram (✓✓✓). The sides of the coil cut the magnetic field lines as the coil turns (✓) so a voltage is induced in the coil (✓). The voltage alternates because the angle between the direction of motion of the coil sides and field lines changes continuously (✓).
   b) (i) See page 209 (✓✓).
      (ii) Any maximum or minimum (✓).
   c) The peaks are higher (✓) and nearer to each other (✓).

8. a) UK – the higher voltage in the UK is more dangerous (✓) but smaller currents for the same power in the UK mean less risk of overheating (✓).
   b) Advantages: no underground trenches need to be dug, no waterproof insulating material needed round cable (✓). Disadvantages: liable to lightning strikes, unsightly (✓).

Your score: ☐ out of 48

Your improvement index: $\dfrac{\boxed{}/48}{\boxed{}/34} \times 100\% = \boxed{}\%$

Index

a.c. generator 209
acceleration 199
acid rain 118–19
acids 110–11, 150
aerobic respiration 11
AIDS (Acquired Immune Deficiency Syndrome) 46
air 11, 115–20, 151
alcohol 63
alkenes 135–6, 138, 156
allergies 58
alloys 129, 153
　see also metals
alpha radiation 179, 182, 184
anaerobic respiration 11
Animal kingdom 12
argon 117
artificial vegetative reproduction 68
asexual reproduction 66, 68–9
atoms 98–101, 180

bacteria 14, 58
bandwidths 195
bases 112–13, 150
beta radiation 179, 182, 184
Big Bang 170
biosphere 16
biotechnology 73–4
blood 46, 59
body temperature 61, 176
body water content 56, 60
bonding 102–4
brain 50
Brownian motion 90

cancer 58, 63, 75
carbohydrates 33–4
carbon dioxide 117
carbon monoxide 118
catalysts 132–3
cells 24–37
　at work 24, 26–7
　division 25, 28–9, 75
　functions and structure 24, 27
　surface area to volume ratio 32
cellulose 33, 34
centre of gravity 200
characteristics of life 11
chemical reactions
　and energy 136
　equations 94
　heat of 136–7
　reaction speeds 131–3, 154
chitin 34
chromatography 96
chromosomes 25, 36, 59, 72
circuit breakers 208
classification of living things 11–14
coal 134
colour 189
comets 168
communications 195
competition between organisms 18–19
composite materials 89
compounds 91
　formulas 92–3
　for life 33
conservation 129
constellations 165
corrosion 128
covalent bonding 103–4
covalent substances 104–5
cracking 135
crystals 90
Curie, Marie 179
current 205, 206
cystic fibrosis 59

Darwin, Charles 76
dichotomous keys 14
diet 39–41
diffusion 90
digestive system 42–5
disaccharides 33
diseases 58–63
distillation 96–7, 135
DNA (deoxyribonucleic acid) 25, 35, 36
Down's syndrome 59
drugs 63, 75
dynamo 210

ears 52–3
Earth
　age of 78
　in space 157, 164–6
　supporting life 10–11
earthing 208
eclipses 166
ecosystems 16–17
efficiency 178
Einstein, Albert 181
elastic behaviour 201
electricity 161, 205–8
electromagnetic induction 209–10
electromagnetic waves 193–5
electrons 98–101
elements 91, 92
　for life 33
　periodic table 106–9, 127, 148
energy
　conservation of 173
　and food 39
　forms of 173
　heat transfer 175–6
　resources 177–8
　thermal energy 174
　and work 172–3
environment 16–17
　human impact on 21–3
enzymes 35
equations for chemical reactions 94
equilibrium 200
evaporation 90

Index

evolution 76–9
extinction 79
eyes 53, 54

Faraday's law 209
fats 34
filtration 95–6
food
  and diet 39–41
  digestive system 42–5
  nutrients 11, 39, 75
force 158, 198–202
formulas of compounds 92–3
fossils 79
fractional distillation 97, 135
frequency 187
frequency bands 195
fuels 134–7, 155, 177
fuses 208

galaxies 170
gamma radiation 179, 182, 184, 194
gases 89, 90
Geiger counters 181
genetics
  genetic code 37
  genetic engineering 74
  genetic variation 75–6
  rules 71
  vocabulary 71
glycogen 33, 34
gravity 168

haemophilia 46, 59
half-life 183
halogen hobs 193
heat transfer 175–6
helium 117
HIV (Human Immunodeficiency Virus) 46
homeostasis 55, 58, 60
Hooke's law 201
hormones 54–5, 56–7
Hubble's law 170
hydraulic brakes 202
hydrocarbons 119–20

infrared light 193
inheritance 70–2
  of sex 72
ionic bond 102–3
ionic substances 104–5
ions 102, 182
iron 127, 128
isotopes 180–1

keys 14–15
kidneys 55
kinetic energy (KE) 173
kinetic theory 89
kingdoms 11–14

land use 23
lead 120
Lenz's law 209
leukaemia 46
light 187–90
  intraspecific competition for 18
limestone 125
Linnaeus, Carolus 14
lipids 34
liquids 89, 96, 97
liver 43, 55
lung diseases 62, 63
Lyell, Charles 78

magnetism 161, 209–10
mains circuits 207
Malthus, Reverend Thomas 78
meiosis 25, 29
Mendeleev, Dmitri 106
metals
  conservation 129
  corrosion 128
  extraction 127–8
  reactions of 108, 126–7
  reactivity series 127
  uses 129
microwave cookers 193
mirrors 188
mitosis 25, 28
molecules 91, 180
monohybrid inheritance 70–2

monosaccharides 33
Moon 166
mutation 37, 75

naming organisms 14
neon 117
nervous system 48, 50–1
neurones 48, 51
neutralisation 112
neutrons 98, 180
Newlands, John 106
Newton's laws of motion 199
nitrogen 117
  oxides 119
noble gases 117
nose 52
nucleic acids 35
nutrition 11, 39, 75

Ohm's law 205
oil (petroleum) 134–5
oils 34
optical fibres 190, 195
organ systems 30–1, 32
oxidation 116–17
oxides of metals 127
oxides of nitrogen 119
oxygen 115–16
  solubility 121–2

pancreas 55
periodic table 106–9, 127, 148
petroleum 134–5
photosynthesis 26
planets 167
plastic behaviour 201
plastics 139, 156
pleurisy 62
pneumonia 62
pollution 23, 118–20, 122
polysaccharides 33–4
population size 19–21
potential difference 205
power 173
predators 19, 20
pressure 202
prey 19, 20

properties of materials 89
proteins 34–5
protons 98, 180

radioactive dating 183
radioactive waste 184
radioactivity 159, 179–84
ray diagrams 188
reactions *see* chemical reactions
red shift 170
reduction 116–17
reflection 187, 188
reflex arc 50
refraction 187, 189
replication 36
reproduction 11, 25, 65–9
resistance 205, 206
respiration 11
RNA (ribonucleic acid) 35
rocks 123–5
rusting 128
Rutherford, Ernest 180

salts 114, 152
satellites 168
saturated fats 34
sense organs 49, 52–3
sexual characteristics 55
sexual reproduction 65–6, 75
sickle-cell anaemia 59

skin 52, 55, 61
smoking 62–3
soil formation 11
solar system 167
solids 89, 90, 95
  strength of 201–2
solvents 63
speed
  and distance 198
  terminal speed 199
  and velocity 198
starch 33, 34
stars 169
states of matter 88
sulphur dioxide 118
Sun 166
sweat pores 61
symbols of elements 92
synapses 51

tarnishing 126
taste buds 52
temperature scales 174
thermal conduction 175
thermal convection 175
thermal energy 174
thermal radiation 175
tissues 30
tongue 52
total internal reflection 190

ultraviolet light 193
Universe 170
unsaturated fats 34

vaporisation 90
variation 75–6
vegetative reproduction 68
velocity 198, 199
voltage 205

water
  body water content 56, 60
  cycle 121
  intraspecific competition for 18
  pollution 122
  pure water 122
wavelength 187
waves 160, 187
  electromagnetic 193–5
weight 199
white blood cells 59
work 172–3

X chromosome 59, 72
X-rays 194

Y chromosome 72
yeast cells 74

TRAIN YOUR BRAIN!

BRAIN TRAINERS

For further information on books, video and audio tapes, support materials and *Brain Trainer* courses, please send for our brochure.

Buzan Centres Ltd, 54 Parkstone Road, Poole, Dorset, BH15 2PX
Tel: 44 (0) 1202 674676, Fax: 44 (0) 1202 674776,
Email: Buzan_Centres_Ltd@compuserve.com